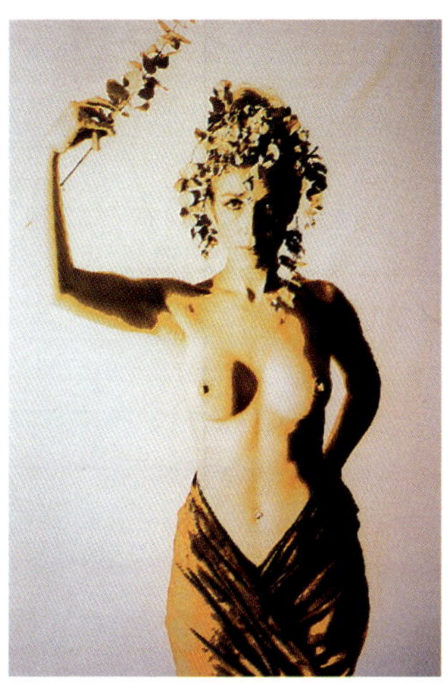

Pro·Lighting

NUDES

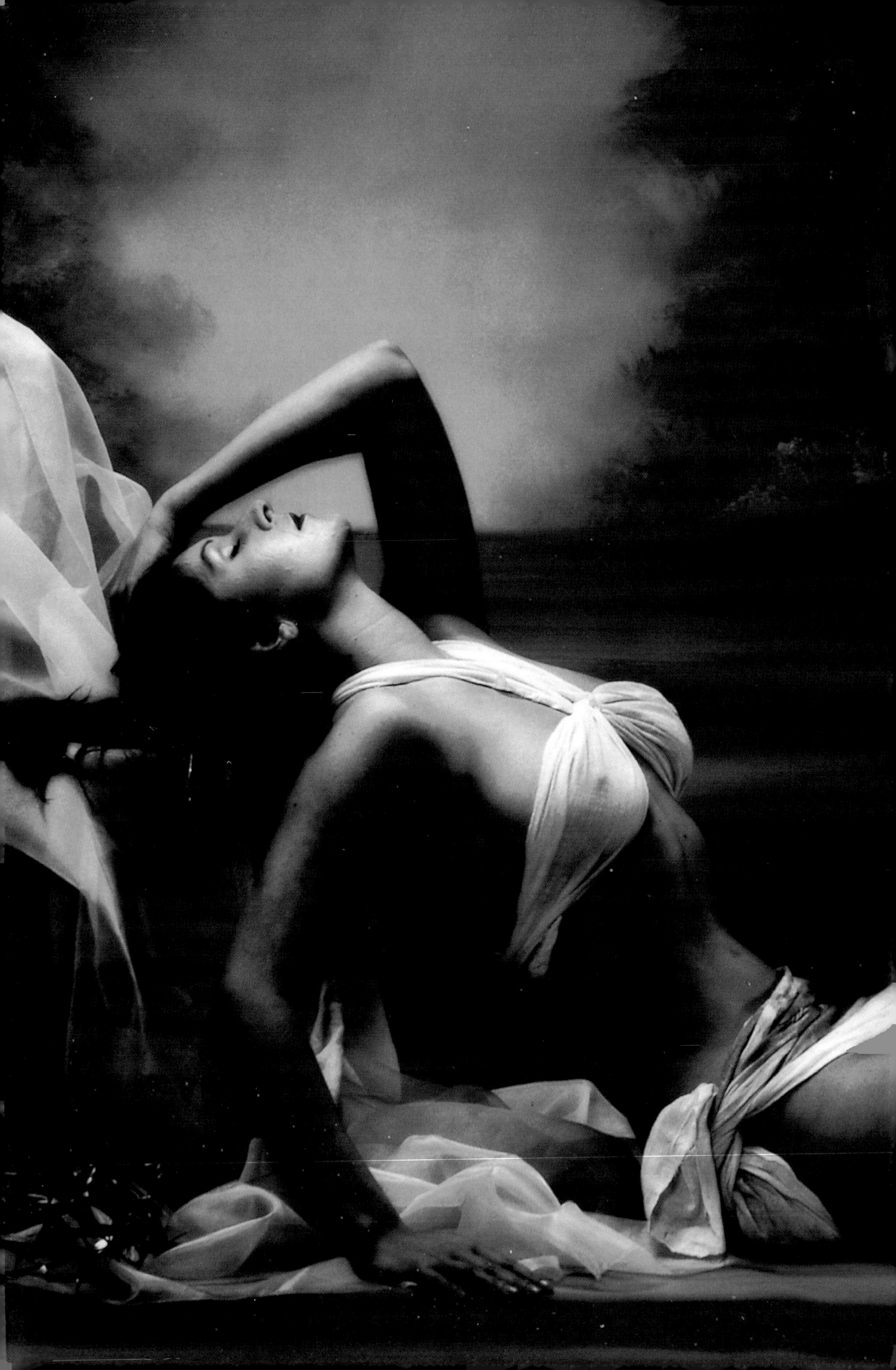

Pro·Lighting

ROGER HICKS and FRANCES SCHULTZ

NUDES

ROTOVISION

A Quarto Book

Published and distributed by:
RotoVision SA
7 rue du Bugnon
1299 Crans
Switzerland

RotoVision SA Sales Office
Sheridan House
112/116A Western Road
Hove, West Sussex BN3 1DD
England
Tel: +44 1273 72 72 68
Fax: +44 1273 72 72 69

Distributed to the trade in the United States:
Watson-Guptill Publications
1515 Broadway
New York, NY 10036

ISBN 2-88046-271-1

This book was designed and produced by
Quarto Publishing plc
6 Blundell Street
London N7 9BH

Creative Director: Richard Dewing
Designer: Fiona Roberts
Senior Editor: Anna Briffa
Editor: Kit Coppard
Picture Researchers: Roger Hicks and Frances Schultz

Typeset in Great Britain by
Central Southern Typesetters, Eastbourne
Manufactured in Singapore by Teck Wah Paper Products Ltd.
Printed in Singapore by ProVision Pte. Ltd.
Tel: +65 334 7720
Fax: +65 334 7721

CONTENTS

▼

THE MOST COMMON RESPONSE FROM THE PHOTOGRAPHERS WHO CONTRIBUTED TO THIS BOOK, WHEN THE CONCEPT WAS EXPLAINED TO THEM, WAS "I'D BUY THAT". THE AIM IS SIMPLE: TO CREATE A LIBRARY OF BOOKS, ILLUSTRATED WITH FIRST-CLASS PHOTOGRAPHY FROM ALL AROUND THE WORLD, WHICH SHOW EXACTLY HOW EACH INDIVIDUAL PHOTOGRAPH IN EACH BOOK WAS LIT.

Who will find it useful? Professional photographers, obviously, who are either working in a given field or want to move into a new field. Students, too, who will find that it gives them access to a very much greater range of ideas and inspiration than even the best college can hope to present. Art directors and others in the visual arts will find it a useful reference book, both for ideas and as a means of explaining to photographers exactly what they want done. It will also help them to understand what the photographers are saying to them. And, of course, "pro/am" photographers who are on the cusp between amateur photography and earning money with their cameras will find it invaluable: it shows both the standards that are required, and the means of achieving them.

The lighting set-ups in each book vary widely, and embrace many different types of light source: electronic flash, tungsten, HMIs, and light brushes, sometimes mixed with daylight and flames and all kinds of other things. Some are very complex; others are very simple. This variety is very important, both as a source of ideas and inspiration and because each book as a whole has no axe to grind: there is no editorial bias towards one kind of lighting or another, because the pictures were chosen on the basis of

impact and (occasionally) on the basis of technical difficulty. Certain subjects are, after all, notoriously difficult to light and can present a challenge even to experienced photographers. Only after the picture selection had been made was there any attempt to understand to understand the lighting set-up.

This book is a part of the third series: PORTRAITS, STILL LIFE and NUDES. The first series was PRODUCT SHOTS, GLAMOUR SHOTS and FOOD SHOTS, and the second was INTERIORS, LINGERIE and SPECIAL EFFECTS. The intriguing thing in all of them is to see the degree of underlying similarity, and the degree of diversity, which can be found in a single discipline or genre.

In portraiture, for example, there is a remarkable preference for monochrome and for medium formats, though the styles of lighting are very varied. In nudes, softer lighting is more usual, though the rendition is very often what painters would call "hard edge". And in still lifes, although few manipulated images are shown in the book, many photographers said that they were either already using computers or were getting in to it.

In none of the books of the third series, though, is there as much of a "universal lighting set up" as was so often detectable in the first two series. This is probably

because all three topics are inclined to be personal pictures, often portfolio shots, and they therefore reflect artistic variety more than commercial necessity.

The structure of the books is straightforward. After this initial introduction, which changes little among all the books in the series, there is a brief guide and glossary of lighting terms. Then, there is a specific introduction to the individual area or areas of photography which are covered by the book. Sub-divisions of each discipline are arranged in chapters, inevitably with a degree of overlap, and each chapter has its own introduction. Finally, at the end of the book, there is a directory of those photographers who have contributed.

If you would like your work to be considered for inclusion in future books, please write to Quarto Publishing, 6 Blundell Street, London, N7 9BH, and request an Information Pack. DO NOT SEND PICTURES, either with the initial inquiry or with any subsequent correspondence, unless requested; unsolicited pictures may not always be returned. When a book is planned which corresponds with your particular area of expertise, we will contact you. Until then, we hope that you enjoy this book; that you will find it useful; and that it helps you in your work.

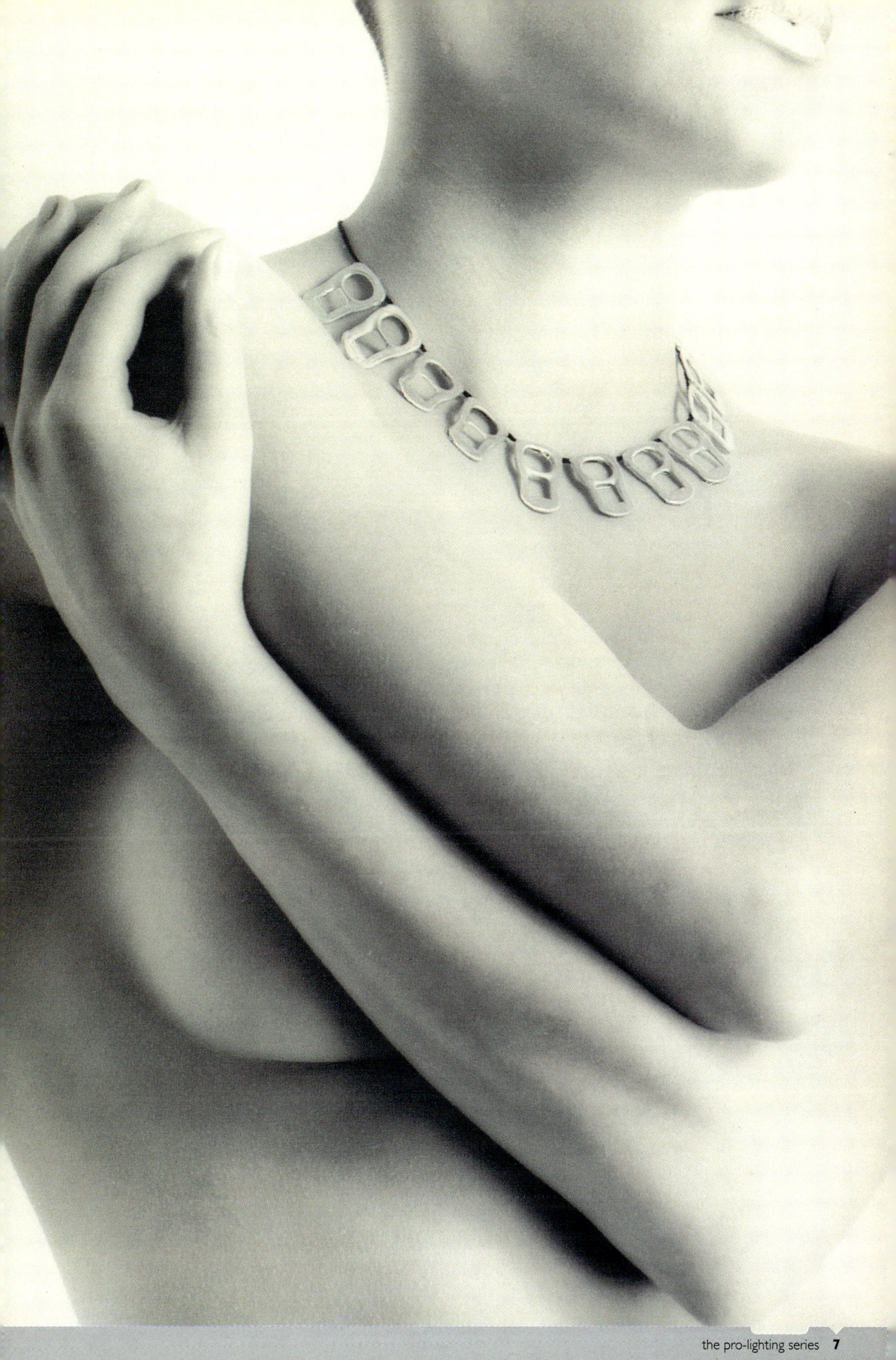

H O W   T O   U S E   T H I S   B O O K

▼

THE LIGHTING DRAWINGS IN THIS BOOK ARE INTENDED AS A GUIDE TO THE LIGHTING SET-UP RATHER THAN AS ABSOLUTELY ACCURATE DIAGRAMS. PART OF THIS IS DUE TO THE VARIATION IN THE PHOTOGRAPHERS' OWN DRAWINGS, SOME OF WHICH WERE MORE COMPLETE (AND MORE COMPREHENSIBLE) THAN OTHERS, BUT PART OF IT IS ALSO DUE TO THE NEED TO REPRESENT COMPLEX SET-UPS IN A WAY WHICH WOULD NOT BE NEEDLESSLY CONFUSING.

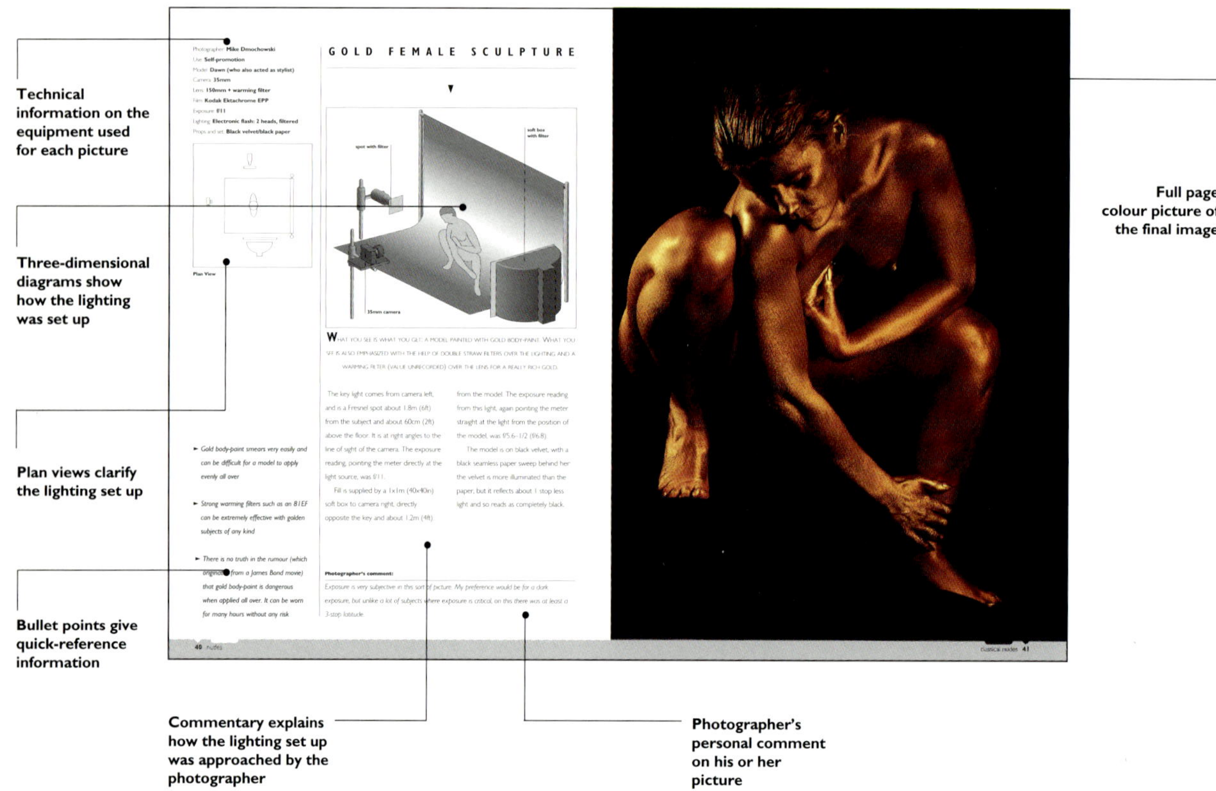

Technical information on the equipment used for each picture

Three-dimensional diagrams show how the lighting was set up

Plan views clarify the lighting set up

Bullet points give quick-reference information

Commentary explains how the lighting set up was approached by the photographer

Photographer's personal comment on his or her picture

Full page colour picture of the final image

Distances and even sizes have been compressed and expanded: and because of the vast variety of sizes of soft boxes, reflectors, bounces and the like, we have settled on a limited range of conventionalized symbols. Sometimes, too, we have reduced the size of big bounces, just to simplify the drawing.

None of this should really matter, however. After all, no photographer works strictly according to rules and preconceptions: there is always room to move this light a little to the left or right,

to move that light closer or further away, and so forth, according to the needs of the shot. Likewise, the precise power of the individual lighting heads or (more important) the lighting ratios are not always given; but again, this is something which can be "fine tuned" by any photographer wishing to reproduce the lighting set-ups in here.

We are however confident that there is more than enough information given about every single shot to merit its inclusion in the book: as well as purely

lighting techniques, there are also all kinds of hints and tips about commercial realities, photographic practicalities, and the way of the world in general.

The book can therefore be used in a number of ways. The most basic, and perhaps the most useful for the beginner, is to study all the technical information concerning a picture which he or she particularly admires, together with the lighting diagrams, and to try to duplicate that shot as far as possible with the equipment available.

A more advanced use for the book is as a problem solver for difficulties you have already encountered: a particular technique of back lighting, say, or of creating a feeling of light and space. And, of course, it can always be used simply as a source of inspiration.

The information for each picture follows the same plan, though some individual headings may be omitted if they were irrelevant or unavailable. The photographer is credited first, then the client, together with the use for which the picture was taken. Next come the other members of the team who worked on the picture: stylists, models, art directors, whoever. Camera and lens come next, followed by film. With film, we have named brands and types, because different films have very different ways of rendering colours and tonal values. Exposure comes next: where the lighting is electronic flash, only the aperture is given, as illumination is of course independent of shutter speed. Next, the lighting equipment is briefly summarized — whether tungsten or flash, and what sort of heads — and finally there is a brief note on props and backgrounds. Often, this last will be obvious from the picture, but in other cases you may be surprised at what has been pressed into service, and how different it looks from its normal role.

The most important part of the book is however the pictures themselves. By studying these, and referring to the lighting diagrams and the text as necessary, you can work out how they were done; and showing how things are done is the brief to which the *Pro Lighting* series was created.

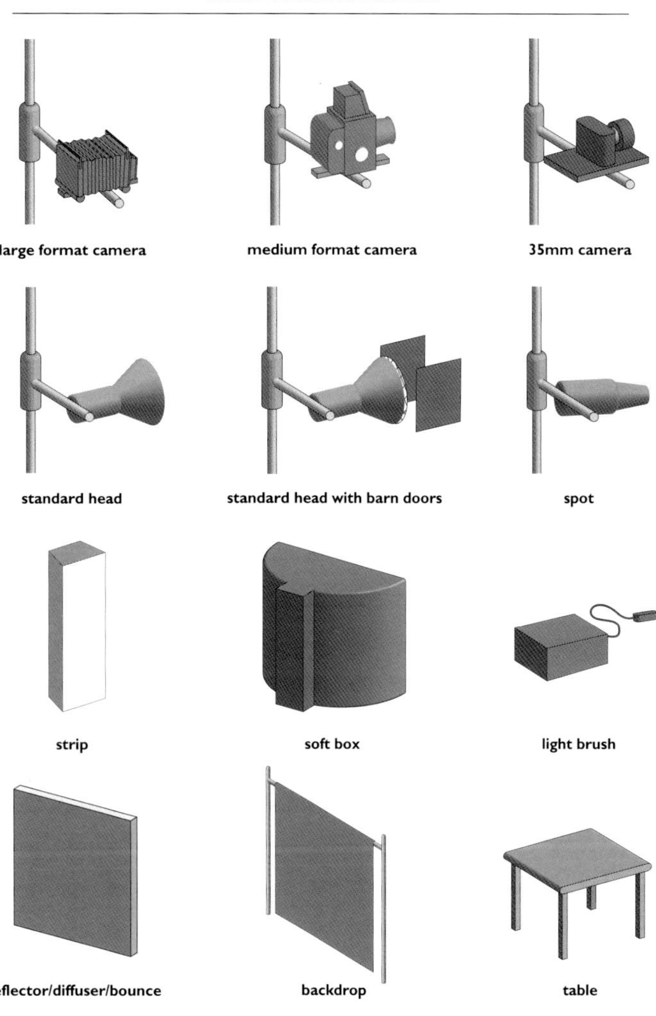

GLOSSARY OF LIGHTING TERMS

▼

LIGHTING, LIKE ANY OTHER CRAFT, HAS ITS OWN JARGON AND SLANG. UNFORTUNATELY, THE DIFFERENT TERMS ARE NOT VERY WELL STANDARDIZED, AND OFTEN THE SAME THING MAY BE DESCRIBED IN TWO OR MORE WAYS OR THE SAME WORD MAY BE USED TO MEAN TWO OR MORE DIFFERENT THINGS. FOR EXAMPLE, A SHEET OF BLACK CARD, WOOD, METAL OR OTHER MATERIAL WHICH IS USED TO CONTROL REFLECTIONS OR SHADOWS MAY BE CALLED A FLAG, A FRENCH FLAG, A DONKEY OR A GOBO — THOUGH SOME PEOPLE WOULD RESERVE THE TERM "GOBO" FOR A FLAG WITH HOLES IN IT, WHICH IS ALSO KNOWN AS A COOKIE. IN THIS BOOK, WE HAVE TRIED TO STANDARDIZE TERMS AS FAR AS POSSIBLE. FOR CLARITY, A GLOSSARY IS GIVEN BELOW, AND THE PREFERRED TERMS USED IN THIS BOOK ARE ASTERISKED.

Acetate

see Gel

Acrylic sheeting

Hard, shiny plastic sheeting, usually methyl methacrylate, used as a diffuser ("opal") or in a range of colours as a background.

***Barn doors**

Adjustable flaps affixed to a lighting head which allow the light to be shaded from a particular part of the subject.

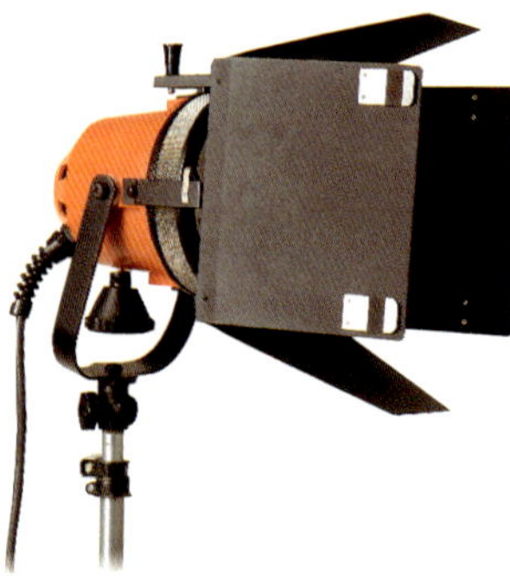

Barn doors

Boom

Extension arm allowing a light to be cantilevered out over a subject.

***Bounce**

A passive reflector, typically white but also, (for example) silver or gold, from which light is bounced back onto the subject. Also used in the compound term "Black Bounce", meaning a flag used to absorb light rather than to cast a shadow.

Continuous lighting

What its name suggests: light which shines continuously instead of being a brief flash.

Contrast

see Lighting ratio

Cookie

see Gobo

***Diffuser**

Translucent material used to diffuse light. Includes tracing paper, scrim, umbrellas, translucent plastics such as Perspex and Plexiglas, and more.

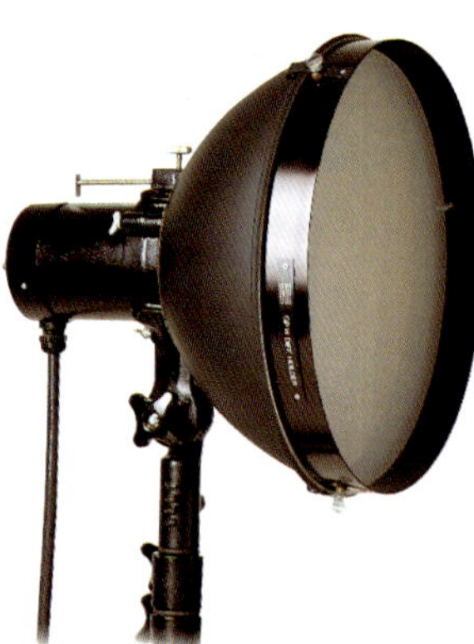

Electronic flash: standard head with parallel snoot (Strobex)

Donkey

see Gobo

Effects light

Neither key nor fill; a small light, usually a spot, used to light a particular part of the subject. A hair light on a model is an example of an effects (or "FX") light.

***Fill**

Extra lights, either from a separate head or from a reflector, which "fills" the shadows and lowers the lighting ratio.

Fish fryer

A small Soft Box.

***Flag**

A rigid sheet of metal, board, foam-core or other material which is used to absorb light or to create a shadow. Many flags are painted black on one side and white (or brushed silver) on the other, so that they can be used either as flags or as reflectors.

***Flat**

A large Bounce, often made of a thick sheet of expanded polystyrene or foam-core (for lightness).

Foil

see Gel

French flag

see Flag

Frost

see Diffuser

***Gel**

Transparent or (more rarely) translucent coloured material used to modify the colour of a light. It is an abbreviation of "gelatine (filter)", though most modern "gels" for lighting use are actually of acetate.

***Gobo**

As used in this book, synonymous with "cookie": a flag with cut-outs in it, to cast interestingly-shaped shadows. Also used in projection spots.

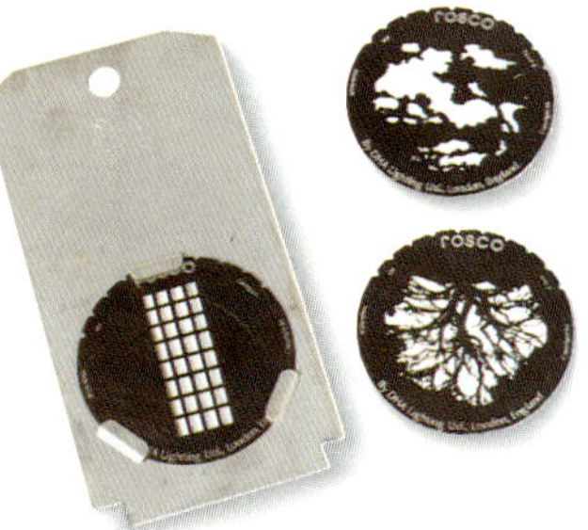

"Cookies" or "gobos" for projection spotlight (Photon Beard)

***Head**

Light source, whether continuous or flash. A "standard head" is fitted with a plain reflector.

***HMI**

Rapidly-pulsed and

effectively continuous light source approximating to daylight and running far cooler than tungsten. Relatively new at the time of writing, and still very expensive.

*Honeycomb

Grid of open-ended hexagonal cells, closely resembling a honeycomb. Increases directionality of

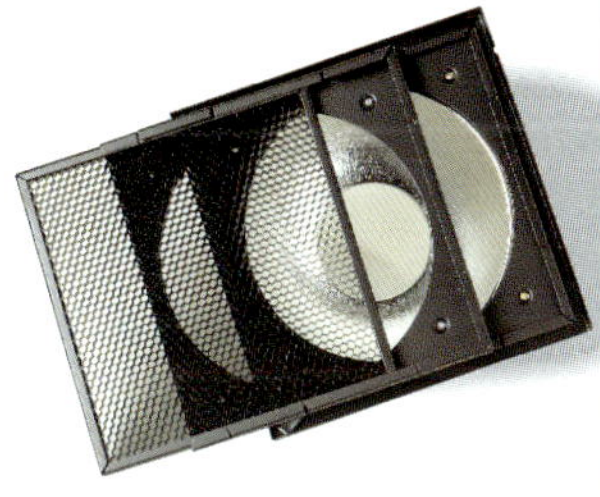

Honeycomb (Hensel)

light from any head.

Incandescent lighting

see Tungsten

Inky dinky

Small tungsten spot.

*Key or key light

The dominant or principal light, the light which casts the shadows.

Kill Spill

Large flat used to block spill.

*Light brush

Light source "piped" through fibre-optic lead. Can be used to add highlights, delete shadows and modify lighting, literally by "painting with light".

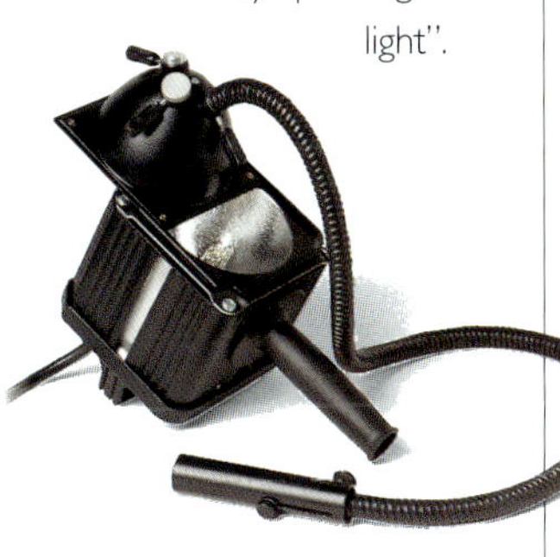

Electronic Flash: light brush "pencil" (Hensel)

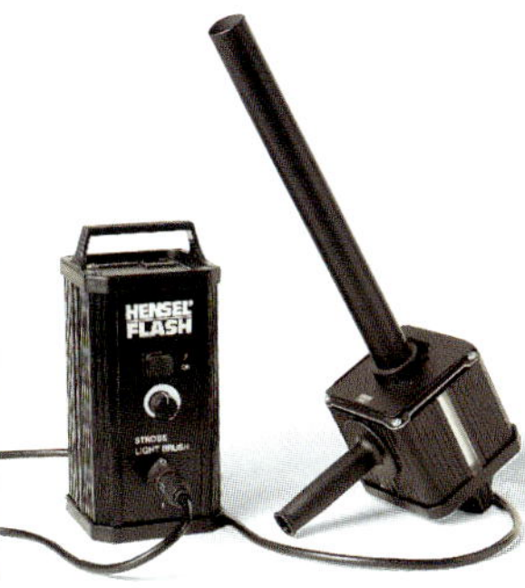

Electronic Flash: light brush "hose" (Hensel)

Lighting ratio

The ratio of the key to the fill, as measured with an incident light meter. A high lighting ratio (8:1 or above) is very contrasty, especially in colour, a low lighting ratio (4:1 or less) is flatter or softer. A 1:1 lighting ratio is completely even, all over the subject.

*Mirror

Exactly what its name suggests. The only reason for mentioning it here is that reflectors are rarely mirrors, because mirrors create "hot spots" while reflectors diffuse light. Mirrors (especially small shaving mirrors) are however widely used, almost in the same way as effects lights.

Northlight

see Soft Box

Perspex

Brand name for acrylic sheeting.

Plexiglas

Brand name for acrylic sheeting.

*Projection spot

Flash or tungsten head with projection optics for casting a clear image of a gobo or cookie. Used to create textured lighting effects and shadows.

*Reflector

Either a dish-shaped surround to a light, or a bounce.

*Scrim

Heat-resistant fabric

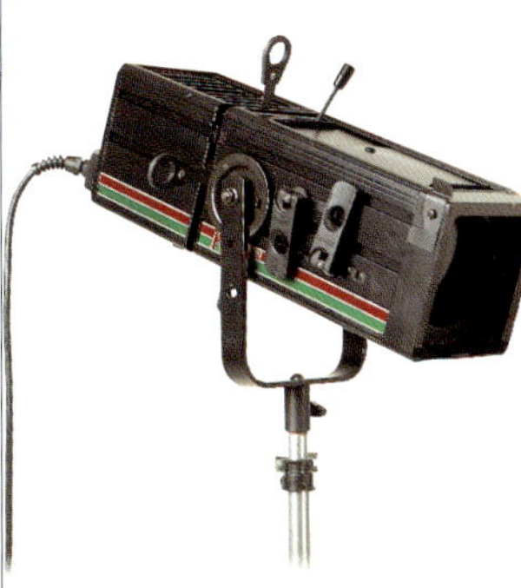

Electronic Flash: projection spotlight (Strobex)

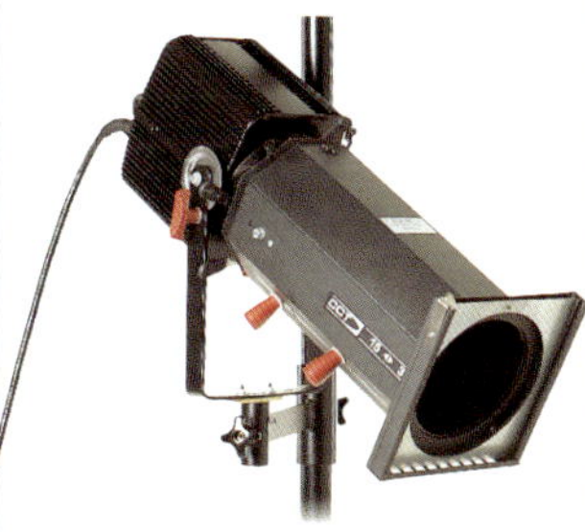

Tungsten Projection spotlight (Photon Beard)

diffuser, used to soften lighting.

*Snoot

Conical restrictor, fitting over a lighting head. The light can only escape from the small hole in the end, and is

therefore very directional.

*Soft box

Large, diffuse light source made by shining a light

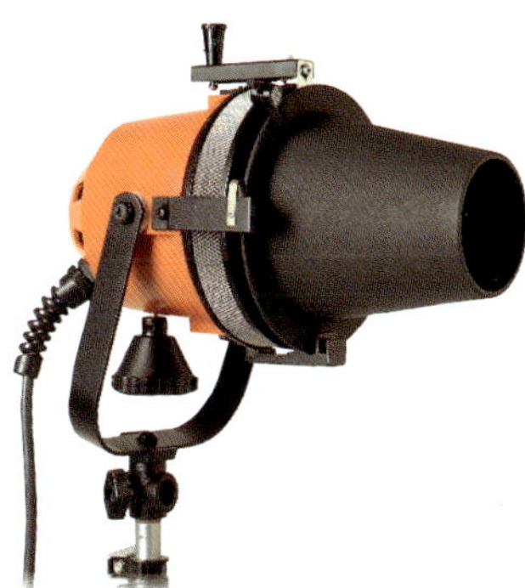

Tungsten spot with conical snoot (Photon Beard)

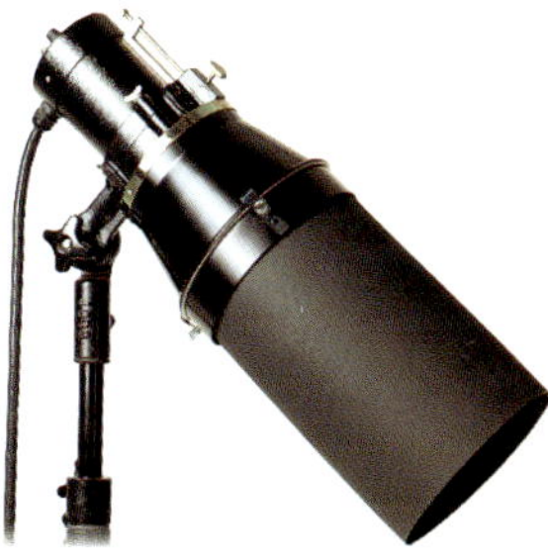

Electronic Flash: standard head with parallel snoot (Strobex)

through one or two layers of diffuser. Soft boxes come in all kinds of shapes

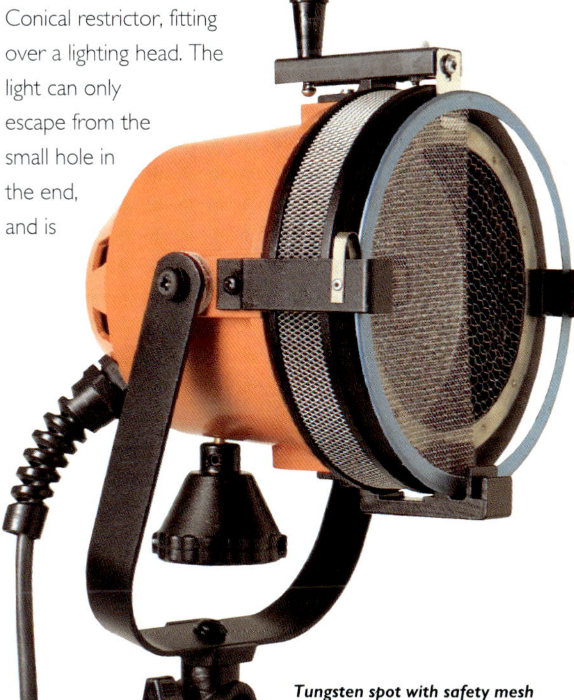

Tungsten spot with safety mesh (behind) and wire half diffuser scrim (Photon Beard)

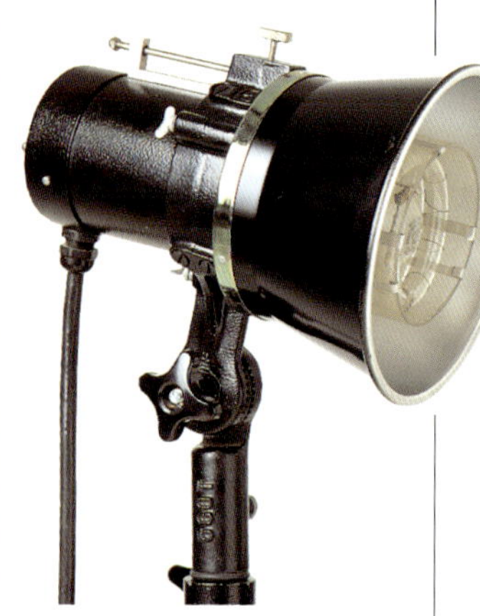

Electronic flash: standard head with large reflector and diffuser (Strobex)

and sizes, from about 30x30cm to 120x180cm and larger. Some soft boxes are rigid; others are made of fabric stiffened with poles resembling fibreglass fishing rods. Also known as a northlight or a windowlight, though these can also be created by shining standard heads through large (120x180cm or larger) diffusers.

***Spill**

Light from any source which ends up other than on the subject at which it is pointed. Spill may be used to provide fill, or to light backgrounds, or it may be controlled with flags, barn doors, gobos etc.

***Spot**

Directional light source. Normally refers to a light using a focusing system with reflectors or lenses or both, a "focusing spot", but also loosely used as a reflector head rendered more directional with a honeycomb.

***Strip or strip light**

Lighting head, usually flash, which is much longer than it is wide.

Electronic flash: strip light with removable barn doors (Strobex)

Strobe

Electronic flash. Strictly, a "strobe" is a stroboscope or rapidly repeating light source, though it is also the name of a leading manufacturer.

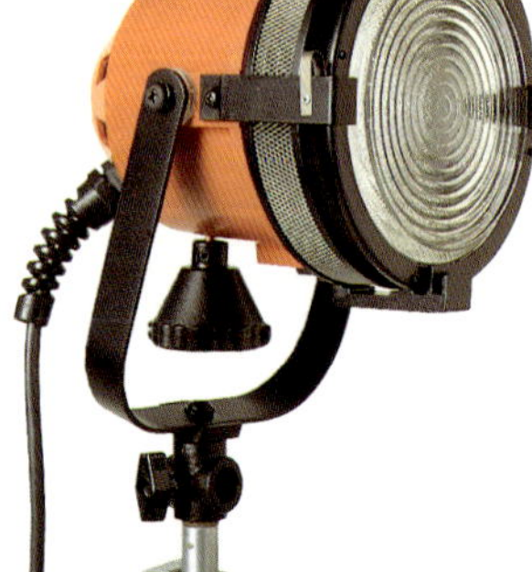

Tungsten spot with removable Fresnel lens. The knob at the bottom varies the width of the beam (Photon Beard)

Strobex, formerly Strobe Equipment.

Swimming pool

A very large Soft Box.

***Tungsten**

Incandescent lighting. Photographic tungsten

Electronic flash: standard head with standard reflector (Strobex)

lighting runs at 3200°K or 3400°K, as compared with domestic lamps which run at 2400°K to 2800°K or thereabouts.

***Umbrella**

Exactly what its name suggests; used for modifying light.

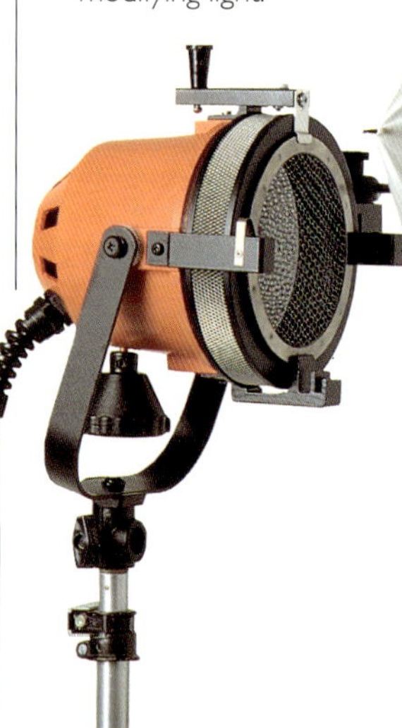

Umbrellas may be used as reflectors (light shining into the umbrella) or diffusers (light shining through the umbrella). The cheapest way of creating a large, soft light source.

Windowlight

Apart from the obvious meaning of light through a window, or of light shone through a diffuser to look as if it is coming through a window, this is another name for a soft box.

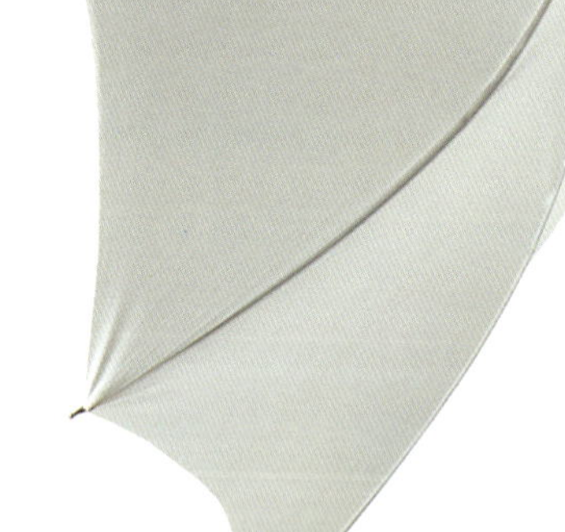

Tungsten spot with shoot-through umbrella (Photon Beard)

NUDES

▼

From the very earliest days of photography, and indeed from the earliest days of representational art, the portrayal of the nude and partially nude human form has exercised an enduring fascination. By the early 1850s there were numerous daguerreotypists in Paris in particular who were noted for their photography of the nude: Auguste Bellocq, Bruno Braquehais, Jean-Louis-Marie-Eugène Durieu, F. Jacques Moulin, Louis Camille d'Olivier and more.

Some of this early work was nothing more nor less than pornography, but co-existing with this was an artistic tradition which stretched back hundreds or even thousands of years: a representation of a nude can after all be attractive without being erotic, or erotic without being pornographic. What is surprising, to the modern eye, is how many of the early photographers seem to have made no particular distinction: Moulin, in particular, produced some quite charming pictures, and others which even his most ardent admirers would be hard pressed to defend on aesthetic grounds.

This is the central problem in all nude photography: which pictures are "acceptable", and to whom. There are no doubt many who would like to see even this book burned, while there are others who will be unable to see why a single image in here could upset anyone. Art, like depravity, is something which is easier to recognize than to define.

This is not, however, the place for such a debate. Nor is it the place for a discussion of why individual photographers take pictures of nudes. You have presumably bought the book, or you are contemplating buying it, and so it is our job to give you as much guidance as possible on how to photograph the nude – which for our purpose includes the partially nude, as a book containing nothing but total nudity would be more use as an anatomy book than as a book on photography. We have drawn work from photographers from numerous countries, all with their own unique styles and ways of working. Our job has been merely to learn from them how they work, to organize that information, and to make it as useful and informative as possible.

STUDIOS AND SETTINGS

It might have been useful – though, unfortunately, it would not have been practical – to include a chapter of historical images in this book. It could have begun with the static nineteenth-century nudes in their stuffy studios; moved on to the Edwardians, with their naturalistic studio sets and locations; then gone on to the period between World War One and World War Two, the heyday of the geometrical nude and the semi-abstract "figure study"; taken in the 1950s, with their emphasis on the outdoors, and the 1960s with their gritty photo-realism; and the self-indulgence which characterized so much of the 1970s…

Of course, as we come nearer to our own times it becomes harder and harder to recognize underlying trends. There also seems to be more diversity than ever before. In this book there are very simple studio nudes, shorn of context or with only the simplest of backdrops, but there are also nudes in natural (or naturalistic) settings; in abandoned buildings; out of doors and indoors; photographed with the utmost in romanticism, or in the grittiest of realism. Unlike the case of some other books in the PRO LIGHTING series, generalizations are very hard to make: photographing the nude is one of the most intensely personal forms of photography.

PHOTOGRAPHY AND PAINTING

More than in almost any other area of photography, the link between the photographed nude and the painted nude is abundantly clear, and the photographer who looks only at the works of other photographers and ignores the works of painters is making a serious mistake. There are pictures in these pages which are reminiscent of Alma-Tadema, Balthus, Hockney and even Liechtenstein. A tour of any art gallery, or a few books on painting, can be worth as much as a visit to a photographic gallery, even if it is showing the works of an acknowledged master such as Bill Brandt, Helmut Newton, or Jock Sturges.

Clothes, Props and Make-up

As already remarked, the totally
unclothed nude is unusual; and there is
quite a lot of fashion and personal
originality in what he or she may be
clothed with. Diaphanous draperies were
always popular with the painters of yore,
and, within the bounds imposed by the
greater literalness of photography, the
same may also be found in these pages:
lengths of fabric, and even sheets, are
pressed into service on a regular basis.
More conventional clothes may be
partially undone, or underwear may be
revealed, or clothes normally regarded as
essential for decency may be omitted.

When it comes to props and
backgrounds, there is a long tradition of
geometrical or semi-abstract nudes,
where props normally look out of place;
but there is no doubt that in the vast
majority of nude studies props are an
essential part of the picture. This is true
whether you are considering the
irreverent humour of Michèle Francken
or the almost apocalyptic intensity of
some of Stu Williamson's pictures; and in
one of Struan's most notable pictures,
the model herself is essentially a prop
because the picture was commissioned
as an advertising photograph for a shoe.

As for hair and make-up, this is
something which dates far faster than
most people (especially most men)
realize. Examples like the old "bee-hive"
hairdo are obvious, but compare the
heavy eye make-up and often unnatural
but often dramatic lipsticks of the 1960s
with the more naturalistic eye-make-up
and washed-out lipsticks of the late
1970s and early 1980s. This is one
reason why timeless-looking young girls
with long hair are often preferred by
photographers. Another is that gravity
has taken less of a toll of their figures.

Cameras, Lenses and Film for Nudes

Commercially, roll-film cameras have it
all: they offer a bigger image than 35mm,
with commensurately better quality, and
the old argument of "big fee — big
camera" has a certain logic to it.

What is interesting, though, is how
many photographers choose 35mm for
their personal work. In particular, even
when Struan has been shooting
commercially with his Hasselblad, he may
switch to 35mm for his personal shots,
several of which appear in here. Likewise,
Julia Martinez said of one set of pictures
(of which two appear in this book), "I
was just working with 35mm, and the
freedom was wonderful; no big, heavy
cameras and no lights to move around.
The model felt more relaxed, too."

Going in the other direction, very few
photographers shoot large format nudes
any more, although there is a handful of
4x5in shots in this book.

Longer-than-standard lenses are very
much the norm, although there are also
plenty of wide-angle shots in the book:
Struan with 35mm and even 28mm on
35mm, Guido Paternò Castello with
50mm on 6x6cm, Peter Goodrum with
90mm on 4x5in.

As for films, a surprisingly high
proportion of pictures in this book were
shot on black and white — or perhaps it is
not quite such a surprise, given the way
in which so many photographers shoot
nudes for fun, rather than for profit.
Many photographers still have a sneaking
suspicion that monochrome is more
"real" than colour, while others simply
maintain that it gives them more control
and better enables them to realize their
personal photographic vision. There
seems to be no overall preference for a
particular type or even brand of black
and white film, and Stu Williamson
makes a particular point of using a wide
range of monochrome films for different
tonal effects.

Lighting Equipment for Nudes

Yet again, generalizations are impossible:
unlike (for example) food or pack shots,
there are not even any particularly
common lighting set-ups. In these pages
you will find everything from available
light to monster soft boxes to on-camera
flash, taking in a number of quite
complex lighting set-ups on the way.

A basic kit would probably consist of
three heads, two of which would be
used for lighting the background, though
everything from single-light pictures to
those using four or five lights will be
found in this book. It is also worth
mentioning Stu Williamson's ingenious
Tri-Flector, which is described more fully
on page 24.

And, of course, many photographers
shoot nudes only by available light; you
will find plenty of examples of these, too.

The Team

Most photographers of the nude work
on their own most of the time. There are
two main reasons for this. The first is
simple economics: a lot of nude
photography is done for personal or
portfolio work, and the budget simply
does not stretch to an assistant. There

are exceptions, as when a personal shot
is grafted onto a commissioned shoot,
but this is the exception rather than the
rule.

The other reason is that nude
photography requires a certain rapport
between the subject and the model, and
it is often difficult to establish that rapport
if a third person is present. On the one
hand, the third person may reassure the
model – this is especially true if the third
person is of the same sex as the model –
on the other, he or she may seem like an
intrusion: the photographer is, as it were,
licensed to see the model in the nude,
but other people are not.

THE NUDE PHOTOGRAPHY SESSION

Because nude photography is so
intensely personal, and because models
vary so widely in temperament and
attitude, only a few general remarks are
appropriate.

The most important ones concern
the facilities for the model. She should be
able to dress and undress in privacy,
because nude modelling is not the same
as doing a strip-tease. This privacy can be
a changing room, or a car with a sheet
draped over the windows and weighted
or taped down at the corners. She
should be able to keep warm between
shots: a clean, soft blanket is a useful
thing to have to hand. She should of
course have been warned beforehand
not to wear tight clothing, as marks on
the skin can take hours to disappear.

Other people should be excluded as
far as possible, though a few models
seem to be born exhibitionists and
deliver their best work in front of a large
and appreciative audience. In some
countries, or in some locations, there
may be a problem with public nudity. At
the very least, this can make a shoot
awkward, and at the worst it may involve
arrest or assault or both. If you are in an
unfamiliar country, check local mores as
far as possible – and remember, what
goes in San Francisco may not go in
Kansas, and what goes at the Cap
d'Antibes most certainly does not go in
the Bois de Boulogne.

Finally, remember this. More than
most kinds of photography, taking
pictures of nudes is a matter of mood.
That mood may be timeless, or
deliberately confrontational, or erotic, or
innocent, or a hundred other things; but
if the mood you want is not the same as
the mood you are getting, this more than
anything else will stop you taking the
pictures you envisioned.

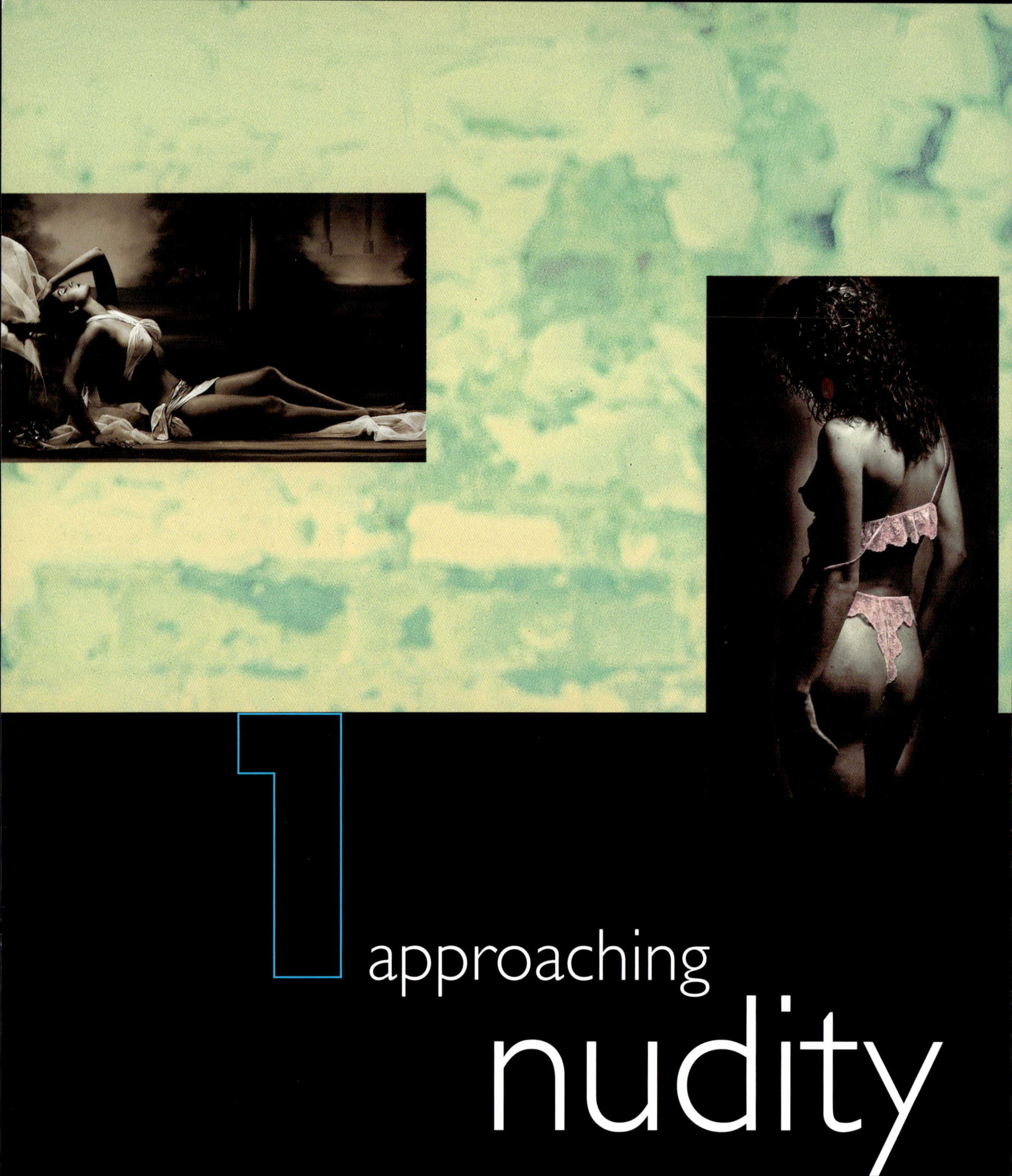

1 approaching nudity

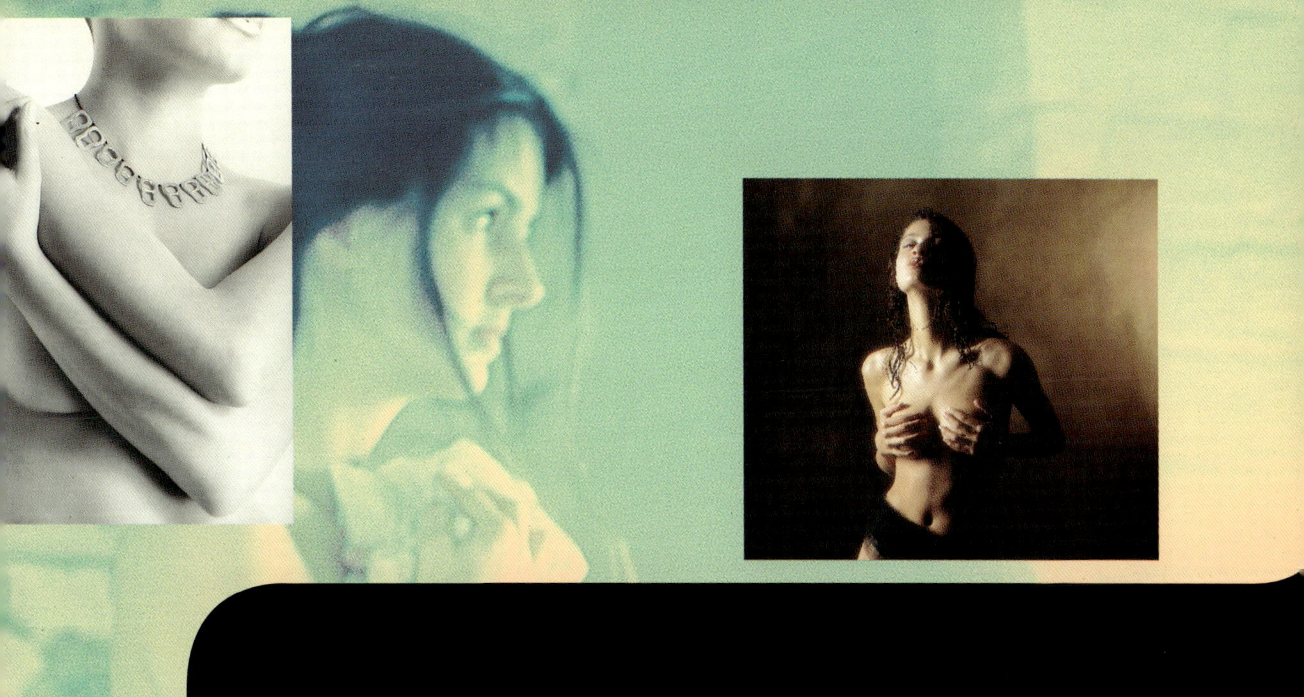

▶ A perennial problem, particularly with inexperienced models, is getting them to feel relaxed about nudity. The first chapter in this book therefore deals with "almost nude" pictures – a means of easing models into nudity gently. If you can show them Polaroids as you go along, this can still further reassure them that they are not being represented in a way which would make them unhappy. Of course, this is not the only reason to take "almost nude" pictures, and (to be fair) it is not the reason why most of the pictures in this chapter were taken. There are portraits here, taken (in the photographer's words) to be "revealing but not too revealing"; there are advertising shots; and there are portfolio and personal shots.

Lighting ranges from outdoor (though most of the outdoor shots in this book are in Chapter 6), through natural indoor light and single-light pictures to a complex four-head set-up. The majority were shot using MF cameras ranging from 645 to 6x7cm, though there are two 35mm shots here. The beginner would be well advised to use medium format, not least because it looks more professional and may well reassure the model; but from a purely technical point of view it does not necessarily matter very much which format you use. There are five monochrome pictures, three in conventional colour, and one cross-processed.

Photographer: **Michèle Francken**

Client: **Mac 3 Company**

Use: **Advertising**

Camera: **6x6cm**

Lens: **110mm with Softar screen**

Film: **Kodak Ektachrome EPP 100**

Exposure: **f/8**

Lighting: **Electronic flash: 1 head**

Props and set: **Hand-painted backdrop**

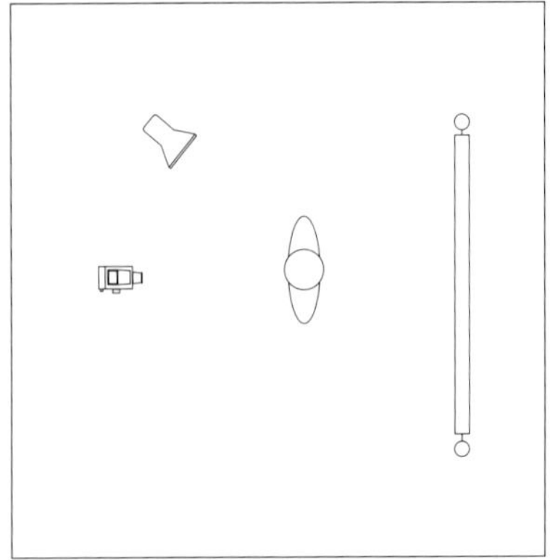

Plan View

▼

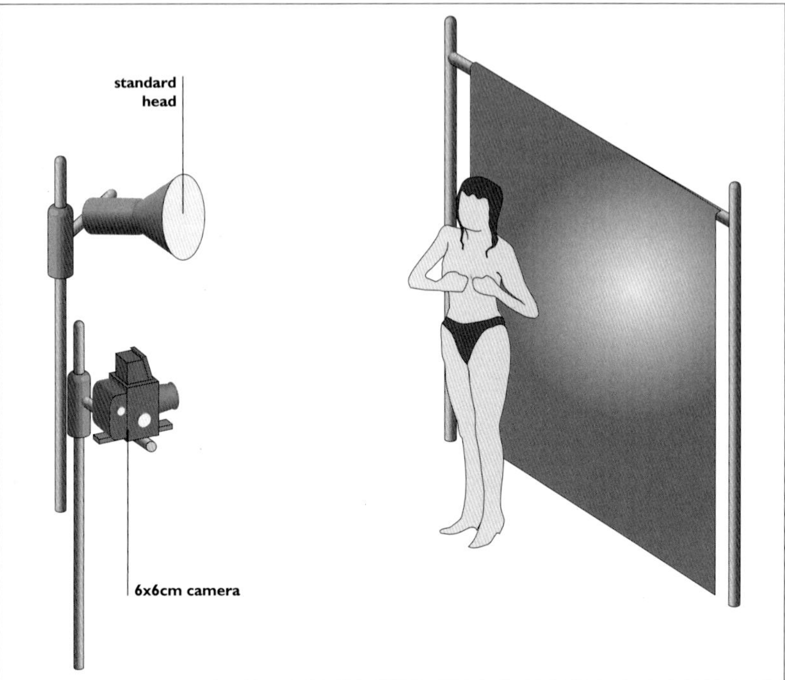

Lighting is subject to Ockham's Razor: lights (like logical entities) should not be multiplied without reason. Here a single light suffices to create a memorable picture. Not even a bounce is used to supplement the lighting plot.

The backdrop is however a little unusual. The model's shadow is just about visible to the lower left, yet the background seems brightly spotlighted. This is normally achieved with additional lighting, but another way to do it is to have a backdrop which is painted as if it were spotlit: in other words, it is painted in somewhat the same way as a graded background, but less smoothly and with more variation in tone. The apparent drawback to such a background is that it is monotonous – but this is only the case for the photographer, because the subjects normally see only their own picture against that ground. Also, considerable differences can be effected, depending on where the subject is placed against the "hot spot."

► *Painted backdrops can be graded, or may give the impression of being spotlit. Some photographers paint their own, but there are manufacturers who specialize in custom or unusual backdrops*

► *The effects obtainable with a painted backdrop can vary widely depending on the subject's distance from the backdrop, the lighting of the backdrop, and the aperture employed*

Photographer's comment:

This sort of lighting is used to create a more sensuous expression. A Softar filter is used to soften the skin.

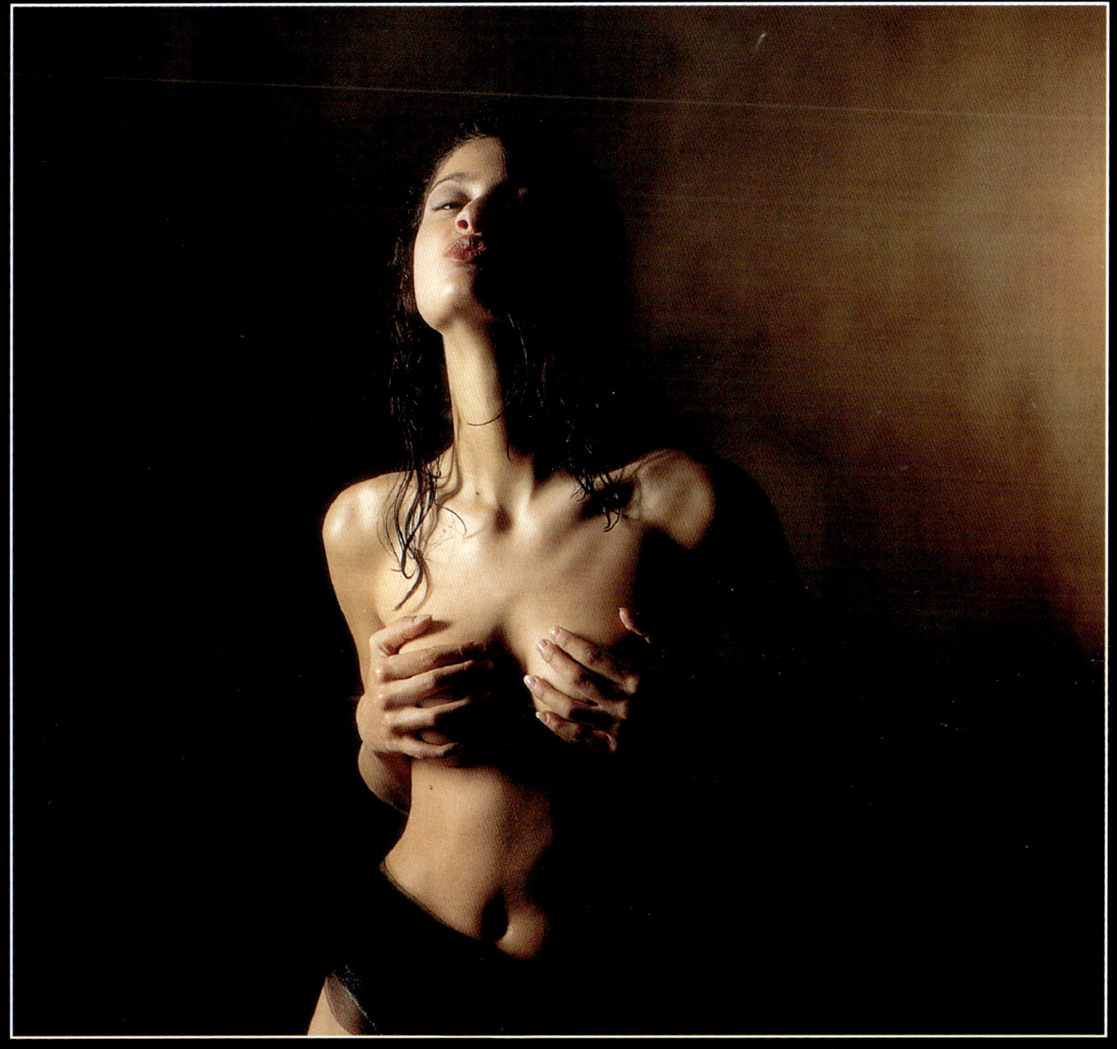

Photographer: **Bob Shell**

Use: **Personal work**

Model: **Audra Fregia**

Camera: **645**

Lens: **80mm**

Film: **Ilford FP4**

Exposure: **1/60 sec at f/8**

Lighting: **Available light**

Props and set: **"My office window!"**

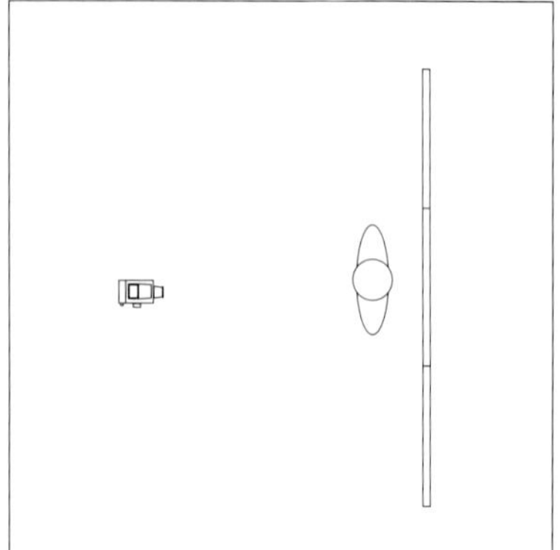

Plan View

A U D R A   A T   T H E   W I N D O W

▼

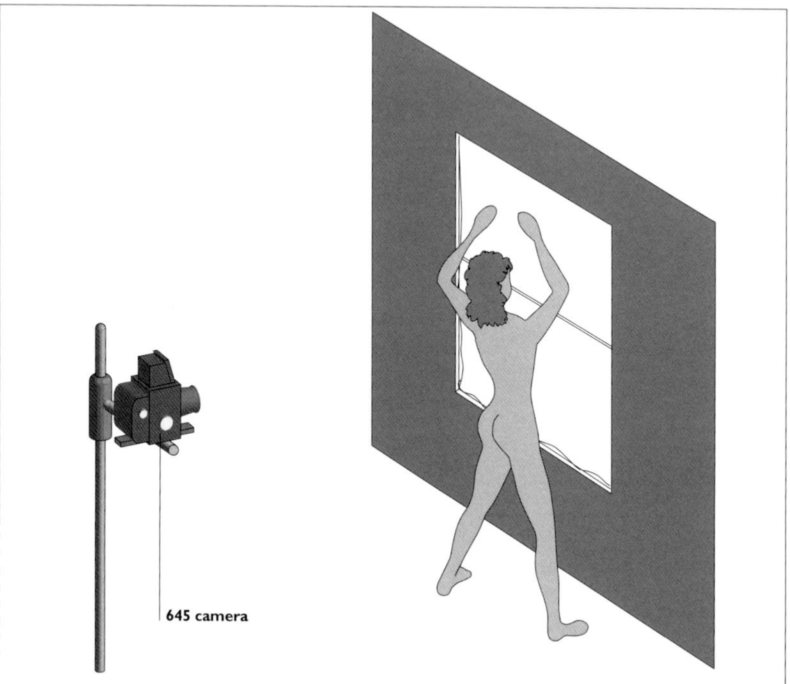

PERHAPS THE MOST IMPORTANT THING TO NOTE HERE IS THAT THE WINDOW IS COVERED WITH FROSTED MYLAR, MAKING IT A NATURAL SOFT BOX AND ALSO MAKING IT OPAQUE SO THAT THE MODEL CANNOT BE SEEN FROM THE STREET.

This sort of silhouette, combined with transillumination of the peignoir, can be extremely effective while still showing remarkably little that could offend any but the most prudish viewer. The shape of the model is beautifully illustrated, and the contrast between the lace of the curtains and the lace of the peignoir is doubly effective. Flare is of course a potential problem and unless the intention is to make a feature of it, the lens must be scrupulously clean; even then, there is some evidence of flare around the model's fingers.

► *Frosted Mylar and Kodatrace are both superb diffusion materials, but in colour Kodatrace introduces a very slight green cast*

► *There is a significant difference between a window receiving direct sun (like this one, which faces north-west) and a window which is illuminated only by sky-light*

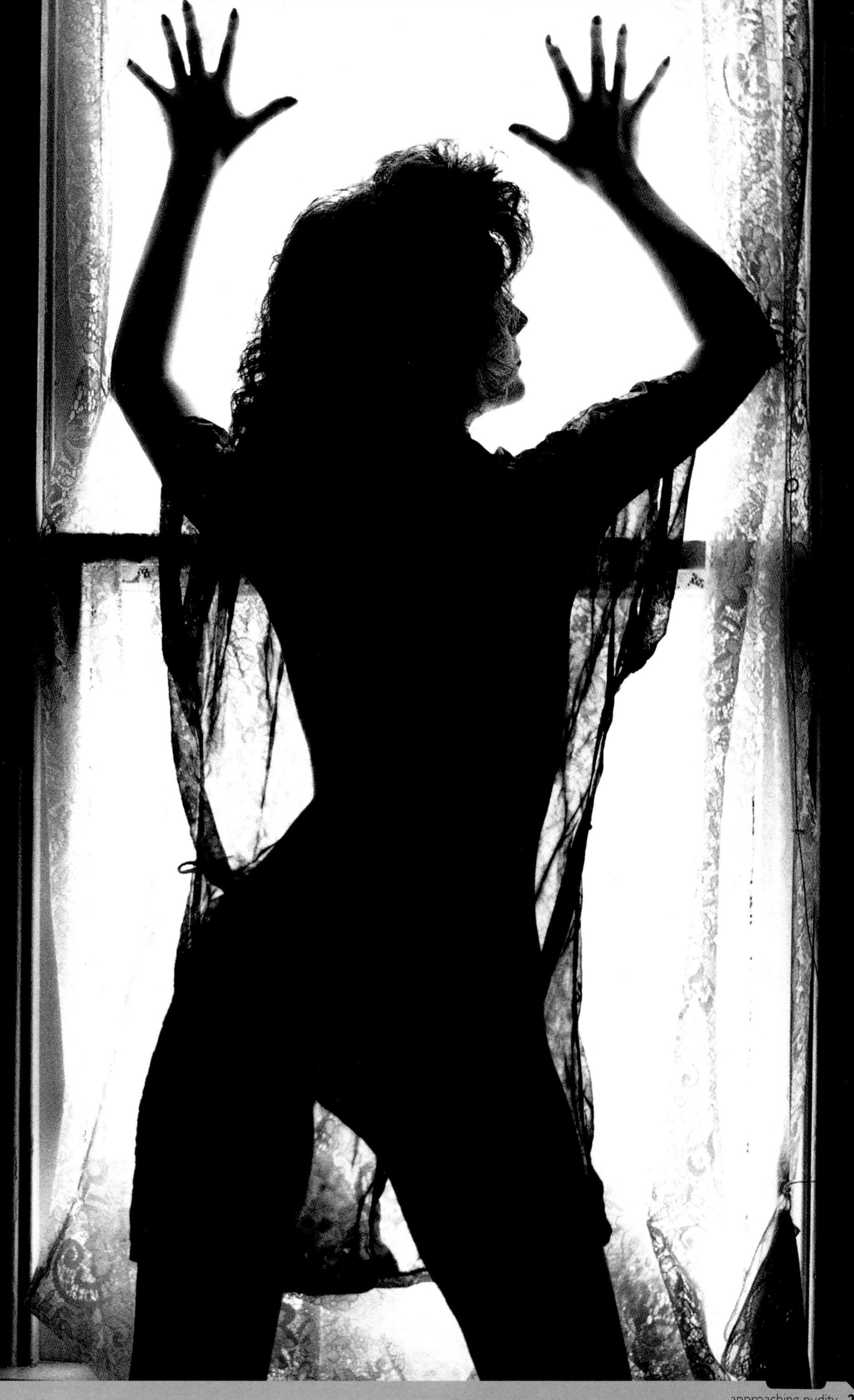

Photographer: **Ron McMillan**

Client: **Beauty Products Catalogue**

Use: **Catalogue**

Model: **Emma Noble**

Assistant: **Paul Cromey**

Camera: **6x6cm**

Lens: **120mm + Softar II soft-focus**

Film: **Kodak Panther X100**

Exposure: **f/16**

Lighting: **Electronic flash: 2 striplights**

Props and set: **Seamless background**

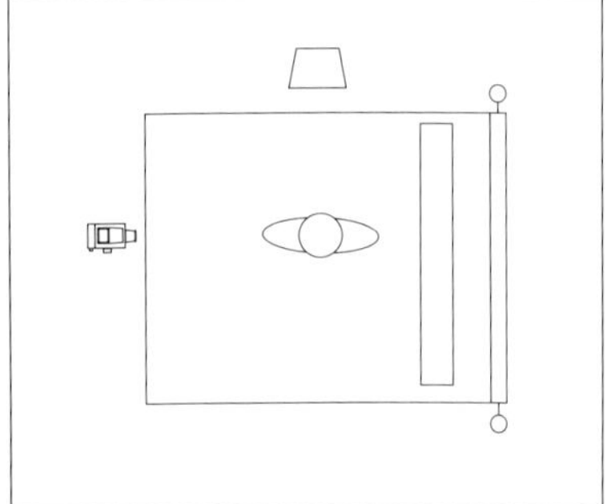

Plan View

E M M A

▼

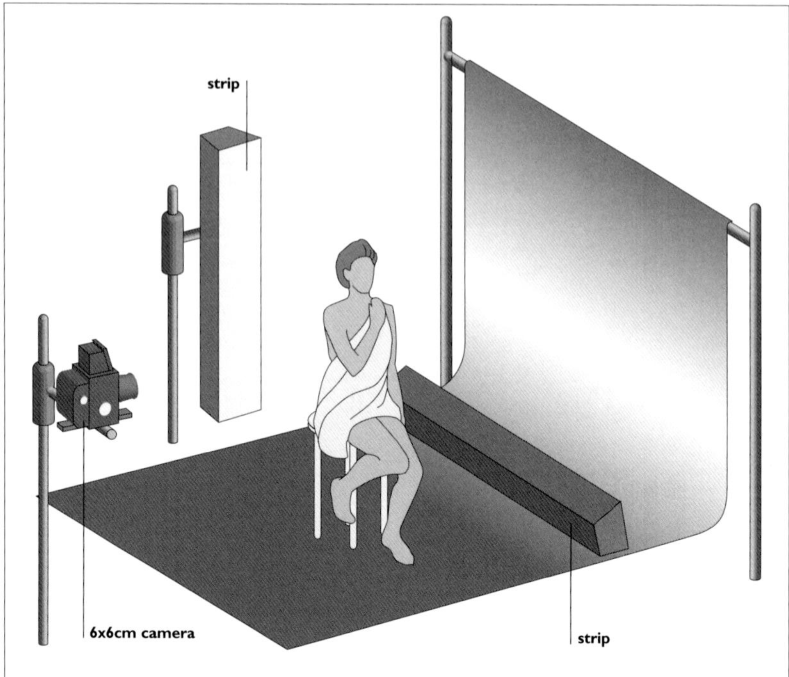

OFTEN, A NUDE SHOT FOR ADVERTISING MUST REVEAL VERY LITTLE; IT MUST LOOK NATURAL AND CHARMING, BUT NOT REVEALING. THIS IS A TIMELESS PICTURE WHICH MIGHT ONCE HAVE SEEMED RISQUÉ BUT WHICH IS ENTIRELY ACCEPTABLE IN THE LATE 20TH CENTURY.

The lighting is certainly simple: a vertical strip light to camera left, illuminating the model's back, and a horizontal strip light on the floor behind the model, illuminating the background and in the process providing a modest amount of fill on the model's arm and on the towel. Compared with the model, the vertical light is very slightly nearer the camera, to provide a glancing light rather than a pure side-light. As so often, it is not the complexity of the lighting which is important, but its appropriateness; and analyzed more carefully, this profile semi-high-key approach is unusual and effective. The use of a white towel on the dark side of the model, away from the light, saves it from being too dark as well as suggesting natural, unaffected beauty.

► *Strip lights are more directional than soft boxes, at least in the short axis*

► *This is an interesting example of white-on-white; the towel is lighter than the background on the left, and darker than the background on the right*

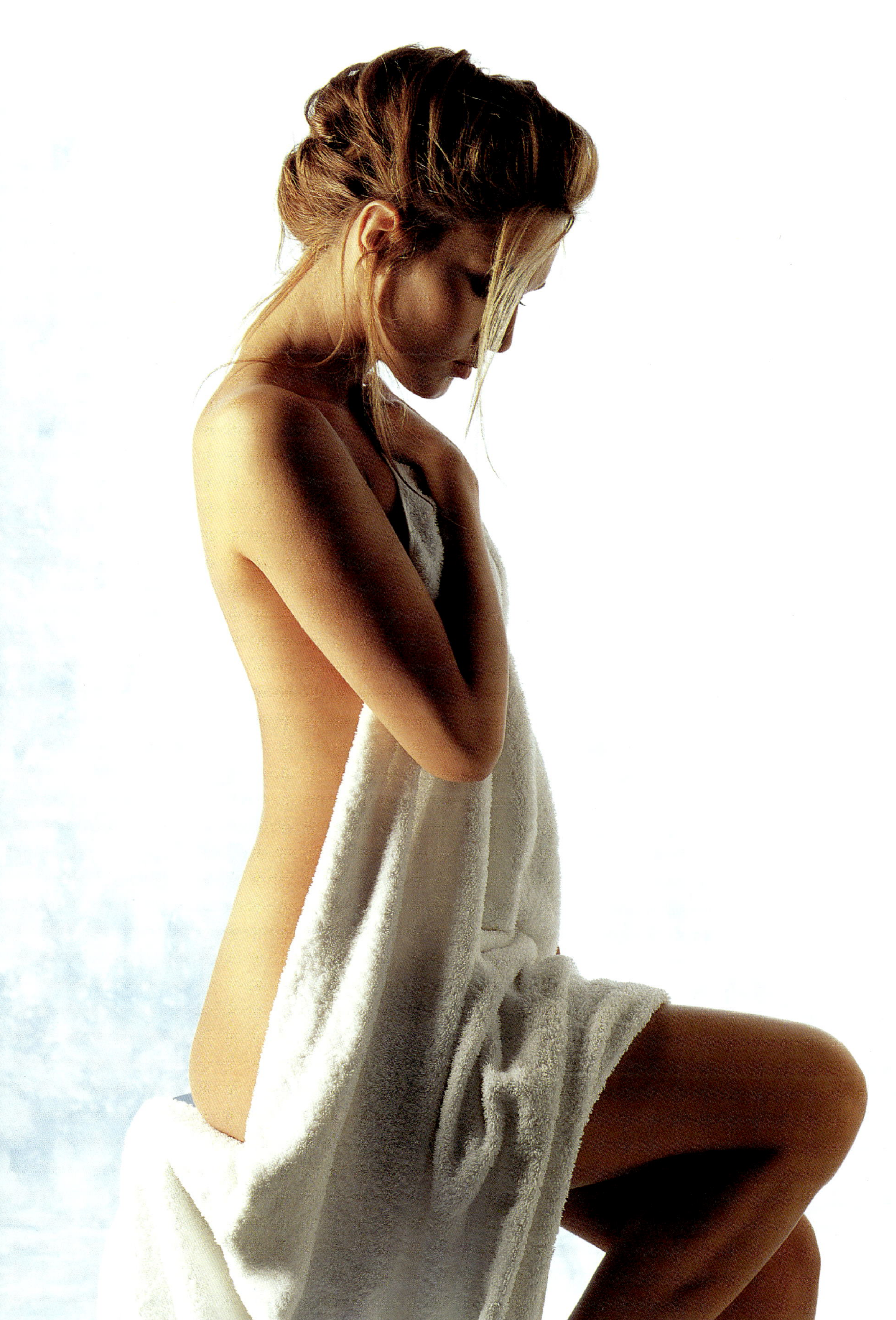

Photographer: **Stu Williamson**

Client: **Andrea (model)**

Use: **Portrait**

Camera: **6x7cm**

Lens: **140mm**

Film: **Ilford FP4**

Exposure: **f/11**

Lighting: **Electronic flash: one head**

Props and set: **Lastolite "Thunder" painted backdrop**

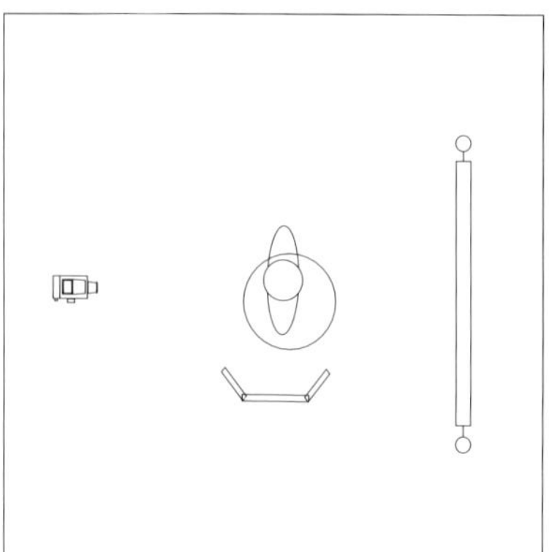

Plan View

A N D R E A

▼

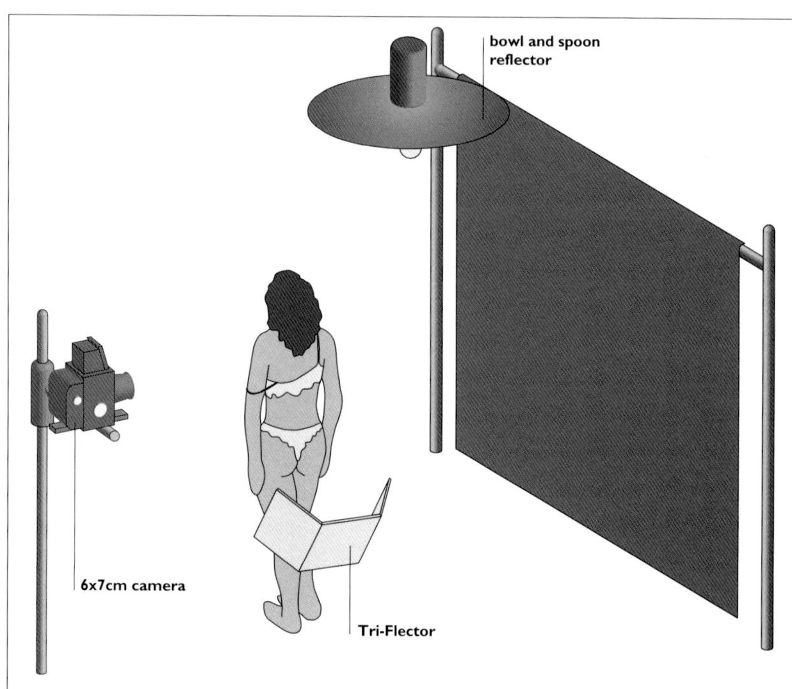

THE SINGLE LIGHT HERE IS A LARGE DISH OF THE TYPE SOMETIMES CALLED A "BOWL AND SPOON" — A LARGE-DIAMETER SHALLOW REFLECTOR WITH A DIFFUSER CAP OVER THE LAMP ITSELF.

This light is well above the model and to camera right, as may be seen from the shadows; but Stu also used his trademark "Tri-Flector" (which he invented and which is manufactured by Lastolite). This has a central panel flanked by two "wings" which allow the light to be directed with considerable precision. The picture was then printed with dramatic dodging – Stu prints all his own work – and the pink colour was added with Fotospeed dyes. The shaped background is more an effect of printing than of lighting.

► *Large reflectors give a different quality of light from soft boxes*

► *Hand colouring can add impact to a monochrome nude*

► *The contrast between tanned and untanned areas (if the model has not got an overall tan) can be used to good effect in some shots*

Photographer's comment:

The model wanted a picture for her boyfriend. It had to be intimate and revealing, without being too revealing.

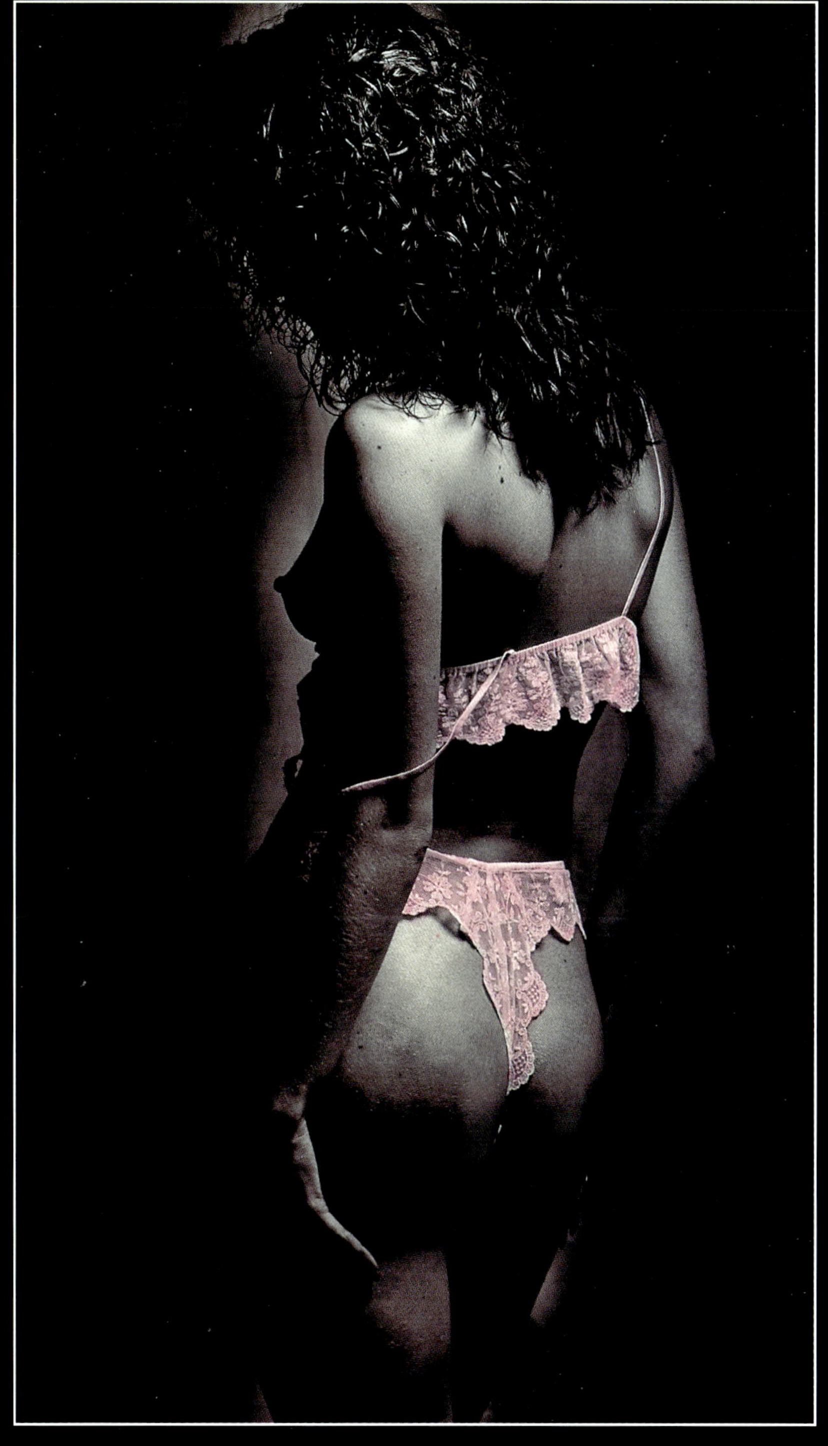

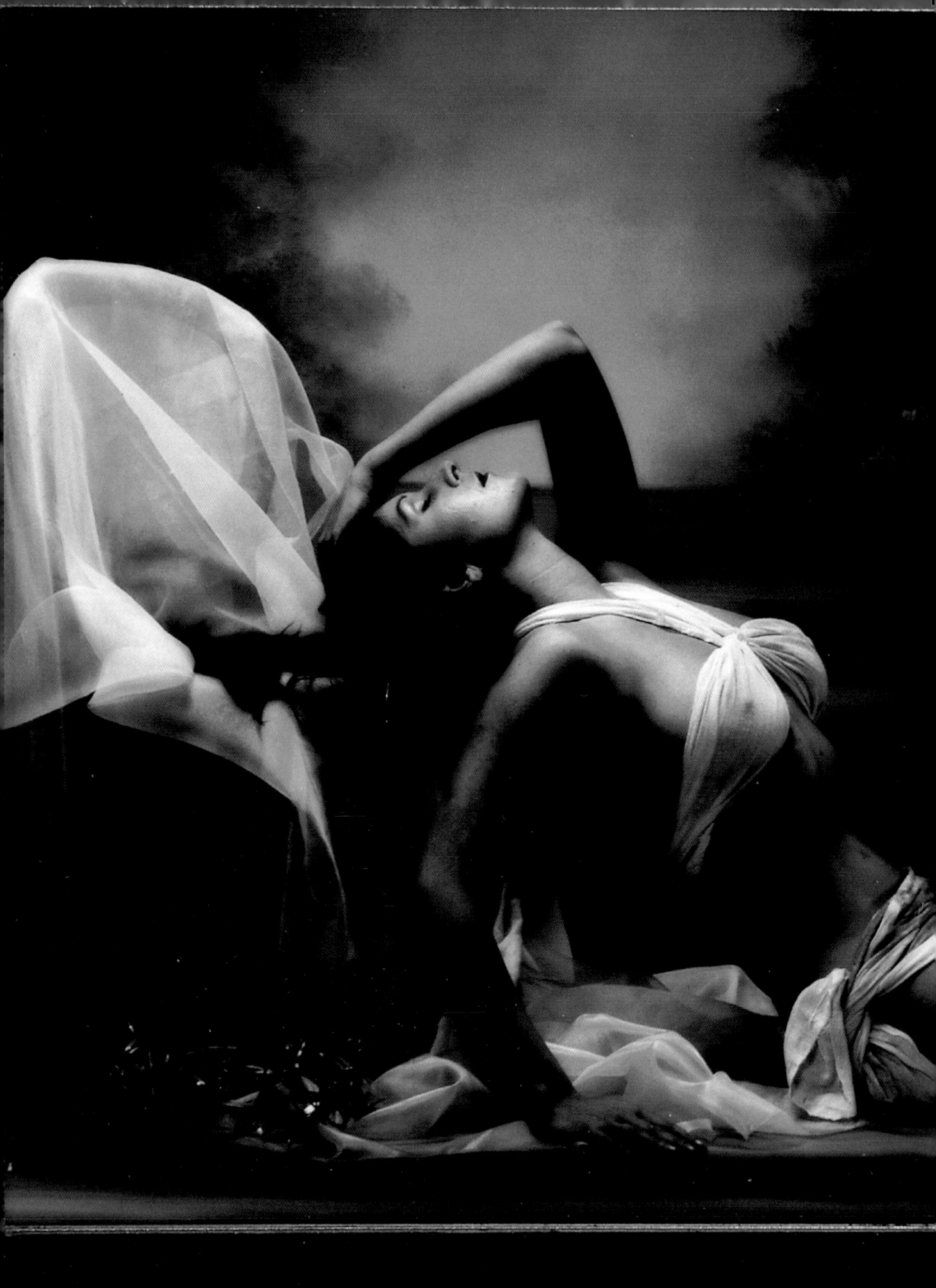

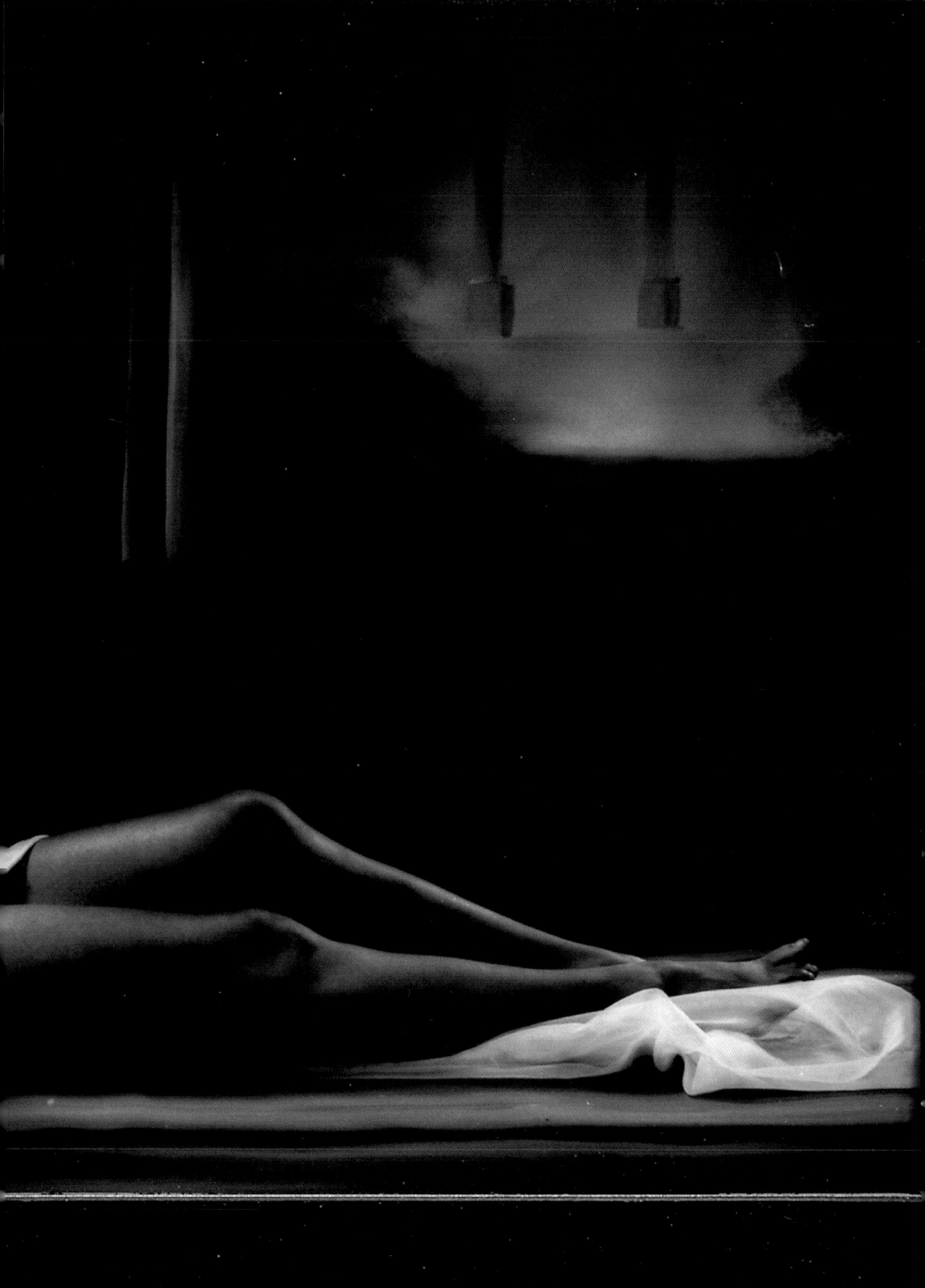

Photographer: **Stu Williamson**

Client: **Tanya**

Use: **Portrait**

Camera: **6x7cm**

Lens: **90mm**

Film: **Ilford Pan F**

Exposure: **f/11**

Lighting: **Electronic flash: 4 heads**

Props and set: **Colorama hand-painted b/g; crown by Terry English, armourer**

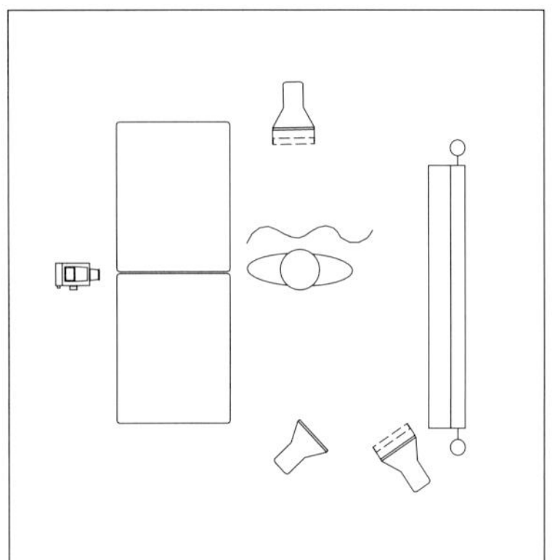

Plan View

T A N Y A

▼

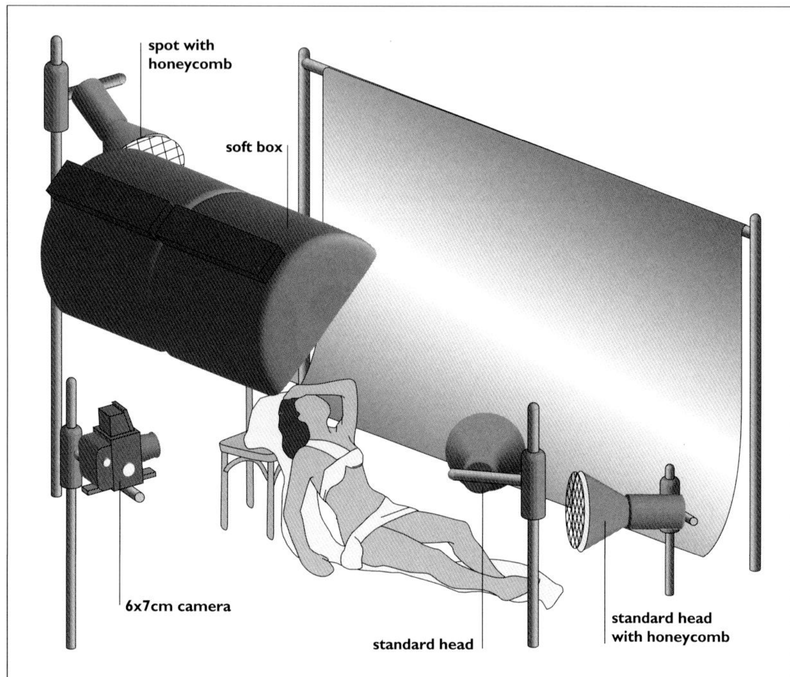

THE MODEL IS SURPRISINGLY FULLY CLOTHED, BUT BECAUSE OF THE WAY THE "CLOTHES" ARE ARRANGED, SHE LOOKS LESS DRESSED THAN SHE IS. THE SEMI-CLASSICAL POSE AND BACKDROP CONTRIBUTE STILL MORE TO THE OVERALL AURA OF SENSUALITY.

The lighting is of course important too. The key is the honeycombed spot to camera left, above the model's head, illuminating (in particular) her face and chest. This is supplemented by another honeycombed head to camera right, rimlighting the model's legs. A large soft box, just above the camera, acts as a general fill and provides some of the illumination of the background, which is also lit with a fourth head coming in from camera right.

This is a good example of a second light being added to the key to create the illusion of one light: the key and the rimlight combine flawlessly, creating the impression of a single light source.

► *If a single light will not do what you want, ask yourself what it would illuminate if it were doing what you want*

► *Painted backdrops can have more than one centre of interest — or two backdrops can sometimes be combined*

Photographer's comment:

I use a wide variety of different black and white films for different tonalities.

Photographer: **Julia Martinez**

Use: **Personal work**

Model: **Sarah**

Camera: **6x7cm**

Lens: **300mm**

Film: **Fuji RDP ISO 100 rated at EI 125 and processed in C41 chemistry**

Exposure: **1/30sec at f/11**

Lighting: **Available light**

Props and set: **Location**

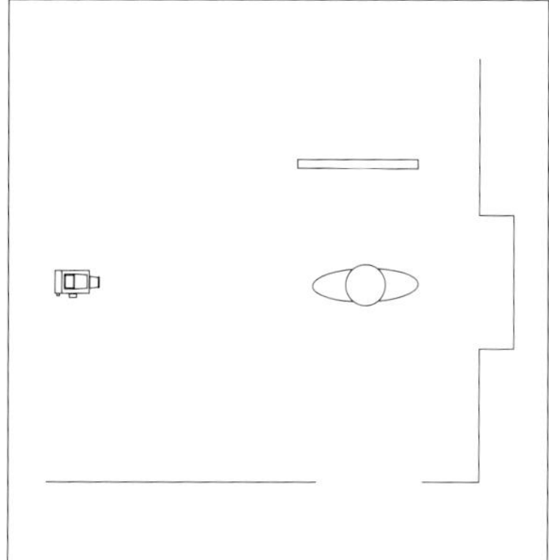

Plan View

- ► *Derelict buildings are a favourite set for photographers, but they have their own dangers*

- ► *Cross-processing adds to the eeriness of the scene*

S A R A H

▼

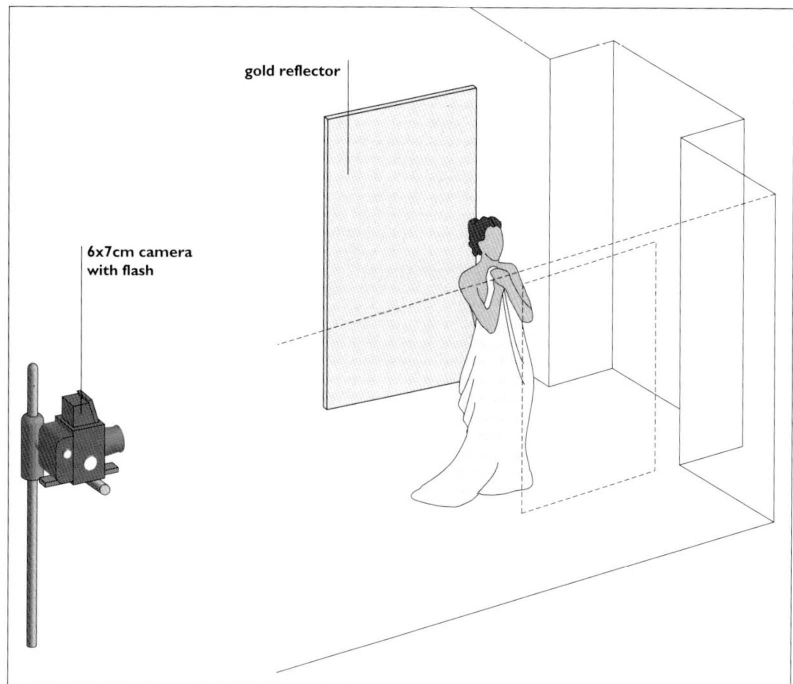

THIS IS AN AVAILABLE-LIGHT SHOT. SUN THROUGH THE WINDOW TO THE RIGHT WAS SUPPLEMENTED BY A LARGE GOLD REFLECTOR TO CAMERA LEFT TO PROVIDE SOME FILL ON THE MODEL'S BACK: IT WAS ABOUT 180CM (6FT) SQUARE.

The lighting, therefore, was as much a matter of selection as anything else: finding the right location, the right window on the right side of the building – but there is a story behind it:

In the photographer's words, "This was shot in a derelict mental hospital. We had to climb several flights of stairs, as the windows on the lower floors were boarded up. At the end of the shoot, we heard noises downstairs, and the model panicked: she dropped the sheet and stood there stark naked in terror. It took me some time to get her to cover up again. We came to no harm: it was homeless people, though the hospital is supposed to be haunted."

Photographer's comment:

I was lucky with the sun coming through the window like that.

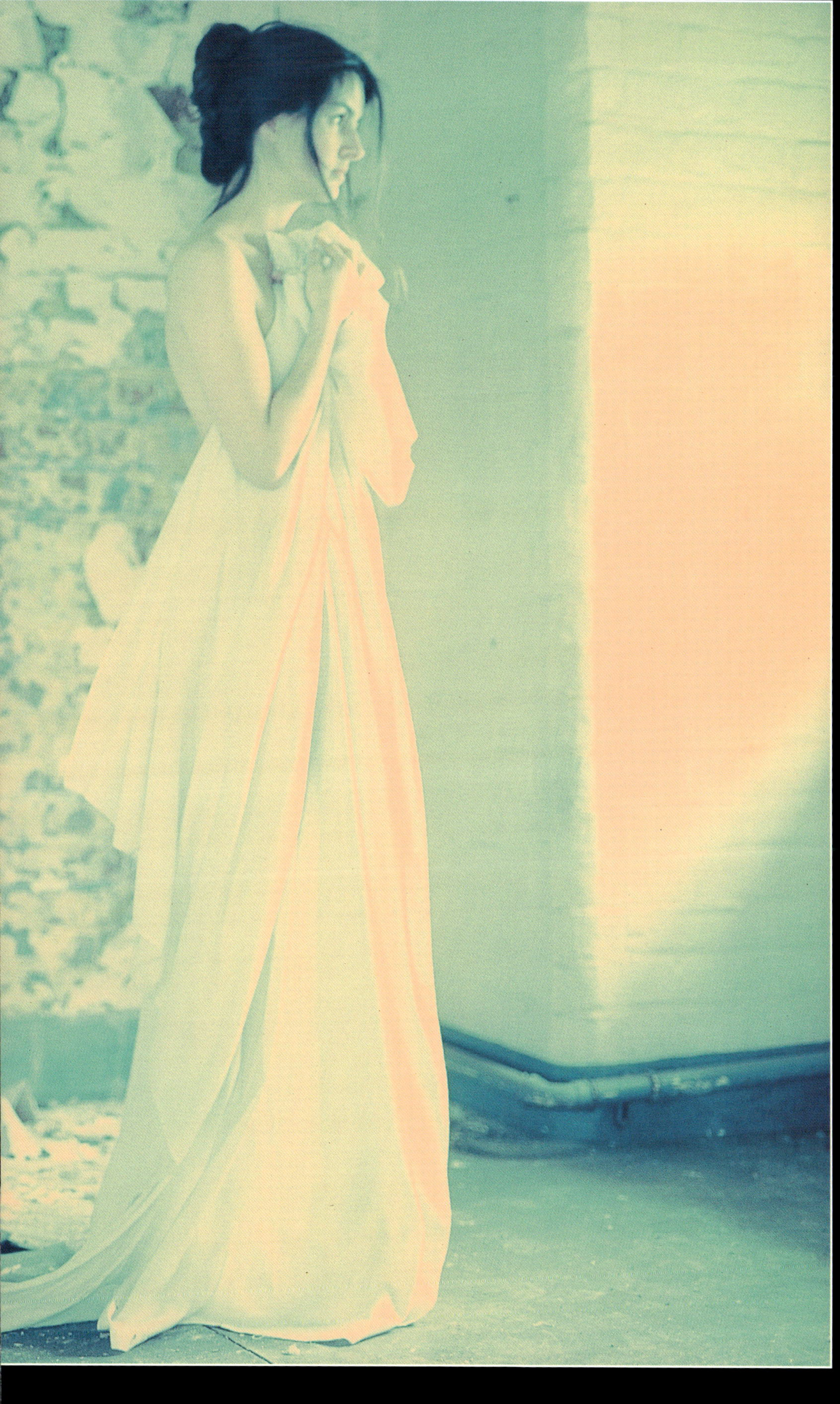

Photographer: **Julia Martinez**

Use: **Personal work**

Model: **Becky**

Camera: **645**

Lens: **300mm**

Film: **Kodak T-Max 100**

Exposure: **f/11**

Lighting: **Electronic flash: 3 heads**

Props and set: **White background – and see**

Photographer's comment

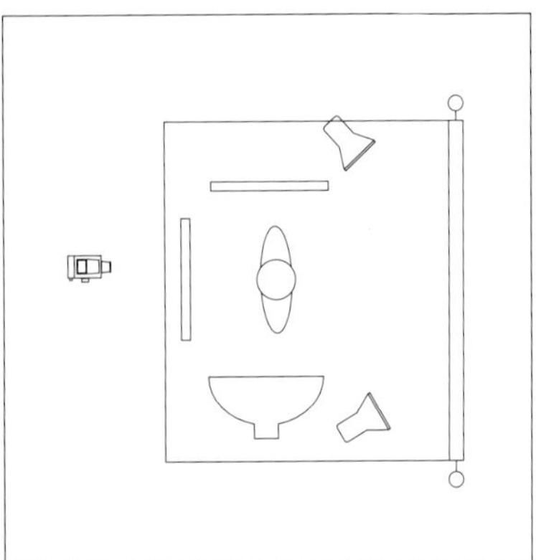

Plan View

► *Chiaroscuro and high key are less incompatible than they might seem*

► *Some photographers' style is intimately bound up with their lighting technique; others are more recognizable from their compositional approach*

RECESSION DRESSING

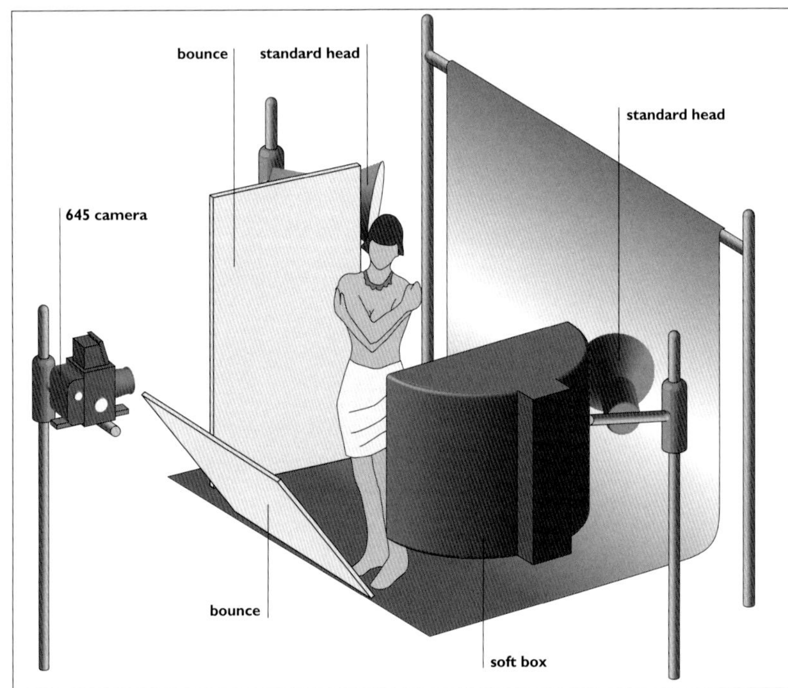

Julia Martinez was at first best known for her gentle available-light pictures but, as the photographs in this book show, she is also quite at home with other light sources — in this case studio flash.

The key and indeed only light on the subject is a 120x120cm (4x4ft) soft box to camera right, beside the model. Two bounces, one to camera left and the other below the camera's line of sight, even out the light considerably while still maintaining strong modelling. Finally, a couple of lights on the background create a classic high-key effect. The printed image was toned blue using Fotospeed materials.

The overall effect is classical and simple. It illustrates, as do most good pictures, that the single most important thing is the photographer's eye. Why is the image framed this way? Would you have framed it this way? And why does it "work" so well?

Photographer's comment:

This was shot for a college assignment on "recession dressing". The necklace is made of Coca-Cola can pulls….

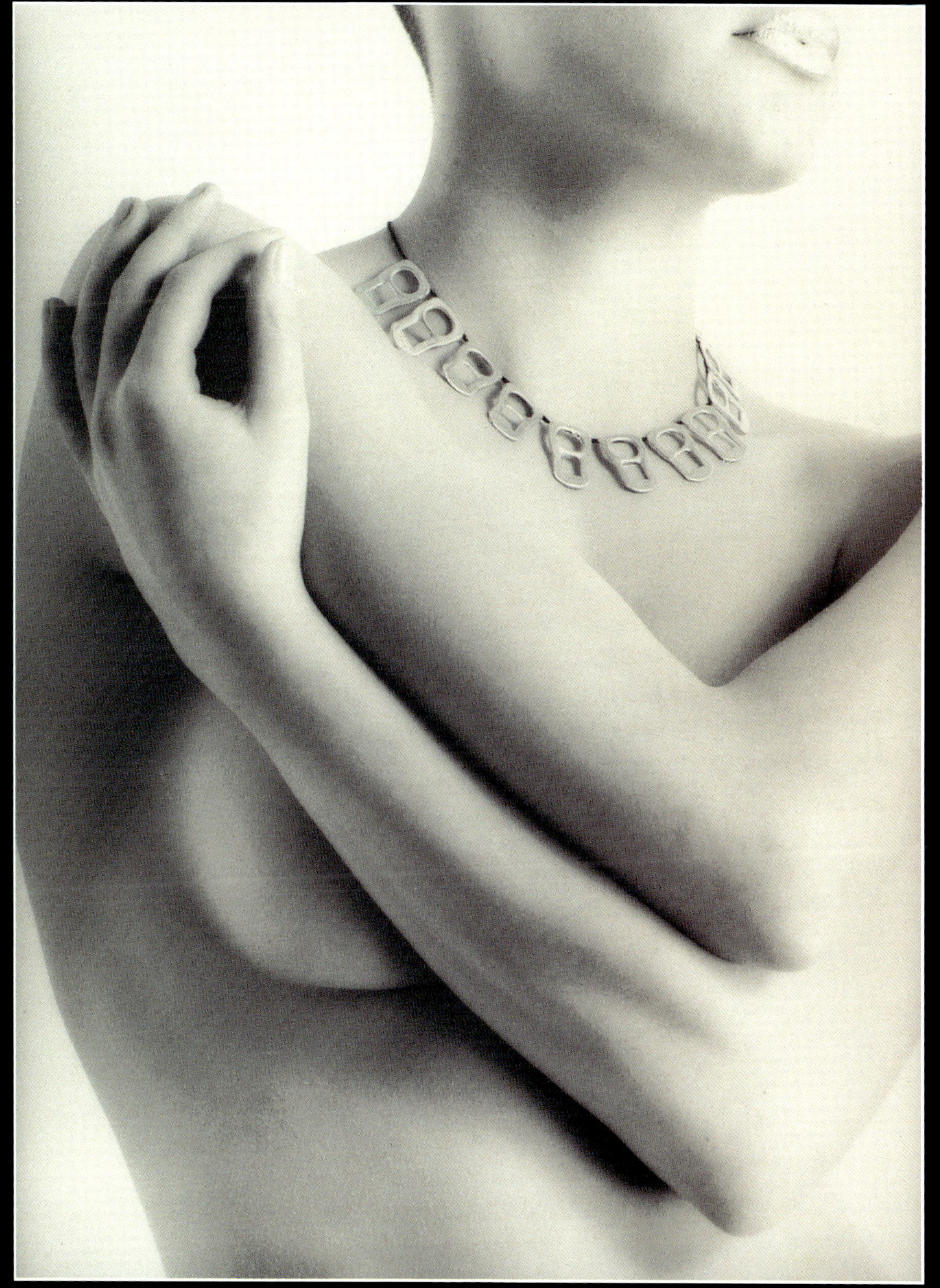

Photographer: **Frank P. Wartenberg**

Use: **Portfolio**

Camera: **35mm**

Lens: **85mm**

Film: **Polaroid Polagraph**

Exposure: **Not recorded**

Lighting: **Late sun**

Props and set: **Location (beach)**

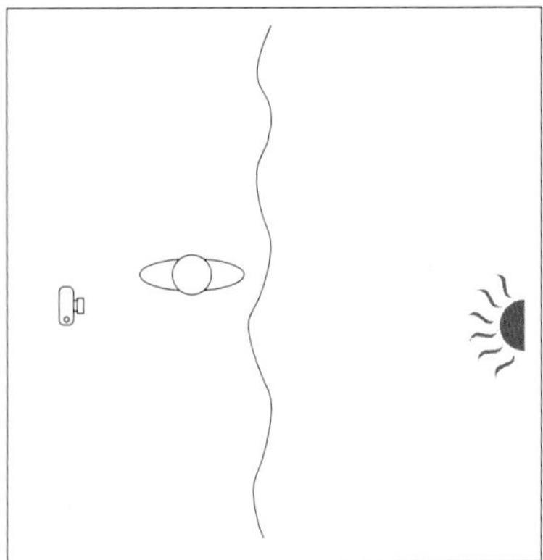

Plan View

L A T E   S U N

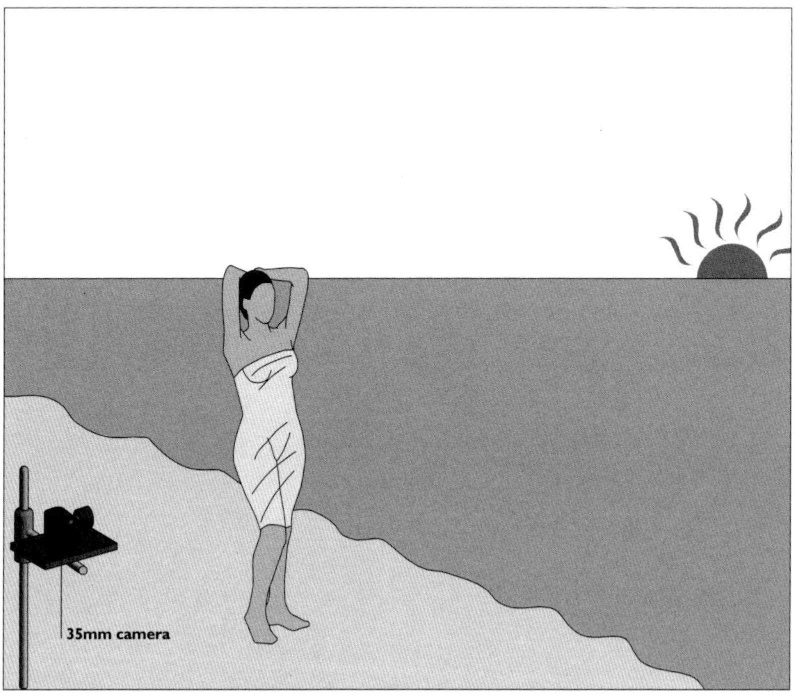

MANY PHOTOGRAPHERS USE POLAROID POLAPAN FOR ITS UNIQUE AND RATHER OLD-FASHIONED TONALITY — WHICH IS OFTEN MORE IMPORTANT THAN "INSTANT" PROCESSING — BUT THE MORE EXPERIMENTALLY MINDED HAVE DISCOVERED JUST WHAT ITS HIGHER-CONTRAST COUSIN, POLAROID POLAGRAPH, CAN DO.

Frank Wartenberg is particularly fond of this film and as he demonstrates here, there is no need to take seriously the warning that it is not intended for general-purpose photography. Even in the relatively contrasty conditions of direct sunlight, it can deliver an excellent tonal range and remarkable subtlety.

Exposure must however be very precise if the highlights are not to be "blown" or the shadows too extensive. Like any high-contrast product, it can be used to expand any part of the tonal range at the expense of both lighter and darker areas; and this is what has been done here

► *With a high-contrast material, the important thing is to know exactly which tones to expand*

► *Polaroid instant-process 35mm films have very tender emulsions and should only be sent out as dupes*

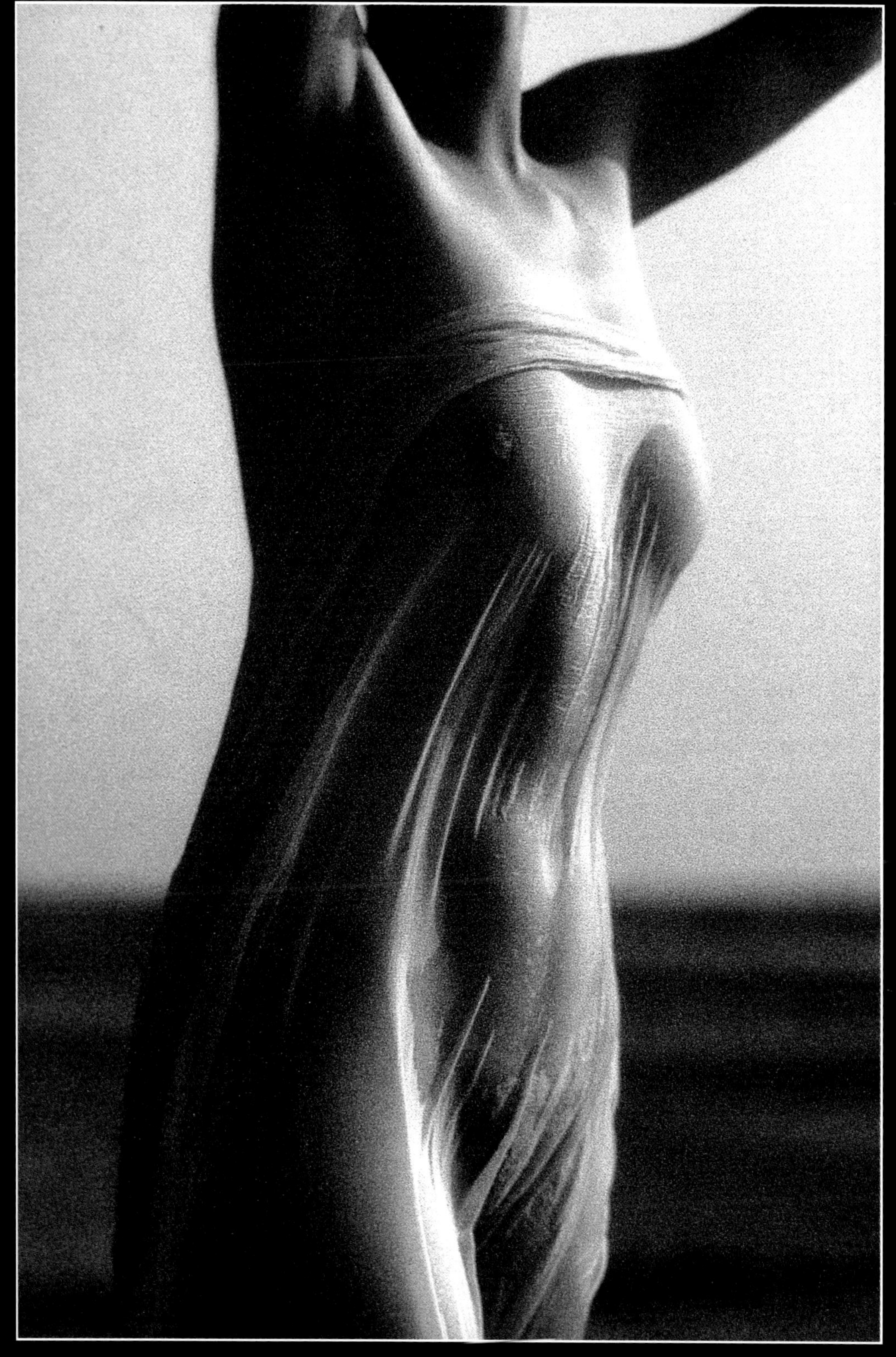

Photographer: **Struan**

Use: **Personal work**

Model: **Krista**

Camera: **35mm**

Lens: **105mm**

Film: **Kodak Tri-X Pan**

Exposure: **1/25 sec at f/4**

Lighting: **Available light**

Props and set: **White studio wall**

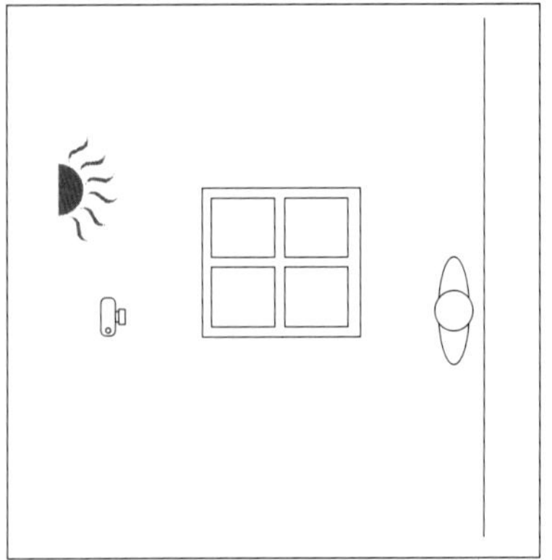

Plan View

J E A N S

▼

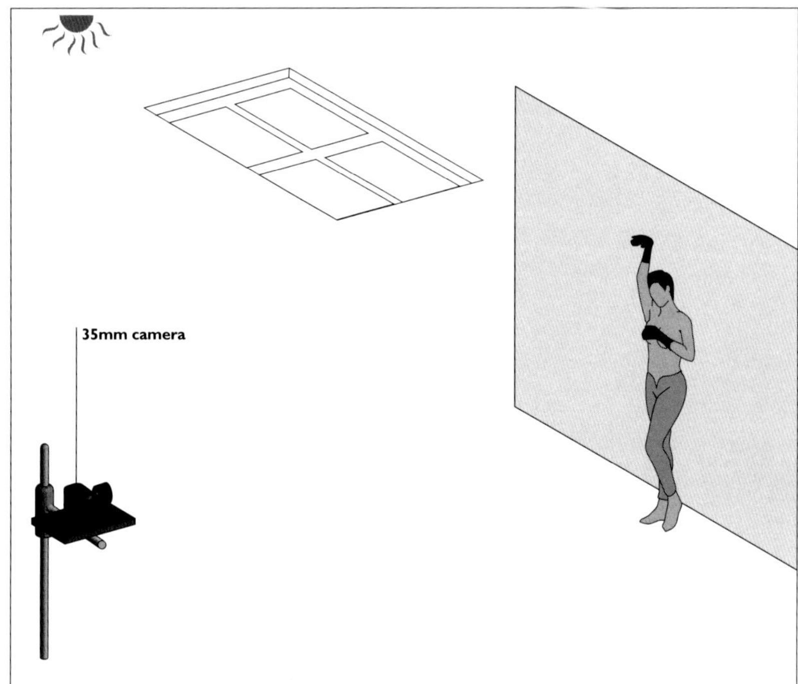

THIS SUCCESS OF THIS PICTURE DERIVES IN LARGE PART FROM ITS PLAYFULNESS. THE MODEL IS DEFINITELY "STRIKING A POSE", BUT THE WOOLLY GLOVES TURN HER INTO A REAL PERSON RATHER THAN JUST A SYMBOL.

Time and again the virtues of our ancestors' daylight studios are revealed: a traditional daylight studio with skylights and blinds is not to be sniffed at. This picture is lit from a skylight on an overcast day.

On the minus side, daylight is less versatile and controllable than artificial light. There are no spotlights, unless it is a sunny day and the windows are in exactly the right place; you need a large studio, in order to take the greatest advantage of light from different directions; light intensity can vary rapidly as clouds blow across the sun; and light colour can vary widely from warm to cold, necessitating filtration in colour.

► *Daylight is a wonderful medium but hard to control*

► *Because of its colour, north light is often of more use in monochrome than in colour*

► *Contrast what people expect with what they don't expect, for arresting effect*

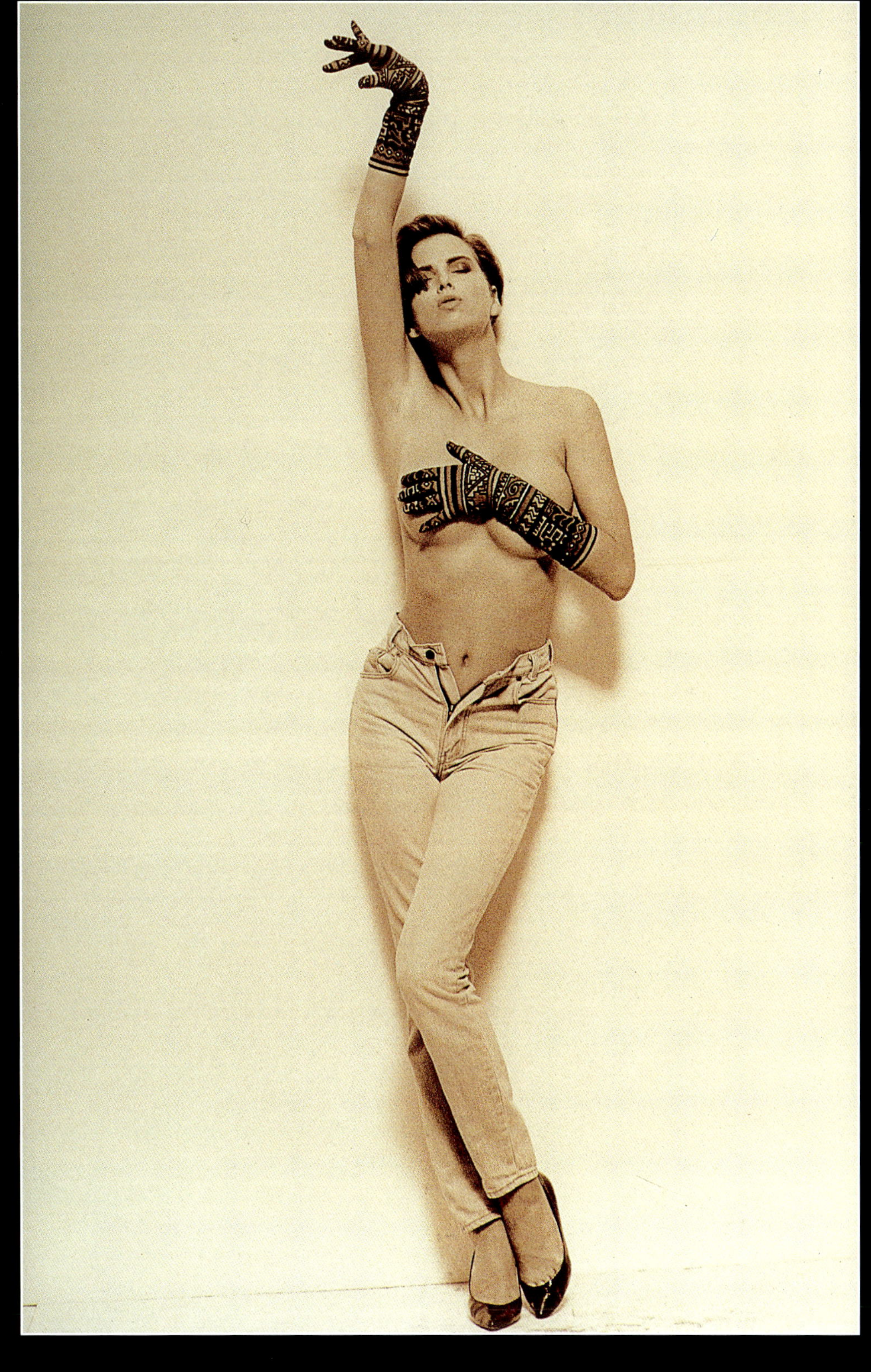

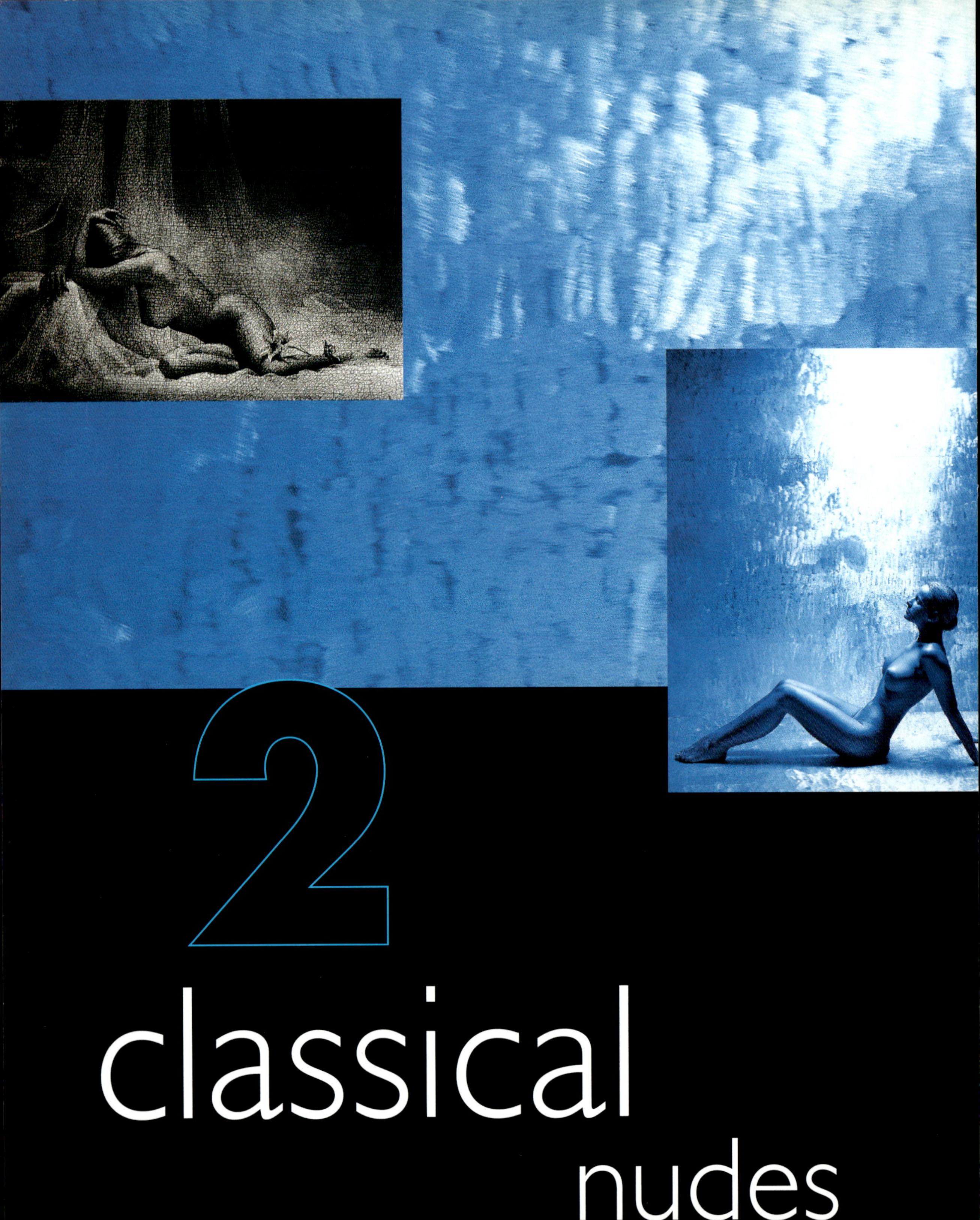

2

classical
nudes

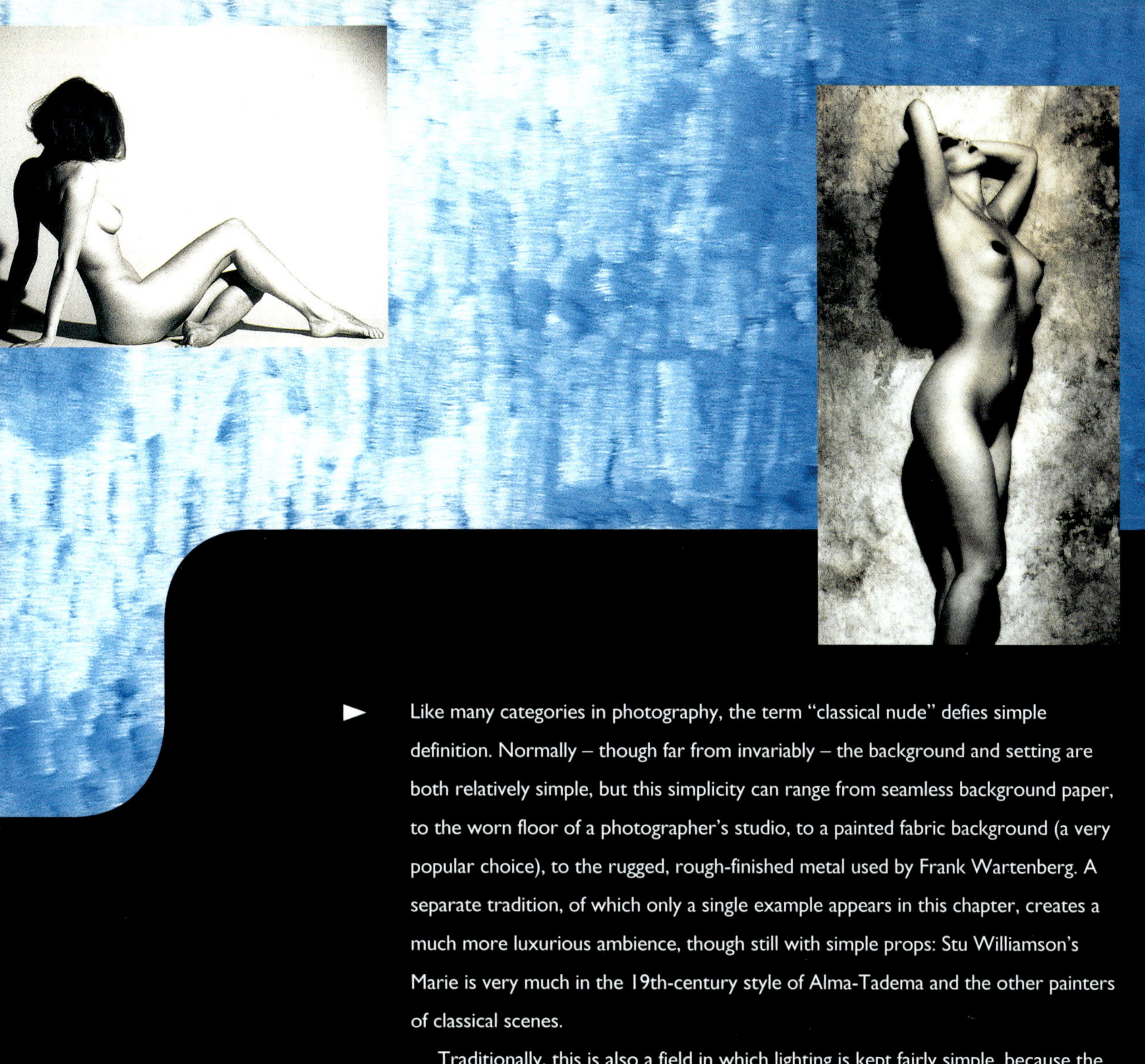

Like many categories in photography, the term "classical nude" defies simple definition. Normally – though far from invariably – the background and setting are both relatively simple, but this simplicity can range from seamless background paper, to the worn floor of a photographer's studio, to a painted fabric background (a very popular choice), to the rugged, rough-finished metal used by Frank Wartenberg. A separate tradition, of which only a single example appears in this chapter, creates a much more luxurious ambience, though still with simple props: Stu Williamson's Marie is very much in the 19th-century style of Alma-Tadema and the other painters of classical scenes.

Traditionally, this is also a field in which lighting is kept fairly simple, because the photographer is often playing with light as much as he (or she) is exploring the graphic possibilities of the nude: half the pictures in this chapter employ only a single light source, and it is not unusual to use two lights together to create the effect of a single, larger light. Rod Ashford's Kay uses a single light on the subject, and another on the background.

The majority of pictures in this chapter were shot on roll-film, with about one-third on 35mm and one on 4x5in. For this kind of image, where texture and gradation are at a premium, 35mm may be a less appropriate choice unless (like the photographers whose work is seen here) you have a particular reason to use it.

Photographer: **Mike Dmochowski**

Use: **Self-promotion**

Model: **Dawn (who also acted as stylist)**

Camera: **35mm**

Lens: **150mm + warming filter**

Film: **Kodak Ektachrome EPP**

Exposure: **f/11**

Lighting: **Electronic flash: 2 heads, filtered**

Props and set: **Black velvet/black paper**

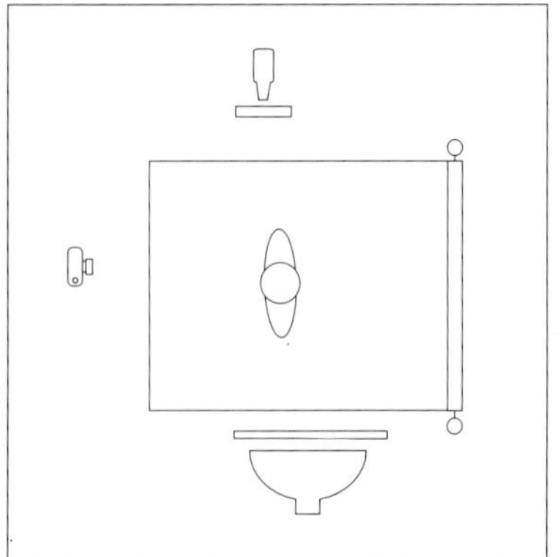

Plan View

> ► *Gold body-paint smears very easily and can be difficult for a model to apply evenly all over*

> ► *Strong warming filters such as an 81EF can be extremely effective with golden subjects of any kind*

> ► *There is no truth in the rumour (which originates from a James Bond movie) that gold body-paint is dangerous when applied all over. It can be worn for many hours without any risk*

GOLD FEMALE SCULPTURE

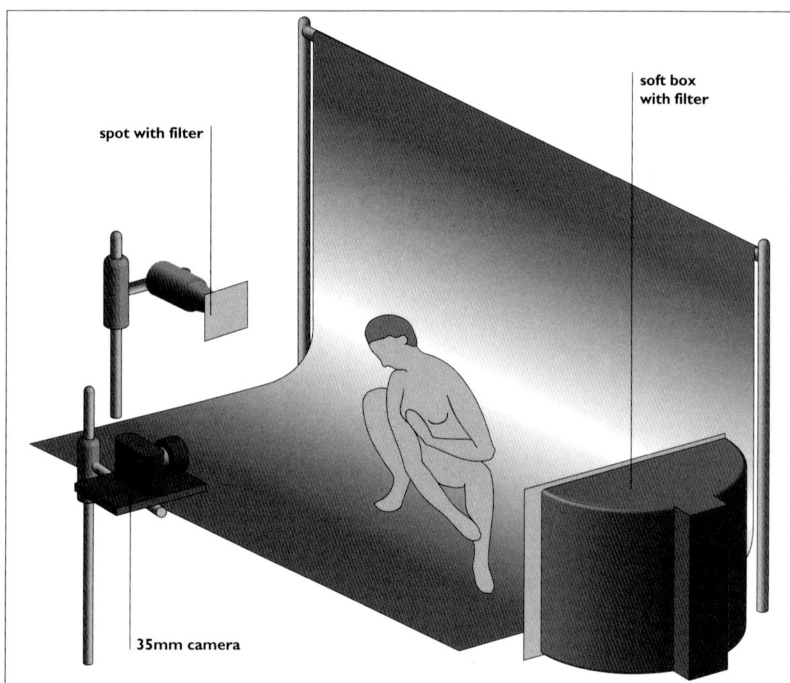

WHAT YOU SEE IS WHAT YOU GET: A MODEL PAINTED WITH GOLD BODY-PAINT. WHAT YOU SEE IS ALSO EMPHASIZED WITH THE HELP OF DOUBLE STRAW FILTERS OVER THE LIGHTING AND A WARMING FILTER (VALUE UNRECORDED) OVER THE LENS FOR A REALLY RICH GOLD.

The key light comes from camera left, and is a Fresnel spot about 1.8m (6ft) from the subject and about 60cm (2ft) above the floor. It is at right angles to the line of sight of the camera. The exposure reading, pointing the meter directly at the light source, was f/11.

Fill is supplied by a 1×1m (40×40in) soft box to camera right, directly opposite the key and about 1.2m (4ft) from the model. The exposure reading from this light, again pointing the meter straight at the light from the position of the model, was f/5.6–1/2 (f/6.8).

The model is on black velvet, with a black seamless paper sweep behind her: the velvet is more illuminated than the paper, but it reflects about 1 stop less light and so reads as completely black.

Photographer's comment:

Exposure is very subjective in this sort of picture. My preference would be for a dark exposure, but unlike a lot of subjects where exposure is critical, on this there was at least a 3-stop latitude.

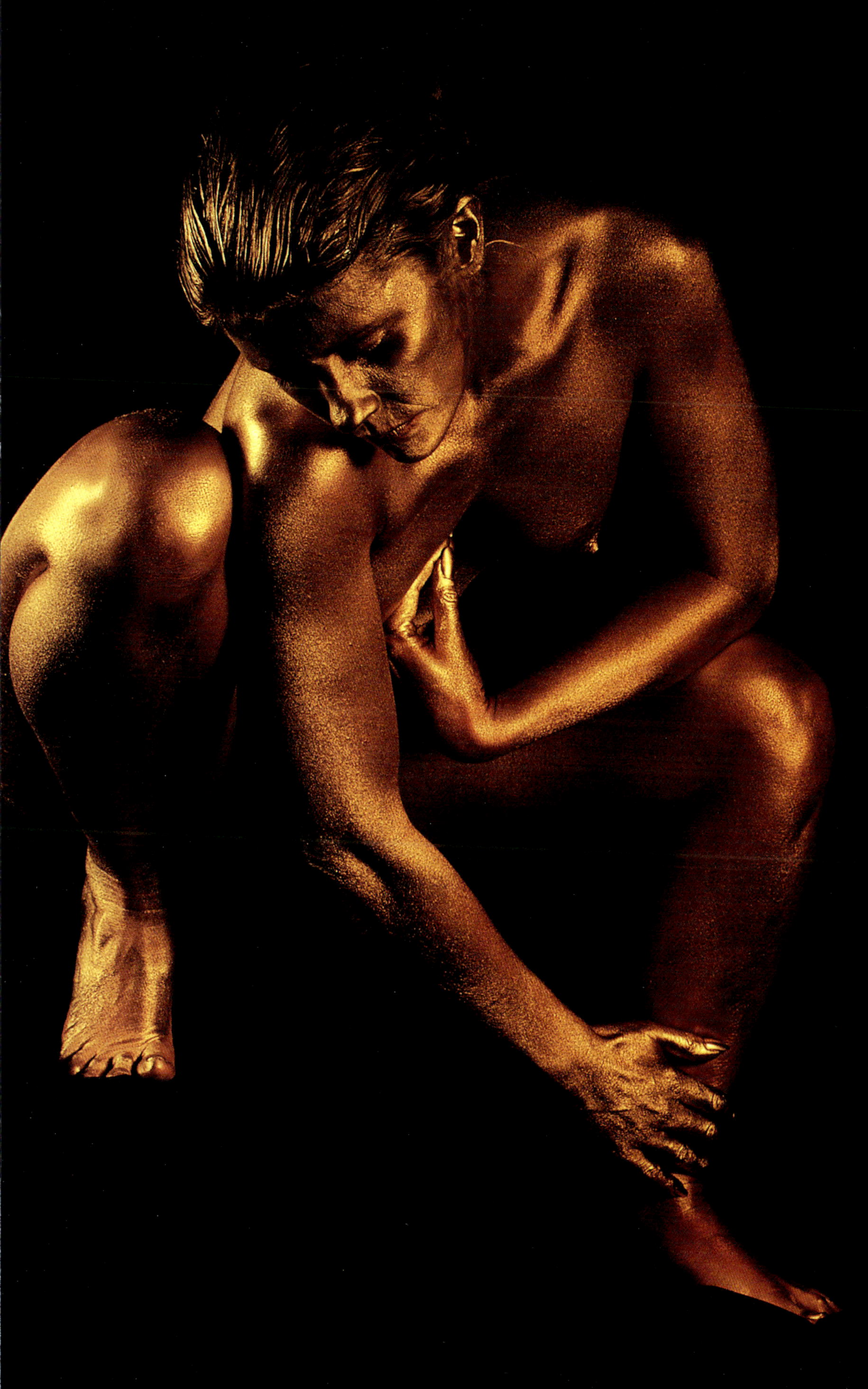

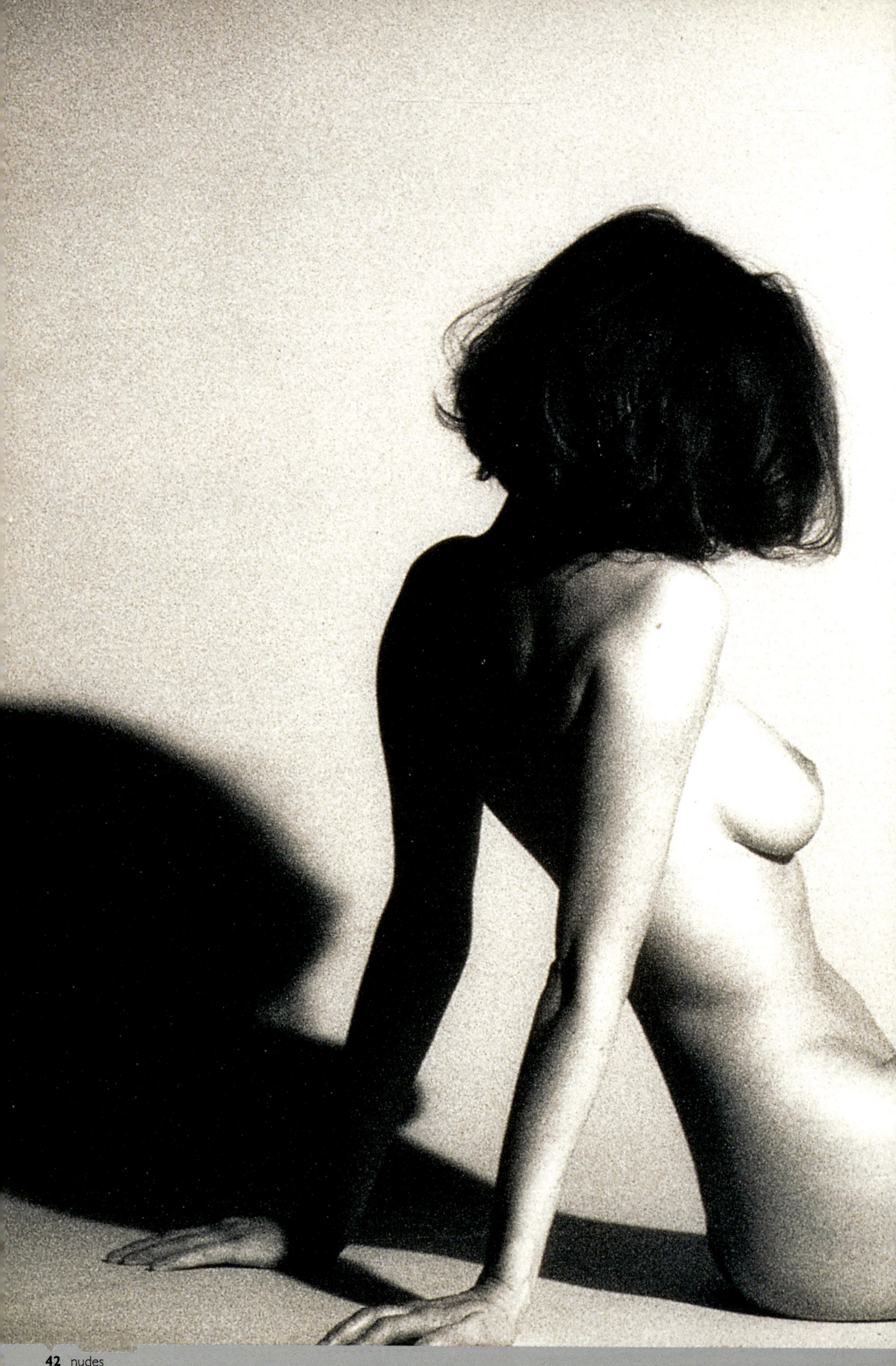

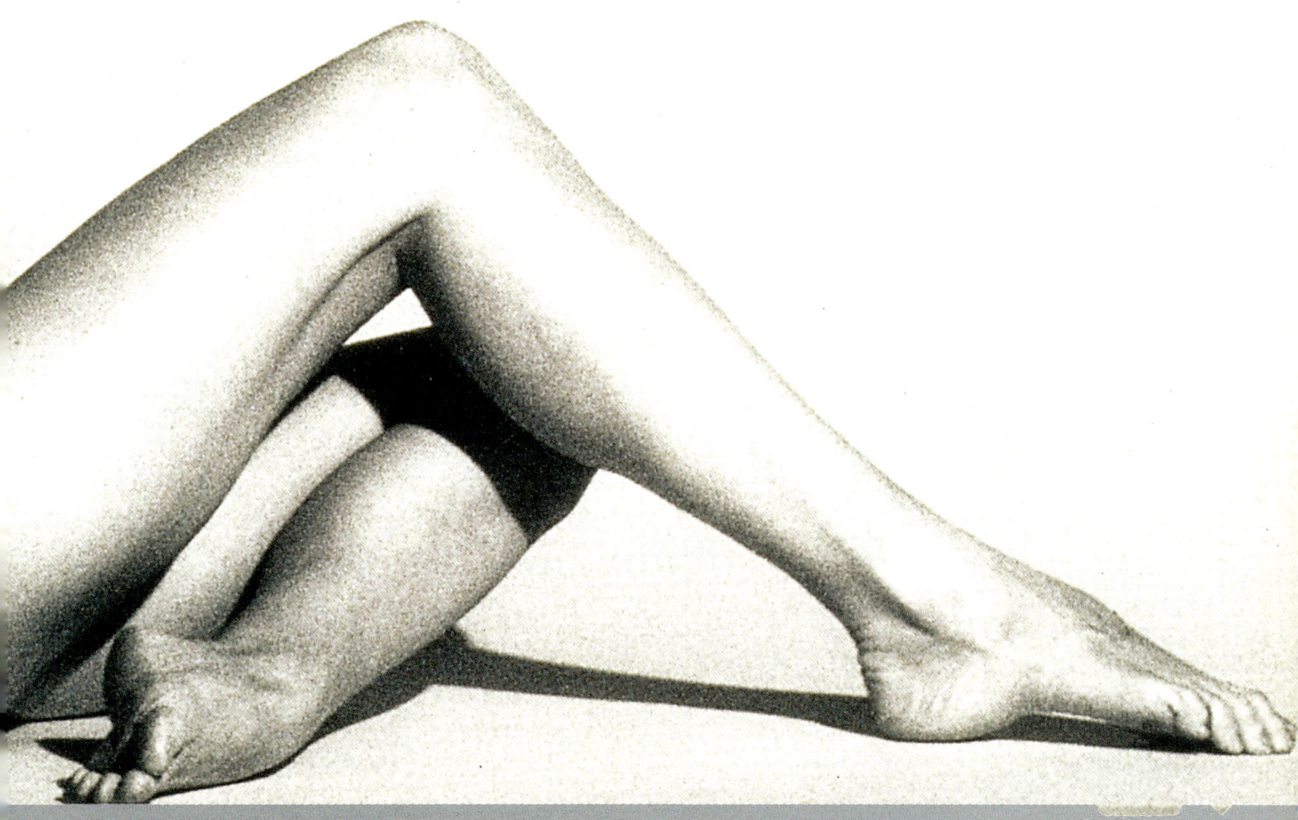

Photographer: **Terry Ryan**

Client: **Jane (the model)**

Use: **Self-promotion**

Camera: **35mm**

Lens: **105mm macro**

Film: **Polaroid Polagraph 400**

Exposure: **1/60sec at f/8**

Lighting: **Tungsten**

Props and set: **White seamless paper**

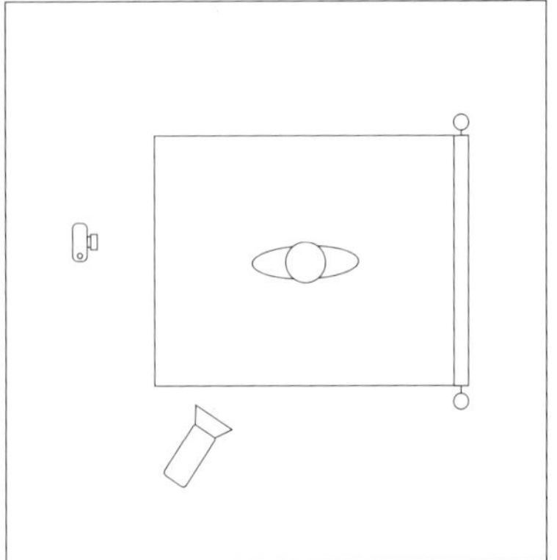

Plan View

J A N E

▼

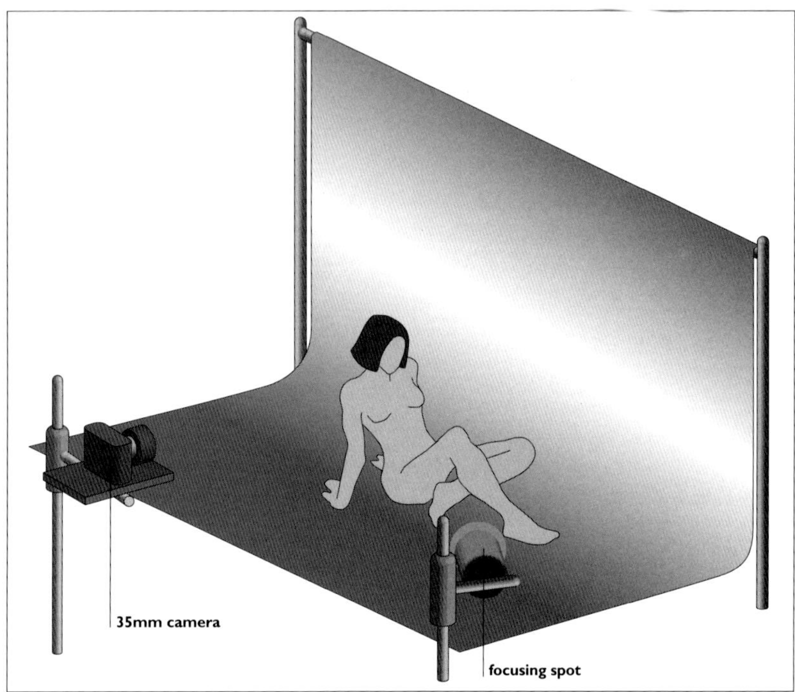

POLAROID POLAGRAPH IS A HIGH-CONTRAST INSTANT-PROCESS SLIDE FILM WHICH CAN NEVERTHELESS BE USED FOR GENERAL PHOTOGRAPHY — *IF* YOU GET THE EXPOSURE ABSOLUTELY SPOT-ON; IN WHICH CASE SOME VERY DRAMATIC HIGH-KEY EFFECTS ARE OBTAINABLE.

The lighting compounds the requirement for ultra-precise exposure: a highly directional 2K tungsten focusing spot creates dramatic chiaroscuro and must be positioned with exquisite care if the outline of the model is to be distinguishable at all points from the background. It is set fairly low, or the tops of the legs would be burned out, and it is fairly oblique in order to create the dramatic shadow which is very much an integral part of the composition. In contrast with most studio pictures, the model must be quite close to the background in order for the shadow to read: normally, of course, one is more concerned with losing shadows than with using them.

► *In any high-key picture there must be some dark tones — and, as this picture illustrates, a high-key picture can even contain a lot of dark tones*

► *When it comes to exposure using high-contrast materials, experience is the best guide, coupled with generous bracketing and (of course) Polaroid tests: a test film can be processed and mounted in a few minutes*

Photographer: **Stu Williamson**

Client: **Marie**

Use: **Portfolio shot for modelling**

Camera: **6x7cm**

Lens: **140mm**

Film: **Ilford FP4 Plus**

Exposure: **f/11**

Lighting: **Electronic flash: three heads**

Props and set: **See text**

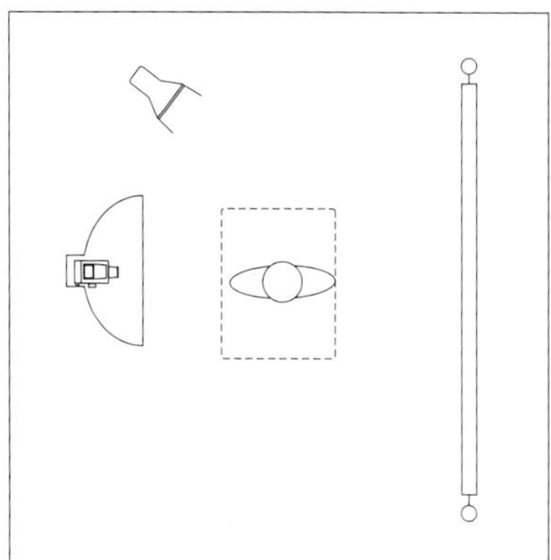

Plan View

► *Photographers can often learn as much from painters as they can from other photographers*

► *Lighting, pose and props are all complemented by the texture screen*

► *Dramatic chiaroscuro characterizes many seraglio scenes*

M A R I E

▼

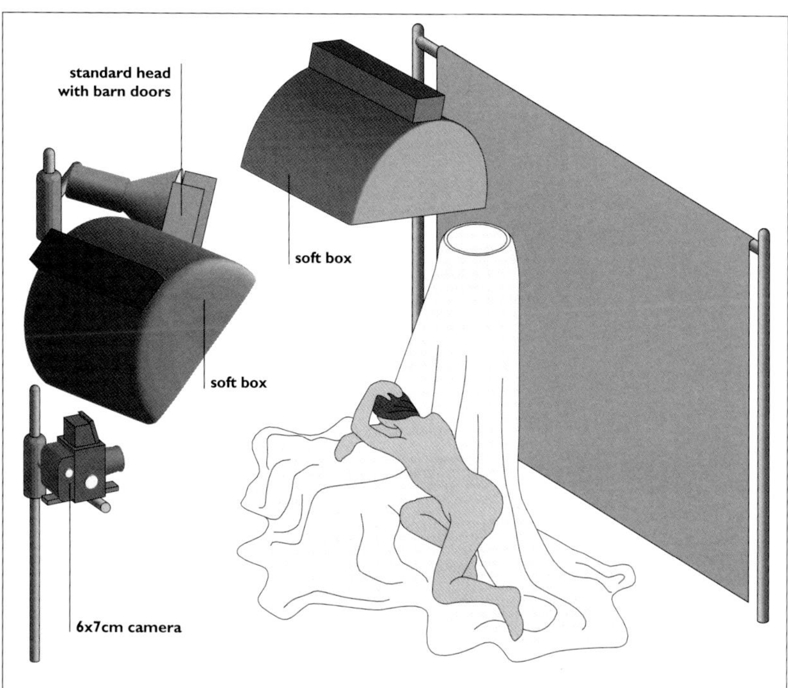

THERE ARE MORE THAN OVERTONES OF 19TH-CENTURY ODALISQUES IN THIS PICTURES; IT IS REMINISCENT OF THE PAINTINGS OF ALMA-TADEMA, WHO WAS FAMOUS FOR HIS VOLUPTUOUS MAIDENS IN CLASSICAL OR EXOTIC SETTINGS.

The key light is from above, almost directly over the model and to her right. The effect is of sunlight streaming through a window. A soft box in front of the model, just above the camera, provides fill. A third light, a standard head with barn-doors, illuminates the background.

The hanging, veil-like material was specially made up by a wedding supply store. It is sewn to a hoop of the kind typically carried by bridesmaids and decked with flowers; as the photographer somewhat unromantically says, "It is like an enormous mosquito net." This hangs in front of a Colorama painted background. To complete the 19th-century effect, the picture was printed through a "Craqueleur" texture screen.

Photographer's comment:

The texture screen is made in the United States and used to be imported into the UK by my father through his business, World Wide Promotions.

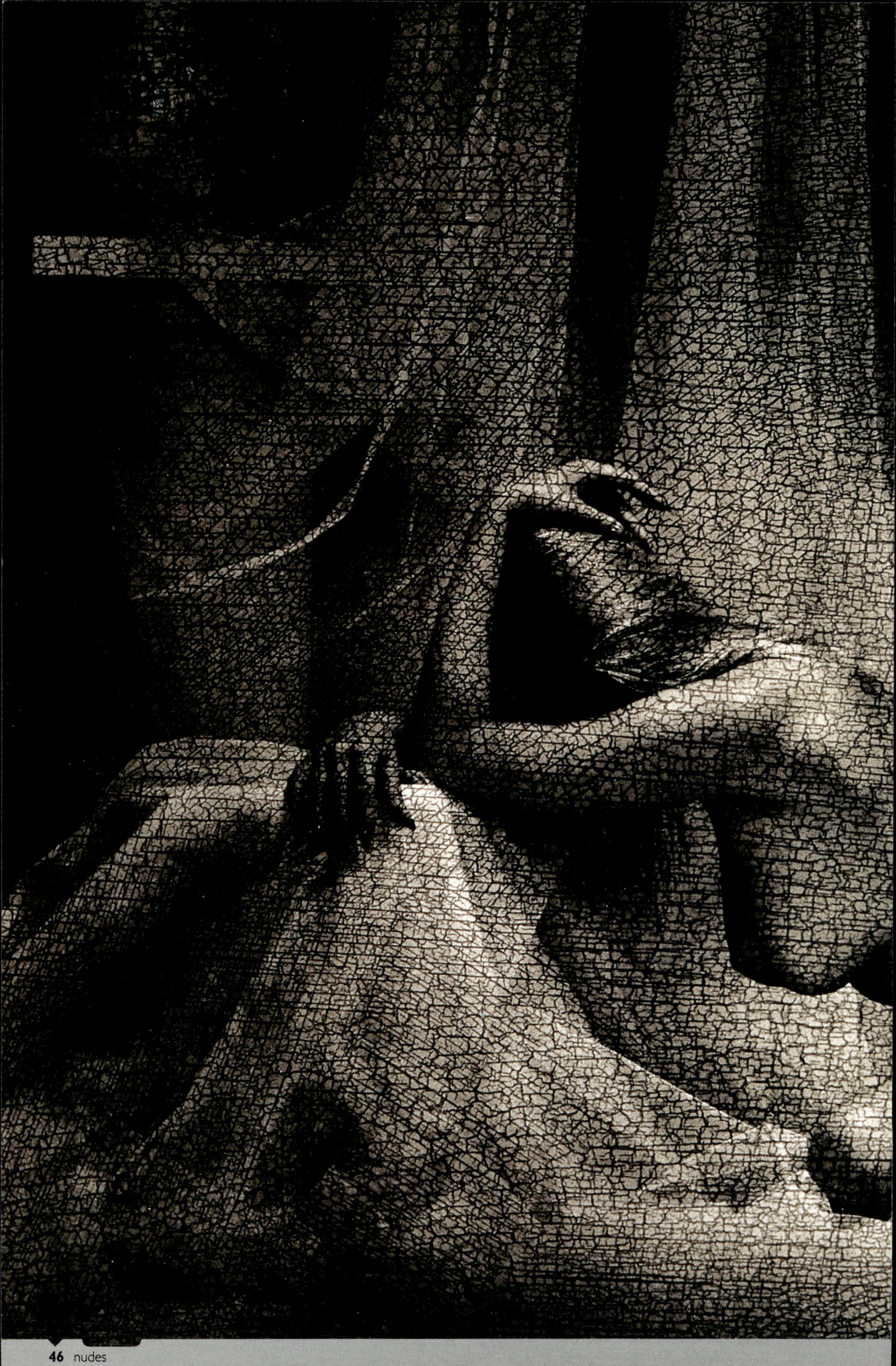

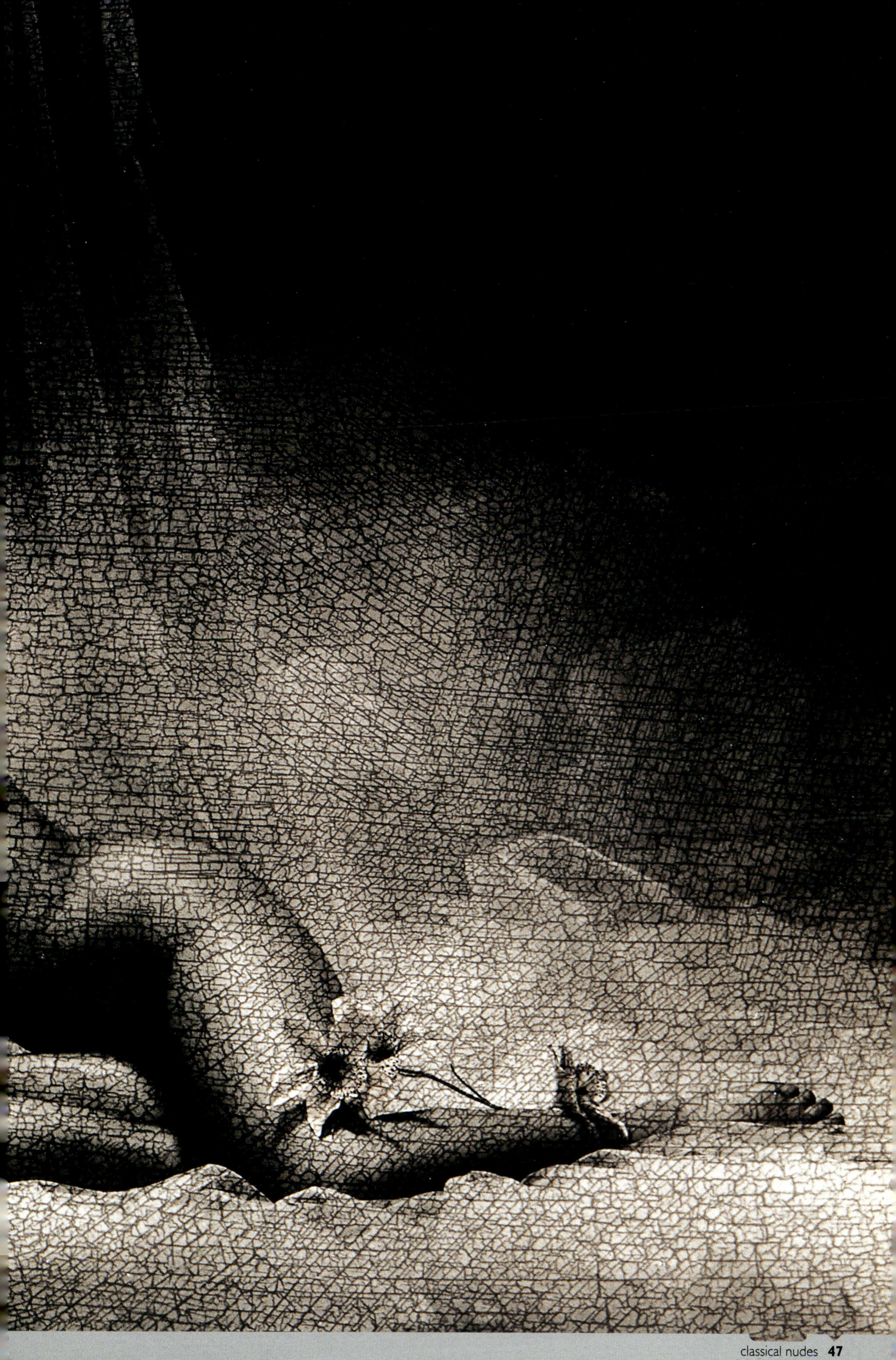

Photographer: **Kay Hurst, K Studios**

Use: **Portfolio**

Model: **Catherine Richardson**

Camera: **4x5in**

Lens: **360mm**

Film: **Polaroid 55 P/N at EI 25**

Exposure: **Not recorded**

Lighting: **Electronic flash: one head**

Props and set: **White background paper**

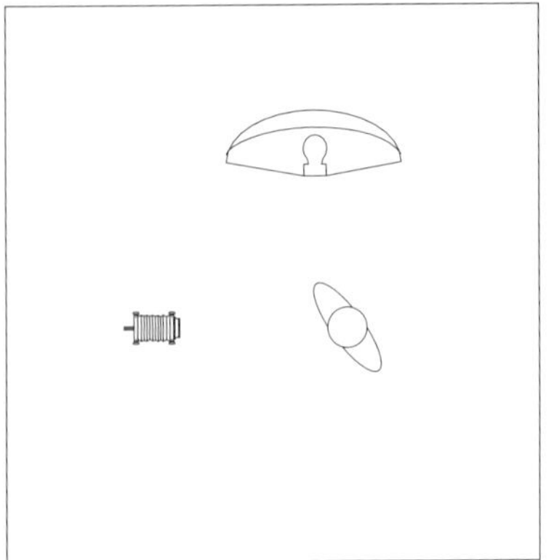

Plan View

▼

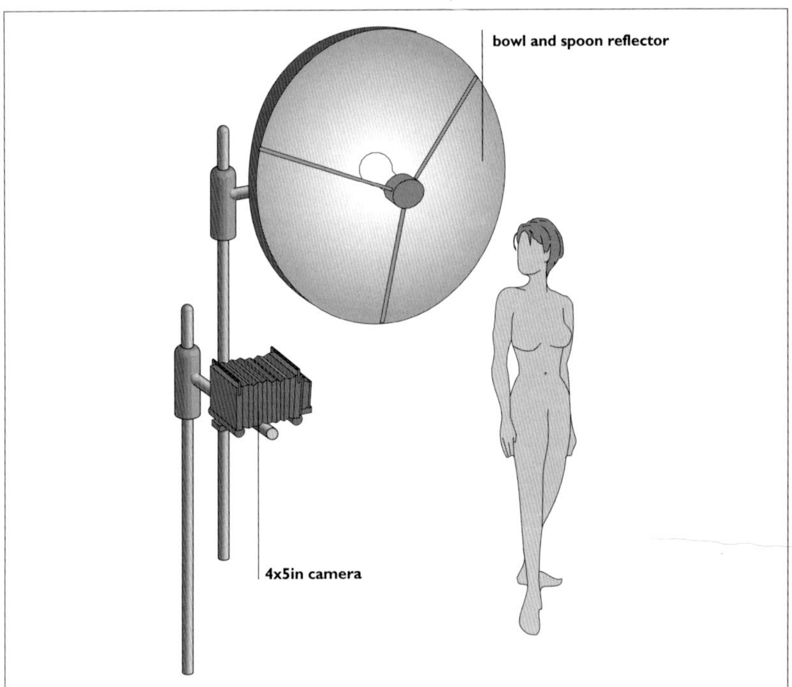

The large (90cm/3ft) "bowl and spoon" gives a "hotter" light than a soft box, especially when used close to the subject, as here. The overall effect of the image is, however, much influenced by the afterwork.

The image was printed onto Kentmere Art Classic, which was then sepia toned, colour photocopied and transferred onto Fabriano Canaletto natural art paper; after treatment with a suitable solvent, the colour copy was burnished down onto the paper. By varying the pressure a solarized effect can be created in the black areas: the pre-treatment is necessary in order to achieve this effect.

► *Quality of light is easier to recognize than to describe, but it is much affected by reflector size and degree of diffusion*

► *Processes such as this are highly idiosyncratic and may require considerable experiment with different papers, toners, photocopiers and transfer papers*

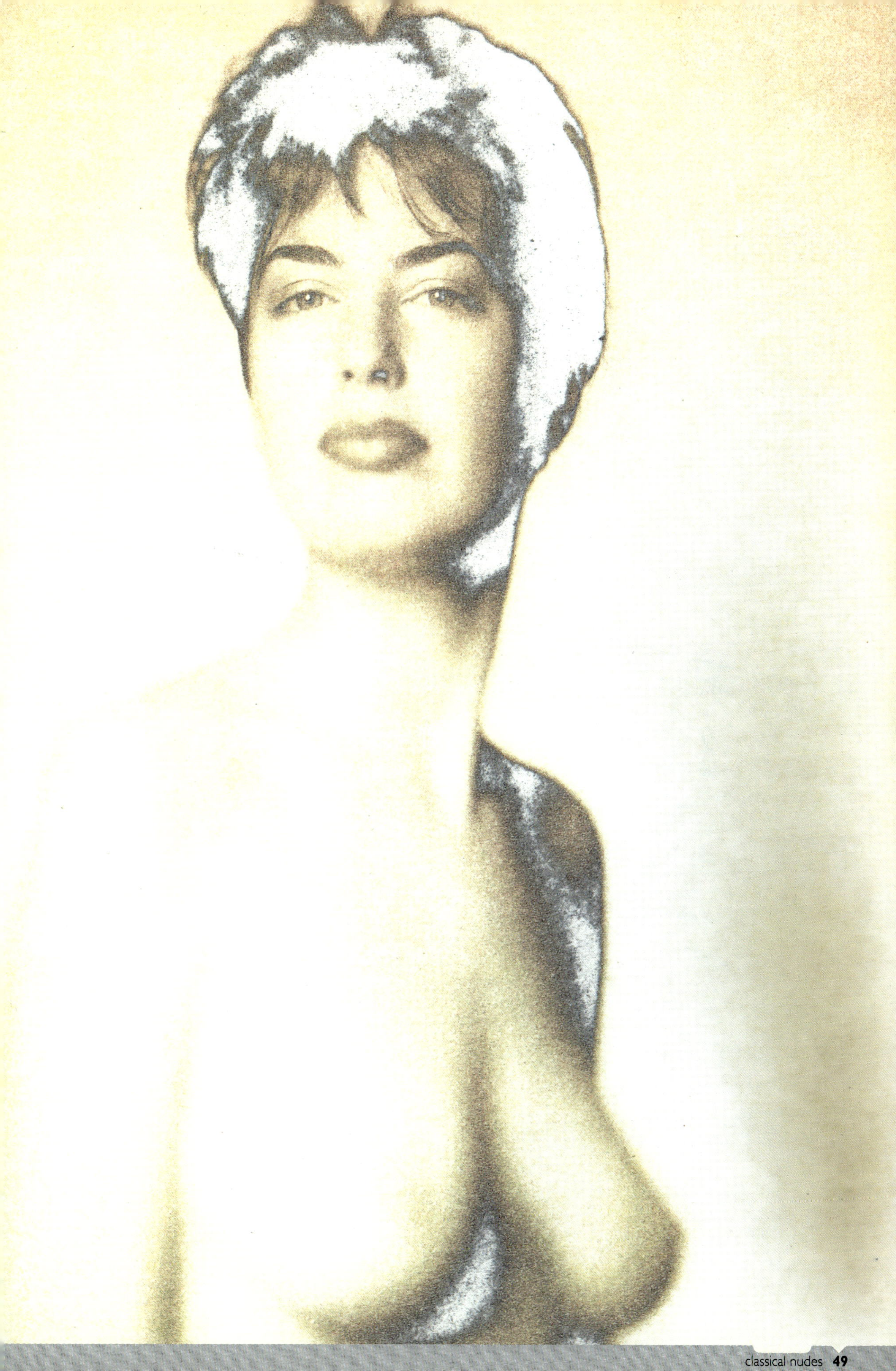

Photographer: **Frank Wartenberg**

Use: **Portrait**

Camera: **6x7cm**

Lens: **350mm + light blue filter**

Film: **Fuji Velvia**

Exposure: **f/5.6**

Lighting: **Mixed: 5 heads (see text)**

Props and set: **Blue painted canvas backdrop**

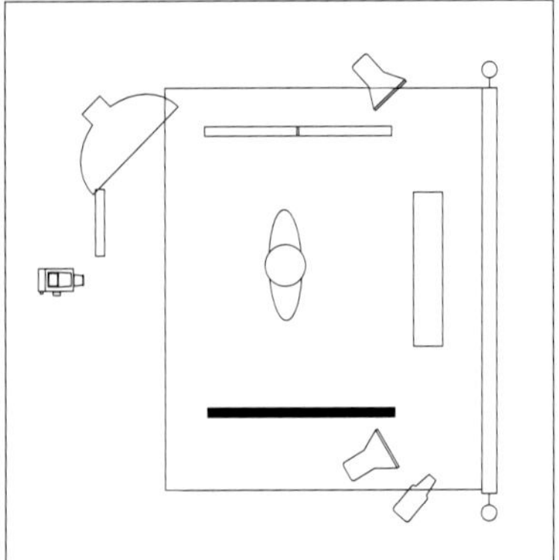

Plan View

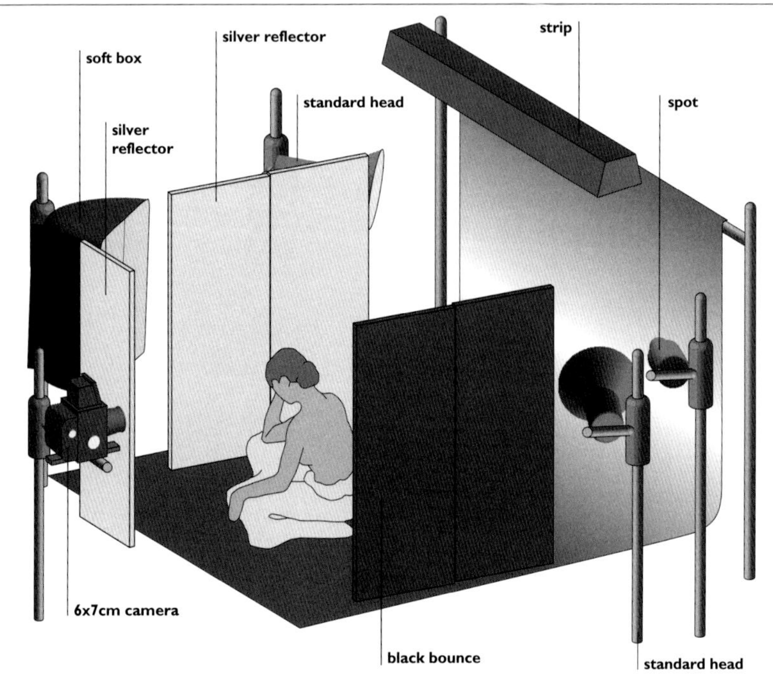

WEAK BLUE FILTRATION ON THE CAMERA LENS AND A BLUE BACKDROP ARE NOT THINGS THAT WOULD OCCUR TO EVERYONE AS BEFITTING A CLASSICAL NUDE; BUT THE RESULT IS A CURIOUSLY EFFFCTIVE COMBINATION OF COLDNESS AND WARMTH.

The key light is a large soft box to camera left, with silver reflectors on either side. The soft box is clearly directional but the big silver bounces on either side of it throw back blue-tinted spill from the other lights to create the illusion of a still larger source. To camera right, large black bounces ensure that the shadow side (the model's back) is as dark as it can be. The remaining lights – two standard flash heads, an overhead strip light, and a daylight (HMI) spot – all combine to illuminate the background fairly evenly but with a small darker area in the upper left to provide a little more variation than comes from the painted canvas alone.

► *Textured canvas creates a mood very different from plain background paper*

► *Evenly illuminating a background can require a great deal of light*

► *The "negative space" around the model creates a good deal of the mood of the picture*

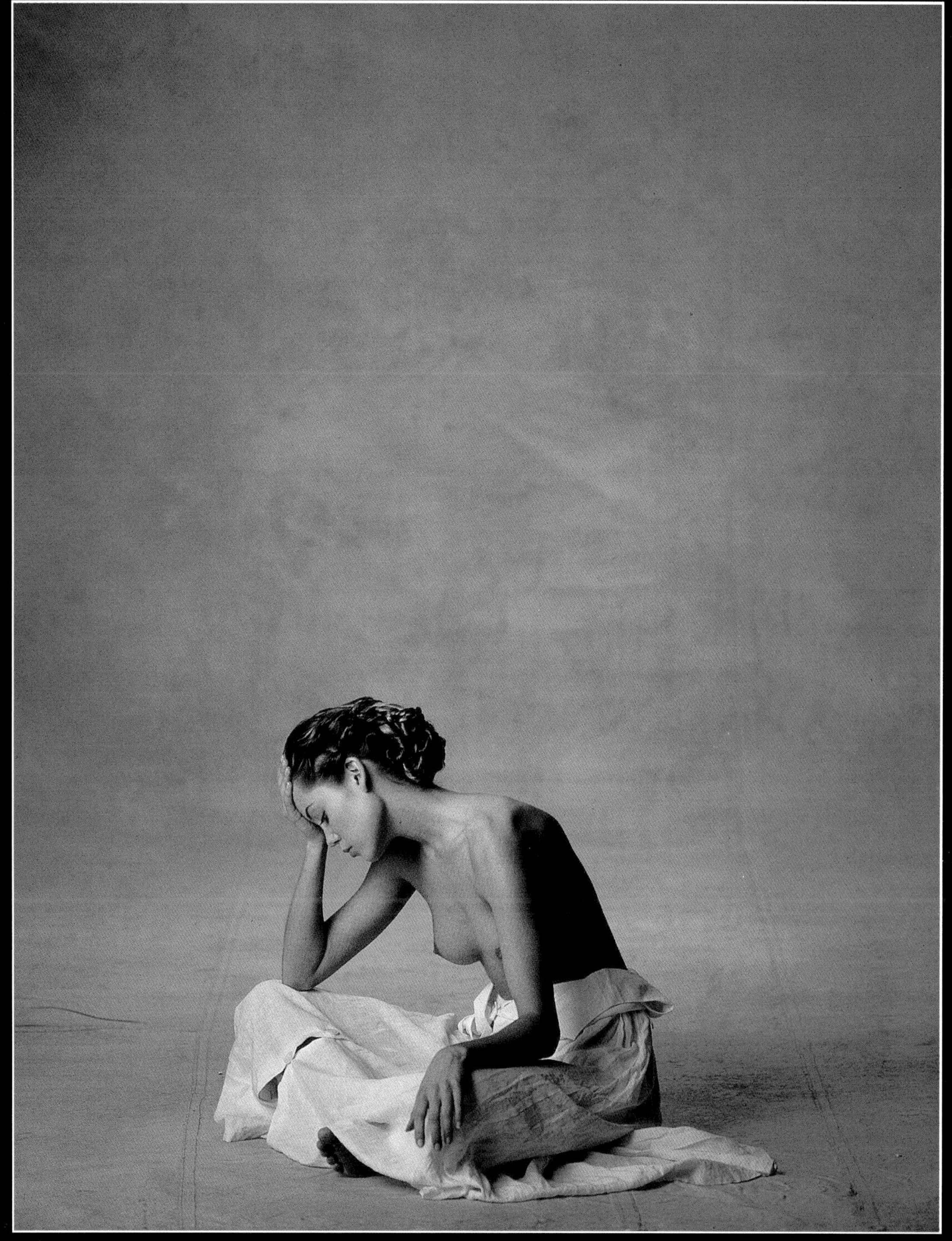

Photographer: **Frank P. Wartenberg**

Use: **Portfolio**

Camera: **RB67**

Lens: **Not recorded**

Film: **Not recorded**

Exposure: **Not recorded**

Lighting: **Daylight plus HMI spot**

Props and set: **White seamless background**

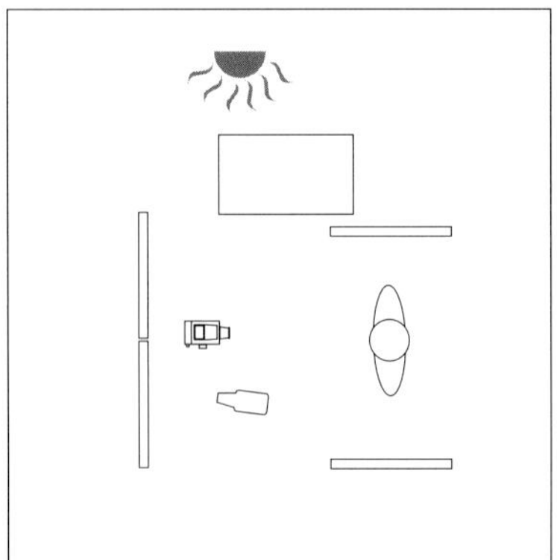

Plan View

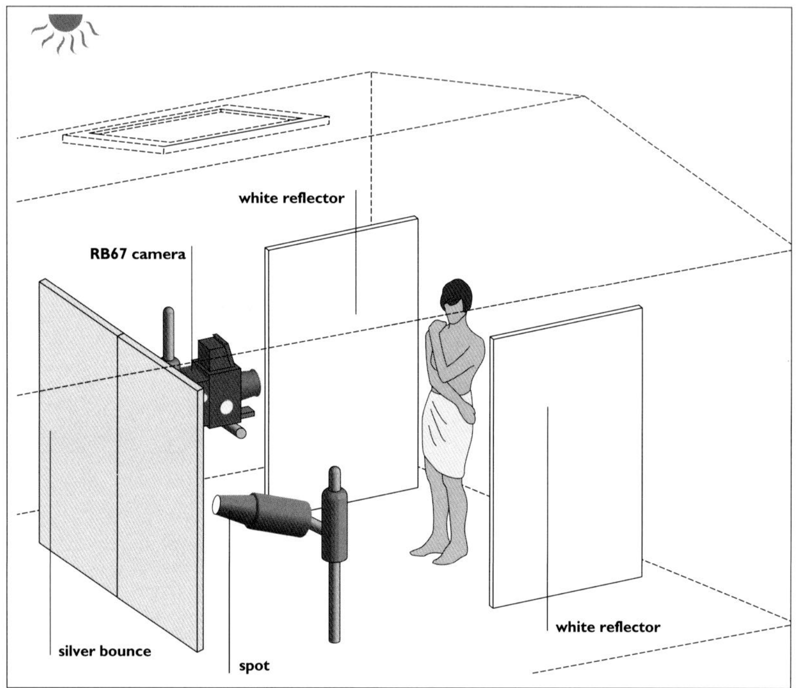

MUCH OF THE POWER OF THIS PICTURE COMES FROM THE MODEL'S DIRECT, CHALLENGING STARE: THE MOOD IS AT ONCE EROTIC AND HUMAN, RATHER THAN DEPERSONALIZING THE MODEL INTO AN EMPTY FANTASY.

Unusually, this was shot in a daylight studio: a large roof window provided the fill. Although such studios are rare today, and although the windows must be capable of being covered when they are not needed, a true daylight studio can be remarkably versatile, as our Victorian ancestors repeatedly demonstrated.

Here, though, the daylight was supplemented by a daylight (HMI) spot bounced off two big silver bounces over the top of the camera to create a very flat, classically high-key light. Two large white reflectors, one on either side of the model, completed the high-key set-up.

► *Normally – though not invariably, as seen here – there are small areas of maximum black even in a high-key picture*

► *The background in a high-key picture is almost invariably lighter than the subject*

► *Generous use of large bounces is commonplace in high-key photography*

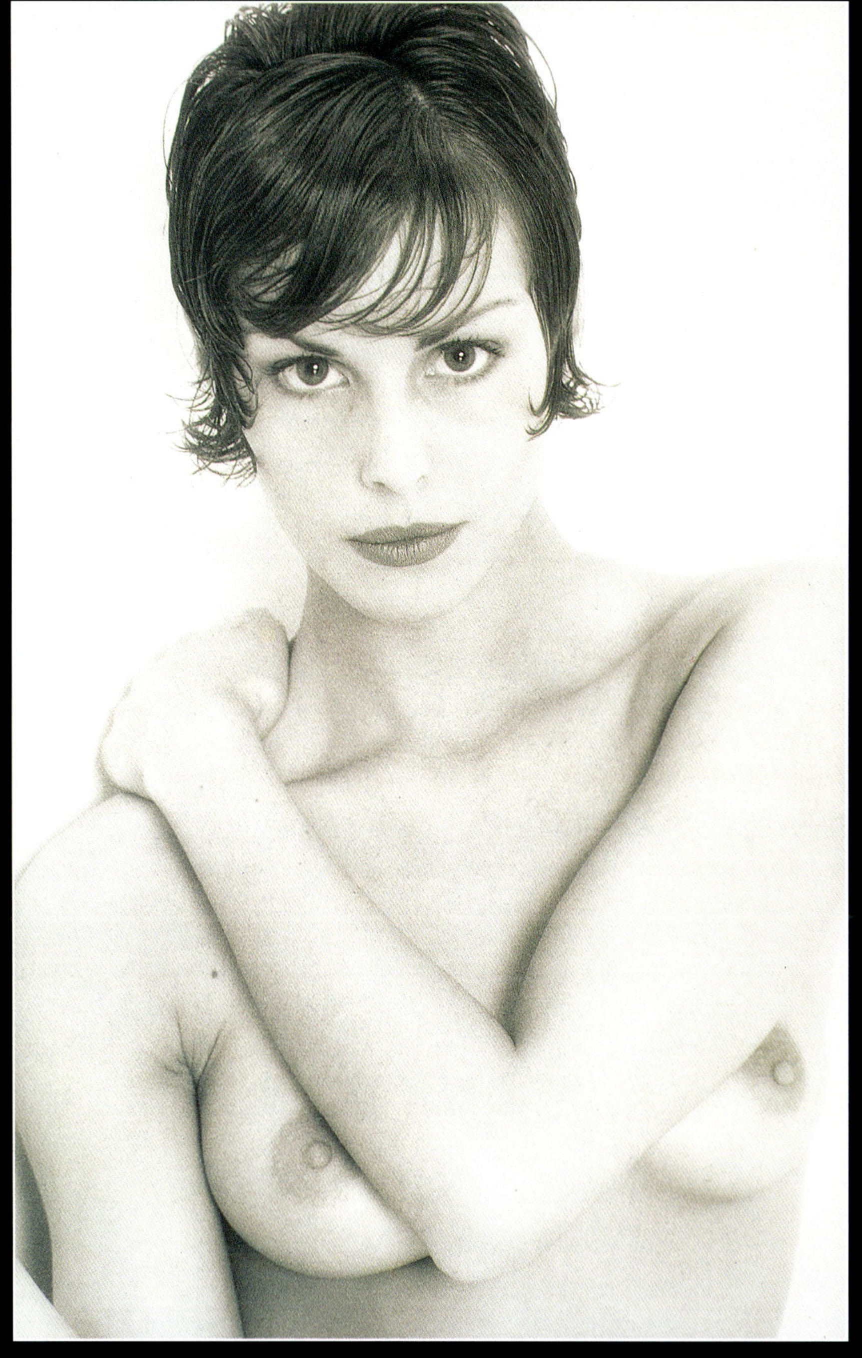

Photographer: **Frank P. Wartenberg**

Use: **Portfolio**

Camera: **6x7cm**

Lens: **185mm with deep blue filter**

Film: **Kodak Ektachrome EPT tungsten balance**

Exposure: **Not recorded**

Lighting: **Large soft box**

Props and set: **Ground metal**

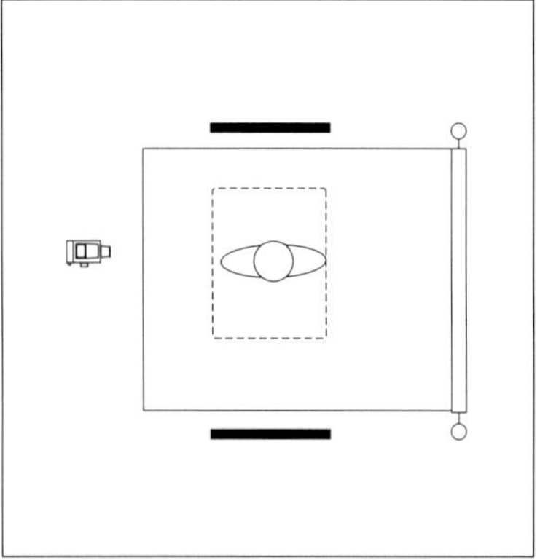

Plan View

B L U E   M E T A L

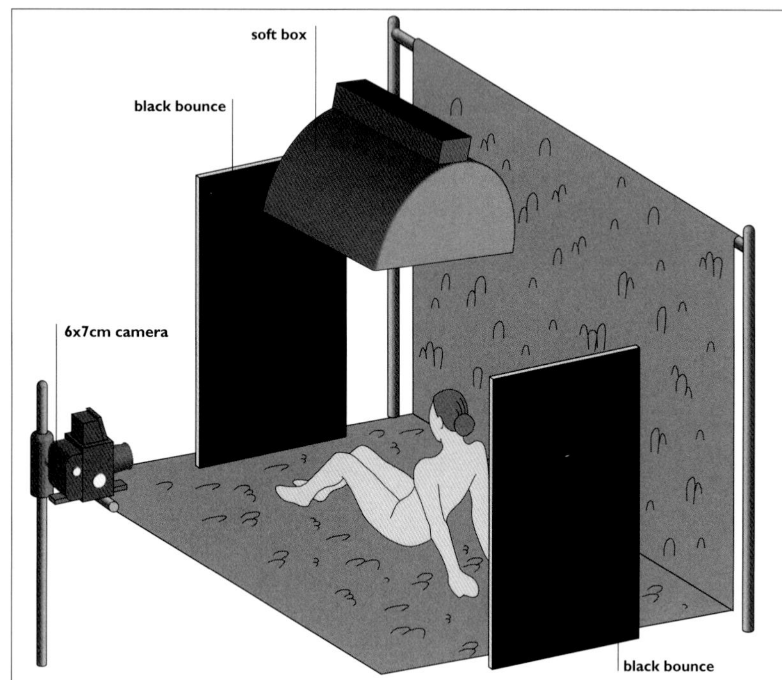

THE SET IS DRAMATIC IN ITS OWN RIGHT: ROUGHLY WORKED METAL. THIS IS NOT THE MOST COMFORTABLE SURFACE TO SIT ON! TO ADD TO HER DISCOMFORT, THE MODEL WAS COVERED WITH SILVER MAKE-UP. THE OVERALL EFFECT IS HOWEVER VERY MEMORABLE.

Tungsten-balance film with daylight-balance flash makes for a very blue image, which is further enhanced here with a deep blue filter. A big soft box is suspended over the model, which explains the shadows: in effect, only the upper part of her body is illuminated, though there is some fill from the reflected light off the background. The flash-back from the background itself burns out the area around the model, creating a semi-silhouette effect.

Painting the model silver may seem curious in the context of a blue picture, but the simple truth is that even the matte silver which is normally attained with make-up is significantly more reflective than normal skin. This is what adds the apparent very high contrast to the figure.

► *In addition to its colour, make-up can greatly affect the reflectivity of skin*

► *Sometimes two separate paths have to be pursued in order to create an intense effect; in this case, blue filtration and the use of tungsten-balance film with daylight-balance lighting*

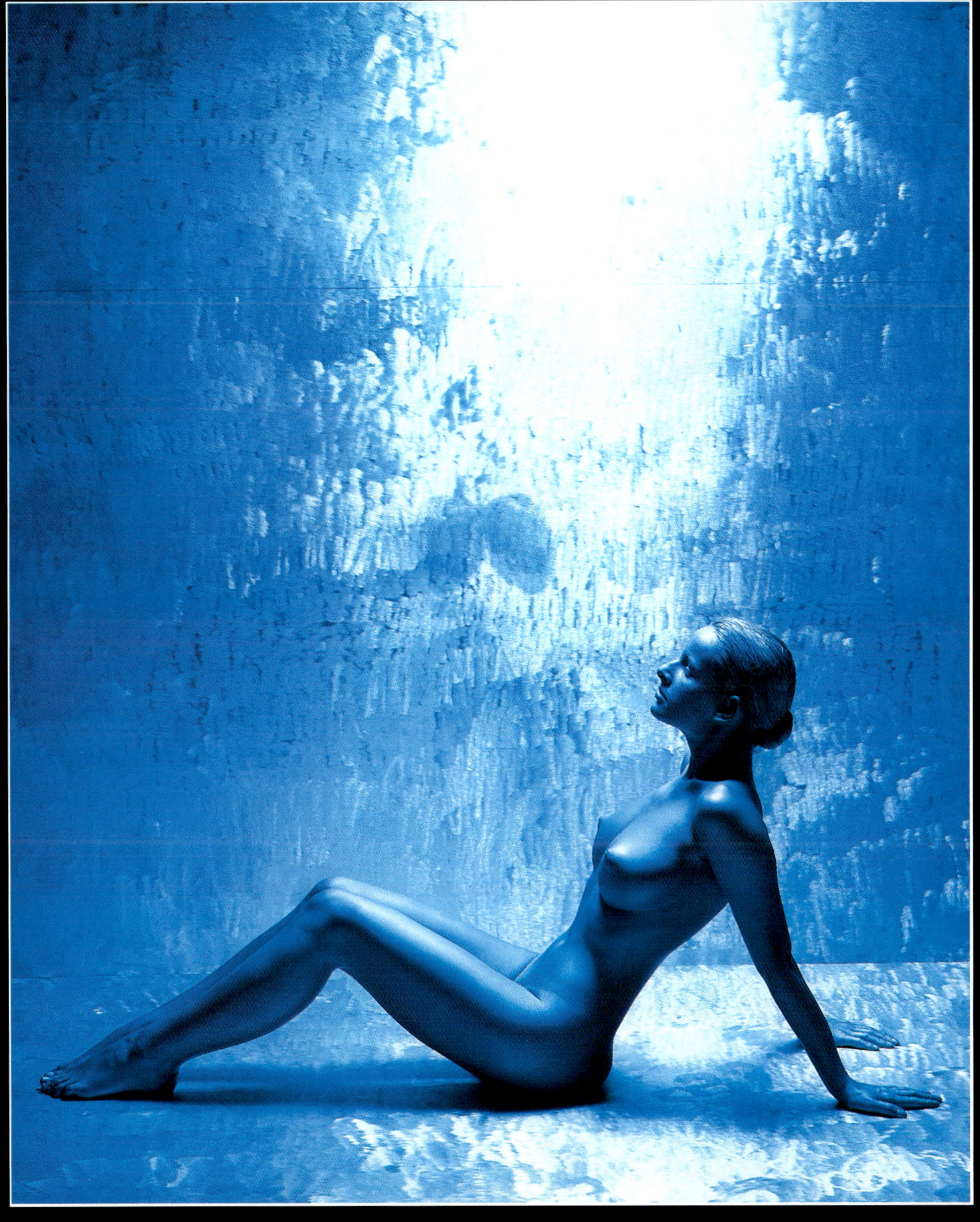

Photographer: **Stu Williamson**

Client: **Correna**

Use: **Model portfolio**

Camera: **6x7cm**

Lens: **105mm**

Film: **Kodak Plus-X Pan**

Exposure: **f/8**

Lighting: **Electronic flash: one spot**

Props and set: **Lastolite hand-painted background**

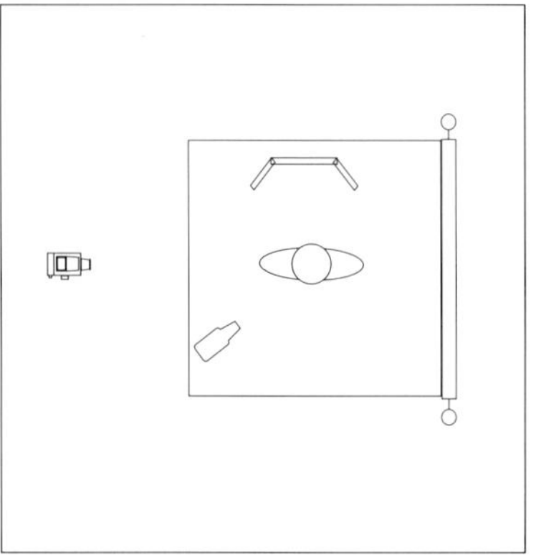

Plan View

► *If there is insufficient room between the model and the background, consider making a feature of the model's shadow*

► *If you want a shadow, it is often best to use the hardest light available to you*

► *Many photographers use a "palette" of films for different effects*

C O R R E N A

▼

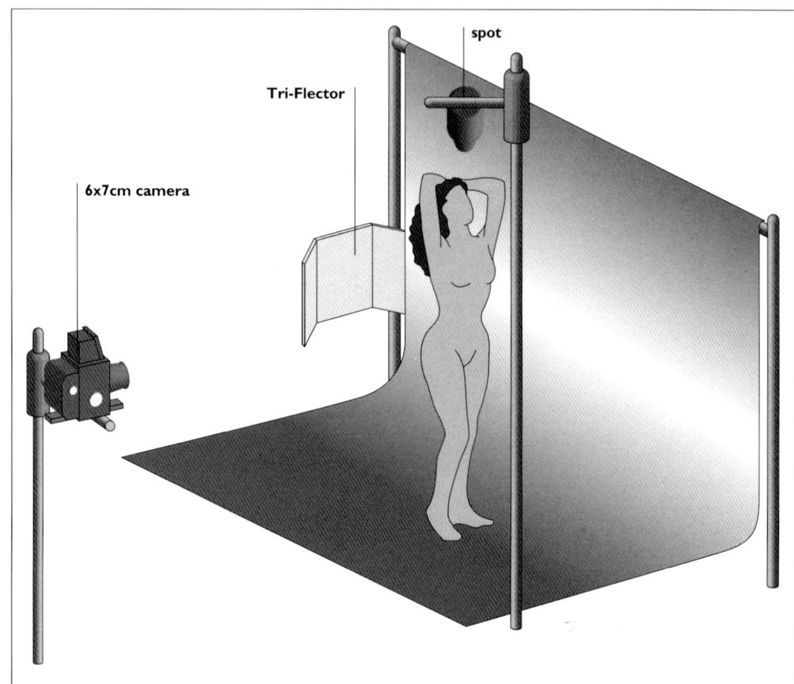

THIS IS THE SORT OF PICTURE WHICH ANY AMATEUR PHOTOGRAPHER COULD TAKE — GIVEN A BEAUTIFUL GIRL, A SPOTLIGHT, AN OFF-THE-SHELF BACKGROUND, ENOUGH TALENT AND A PAINSTAKING ATTENTION TO DETAIL.

It shows that rules are made to be broken – the "rule" in this case being that the model should be a long way from the background so that she casts no shadow. If you are going to break a rule it is often as well to break it thoroughly: Stu used a very hard light to cast a clear, strong shadow which echoes the model's shape on the background. A "Tri-Flector" (see page 24) provides some fill.

The light is very high over the camera, as can be seen from the shadow, and the light is harsh; and yet the modelling is exquisite. The choice of Plus-X Pan, an "old technology" film, allowed maximum control of tonality in development.

Photographer's comment:

The picture was toned using Fotospeed Sepia toner.

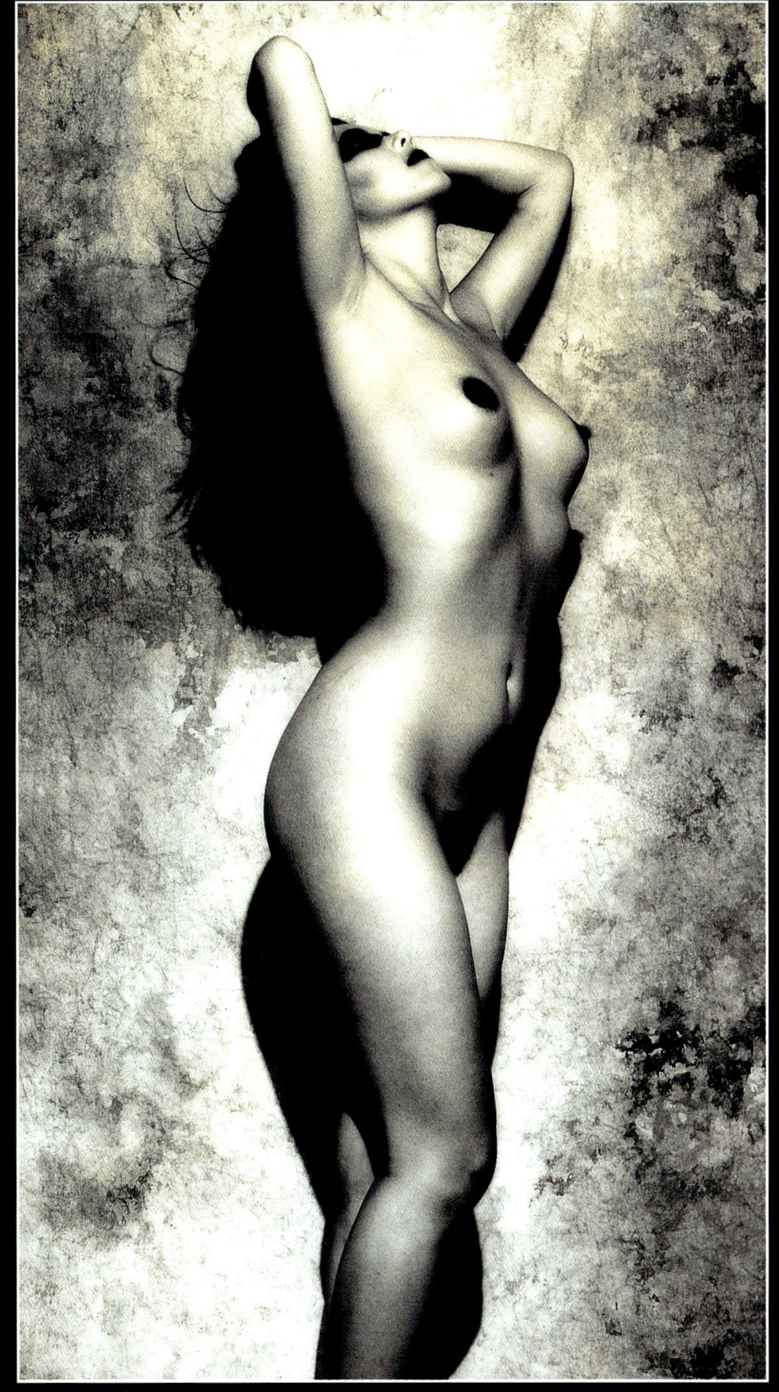

Photographer: **Rod Ashford**

Client: *Professional Photographer* **magazine**

Use: **Review of toners; subsequently used as book cover in Norway**

Model: **Kay Holmes**

Hair/Make-Up: **Sandra Ashford**

Camera: **35mm**

Lens: **70–210mm**

Film: **Ilford FP4 Plus**

Exposure: **f/16**

Lighting: **Electronic flash: 2 heads**

Props and set: **Painted background by Fantasy Backgrounds, Eastbourne**

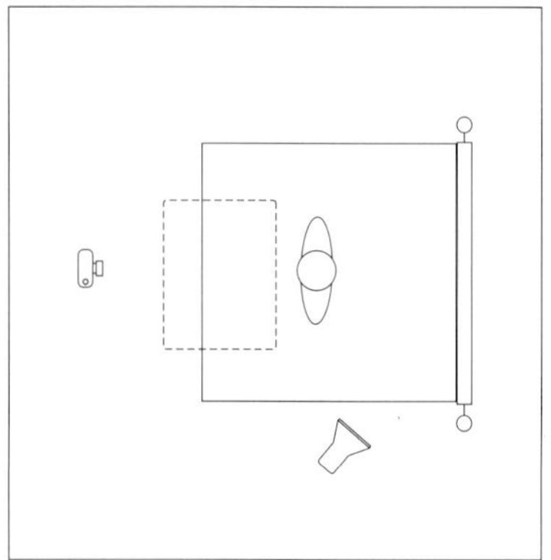

Plan View

► *As with many of the monochrome pictures in this book, this one owes a great deal to the printer (who was also the photographer)*

► *With split toning and "freeze grey", a neutral grey can appear warm toned when contrasted with a cold blue*

K A Y

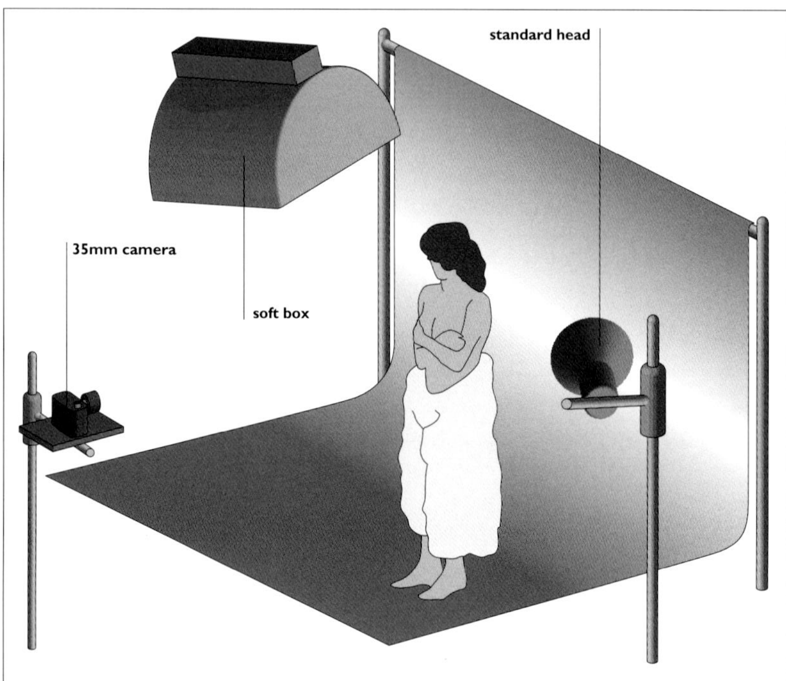

WHEN MOST MAGAZINES TEST TONERS, THEY USE BORING SHOTS FROM THEIR FILES. *PROFESSIONAL PHOTOGRAPHER* HIRED A REAL PHOTOGRAPHER WHO CAN ALSO WRITE, AND GOT HIM TO TEST COLORVIR TONERS IN REAL-WORLD CONDITIONS.

Rod used two lights, a 40x50cm (16x20in) Photoflex Litedome soft box and a standard head. The standard head was used as a background light, while the soft box was the key and only light on the model; as can be seen from the shadows, it was high above the camera and very slightly to the left. Both lights, he notes, were Bowens Esprit units, which he particularly likes.

Contrary to immediate appearances, the background light was not snooted or tightly honeycombed behind the model's head. There was some gradation, but it was much enhanced in printing and then further enhanced (somewhat to the photographer's surprise) by the toning chemistry: a brief dip in "freeze grey" held the highlights, followed by blue toning for the shadows.

Photographer's comment:

The model, Kay Holmes, had contacted the editor of the magazine, asking how to become a model. He referred her to me, and this was from the very first session.

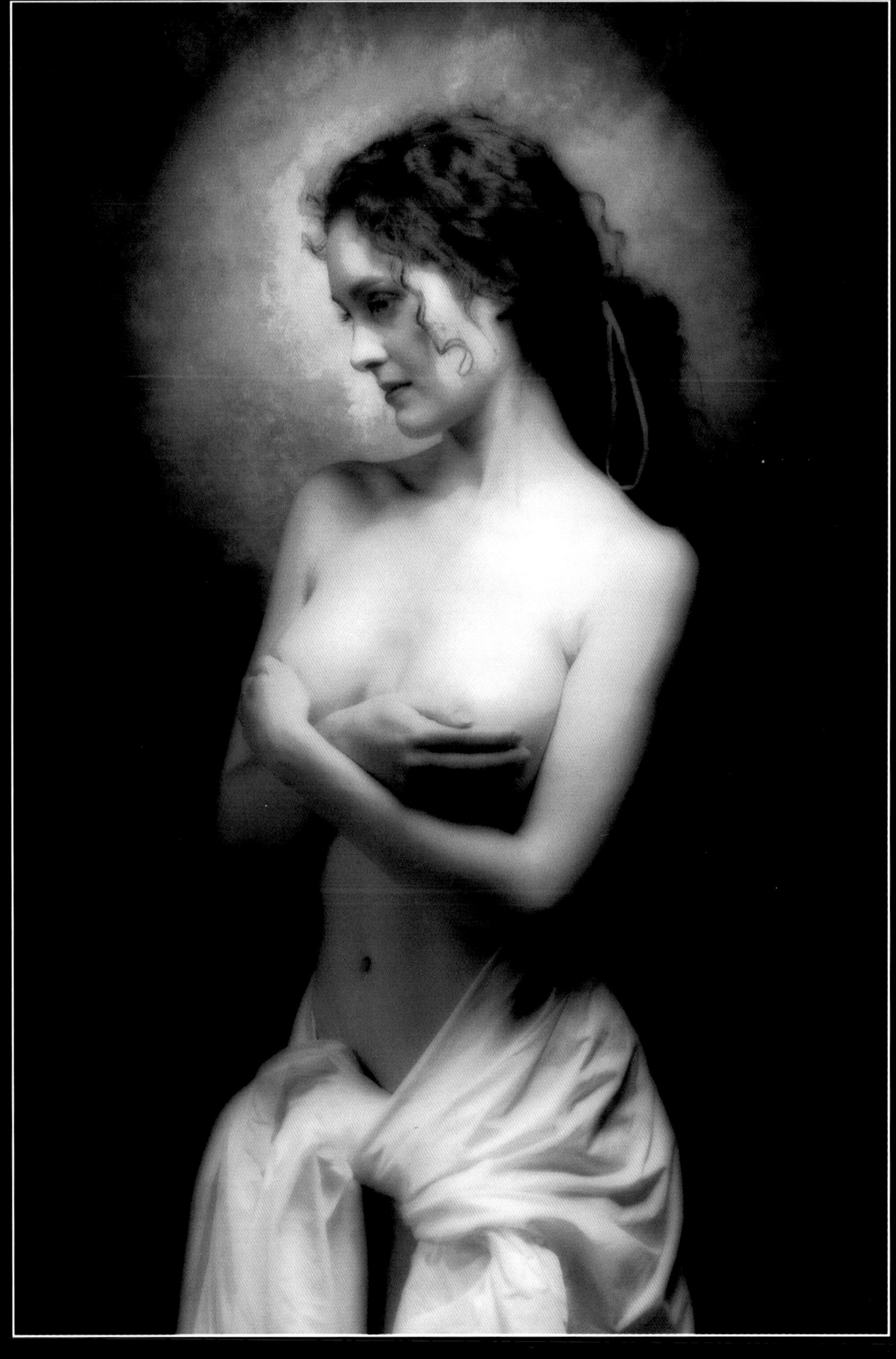

Photographer: **Frank P. Wartenberg**

Use: **Portfolio**

Camera: **6x7cm**

Lens: **185mm**

Film: **Agfa Scala**

Exposure: **Not recorded**

Lighting: **Large soft box**

Props and set: **Ground metal**

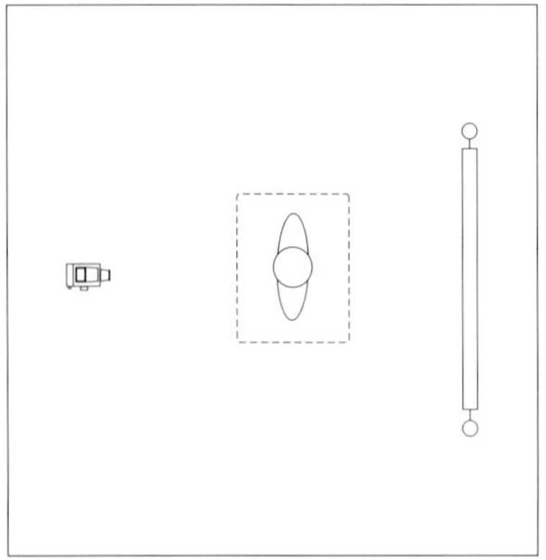

Plan View

SILVER

▼

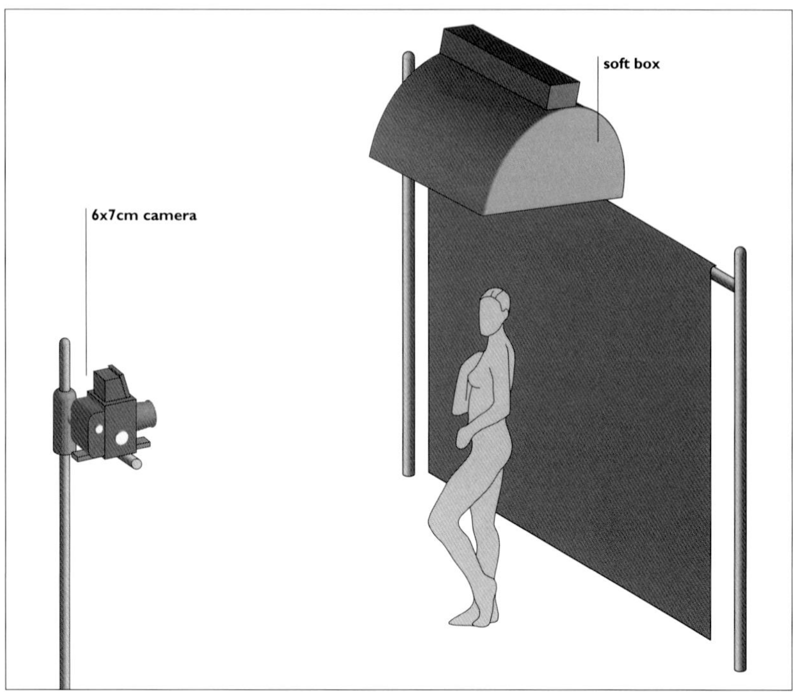

This picture clearly illustrates the relationship between high contrast and high key. In one sense, the two are quite different; and yet in another, effective high key depends on effective high contrast.

Also, there is a great deal of difference between a picture with a full tonal range, but where the main interest lies in the extremes of tone, and one which lacks mid-tones and is reduced to 'soot and whitewash'. Controlling contrast means controlling lighting.

Here the sole light is a big soft box which is suspended over the model. She is painted silver in order to bring her reflectivity up to that of the background.

Roughly equal (and high) reflectivities of subject and background are one of the essential requirements of a high-key picture. In effect, only the upper part of her body is illuminated, though the highly reflective rough-ground metal background provides fill. Choice of film was important: the long tonal range of a transparency film allows more subtlety, more easily, than using a print film.

► *With long tonal ranges, a low-contrast material is essential*

► *With high-contrast materials, low-contrast lighting is essential if you want a good tonal range*

► *Compare this with the picture on page 55, which is lit the same way but uses colour transparency film*

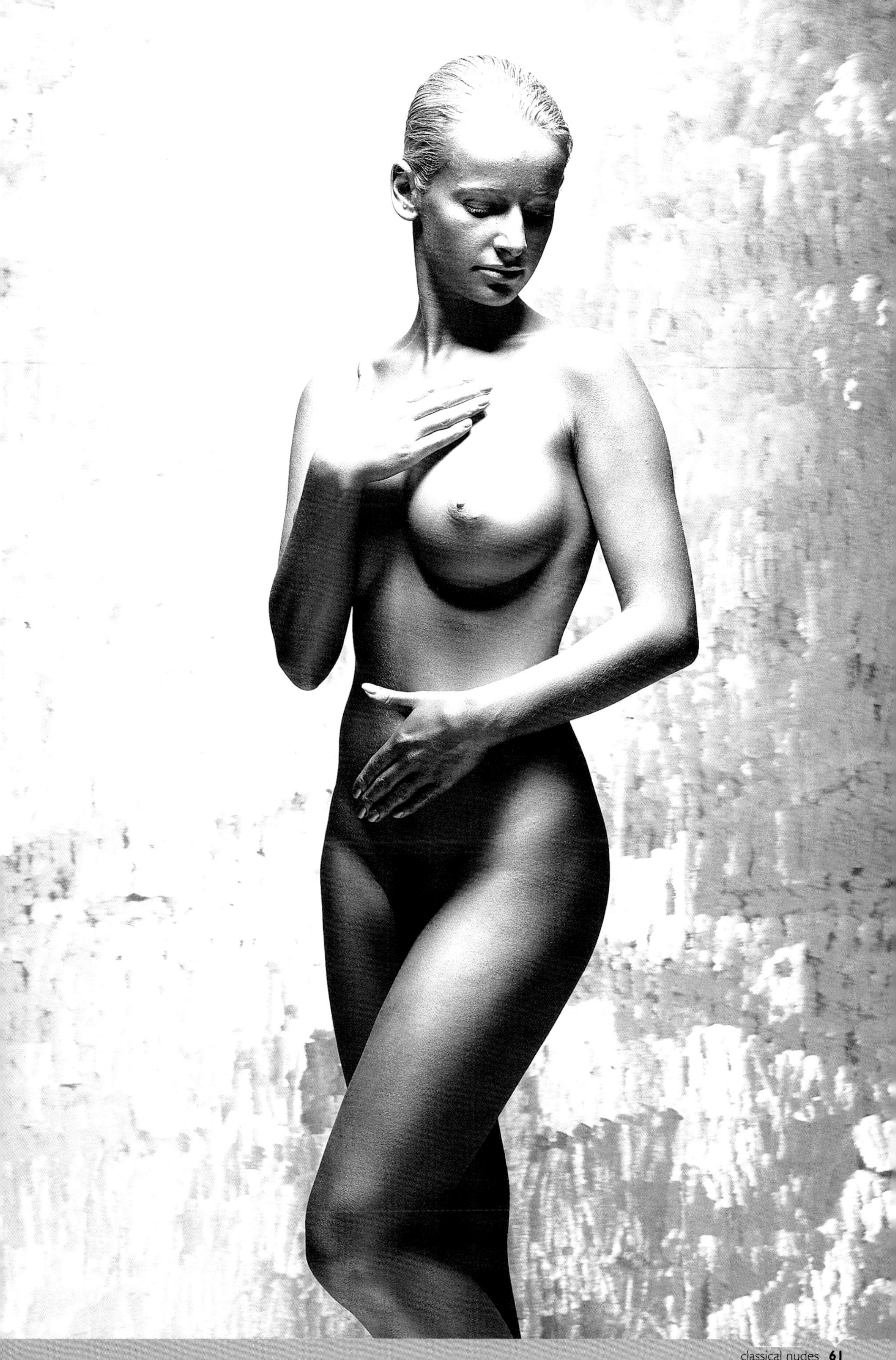

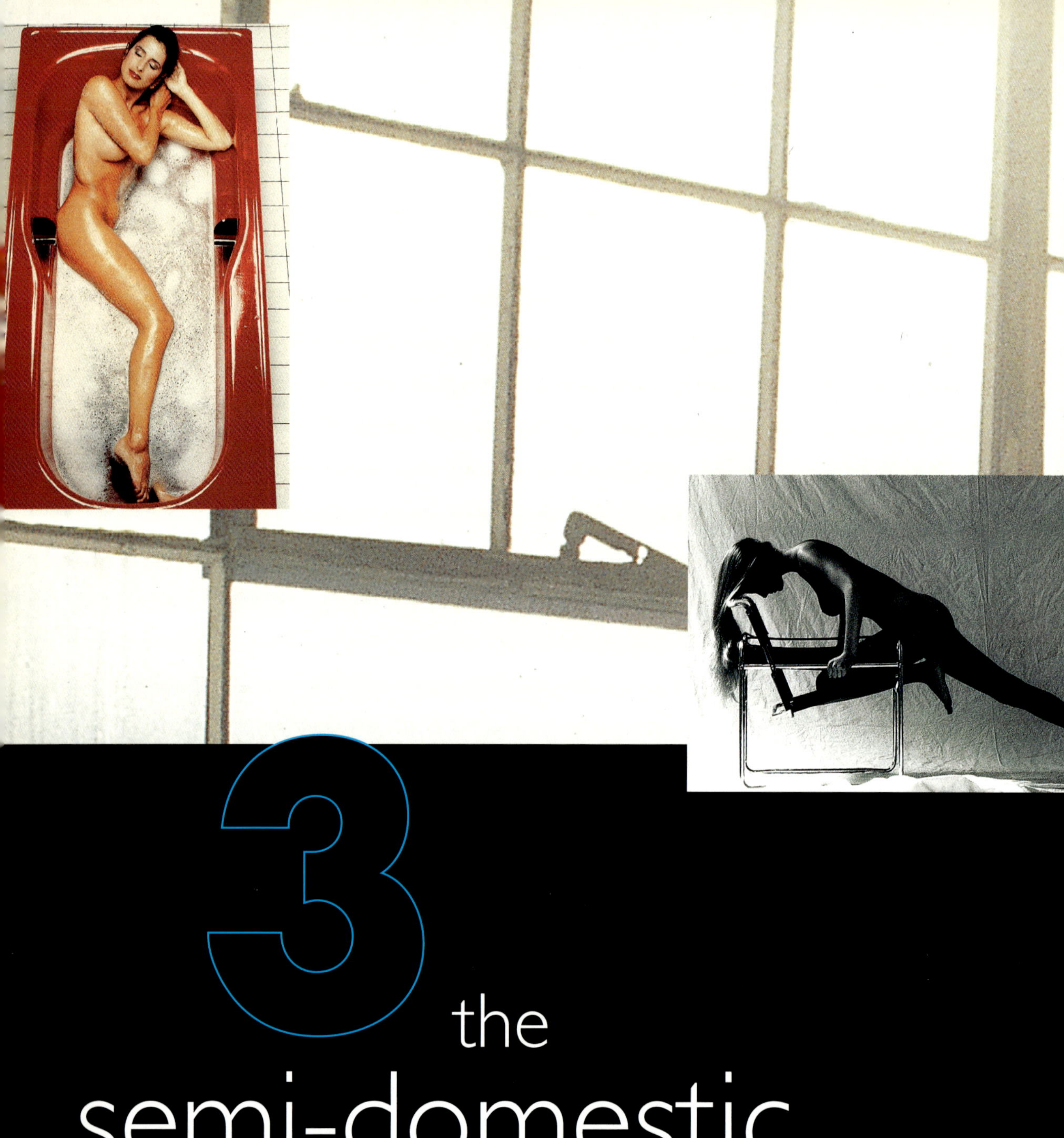

3

the
semi-domestic
nude

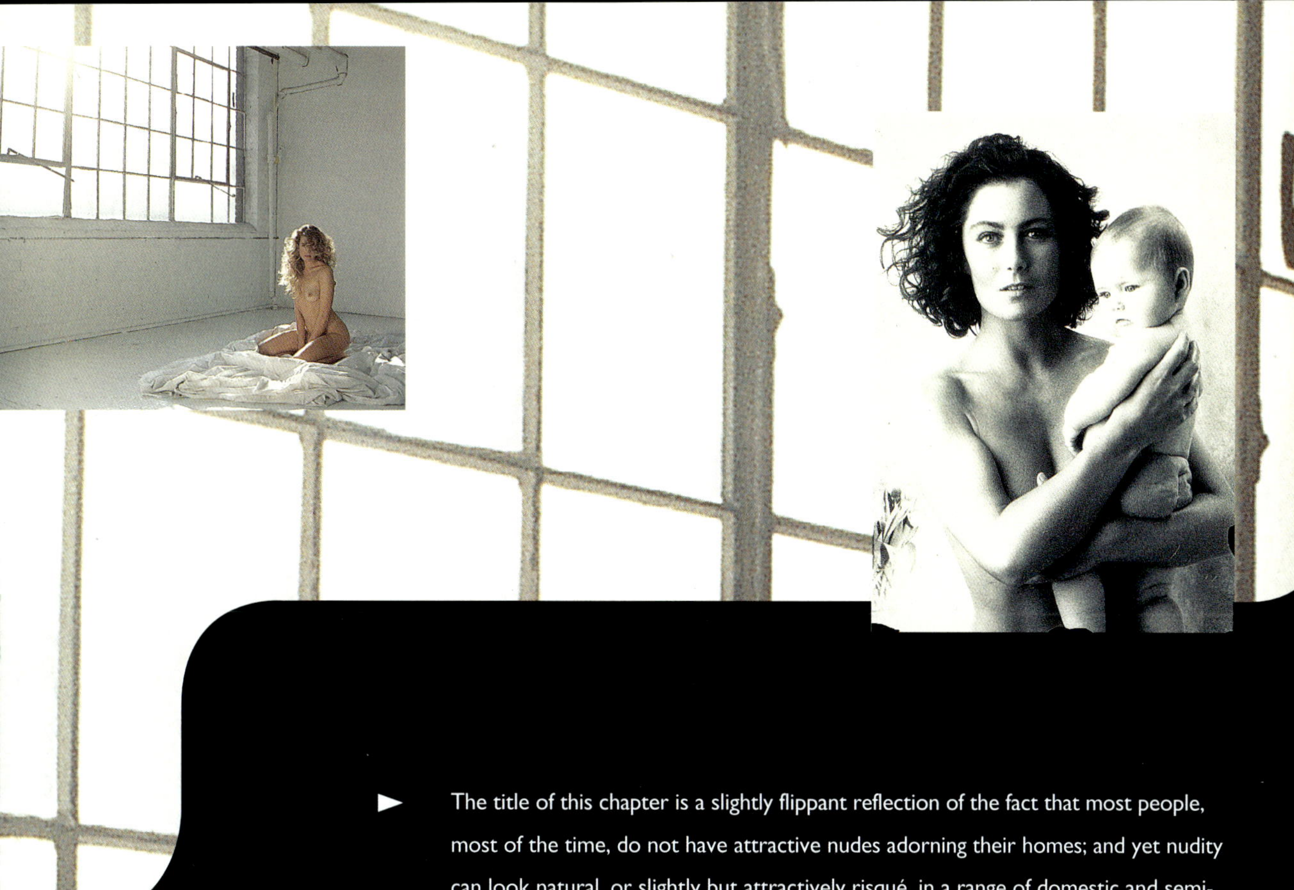

The title of this chapter is a slightly flippant reflection of the fact that most people, most of the time, do not have attractive nudes adorning their homes; and yet nudity can look natural, or slightly but attractively risqué, in a range of domestic and semi-domestic settings.

Inevitably, the definition has been stretched: Frank Wartenberg's Nude with Chair is photographed against a plain fabric backdrop, but was included because it is essentially a picture which could have been taken at home; Terry Ryan's Mother and Child is a studio picture taken against a white background which is included because of the implications of domesticity inherent in motherhood. Often any picture in any chapter in this book could as well be assigned to another chapter; but as long as the pictures are attractive in themselves it is more important that they are included, rather than that they should precisely reflect the title of the chapter.

There is a wide variety of lighting, from daylight (used in half the shots in the chapter) through a single artificial light source to complex set-ups, particularly in Morning Tea from Jordi Morgadas, where the "bedroom" is actually a built set with big soft boxes outside the windows. In general, it must be said, daylight is harder to handle than it looks and such subterfuges as white furnishings (see Peter Barry's Room) are needed to even out the light.

Photographer: **Jordi Morgadas**

Client: **Penthouse Magazine**

Use: **Editorial**

Model: **Karin**

Make-up: **Susana Muñoz**

Stylist: **Maria Rowen**

Camera: **35mm**

Lens: **85mm with A-2 filter**

Film: **Kodak Ektachrome EPR ISO 64**

Exposure: **f/16**

Lighting: **Electronic flash: 3 heads**

Props and set: **Built set**

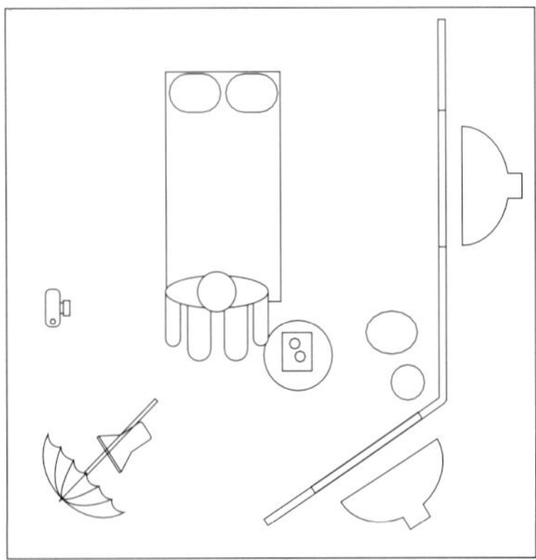

Plan View

► *Very large umbrellas can be a convenient alternative to soft boxes for some applications*

► *Tight lighting ratios can still exhibit a surprising degree of modelling if one light is very diffuse and the other is more directional*

MORNING TEA

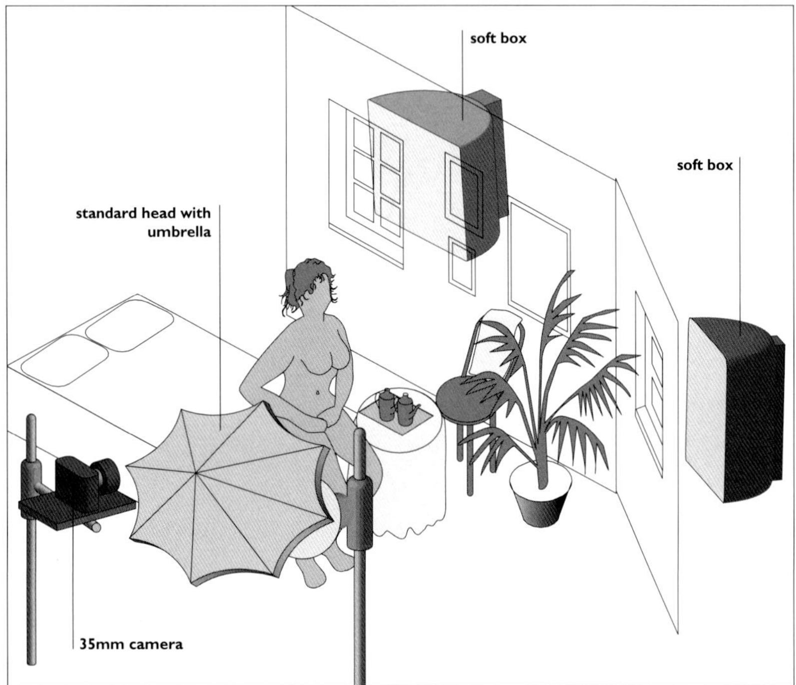

THE BUILT SET, WITH SOFT BOXES SHINING THROUGH WINDOWS, IS A MORE COMMON PLOY THAN MOST AMATEURS IMAGINE: IT GIVES THE PROFESSIONAL THE MAXIMUM POSSIBLE CONTROL, WITHOUT WORRYING ABOUT WEATHER OR TIME OF DAY.

Here there are two "windows", one of which is in shot and the other of which is clearly implied by the light from camera right. Both are transilluminated by large soft boxes, each 100x200cm (40x80in), and they create the many highlights on the model.

If these had been the only lights, however, there would have been very little rendering of the exquisite skin textures, and the drapes of the table beside the bed would have been flat and lifeless. A giant 2m (80in) umbrella to camera right therefore provided what is arguably the key light, although it is only marginally so because the overall lighting ratio is so tight. This picture clearly demonstrates that quality of light – directionality or harshness – can define which light is a key and which are fills or effects lights.

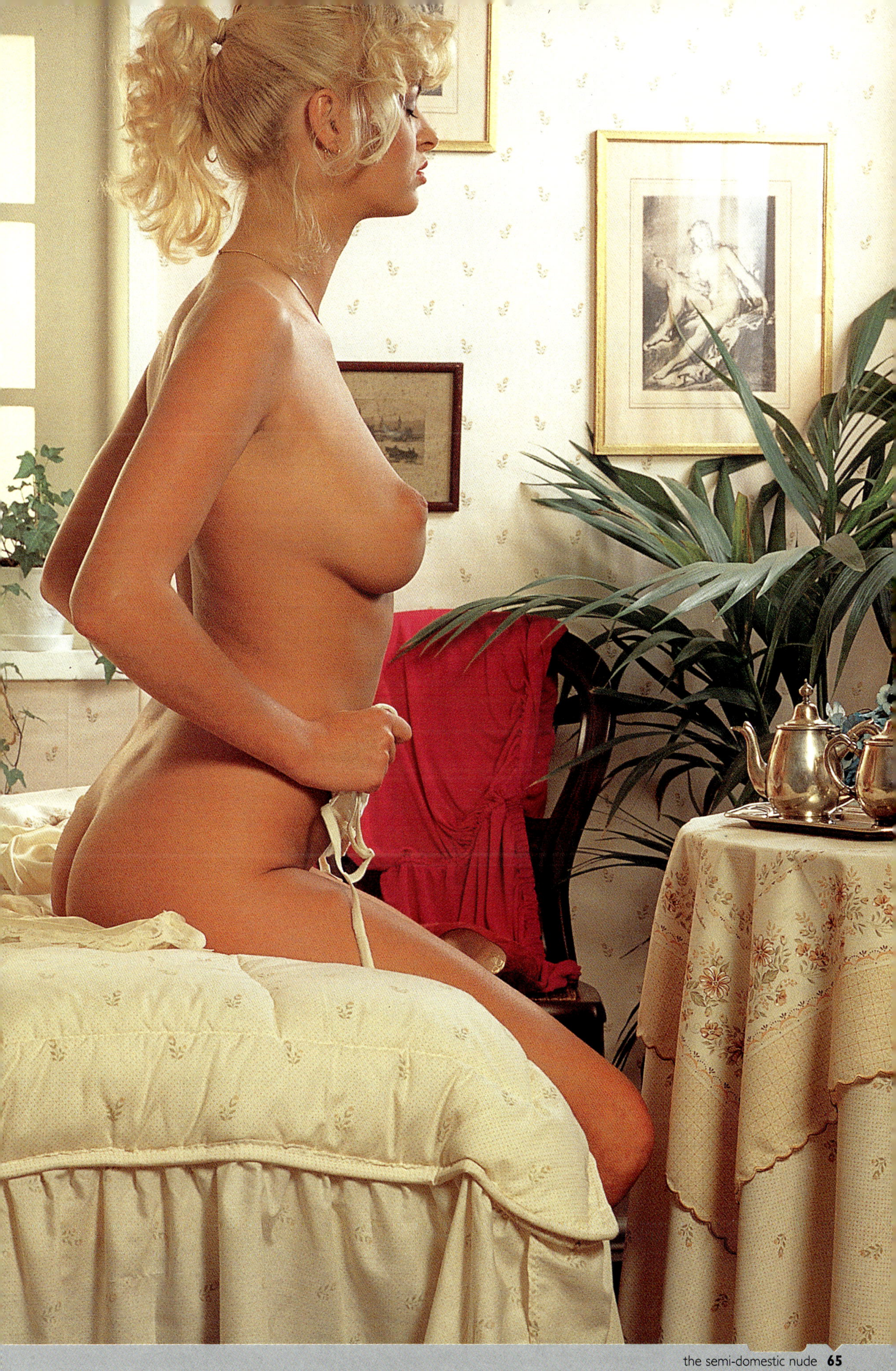

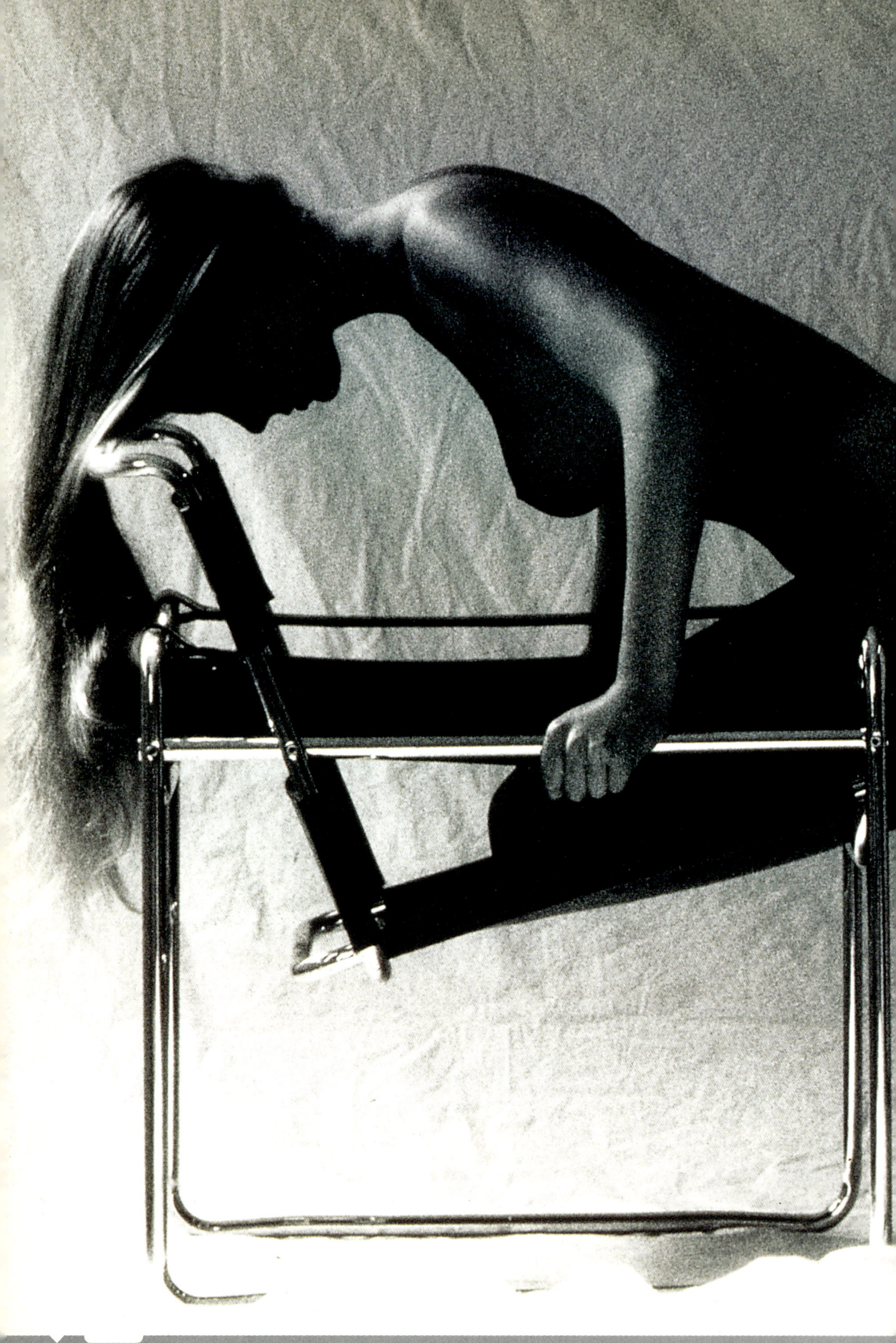

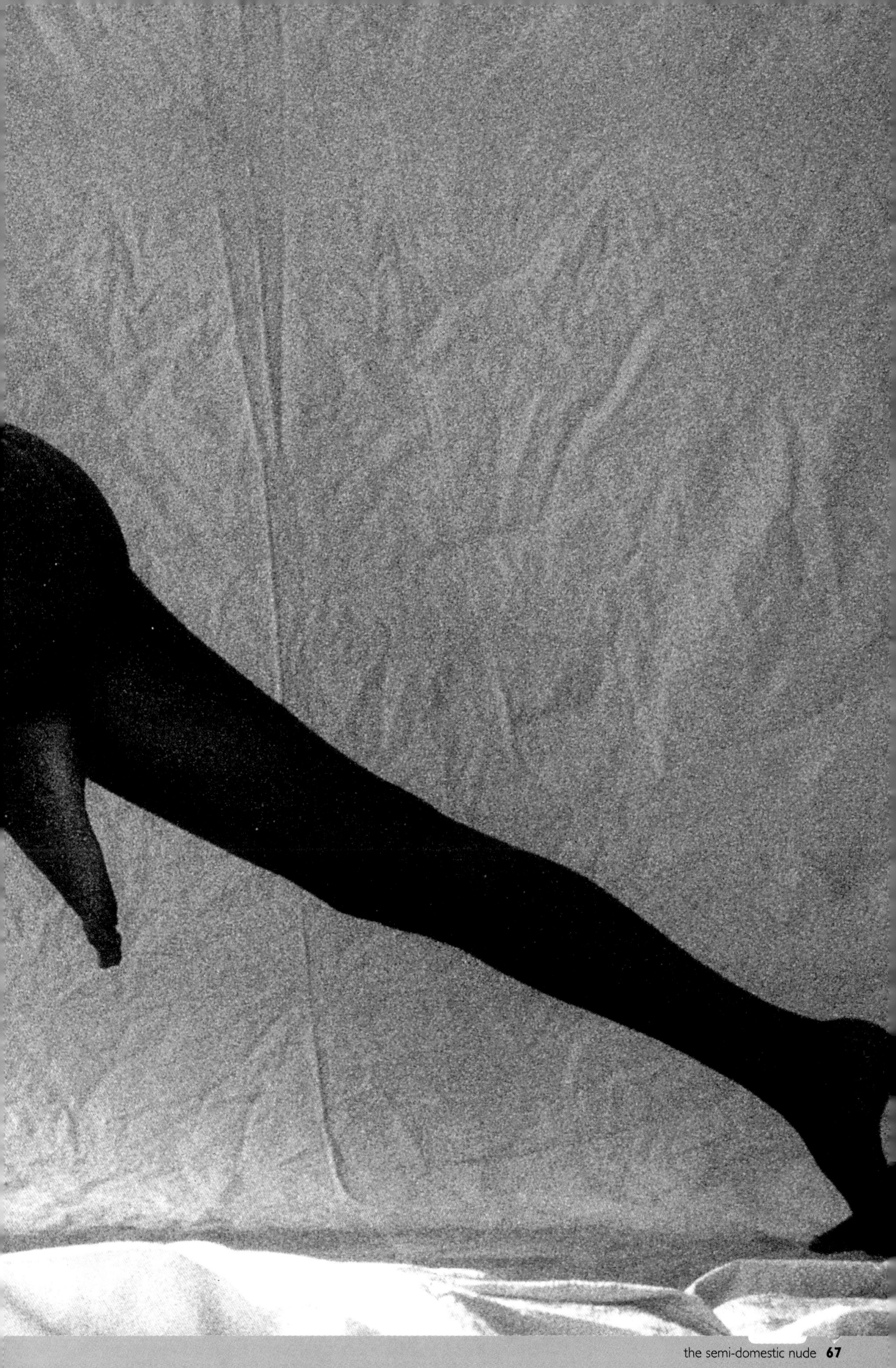

Photographer: **Frank P. Wartenberg**

Use: **Portfolio**

Camera: **35mm**

Lens: **200mm**

Film: **Polaroid Polagraph**

Exposure: **Not recorded**

Lighting: **Daylight**

Props and set: **Natural canvas, chair**

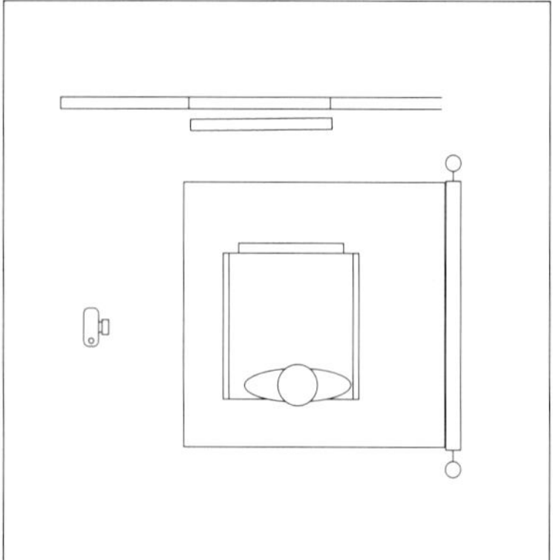

Plan View

N U D E   W I T H   C H A I R

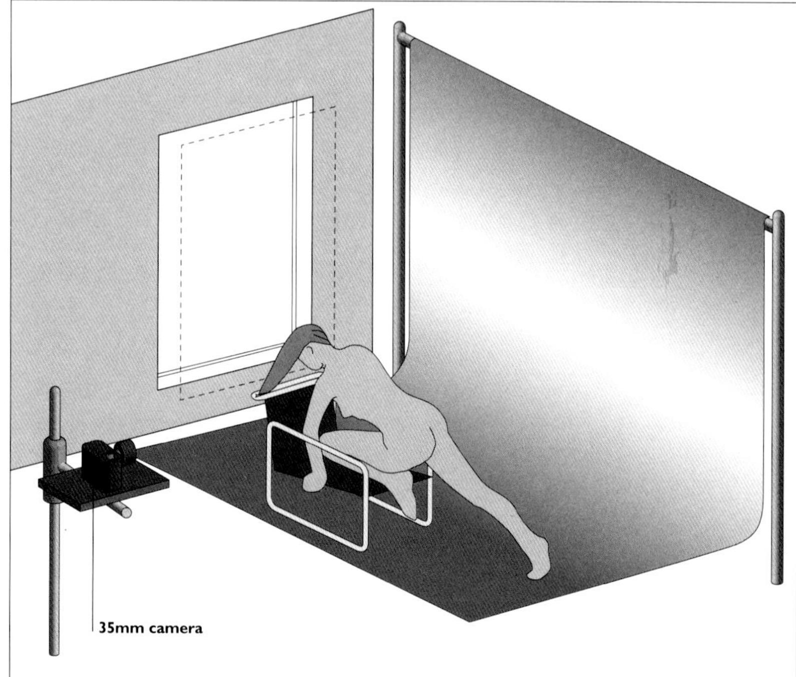

A DAYLIGHT STUDIO REQUIRES MORE THAN JUST DAYLIGHT. IT ALSO NEEDS ENOUGH SPACE TO ENABLE ONE TO CHOOSE THE BEST ANGLE FOR THE LIGHT AND THE CAMERA — WHICH IS ONE OF THE REASONS DAYLIGHT HAS FALLEN OUT OF FAVOUR.

When daylight is feasible, though, it can be delightful: big, soft light sources (and no running costs!). This is shot in front of one of the windows in Frank Wartenberg's studio, with a diffuser over the window to soften the light still more: the model's head is towards the window. It is, however, worth adding that while daylight can work superbly with monochrome, it can vary quite widely in colour from distinctly warm to quite cold and unpleasant.

Although the Victorians were fond of elaborately painted backdrops, they sometimes used plain canvas, as here. The combination of shapes is superbly executed: the timelessness of the human form against the formal chrome-and-leather chair.

► *The use of high-contrast Polagraph film has accentuated the contrast between the form of the model and the background*

► *Daylight studios generally require plenty of room for manoeuvre*

► *A long lens emphasizes graphic form*

Photographer: **Struan**

Client: **Amanda**

Use: **Portrait**

Camera: **35mm**

Lens: **35mm**

Film: **Kodak Ektachrome EPN ISO 100**

Exposure: **1/125sec at f/8**

Lighting: **Available light**

Props and set: **Large daylight studio**

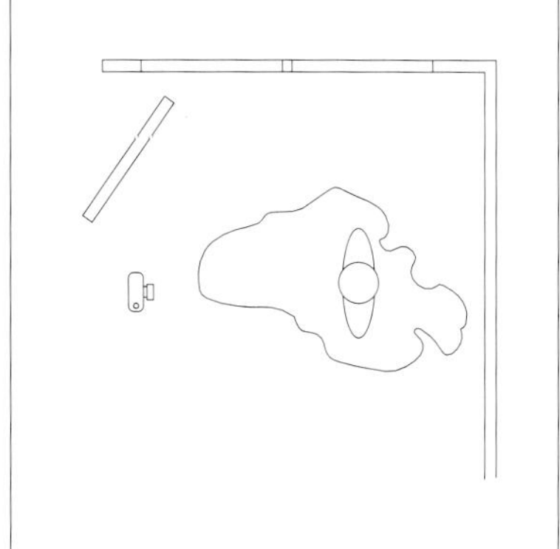

Plan View

▼

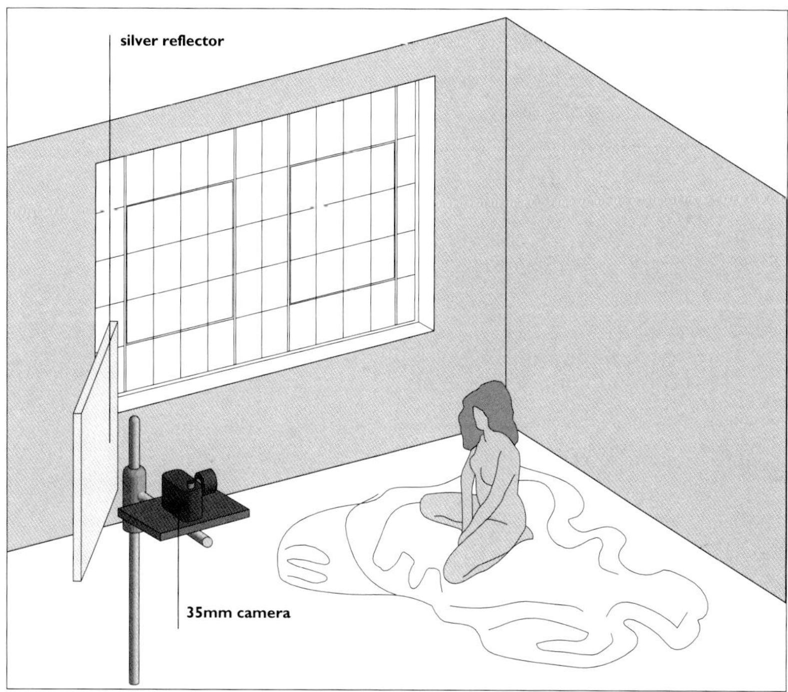

MODERN STUDIOS OFTEN BEAR MORE RESEMBLANCE TO A FACTORY THAN TO A 19TH CENTURY ARTIST'S *ATELIER*. SOME PHOTOGRAPHERS PAINT THEIR WINDOWS BLACK OR OTHERWISE BLOCK THEM PERMANENTLY, WHILE OTHERS FIT BLINDS TO ALLOW THE OPTION OF DAYLIGHT.

Here, sunlight is supplemented by a 120x120cm (4x4ft) silver movie-type reflector to camera left. One might have expected another reflector to be to camera right to provide fill on the side away from the window, but the white interior of the studio took care of this. Besides, this is a much more directional reflector than a white bounce: you can see the secondary shadow behind the model on the wall. Its purpose is to fill the front of the model: without it, the choice would be between wildly overexposing the sunlit portions, or underexposing the model.

The model is kneeling on a white sheet, almost one of Struan's trade-marks; he always carries a few white sheets with him, as props, backgrounds, reflectors, screens for the model to change behind, and so forth.

► *Silver (and gold) reflectors are much more directional than white*

► *Different films have different responses to wide lighting ratios*

► *A white sheet can have numerous uses*

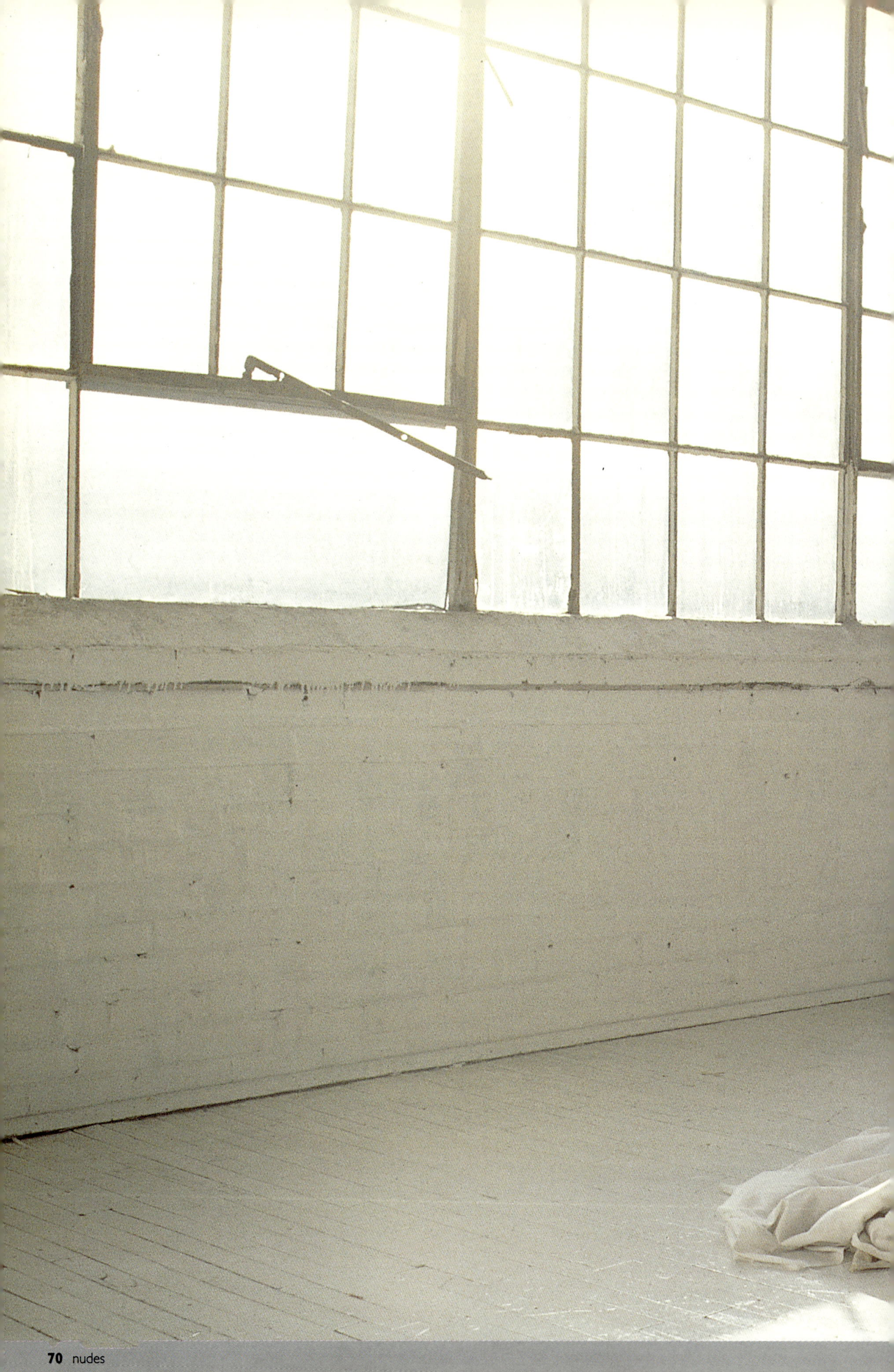

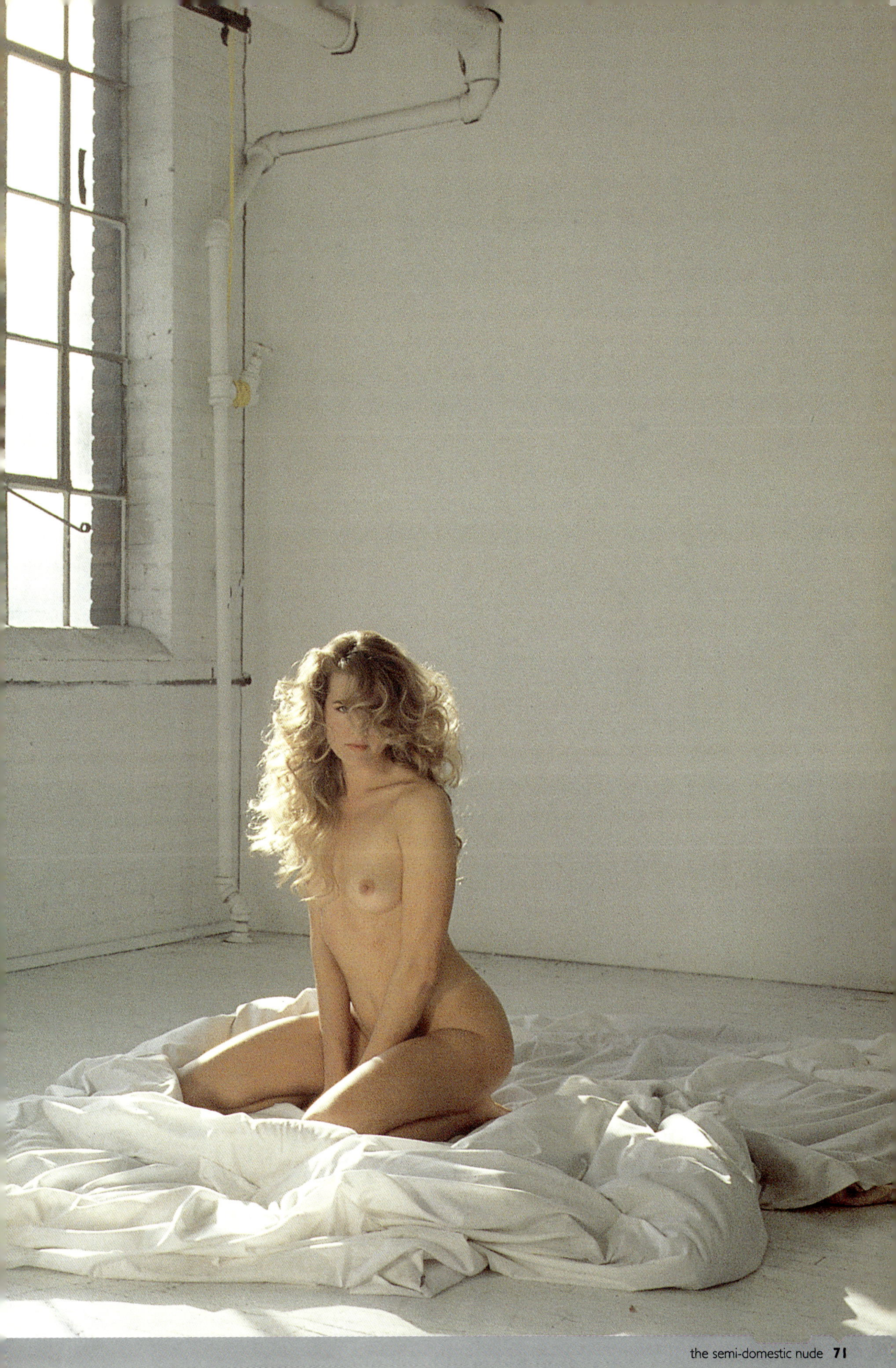

Photographer: **Peter Barry**
Use: **Model test**
Camera: **6x6cm**
Lens: **80mm**
Film: **Kodak Ektachrome EPR ISO 64**
Exposure: **1/4sec at f/4**
Lighting: **Available light**
Props and set: **Location**

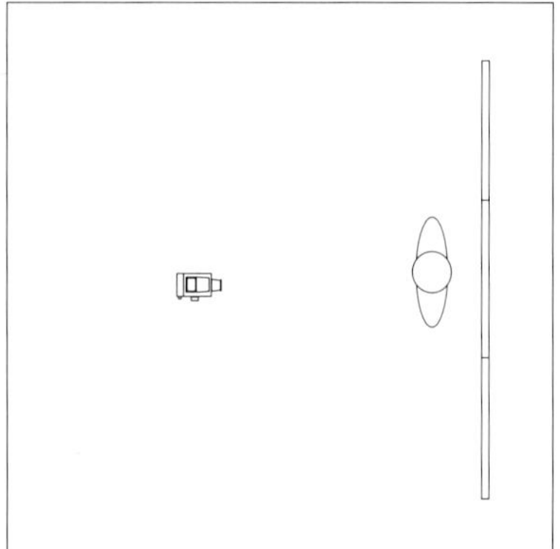

Plan View

▼

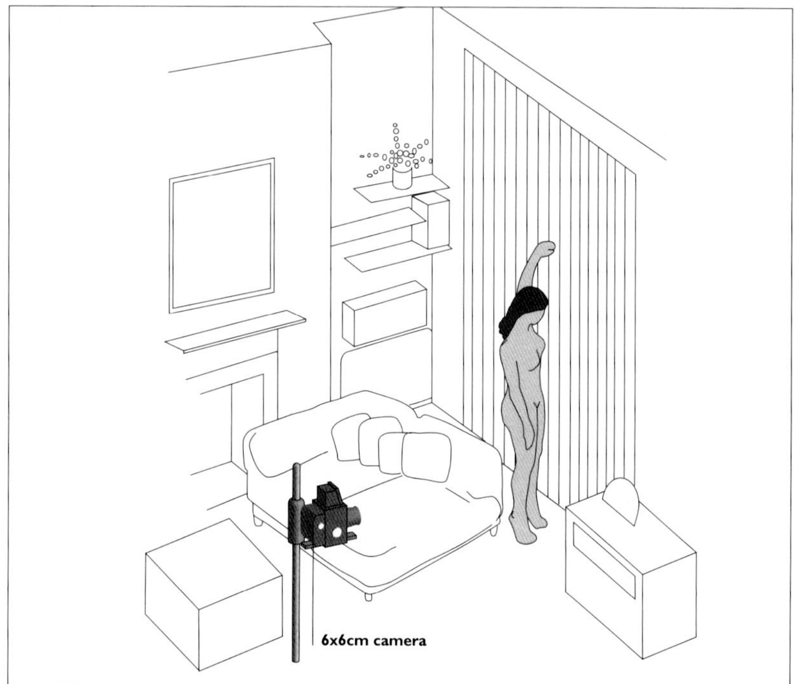

THE LIGHTING HERE IS SO SMOOTH, AND THE MODELLING SO GOOD, THAT IT IS HARD TO BELIEVE THAT IT IS "ONLY" AVAILABLE LIGHT. BUT THERE IS MORE HERE THAN MEETS THE EYE….

Two important factors are the vertically slatted window blinds and the light-coloured chair and cushions behind the model. The slatted blinds can create a surprisingly directional light, and they can also be angled so that the direction can be controlled. These two factors together help to explain a great deal of the success of the photograph.

Exposure is critical and a film of relatively low contrast is needed if the highlights are not to burn out and be "blown"; some modern films would be too contrasty to handle this sort of tonal range. Also, extreme neutrality is needed: some films run slightly blue, others slightly magenta, and, with flesh tones and light highlights, colour casts would soon become very obvious.

► *Do not neglect the possibilities of manipulating blinds and curtains to control "available" light*

► *Over-exposure would "blow" the highlights, but under-exposure would not give adequate skin tones*

► *The tiptoe pose and outstretched arm of the model echo the verticality of the blind*

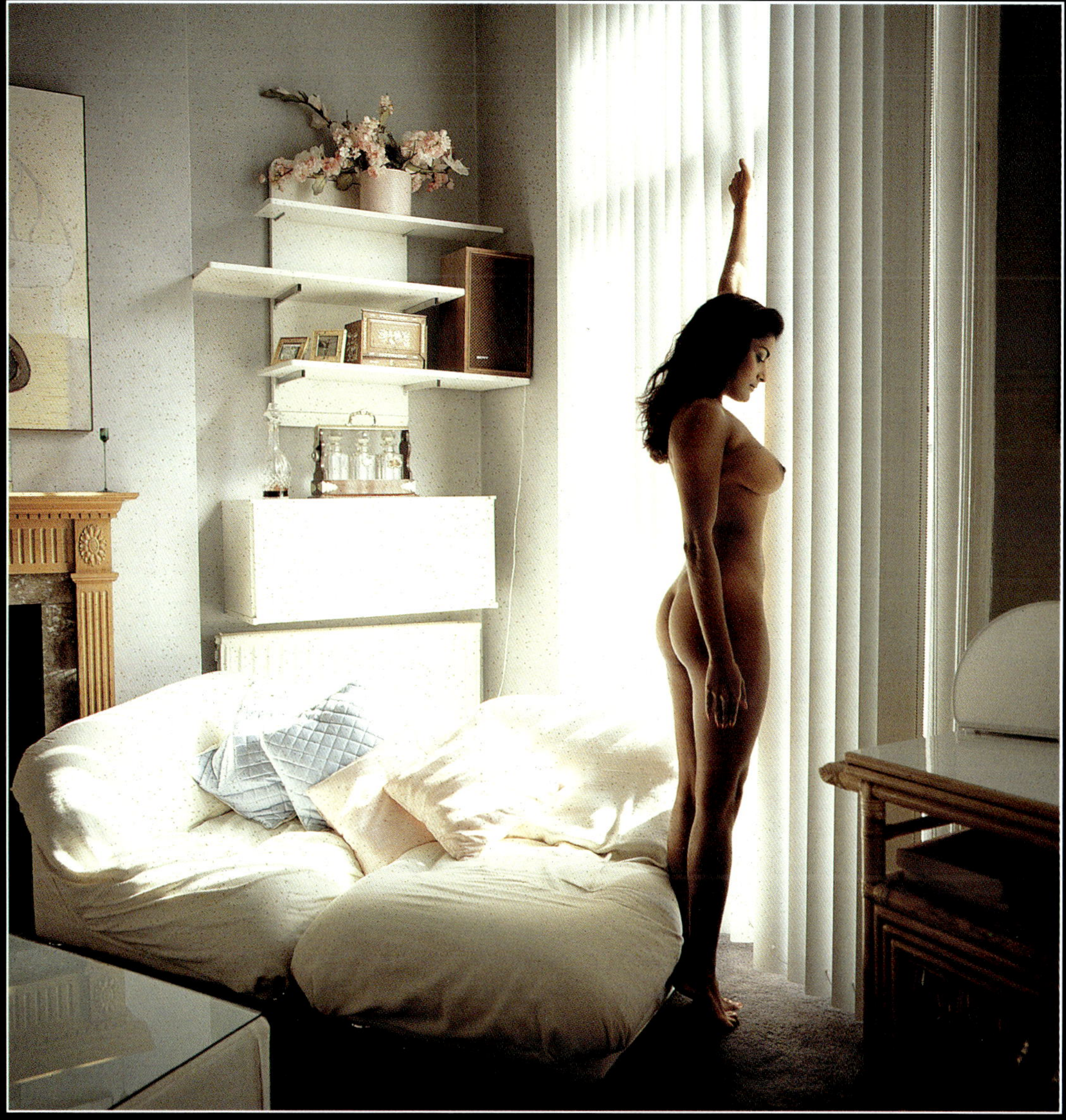

Photographer: **Terry Ryan**

Use: **Self-promotion**

Model: **Amanda Benson**

Camera: **35mm**

Lens: **105mm**

Film: **Polaroid Polagraph 400**

Exposure: **f16**

Lighting: **Electronic flash: 1 head**

Props and set: **White background paper**

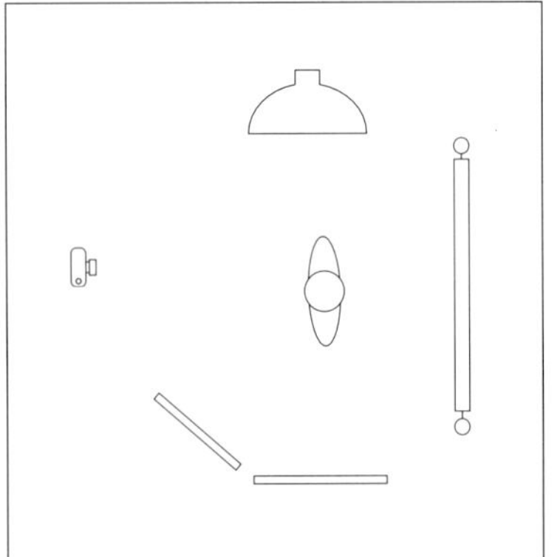

Plan View

▼

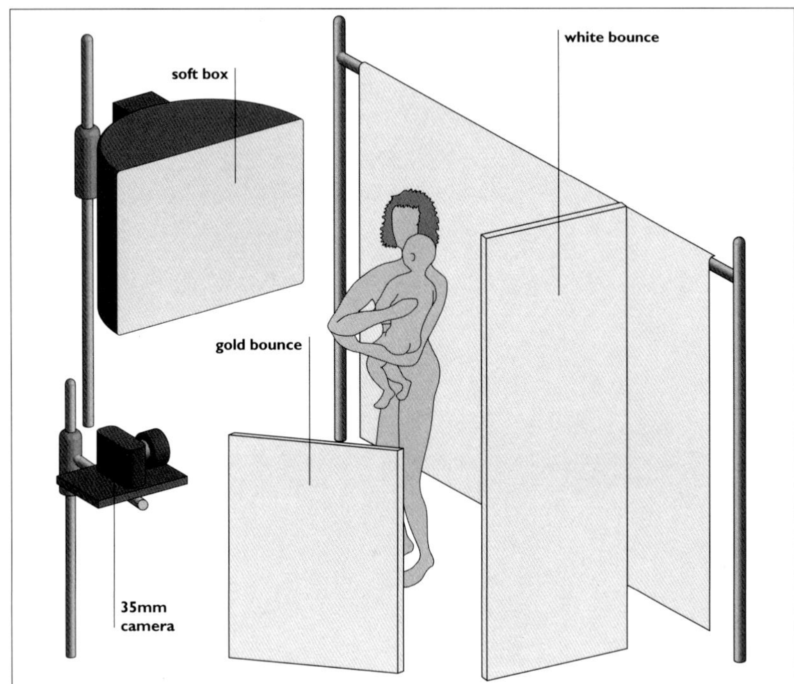

POLAROID'S ISO 400 POLAGRAPH FILM IS DESIGNED FOR TECHNICAL USE, BUT TERRY RYAN HAS DEVELOPED CONSIDERABLE EXPERTISE IN EXPLOITING ITS UNIQUE TONALITY FOR GENERAL PHOTOGRAPHY. THE SECRET LIES IN A VERY TIGHT LIGHTING RATIO AND EXTREMELY CAREFUL EXPOSURE.

The only light here is a big "swimming pool" soft box to camera left, but immediately to camera right there is a big white bounce – a 120x240cm (4x8ft) sheet of expanded polystyrene – and a gold bounce as well. The background, which looks burned out and high-key, as if it were illuminated separately, is in fact very close to the model and is lit only by spill from the key light.

A problem with all Polaroid emulsions is that they are very, very tender and easily scratched, so it makes sense to duplicate them immediately and never to send out originals to clients. In this case the scratches and the processing artifacts (the marks around the edge of the image) are presented as a part of the image – as though it were an old picture that had been rediscovered.

► *High-contrast films require very tight lighting ratios*

► *Lighting backgrounds with spill is not always easy*

► *Flaws and marks can be an integral part of a picture*

Photographer's comment:

This shot was taken whilst working on a shot for Boots the Chemist plc. It was decided to use Polagraph, and although a series of shots was taken, the effect on this particular frame – the borders, etc – seemed to me to add that extra something to the shot.

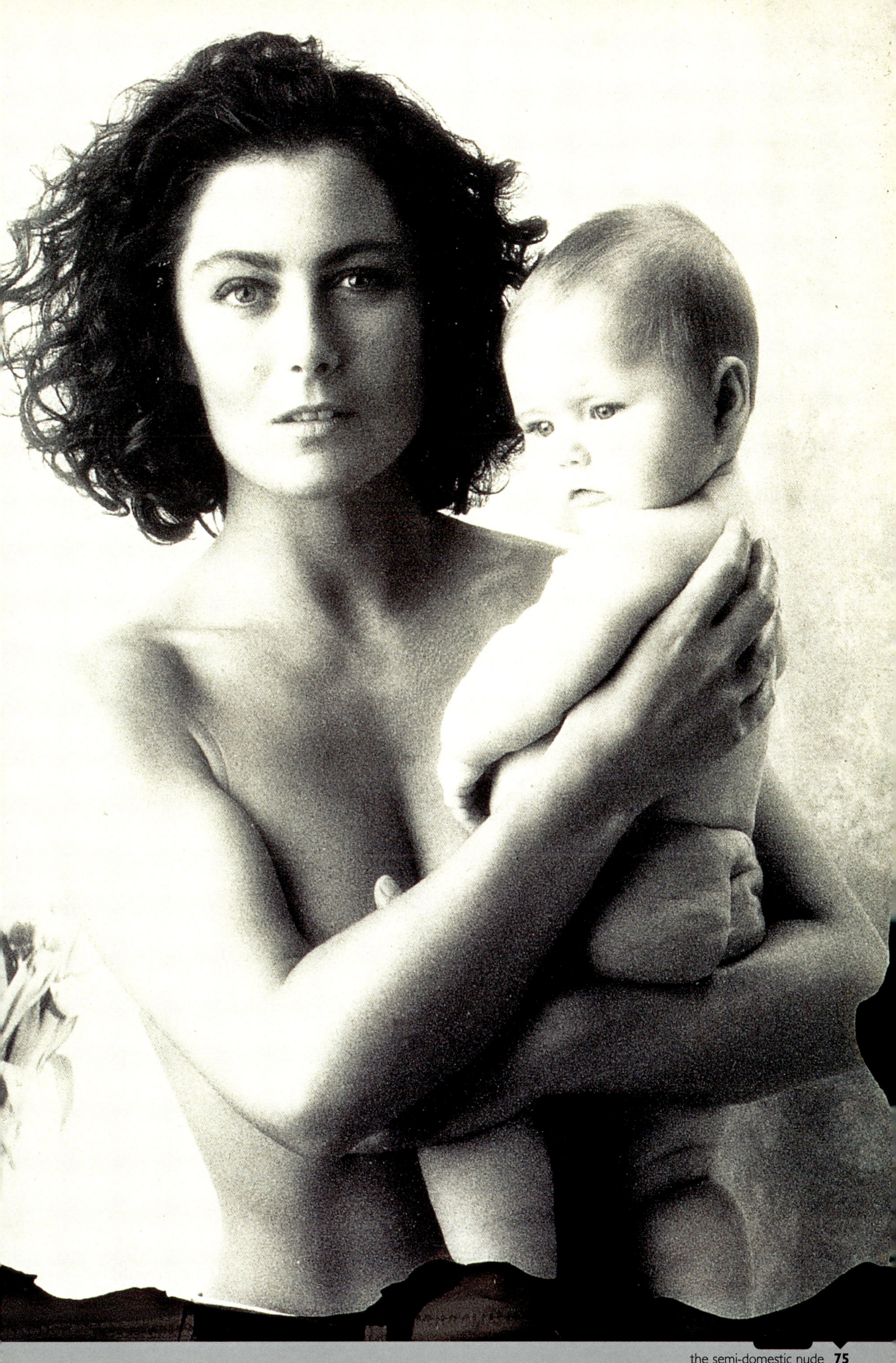

Photographer: **Struan**

Use: **Personal work**

Model: **Lorraine**

Camera: **35mm**

Lens: **50mm**

Film: **Kodachrome 64**

Exposure: **f/11**

Lighting: **Electronic flash: 3 heads**

Props and set: **Bath, tile flats**

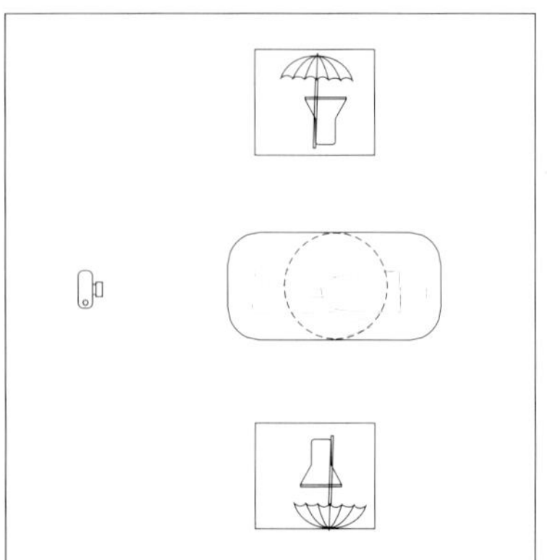

Plan View

► *Vivid colours sometimes speak for themselves, but they can also be enhanced by skillful lighting*

► *Portrait (vertical) compositions are often more energetic than landscape (horizontal)*

RED BATHTUB

▼

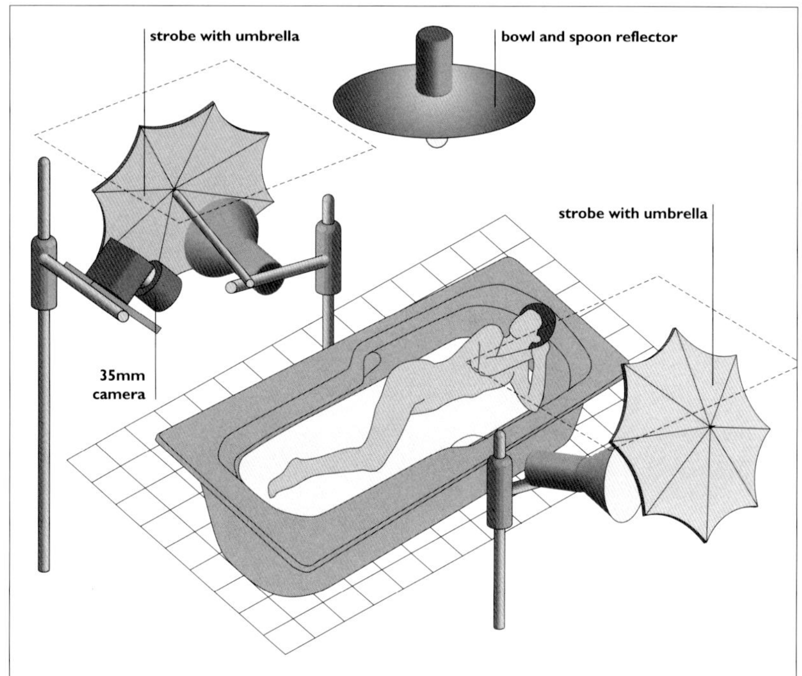

He continues: "We bought a couple of sheets of 240×120cm (8×4ft) tile board for the "floor". There's a single light over the top – my big, circular reflector, 90cm (3ft) across – and then there's a strobe on either side with an umbrella to light the tiles. I tried it without but there was too much shadow beside the bath."

The big round reflector creates the highlights on the model and (even more importantly) on the bath, and choosing Kodachrome really "pops" the red – Kodachrome is famous for its reds.

Baths are normally shot "landscape", which emphasizes their stability and restfulness. Adopting the unusual technique of shooting from one end gives a much more energetic composition.

Photographer's comment:

I shot this on both 35mm and with the Hasselblad; the Hasselblad shot won second prize in a national Hasselblad contest.

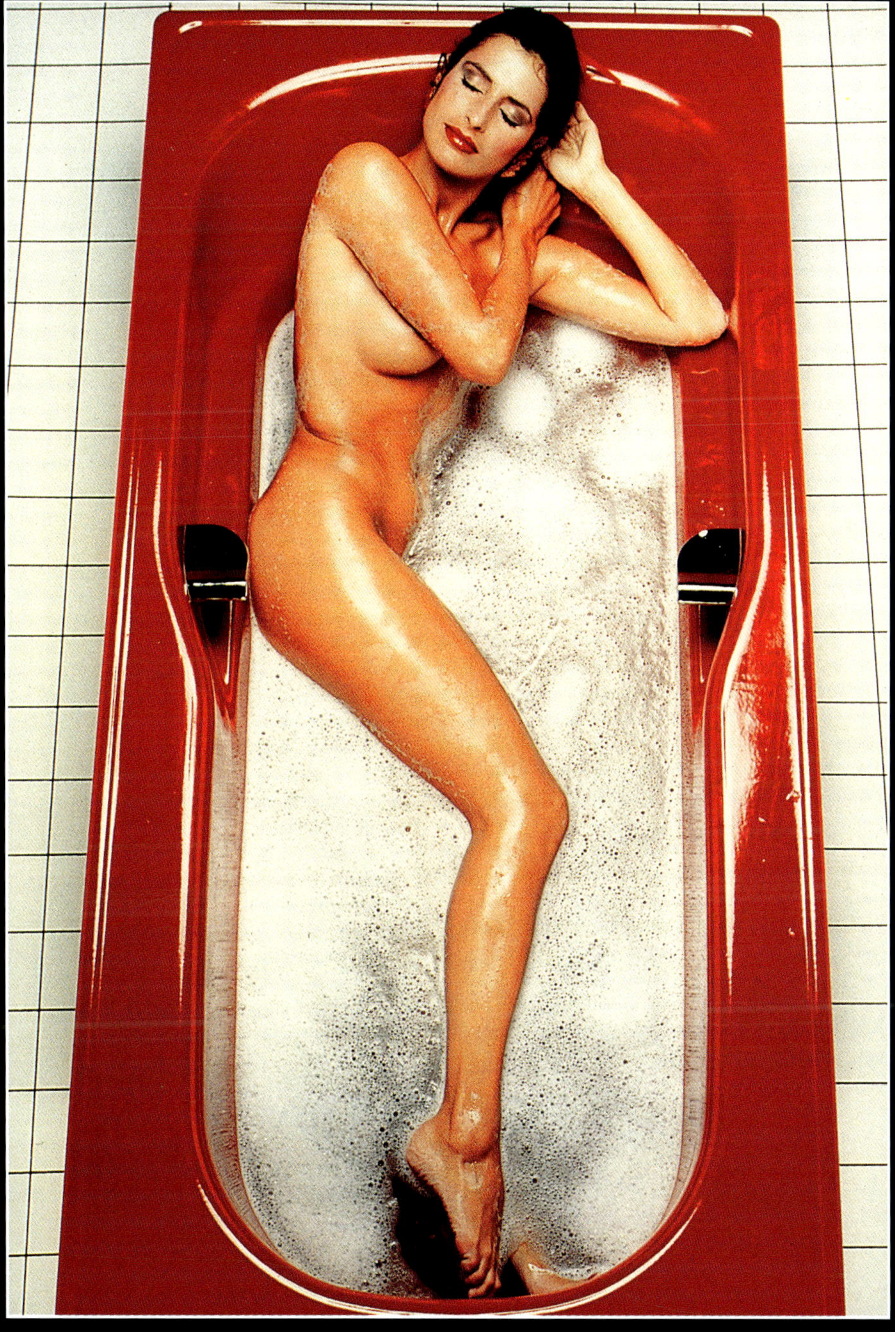

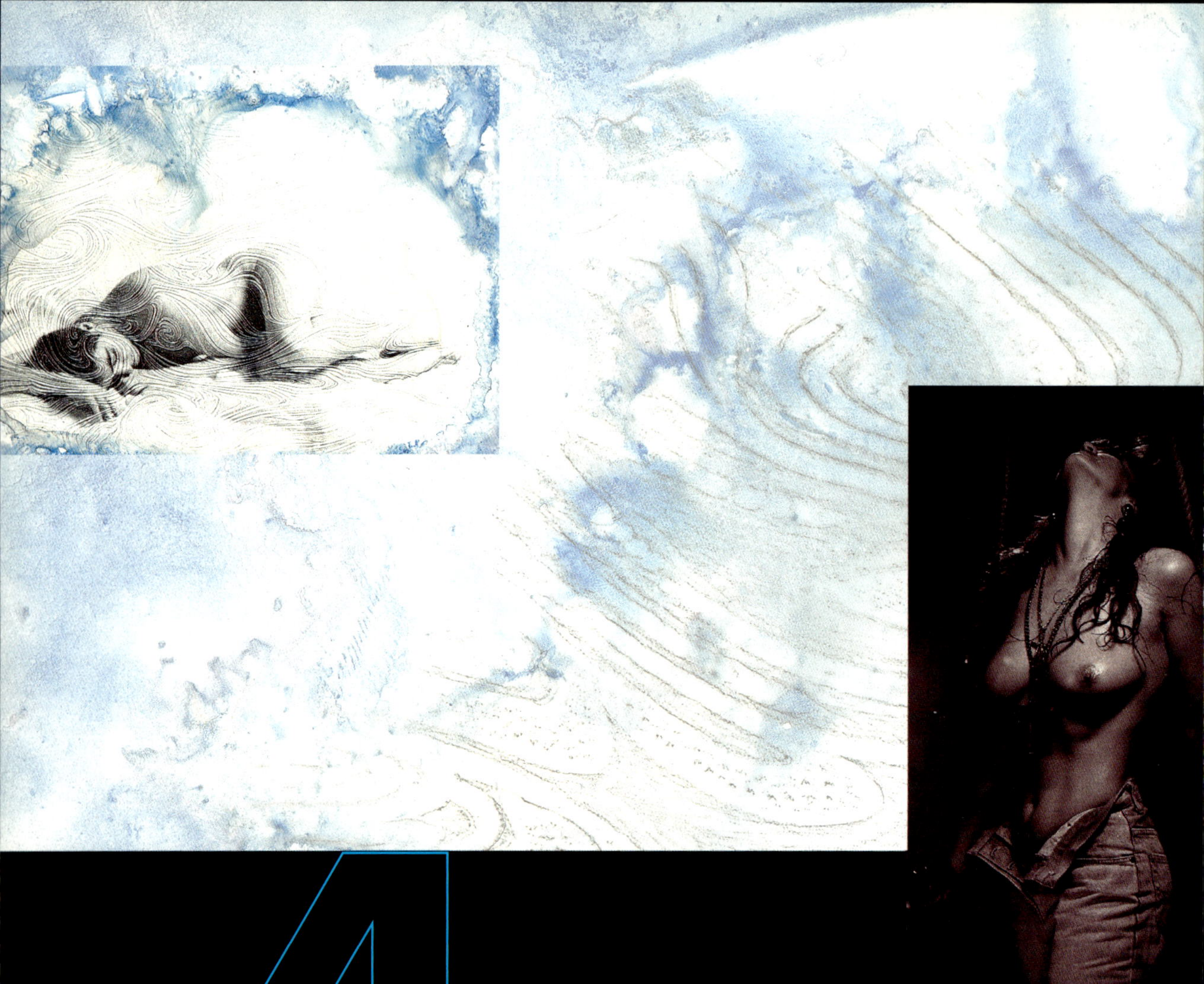

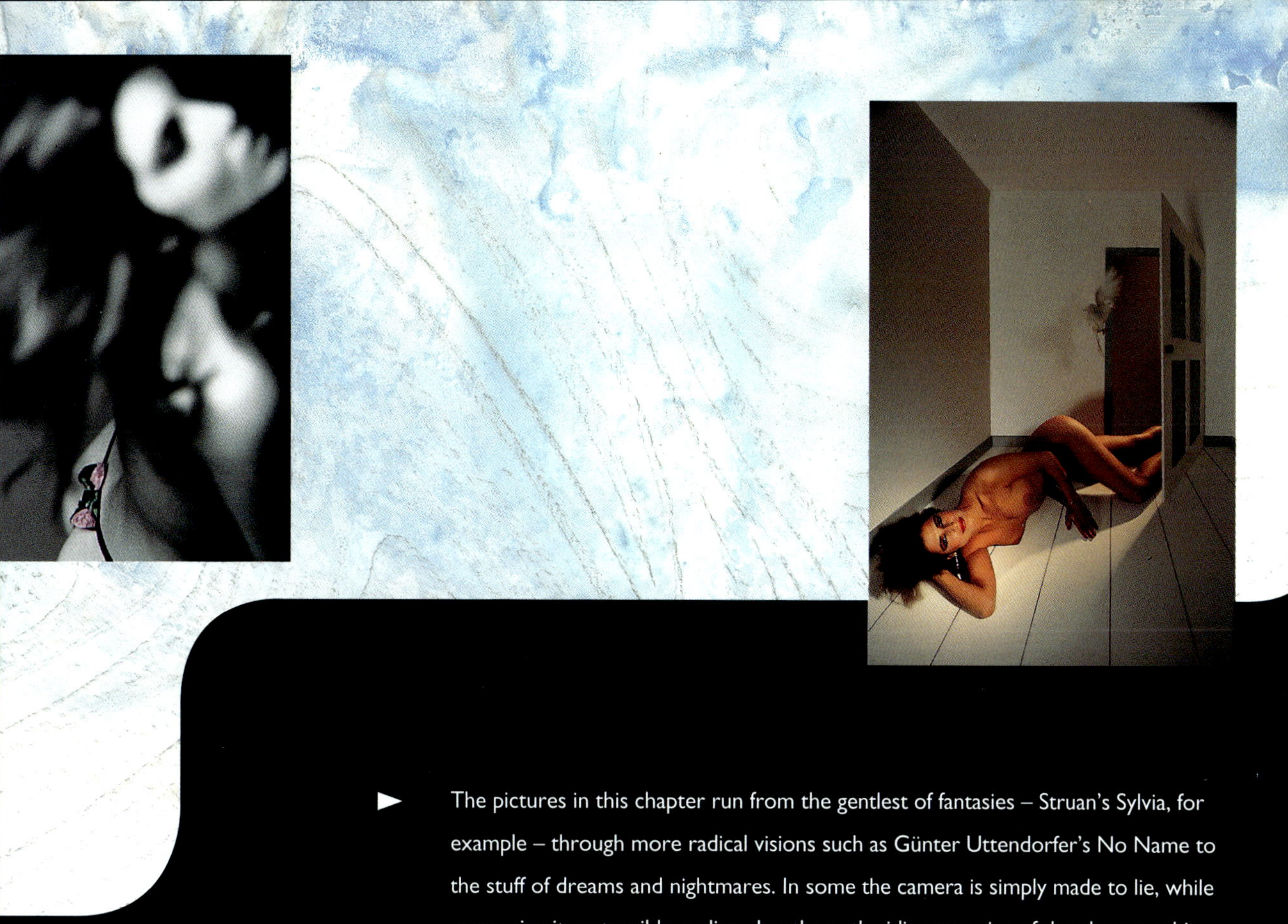

The pictures in this chapter run from the gentlest of fantasies – Struan's Sylvia, for example – through more radical visions such as Günter Uttendorfer's No Name to the stuff of dreams and nightmares. In some the camera is simply made to lie, while preserving its ostensible realism. In others, the idiosyncracies of the photographic process, or the possibilities for manipulation during printing, are the secret. Yet others are simply straight shots: the secret lies in the set-up (and, of course, in the lighting).

Some are definitely disquieting, while others are curiously tranquil; and which ones seem disquieting to a particular person, and which ones seem tranquil, will depend very much on that individual's outlook on life. All illustrate the necessity of learning to meld vision and technique, as either on its own is insufficient: far too many pictures are spoiled by an absence of one or the other, so that a good idea is poorly realized or faultless execution betrays a woeful lack of aesthetic feeling.

Rollfilm and 35mm are neck and neck, with one 4x5in shot. It is particularly interesting to compare two superficially similar pictures, Stu Williamson's Vicky and Günther Uttendorfer's No Name, to see how technically and stylistically different they are – as well as to see that on closer examination, the content and pose of the two pictures differ considerably more than they at first seem.

Photographer: **Harry Lomax**

Use: **Promotional card**

Model: **Jo**

Camera: **4x5in**

Lens: **65mm and 360mm**

Film: **Fuji RDP ISO 100**

Exposure: **f/16 double exposure: see text**

Lighting: **Flash: see text**

Props and set: **Dragon "set"; girl on seamless paper**

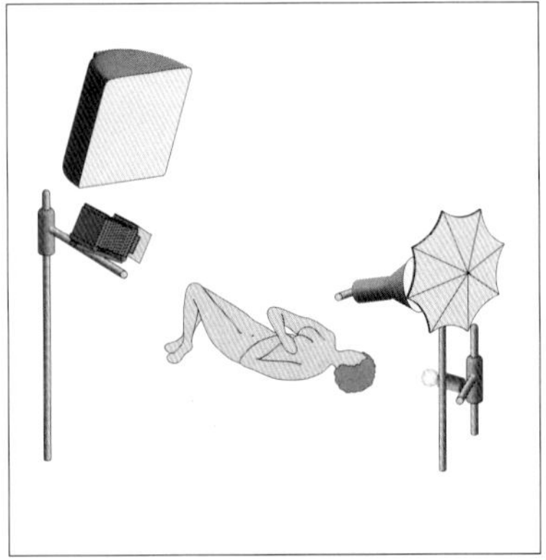

Second Exposure

► *Switching focal lengths is a useful way to control image size in a multiple exposure, provided perspective is not a problem*

► *When switching focal lengths, the relative distances of lights and subject may need to be changed to maintain consistent lighting – although the orientations should remain as constant as possible*

D R A G O N

▼

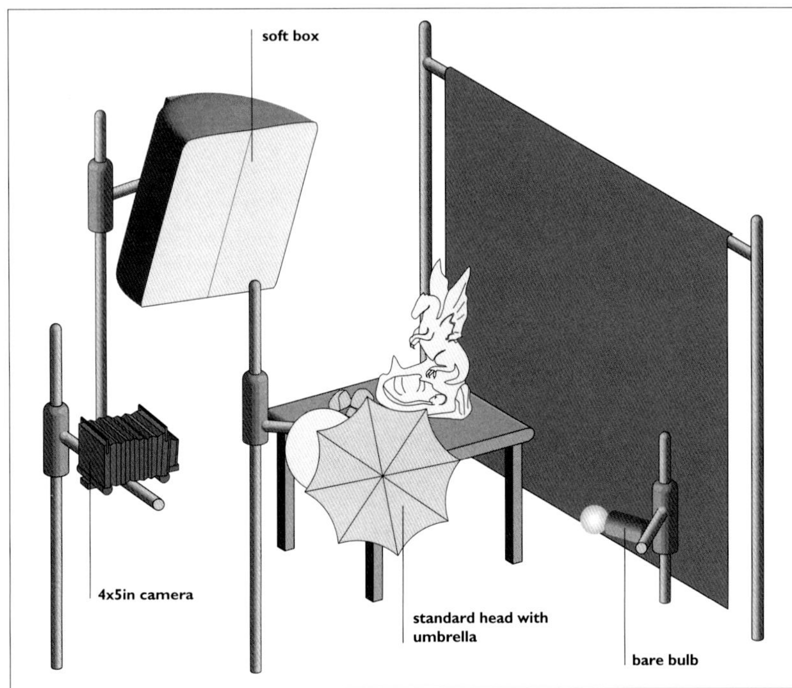

ELECTRONIC IMAGE MANIPULATION IS SO COMMONPLACE NOWADAYS THAT WE MAY FORGET HOW A GOOD PHOTOGRAPHER CAN OFTEN OBTAIN BETTER RESULTS, FASTER AND MORE ECONOMICALLY, USING TRADITIONAL PHOTOGRAPHIC TECHNIQUES. THIS IS A DOUBLE EXPOSURE.

The dragon "set" is a sculpture less than 30cm (12in) high, with a foreground of moss and pebbles and a graduated background. The key light is a big soft box to camera left, very slightly back lighting the subject, while fill comes from an umbrella to camera right set one stop down from the key. A bare bulb behind and below the dragon differentiates the background. The area to be occupied by the girl is masked off and marked on the ground glass. This was shot with a 360mm lens. The girl was then shot through a "keyhole" screen so that only she recorded on the film, the rest going black. The lighting was similar – a soft box to camera left, an umbrella to camera right and a bare bulb behind her – but lighting distances were adjusted to compensate for the fact that she was shot with a 65mm lens in order to get the scale right.

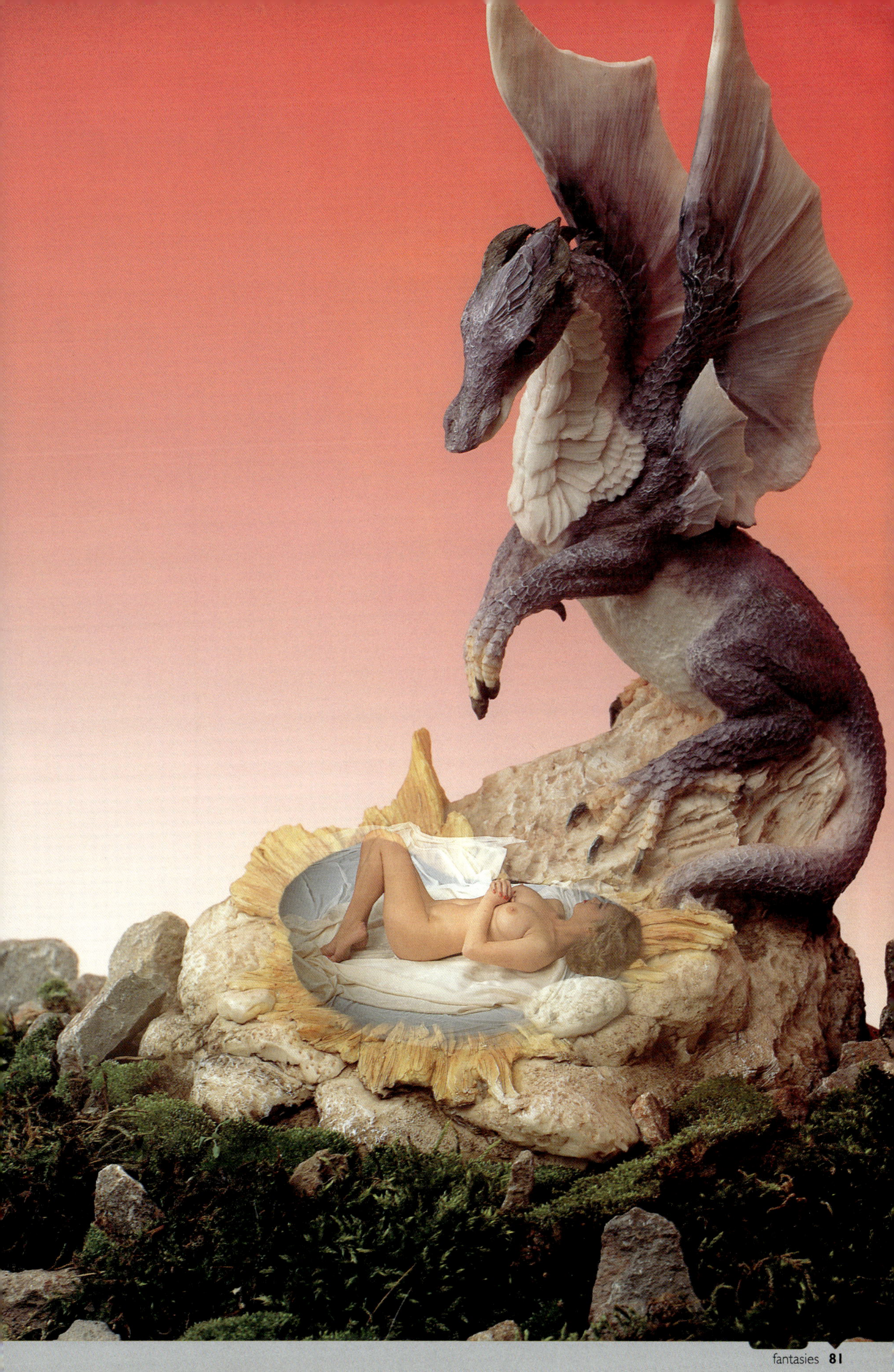

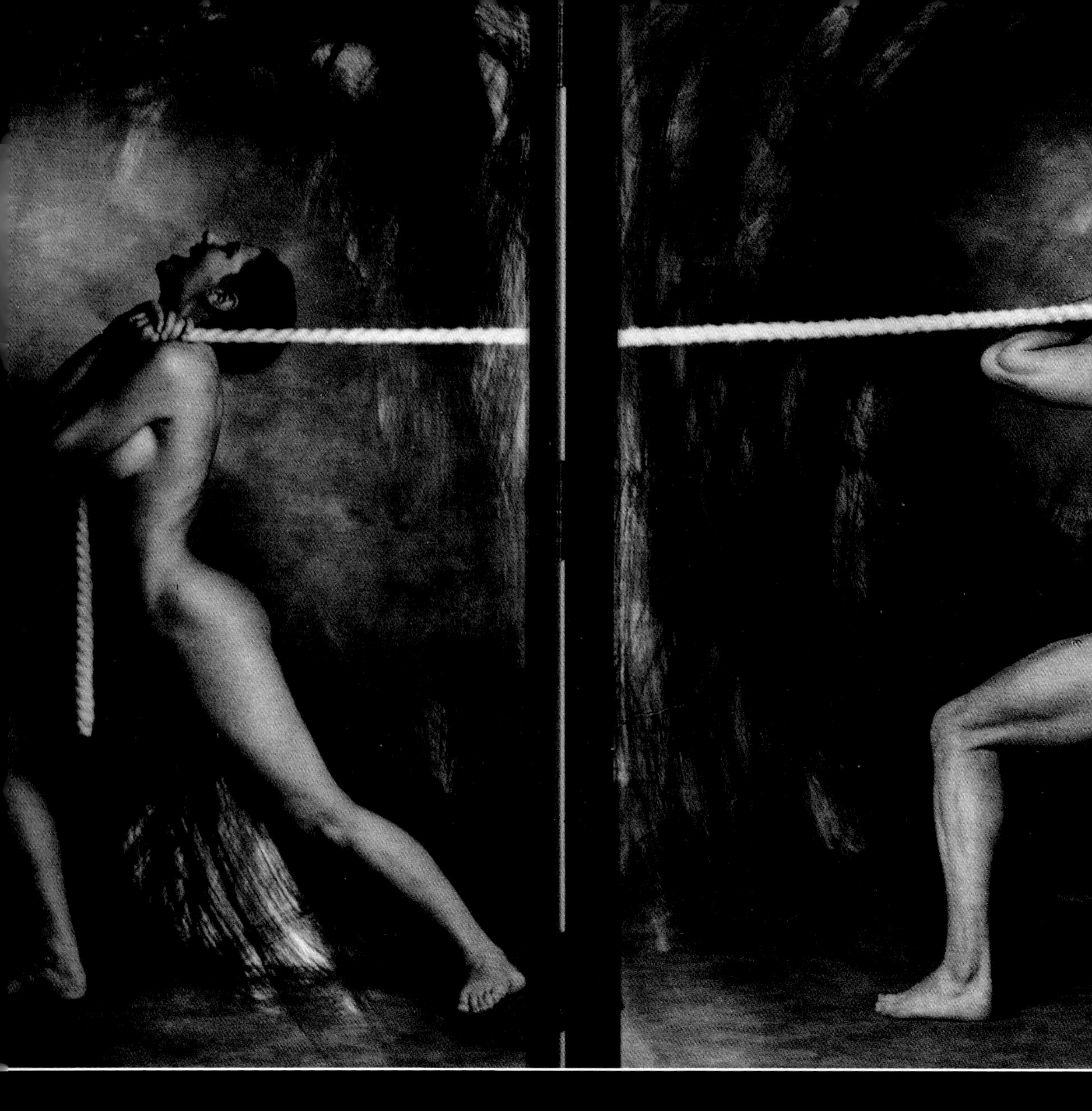

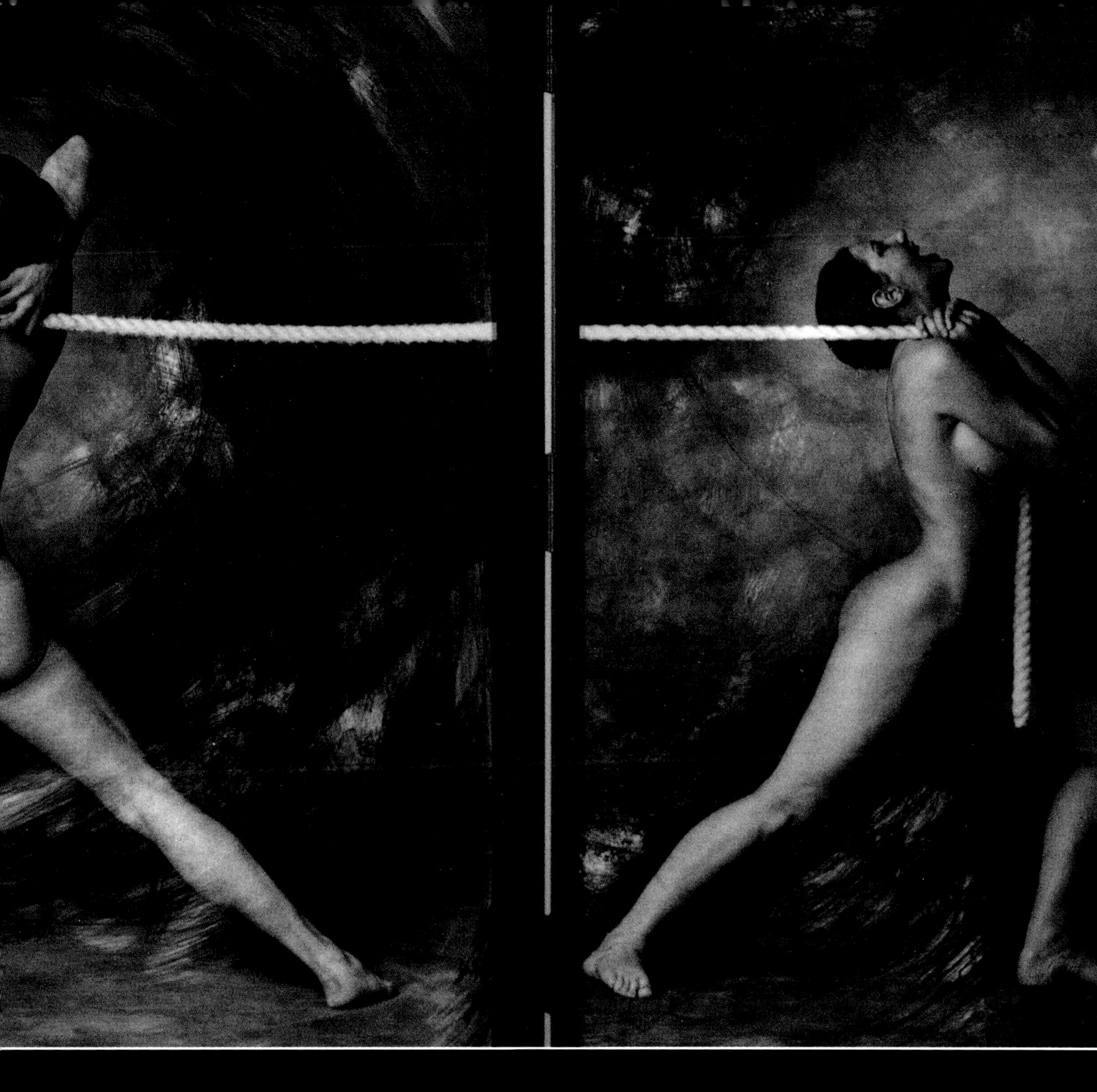

Photographer: **Benny De Grove**

Use: **Exhibition**

Assistant: **Astrid van Doorslaer**

Stylist: **An De Temmerman**

Camera: **6x6cm**

Lens: **150mm**

Film: **Kodak T-Max ISO 400**

Exposure: **f/8**

Lighting: **Electronic flash**

Props and set: **Painted background; rope**

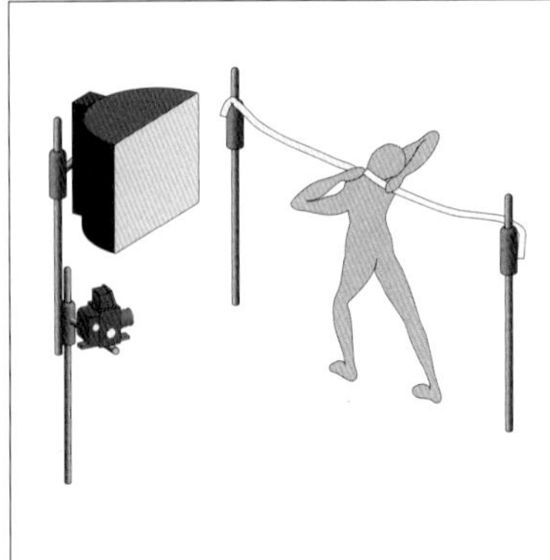

Centre panel

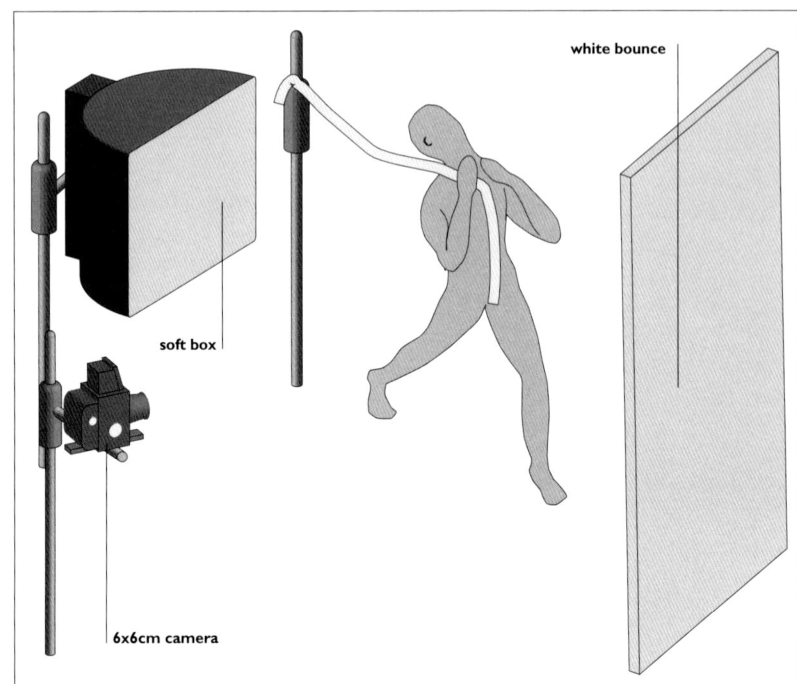

THE TRIPTYCH IS AN UNUSUAL FORM IN PHOTOGRAPHY, BUT IN THIS CASE IT SOLVED A TECHNICAL PROBLEM AS WELL AS MEETING AN AESTHETIC REQUIREMENT. THE TRIPLE PANEL (PREVIOUS PAGE) IS THE TRIPTYCH OPEN; THE DOUBLE PANEL (OPPOSITE) IS THE SAME THING CLOSED.

► *Like any other form of composite image, a triptych must be internally consistent in its lighting*

► *The triptych form allows pictures which would otherwise require more studio space than is available, and also allows supports, etc., to be used out of shot but in the middle of the picture*

► *Although the traditional form of the triptych is in folding "icon" style like this, there is no reason why it has to be*

Making the picture in one shot was not possible: the tension of the rope and the sheer scale of the picture made this impracticable. It was therefore shot as two images, one of the man and one of the woman. Both were lit with a single 80x80cm (32x32in) soft box to camera left, supplemented by a white bounce to camera right in the case of the woman; the woman pulling in the other direction (towards camera right) is merely a flopped image of the woman pulling towards camera left, so the same image is used in effect four times, twice right-way-around and twice flopped.

Getting the level of the rope precisely right in the picture of the man was the most difficult part: it had to match with the level of the rope in the other two pictures.

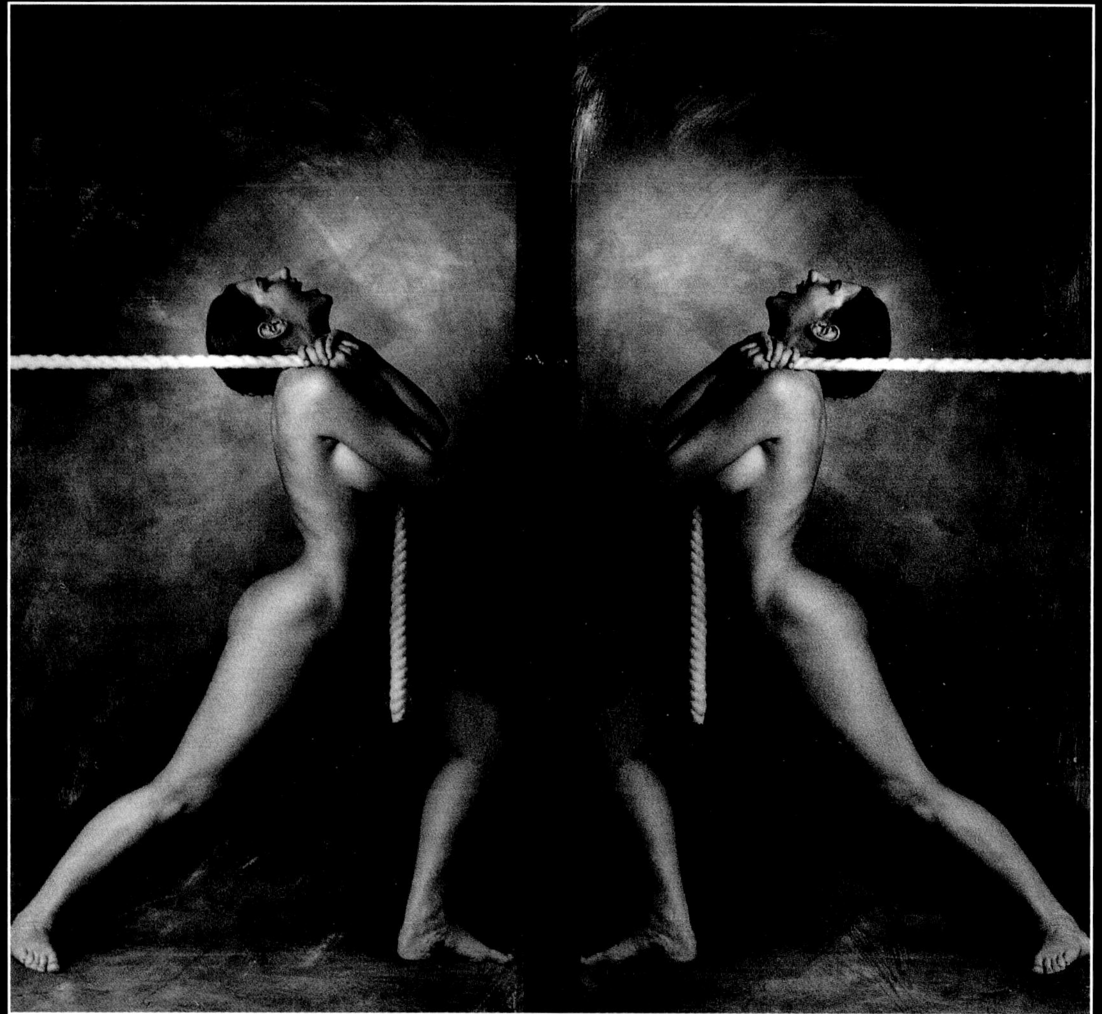

PAISLEY NUDE

Photographer: **Kay Hurst, K Studios**

Use: **Portfolio**

Model: **Julia Spencer**

Camera: **645**

Lens: **75mm**

Film: **Ilford FP4**

Exposure: **f/11**

Lighting: **Electronic flash: single large soft box**

Props and set: **Curtain material; print heavily reworked**

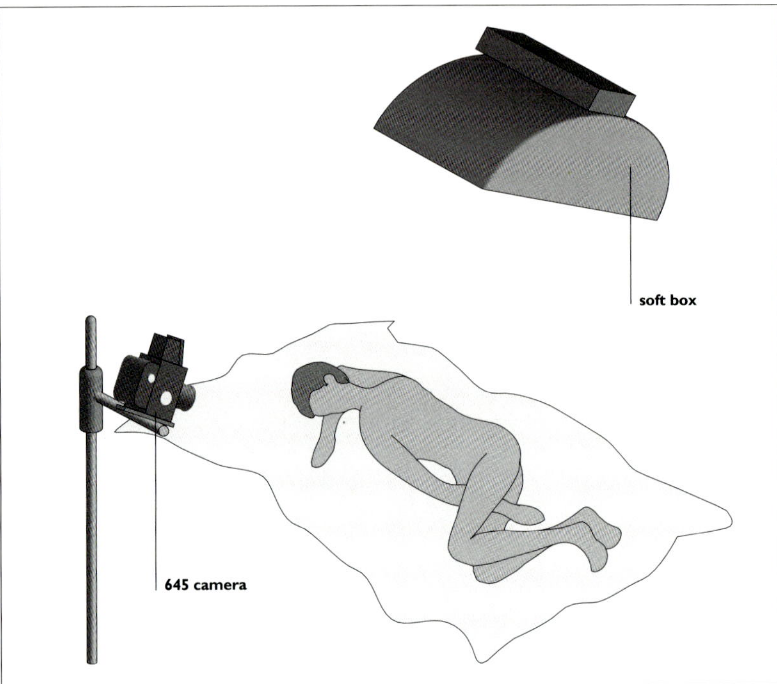

THIS IS FAIRLY TYPICAL OF THE KIND OF PORTRAIT AND NUDE WORK PRODUCED BY K, THOUGH IT IS ACTUALLY A VERY EARLY EXAMPLE OF THE STYLE FOR WHICH SHE HAS SINCE BECOME KNOWN: IT WAS MADE WHEN SHE WAS AT COLLEGE.

The sole light is a large soft box, back lighting the model slightly from camera right and mounted high: the model is lying on "some curtain material which I still have and which I am still using – good value, that!" The print was made on a Kentmere document paper without any baryta layer, which makes for an interesting texture. It was printed through a piece of patterned glass of the type sold for bathroom doors and windows: the print was sized so that the curves of the pattern matched the shape of the model.

The next stage involved floating oily inks on the wet print, manipulating them with cotton swabs. Finally, the distressed or aged effect was added with different-coloured water-based pigments, using special techniques for both application and removal.

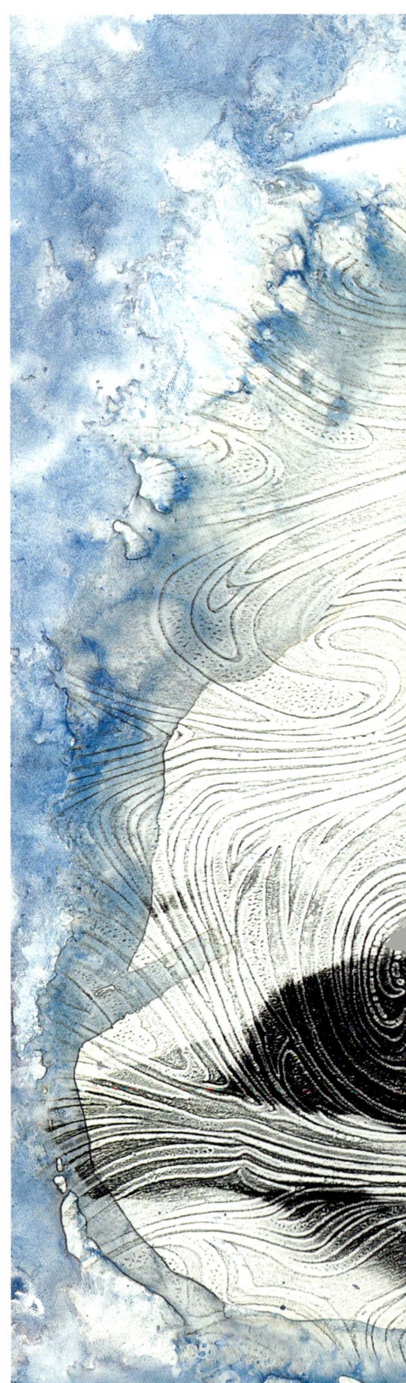

▶ *Printing through textured glass is a well-established technique, but matching the texture to the subject in this way is another matter*

▶ *Different types of brushes create different effects when laying down and removing colour: consider stiff brushes for laying down, and soft Japanese brushes for removal*

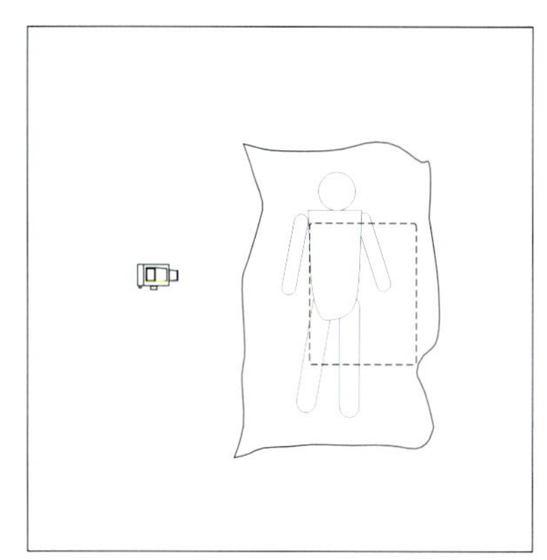

Plan View

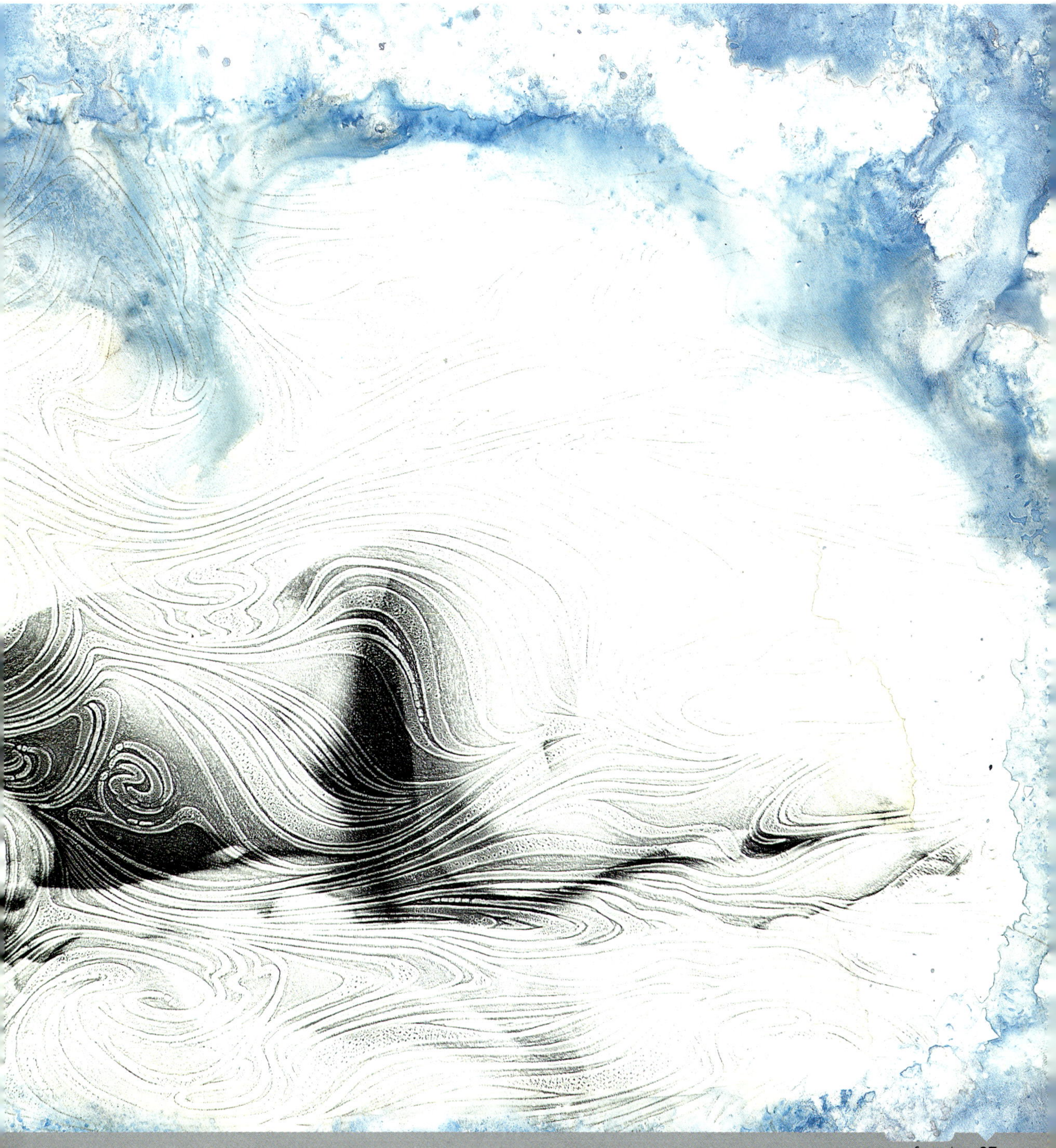

Photographer: **Günther Uttendorfer**

Client: **Mögges Chair Factory**

Use: **Poster**

Model: **Svetlana Hassanin**

Assistant: **Jürgen Weber**

Stylist: **Genevieve Hawtry**

Art director: **Florian Lehner**

Camera: **35mm**

Lens: **55mm**

Film: **Polapan 35**

Exposure: **Not recorded**

Lighting: **Electronic flash: 2 heads**

Props and set: **Built set: metal sheeting, chains, water spray**

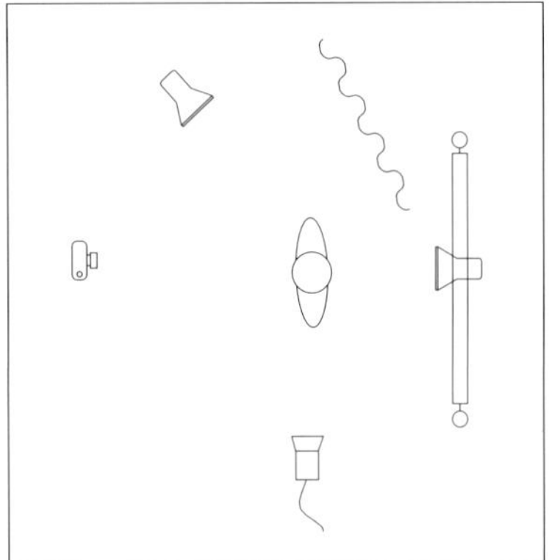

Plan View

N O   N A M E

▼

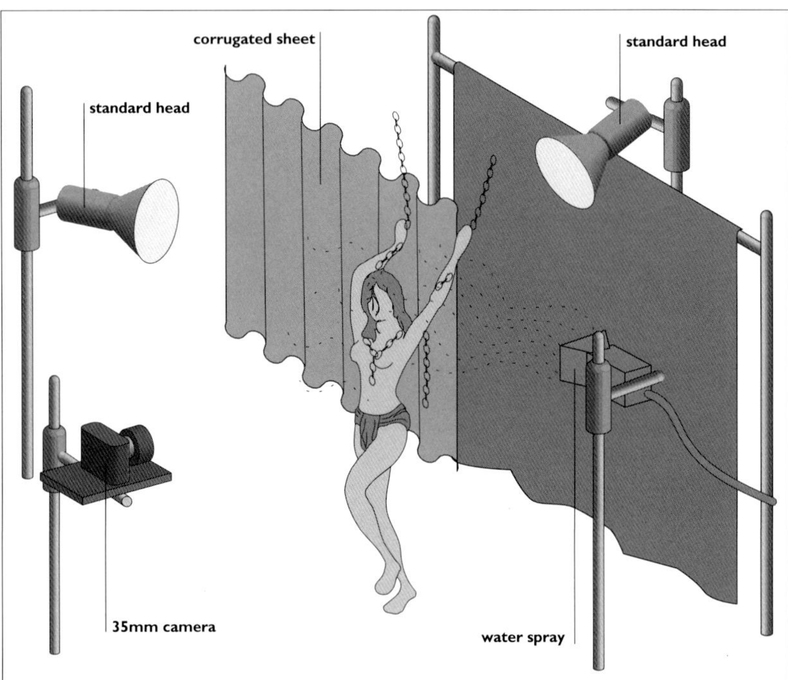

"THIS WAS SHOT AS AN IMAGE-POSTER FOR ONE OF MY CLIENTS. THEY HATED THE IDEA OF NORMAL, STERILE, PREDICTABLE ADVERTISING — SO WE DECIDED TO SHOOT SOMETHING DIFFERENT, SOMETHING MORE LIVELY."

There are only two lights, a 500 Joule unit to camera left at about 45° to the line of sight and about 2m (6ft) from the model, and another 500 Joule unit back lighting the model (and the water spray) some 4m (13ft) from the model. Both lights are set above the model's eye line, the key only slightly above and the back light well above. The key light has a standard head with a honeycomb and a frost, whereas the back light has barn doors and a frost.

The set is built of galvanized corrugated iron sheeting and black fabric. Clearly, when mixing water and electronic flash, considerable care must be taken to avoid the risk of potentially fatal shock.

► *Modern studio flash units typically have a flash duration of 1/300 to 1/800sec, which will not fully "freeze" spraying water*

► *The tonality of Polaroid Polapan has a Hollywood quality to it*

Photographer's comment:

Most of the time I use direct lighting with standard reflectors, honeycombs and frost filters.

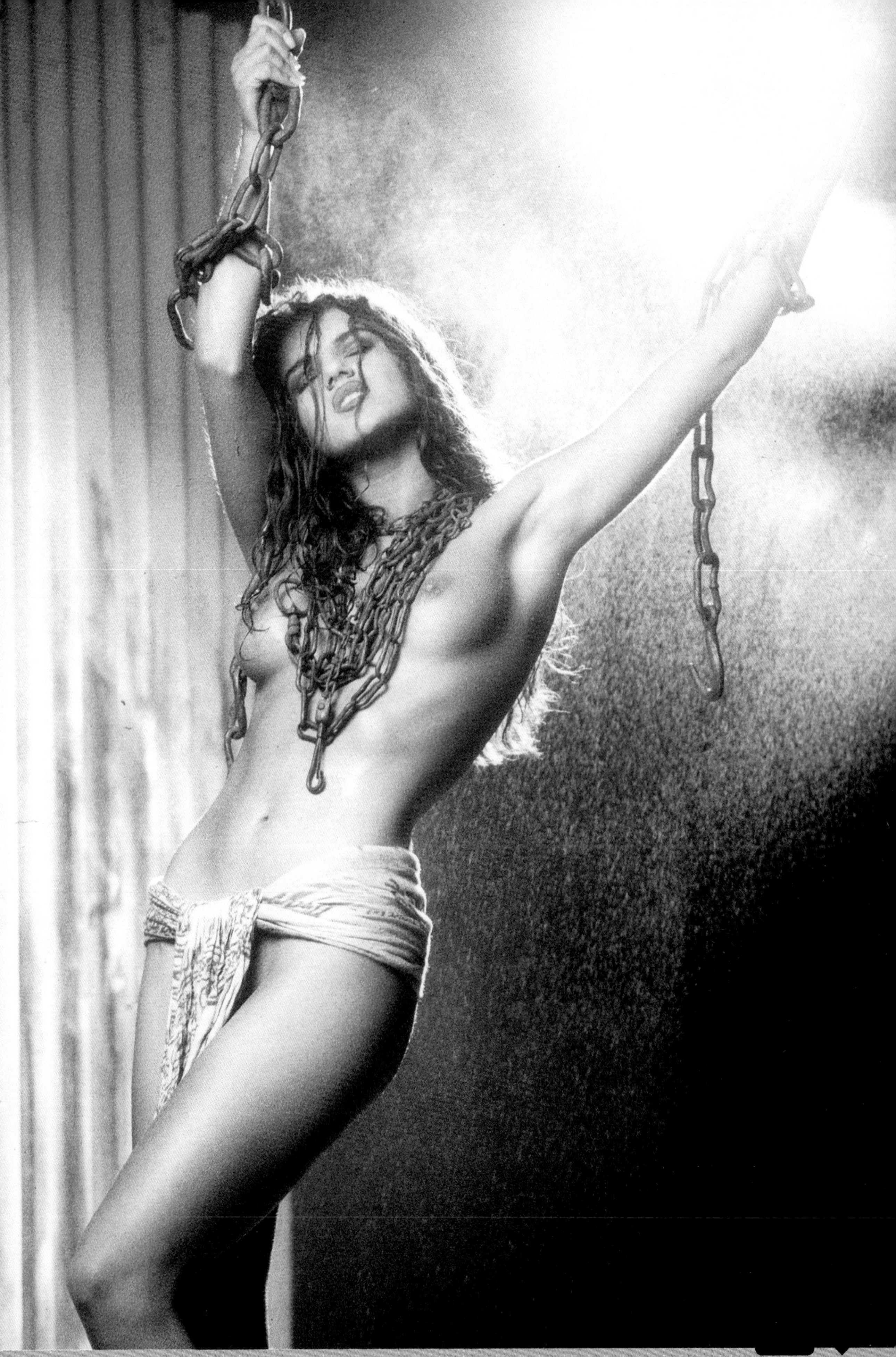

Photographer: **Stu Williamson**

Client: **Vicky**

Use: **Model portfolio**

Camera: **6x7cm**

Lens: **105mm**

Film: **Ilford Pan F**

Exposure: **f/11**

Lighting: **Electronic flash: 2 heads**

Props and set: **Rope; Lastolite hand-painted background**

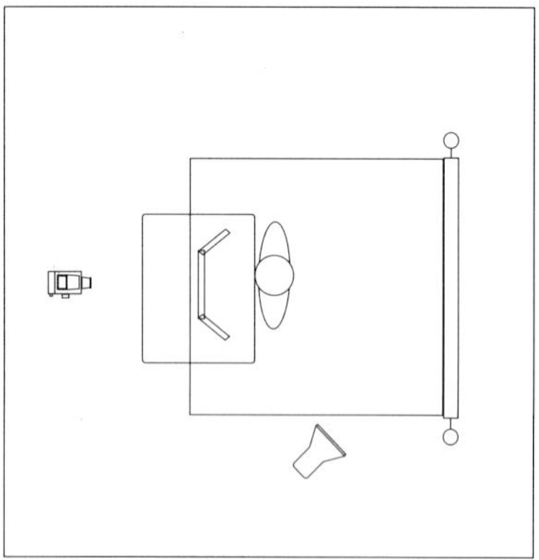

Plan View

V I C K Y

▼

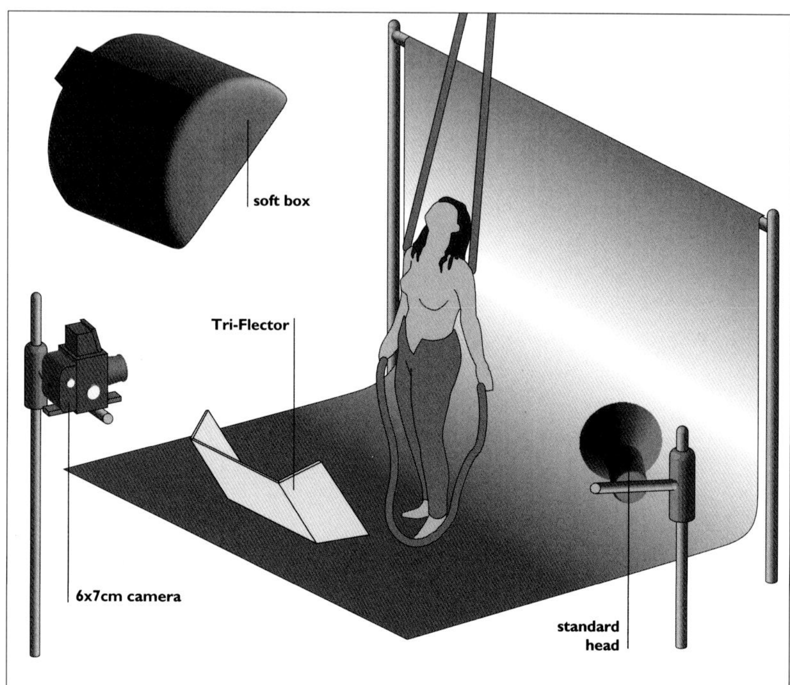

THIS PICTURE IS ALMOST ICONIC, PORTRAYING THE EMERGENCE OF THE ETERNAL FEMININE FROM A WELTER OF SYMBOLS SUCH AS ROPES, JEANS, CHAINS (AROUND HER NECK), THE CROSS AND THE FINGERLESS GLOVES.

There are only two lights, and one of those is no more than a background light; but the key, a soft box almost directly over the camera, is supplemented by a "Tri-Flector".

Invented by the photographer, the Tri-Flector (see page 24) is made in a number of different reflectivities to allow a range of lighting effects from hard to soft. The enterprising photographer may be able to improvise an imitation for himself, from cardboard and gaffer tape, but the purpose-made item is more durable and much easier to use. Because it is (or can be) so directional and so controllable, it functions almost as another light.

► *Lighting creates chiaroscuro and modelling, while photographic technique (and the use of the 6x7 format) captures texture and detail*

► *By all but concealing the model's face, the photographer has portrayed Woman instead of a woman*

► *The sky-gazing pose is open to many interpretations by the viewer*

Photographer's comment:

I suppose one background is much the same as another, but I prefer Lastolite. They are hand-painted in India and they have a certain vibrancy which I find lacking in some others.

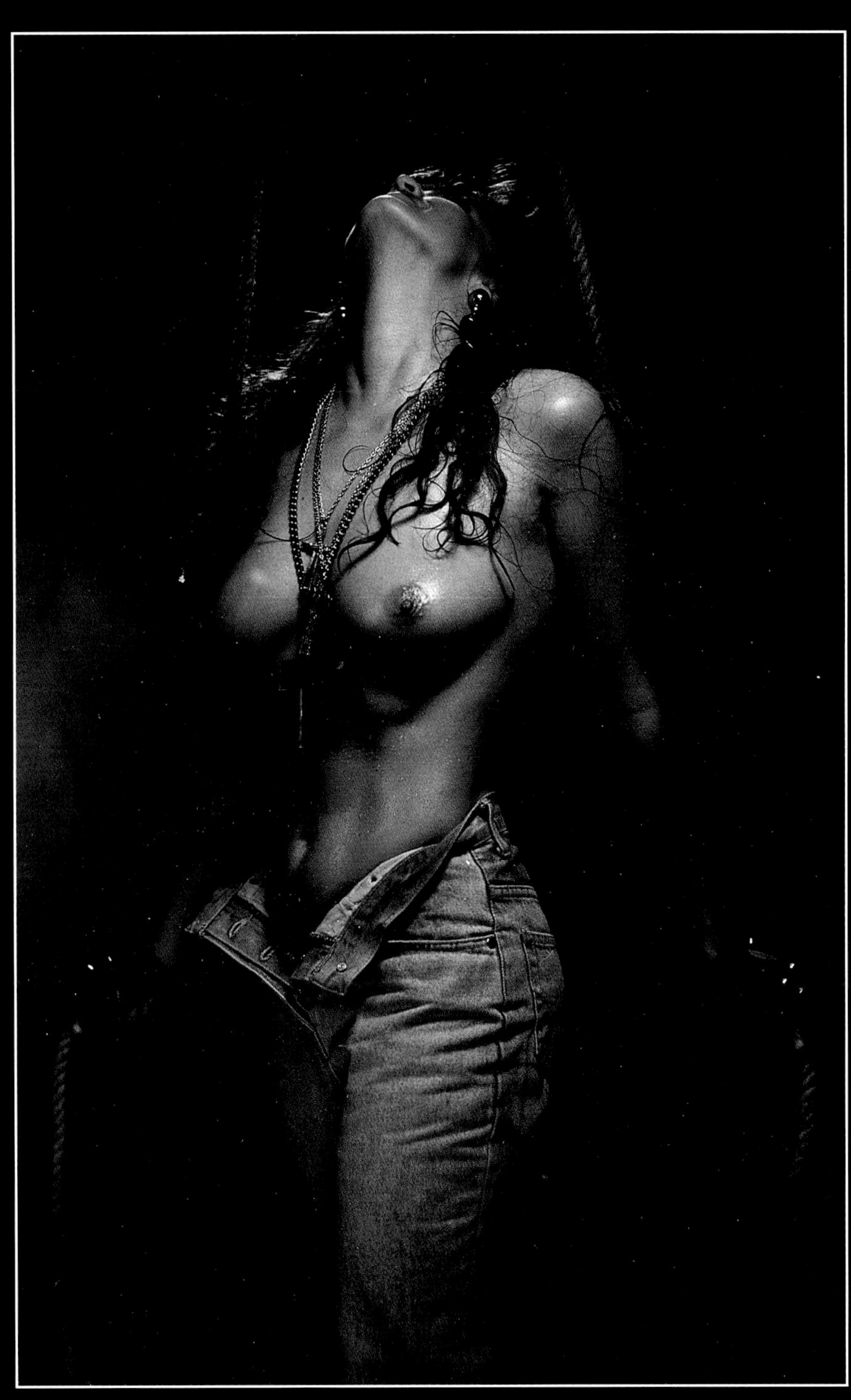

Photographer: **Peter Barry**

Use: **Model test**

Assistant: **Jon Sturdy**

Camera: **6x6cm**

Lens: **110mm with soft screen**

Film: **Kodak Ektachrome EPR**

Exposure: **f/8**

Lighting: **Electronic flash: one very large soft box**

Props and set: **White background; white fabric as "dress"**

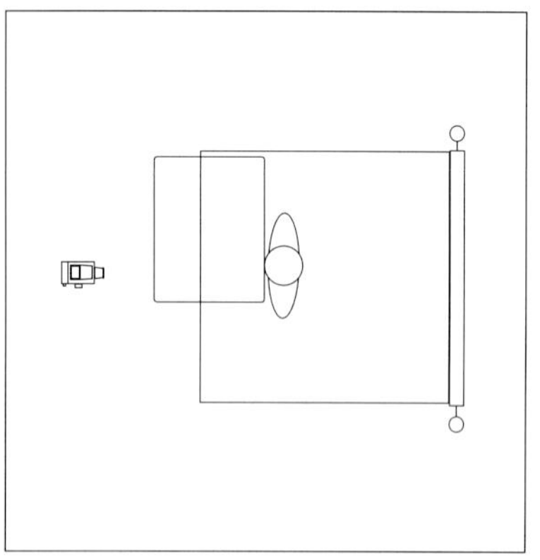

Plan View

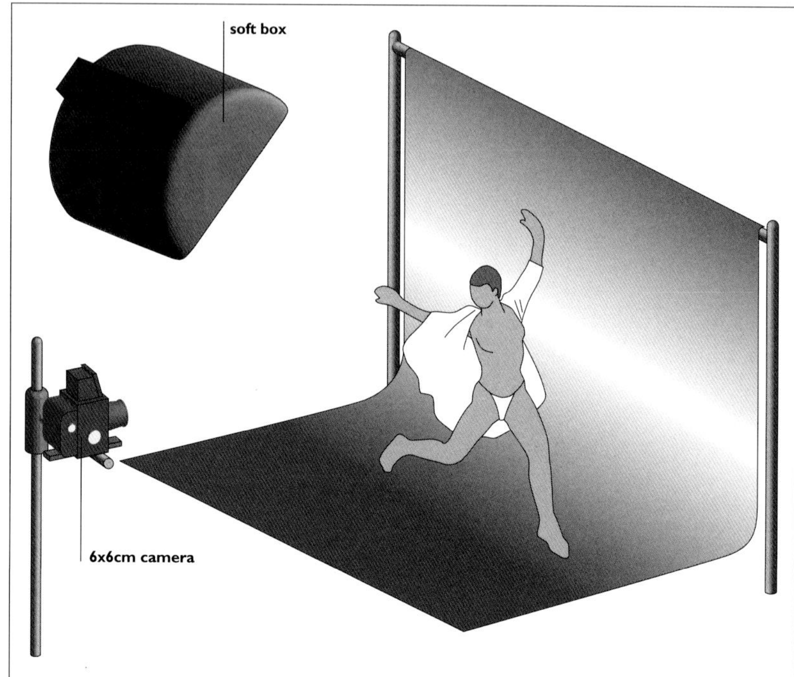

JUMPING MODELS CAN BE VERY ATTRACTIVE IF THEY ARE WELL DONE — AS, OF COURSE, PETER BARRY'S SHOT IS. YOU NEED PLENTY OF ROOM, THOUGH: A WIDE BACKGROUND, AND A LONG LENS, SO YOU NEED A FAIR-SIZED STUDIO.

The light is a very large "Wafer" soft box directly above the camera and very slightly to the left, so the shadows are very soft but the modelling is surprisingly good. Because the source is so big, it also lights the background with minimal shadowing.

Shooting this sort of motion — or any sort of action, for that matter — with a rollfilm SLR requires a certain amount of experience, as the delay between pressing the shutter release and taking the picture can be as much as 1/10sec. At least with flash lighting you can see whether the model was in more or less the right position as the flash goes off: with continuous light, early attempts at action can be very hit-or-miss.

► *Very large soft boxes create a different quality of light from smaller ones*

► *Anticipation and experience are important when shooting movement*

Photographer's comment:

The Quad unit I used has quite a long flash time — about 1/700sec — so there is a tiny bit of blur which I find to be very attractive.

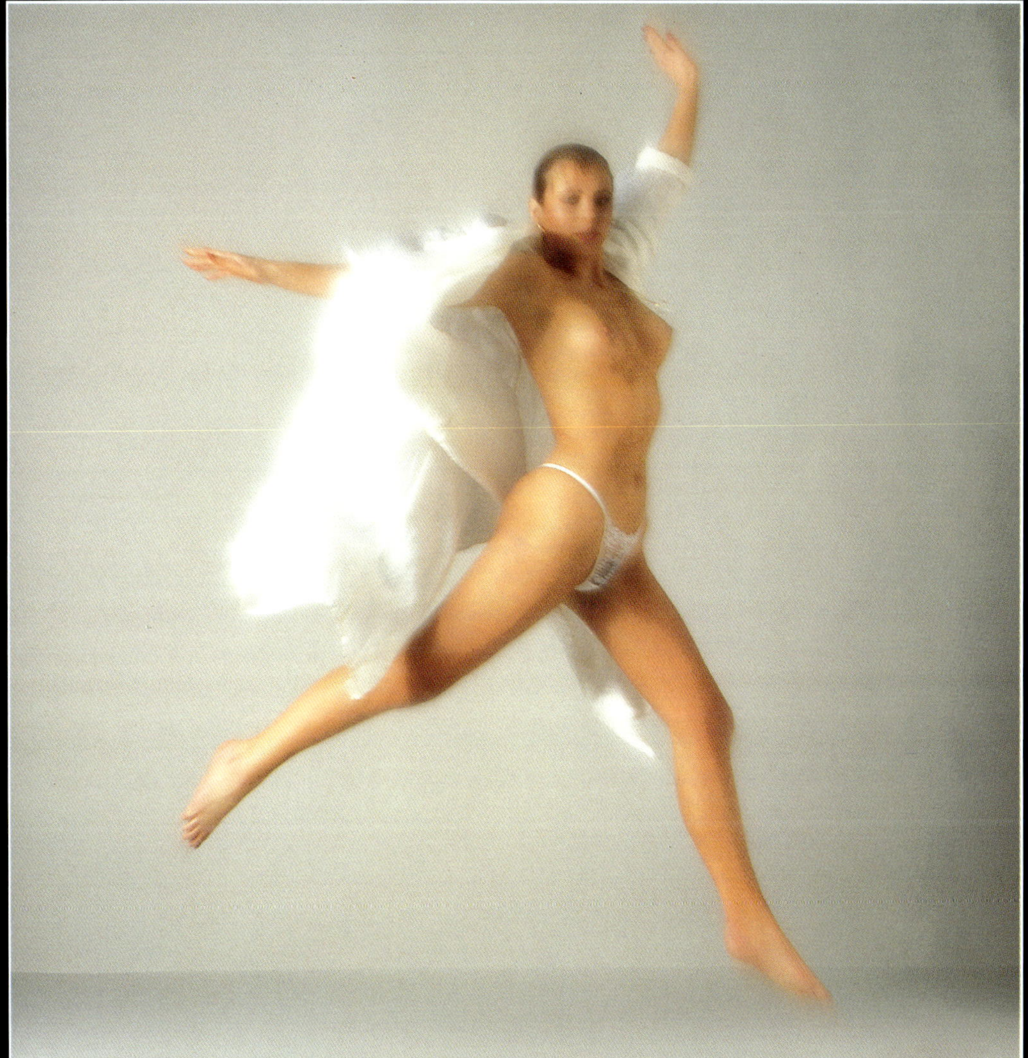

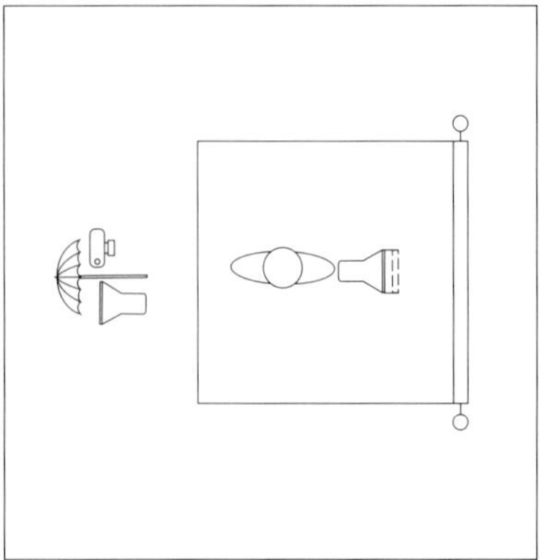

Plan View

▼

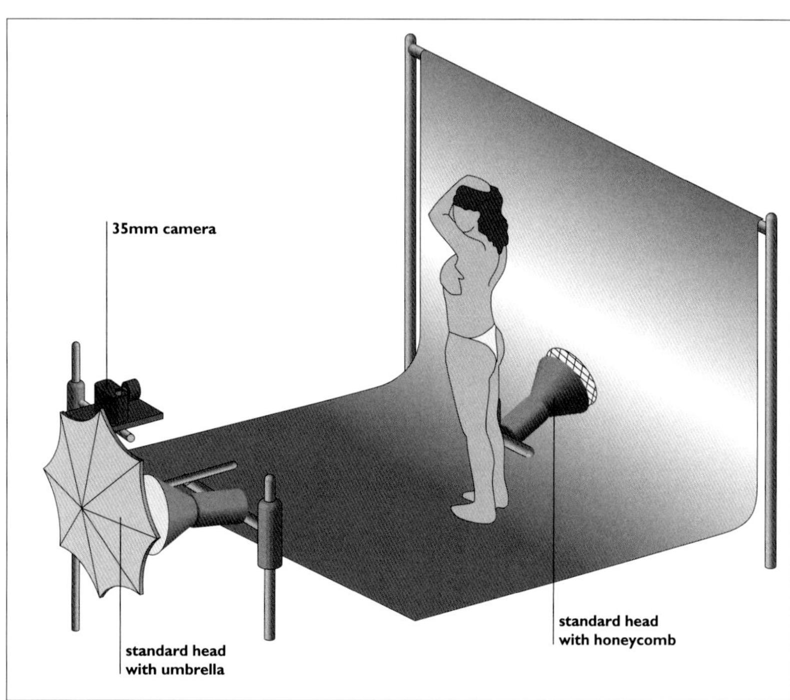

Lighting from below is often known as "horror film" lighting, and beginners' books on portraiture caution against it in the strongest terms; but if it is a big, soft light, it can work.

In this case it is an umbrella just below the camera, and it works very well indeed: look at the contrast between the model's face and the upper part of her arm, or at the small of her back. The modelling is quite unlike what you would expect from fairly diffuse frontal lighting, but this is precisely because the light is below the camera. The lighting plot is completed by another light on the background, with a modest honeycomb (maybe 30°) to limit the spread and grade the light across the background from bottom to top. Note the contrast between the small of Sylvia's back and the background.

► *Point sources are often recommended to give jewels "fire", but large sources can sometimes work better*

► *Exoticism (the gloves and the jewels) can "punch up" even quite modest nudity*

► *Direct eye contact is literally eye-catching*

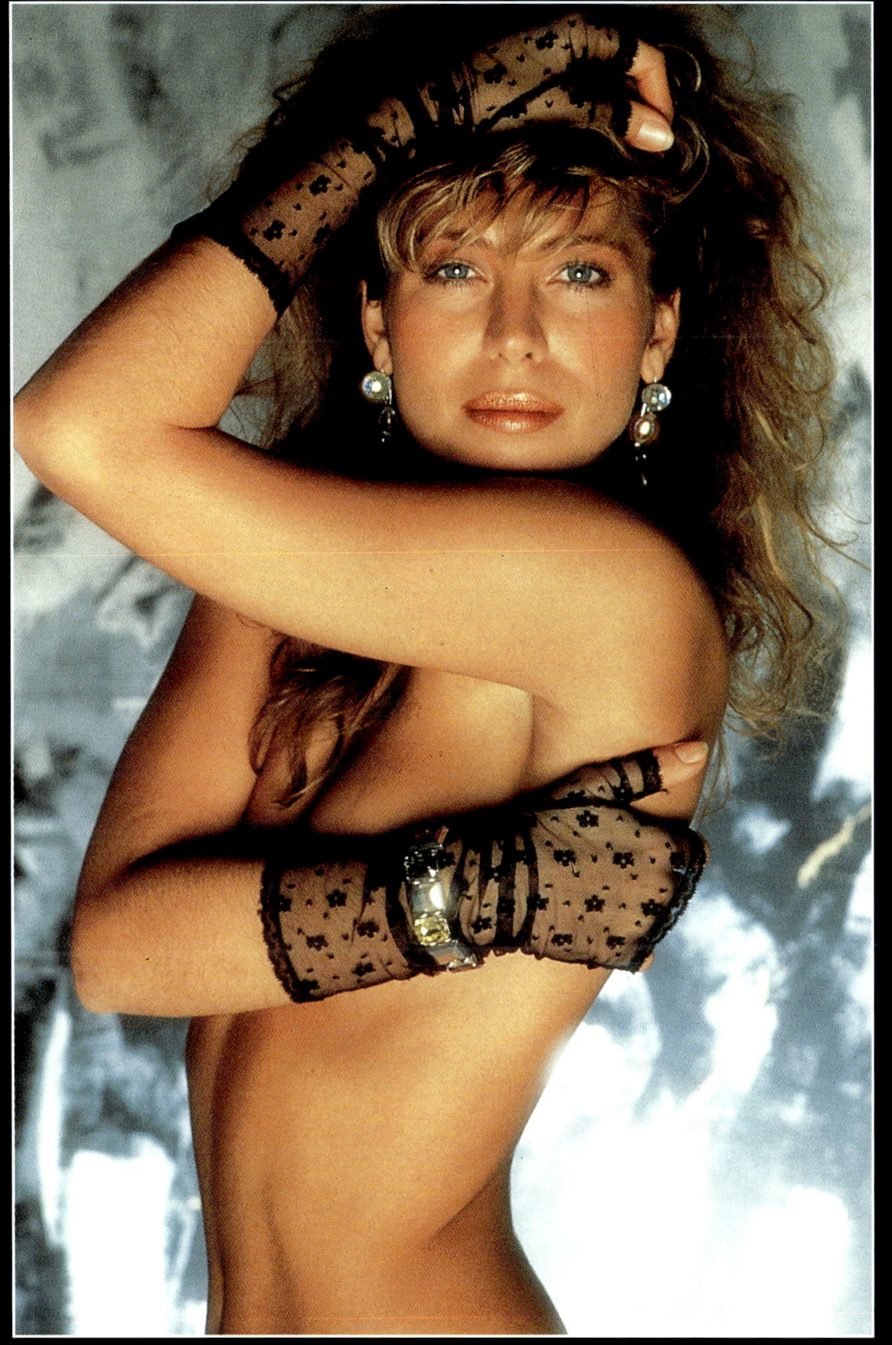

Photographer: **Struan**

Client: **Adagio**

Use: **Lingerie advertising**

Model: **Brenda**

Assistant: **James Fraser**

Camera: **35mm**

Lens: **50mm**

Film: **Kodak Tri-X Pan**

Exposure: **1/60sec at f/1.4**

Lighting: **Electronic flash: 2 heads (but see text)**

Props and set: **Black background**

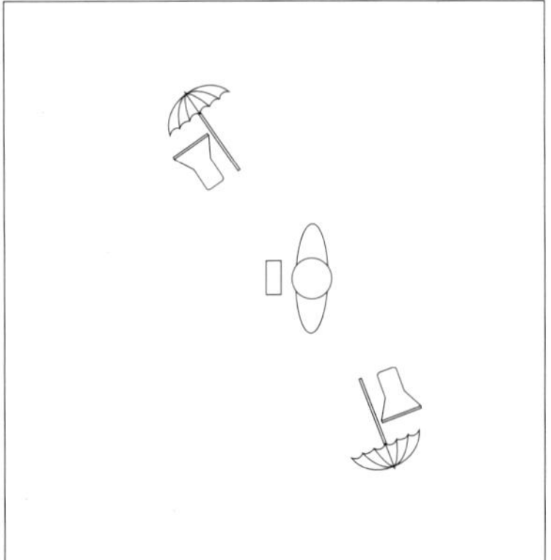

Plan View

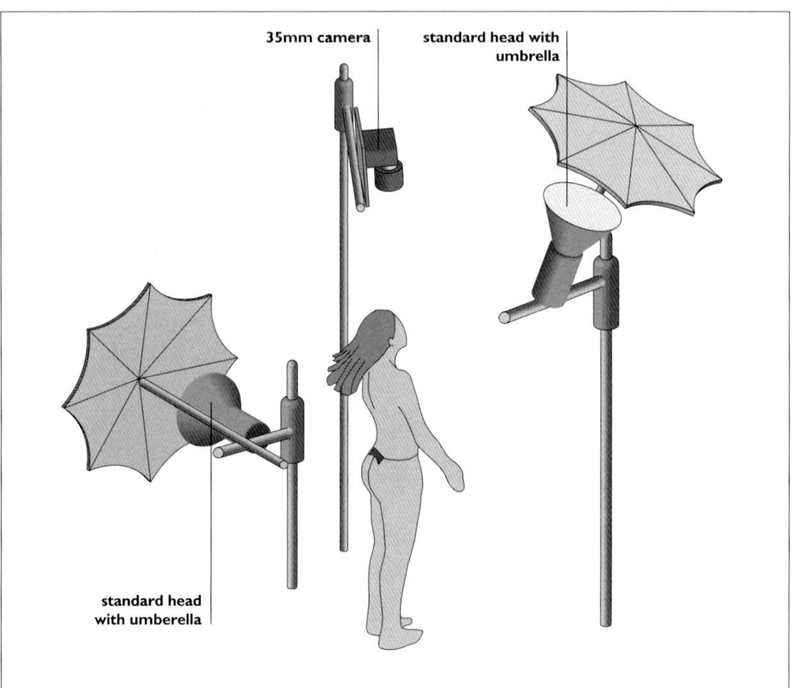

STRUAN HAS SHOT A GOOD DEAL OF ADVERTISING MATERIAL FOR ADAGIO, AND THIS IS FROM A EUROPEAN CAMPAIGN. EXPERIMENTAL INTERPRETATIONS, LESS LITERAL THAN STRAIGHT SHOTS, ARE OFTEN MORE READILY ACCEPTED IN EUROPE THAN IN NORTH AMERICA.

The lighting here was intended to be by flash, using two umbrellas: one directly above the model (look at the shadows) and one to illuminate the rose on the lingerie. But (in Struan's words) "I just kept turning the lights down and down, to allow shooting Tri-X at f/1.4, and suddenly I realized that the modelling lights were all I needed."

The model was asked to keep tossing her head to make her hair fly out – in such circumstances, one has to "shoot for the percentages", selecting the best from a large number of shots – and the image was printed conventionally. The bow was then hand-coloured to match its actual colour as closely as possible.

► *Differential focus with standard and wide-angle lenses requires very wide apertures*

► *Blur, whether from focus or from movement, is more acceptable to some clients than to others*

► *Strong contrasts often work best on out-of-focus images*

Photographer's comment:

Adagio are among my favourite clients. They just send me the lingerie and trust me to shoot it, which is always a great way to work.

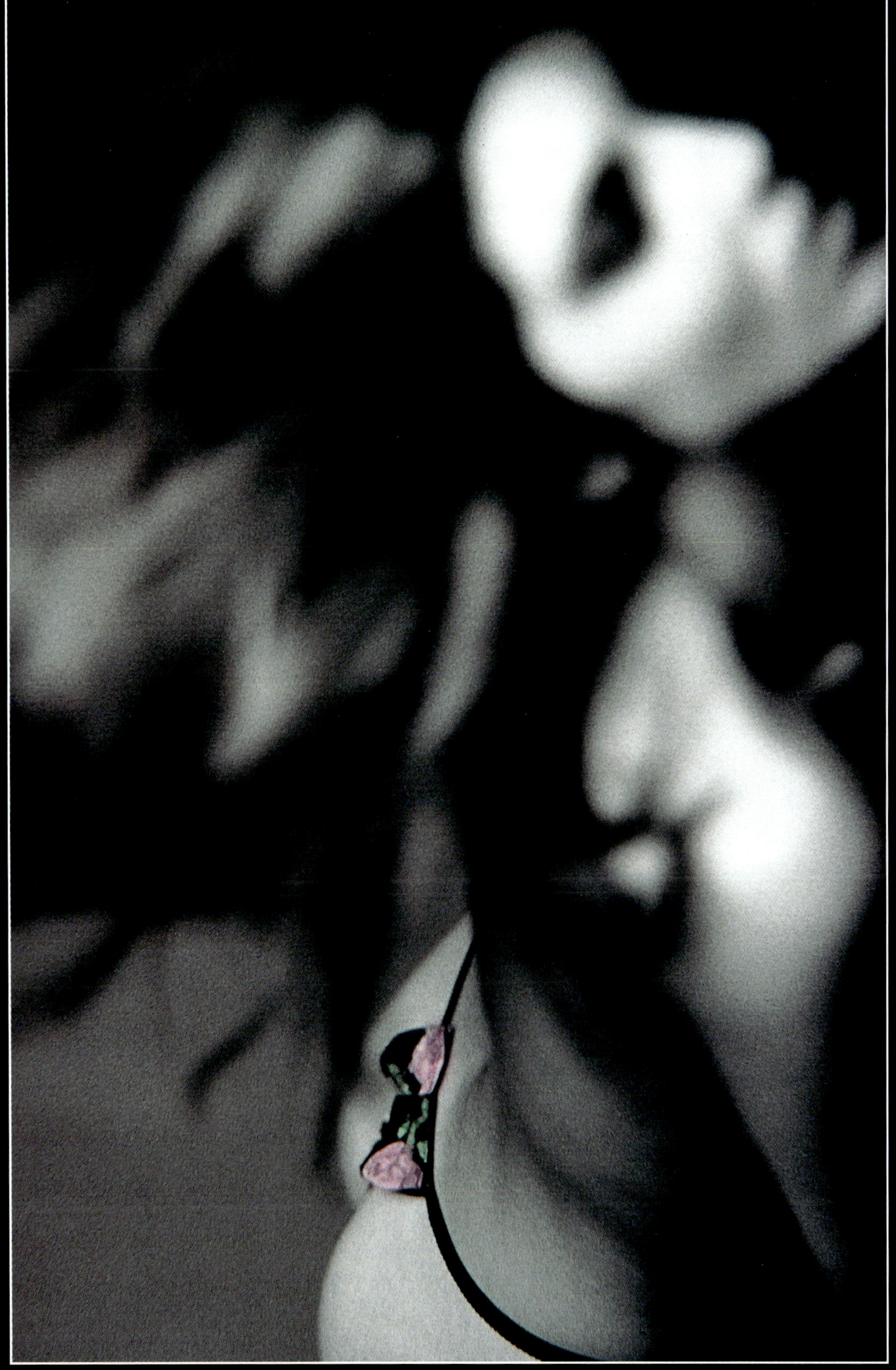

Photographer: **Struan**

Use: **Personal**

Camera: **35mm**

Lens: **28mm with lens shade for 35mm lens**

Film: **Kodachrome 64**

Exposure: **f/16**

Lighting: **Electronic flash: 2 heads**

Props and set: **Built set**

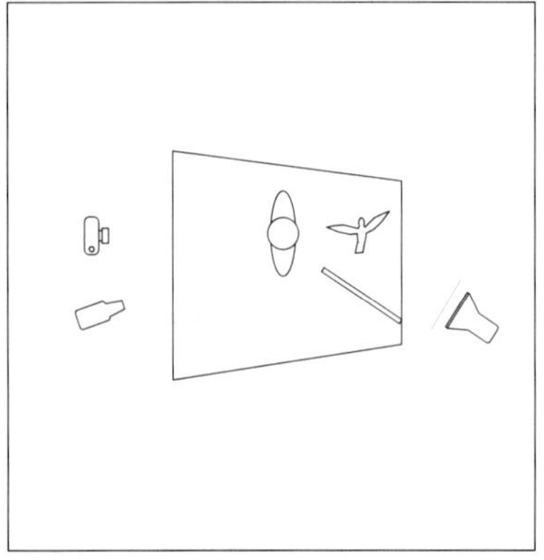

Plan View

▼

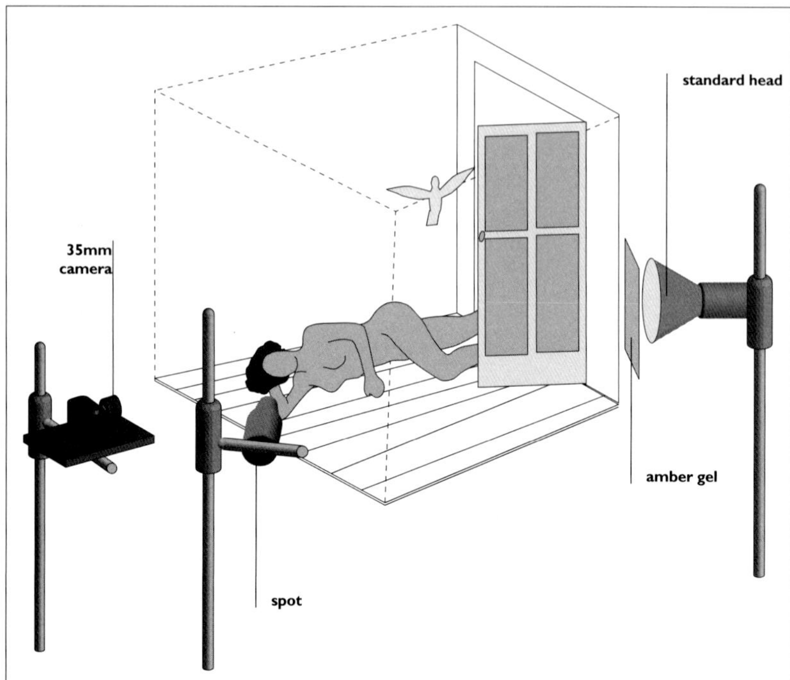

THIS IS ONE OF A NUMBER OF IDEAS WHICH STRUAN TRIED OUT WHEN HE WAS WORKING ON SURREAL AND DREAMLIKE IMAGES. THE SET IS BUILT OUT OF FOAMCORE; THE LINES ARE RIBBONS PINNED TO THE FLOOR; AND THE DARK AREAS ARE GREY BACKGROUND PAPER.

The set is, of course, built in exaggerated perspective, including the cut-out "door". Using ribbons for the lines between the "floorboards" allowed them to be moved so that they could be set to camera for the most convincing effect.

As for the lights, there is a tight (20°) grid spot on the model's face and an open-head flash outside the "door".

A 28mm lens provided the necessary exaggerated perspective. The shading in the corners comes from using the lens shade from a 35mm lens: Struan originally shaded the lens with his hand; he liked the cut-off effect, and used a shade from a lens of longer focal length to create it.

► *Building sets in exaggerated perspective is often a question of building "to camera"*

► *Birds' wings move very fast — too fast to freeze with most flash units*

► *An amber gel on the flash outside the door creates "sunlight"*

Photographer's comment:

We once had a shoot where we needed birds. We couldn't hire them — they were ring-necked turtle doves — so we bought them. We then spent $200 on an aviary and kept them for 15 years, until the last one died. This is one of those birds.

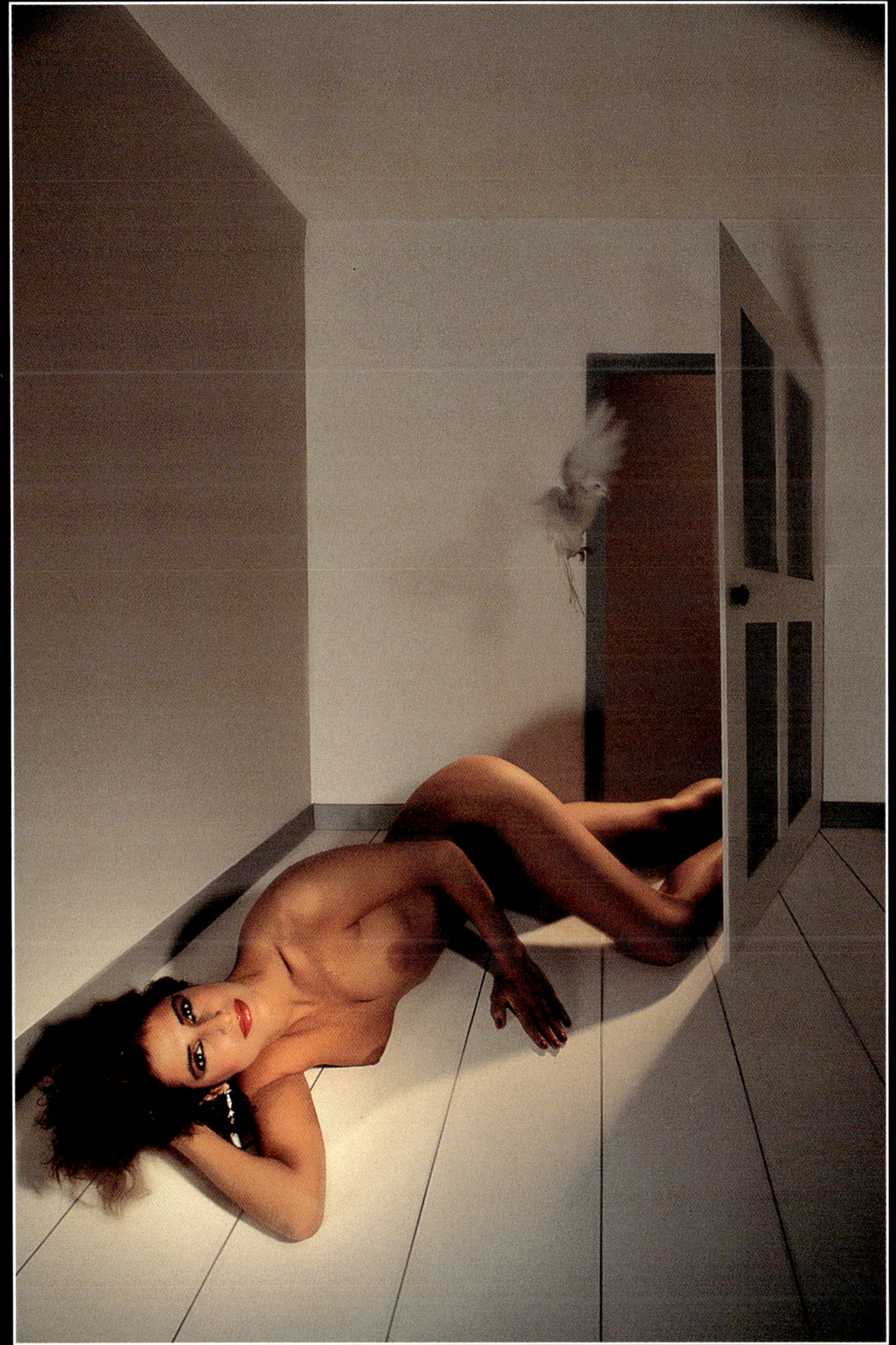

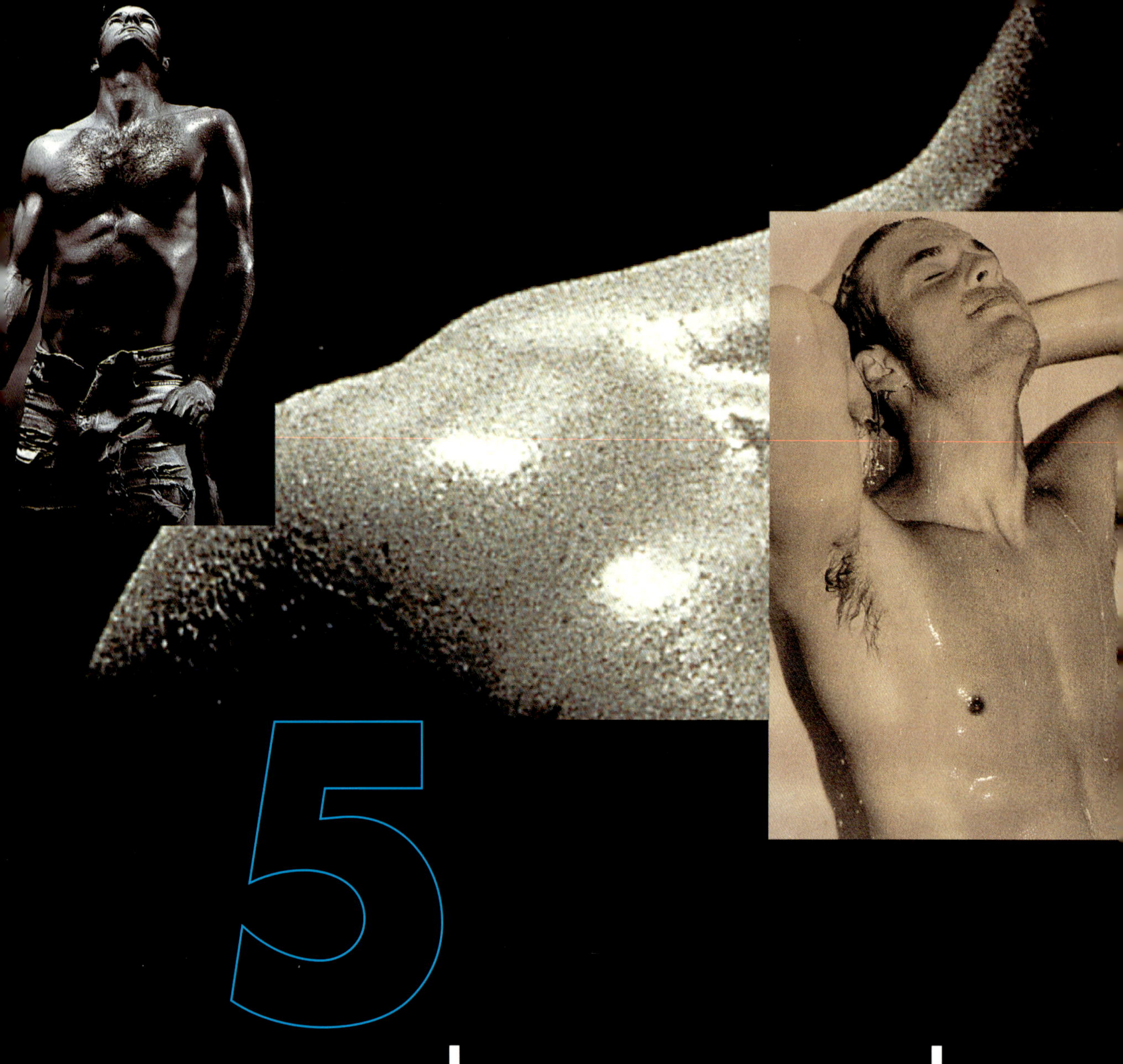

5

male nudes
and couples

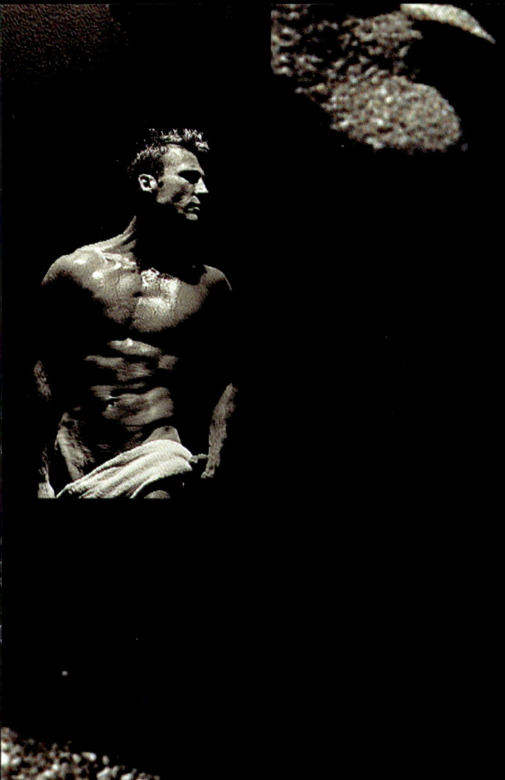

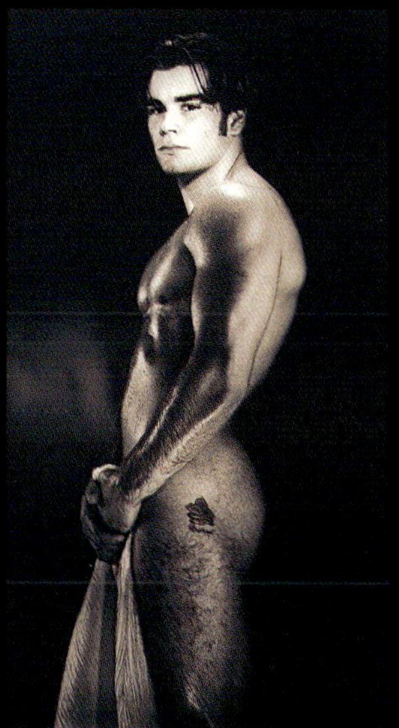

The male nude is a much less common subject than the female nude, and when we were putting the book together we were concerned that there might be a dearth of photographers who chose to submit male nudes; but we need not have worried.

An intriguing point is that all eight of the nudes and couples in this chapter were shot in monochrome, though subsequent toning was the exception rather than the rule. We did receive some male nudes in colour, and they were every bit as good as the black and whites, but they were considerably outnumbered by monochrome.

There is one calendar shot, and one advertising shot, while the others are either personal work or portfolio shots for male models. This indicates that there is still a smaller commercial demand for male nudes than for female; even so, it shows that photography of the male nude is not as rare as it might seem.

Full male nudity is however considerably rarer than full female nudity, and frontal male nudity without benefit of a strategically placed towel or something similar is very rare indeed – an interesting comment on what is "acceptable", and to whom. For all that it is a sexist cliché, it seems true that there are more men who are willing to go out of their way to look at a nude woman than there are women who can be bothered to go out of their way to look at nude men, though this is not the same as saying that women are averse to pictures of nude men.

Photographer: **Mike Dmochowski**

Use: **Self-promotion (poster)**

Models: **Dawn & Del**

Camera: **35mm**

Lens: **150mm**

Film: **Kodak T-Max 100**

Exposure: **1/125sec at f/11**

Lighting: **Electronic flash: Fresnel head**

Props and set: **Black seamless paper background (Colorama)**

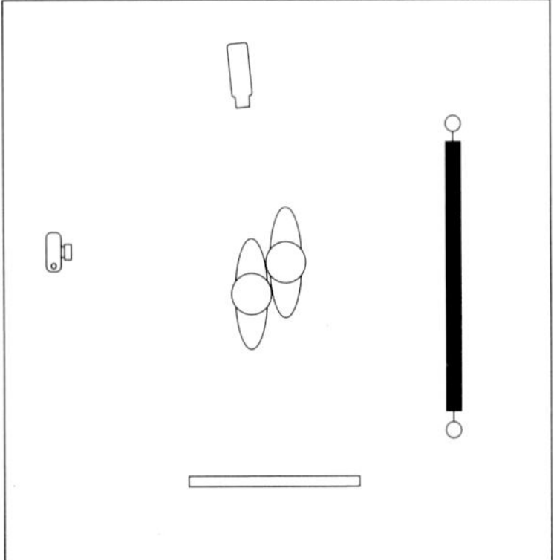

Plan View

BLUE TONE OF WOMAN AND MAN

▼

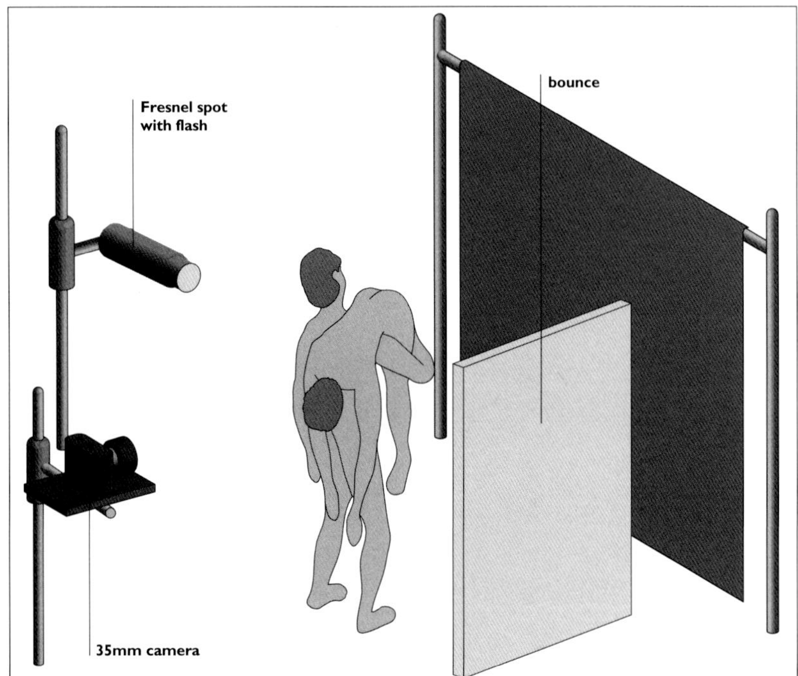

THIS POWERFUL IMAGE IS RATHER LIKE A RORSCHACH DIAGRAM: YOU CAN READ INTO IT WHATEVER YOU LIKE. LOVE … SUPPORT … WAR … LOSS — IT IS BOTH HEAVEN AND HELL. TECHNICALLY, THE ORIGINAL MONO IMAGE WAS PRINTED WITH A BLUE CAST ONTO COLOUR PAPER AND THEN COPIED ONTO TRANSPARENCY.

Going via the Kodak C-type introduced the original colour while the duplication onto 4x5in Kodak Ektachrome EPP further "popped" both contrast and colour. A Fresnel head flash some 8 feet (2.4 metres) to camera left created the highly directional lighting: a Fresnel flash is harder than even the tightest honeycomb or snoot. A 240x120cm (8x4ft) bounce to camera right, about 1m (3ft) from the models, provided a degree of fill and stopped them from merging with the black background, which was of black paper and well behind the models — 240cm (8ft) again — so that it would not be lit by spill.

The tall, thin crop further emphasizes the originality of the image: everything is taken to extremes to create a very eye-catching photograph.

► *Fresnel flash heads provide about the most directional lighting that is available from general-application flash equipment*

► *The danger with highly directional light sources and black backgrounds is that the dark side of the subject can merge into the background — an effect which may or may not be desired*

Photographer's comment:

The objective was to create a sensual, sculptural image.

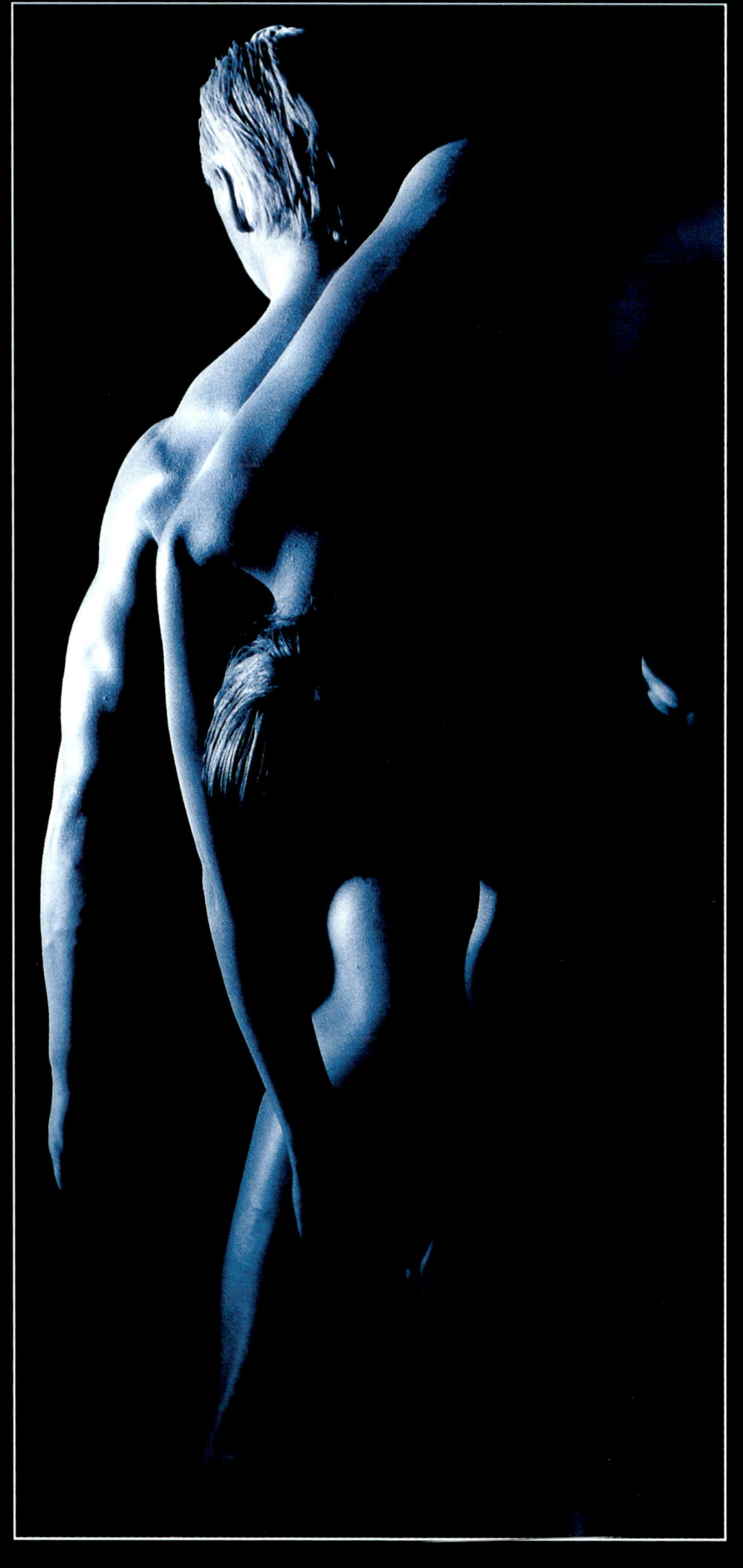

Photographer: **Nick Wright**

Client: **Directors' Cut '95**

Use: **Calendar**

Model: **Kenny**

Assistant: **Al Deane**

Art director: **Wayne Campbell**

Camera: **6x7cm**

Lens: **90mm**

Film: **Kodak T-Max 100**

Exposure: **f/16**

Lighting: **Electronic flash: single head**

Props and set: **White seamless paper**

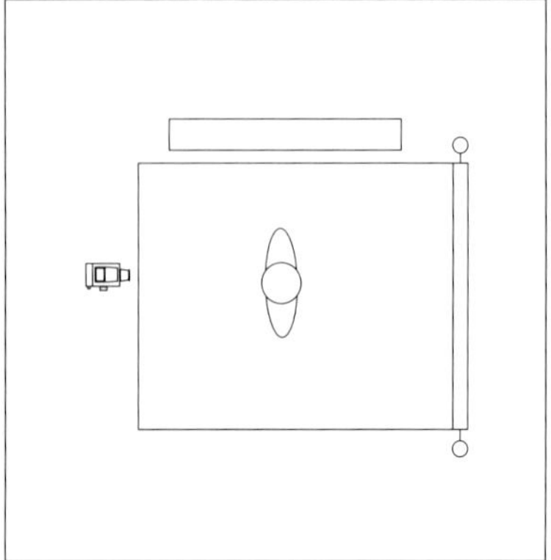

Plan View

K E N N Y

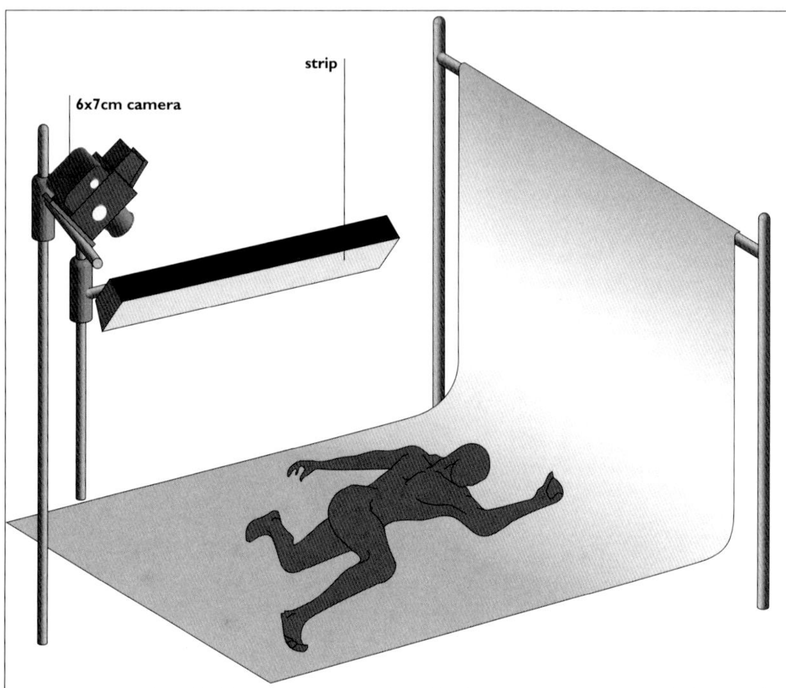

THIS TIMELESS NUDE IS LIT SURPRISINGLY SIMPLY, BUT GETTING A TOTALLY CLEAN, WHITE GROUND WAS A PROBLEM: IN THE EVENT, THE PRINT HAD TO BE MADE VERY CAREFULLY IN ORDER TO LOSE A COUPLE OF MARKS ON THE PAPER.

There is a single light, but it is a 120cm (4ft) long strip light, only about 20cm (8in) wide. Once you know this, you can work out exactly where the light is: in essence, parallel with Kenny's right arm and set at the right height to give the most dramatic shadow; note also how neatly it delineates the face. A linear light source like this gives much sharper shadows than a soft box, but without the splaying of shadows that you would get with a standard reflector. It also gives beautifully controllable highlights.

► *Strips are normally associated with large studio lights such as Strobex, but they can be approximated with appropriately-shaped soft boxes on standard heads*

► *Careful control of exposure and development is needed to control gradation in a shot like this*

Photographer's comment:

I was standing on a ladder with a high tripod, but Kenny is a very big man and I needed the 90mm to get him in.

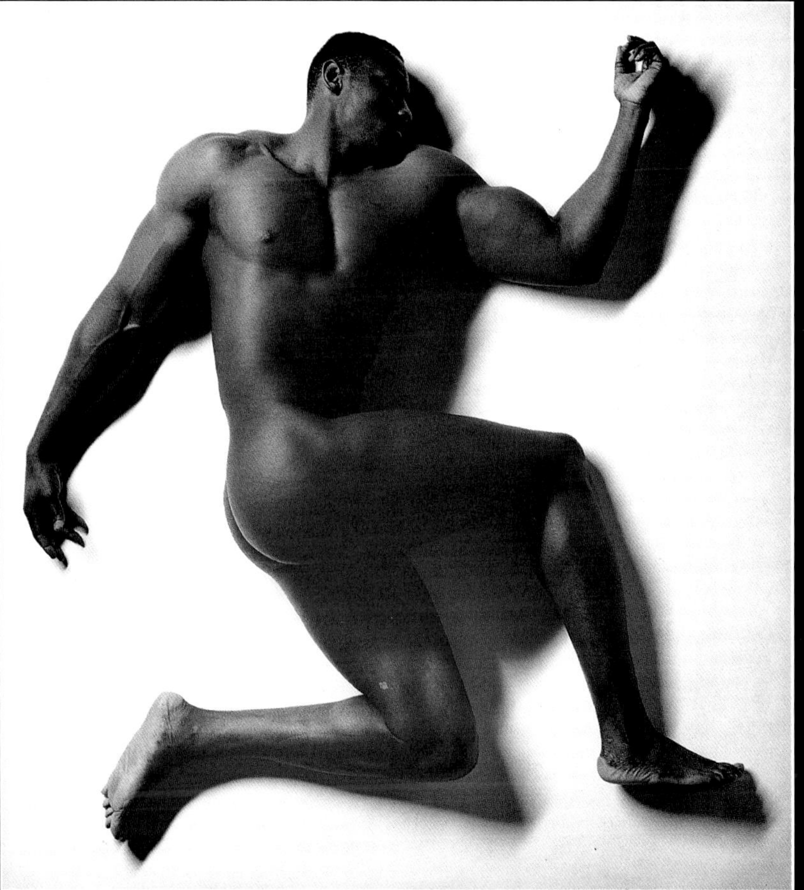

Photographer: **Stu Williamson**

Client: **Brendon**

Use: **Modelling portfolio**

Camera: **35mm**

Lens: **85mm**

Film: **Ilford HP5 Plus**

Exposure: **f/8**

Lighting: **Electronic flash: 4 heads**

Props and set: **Lastolite black background**

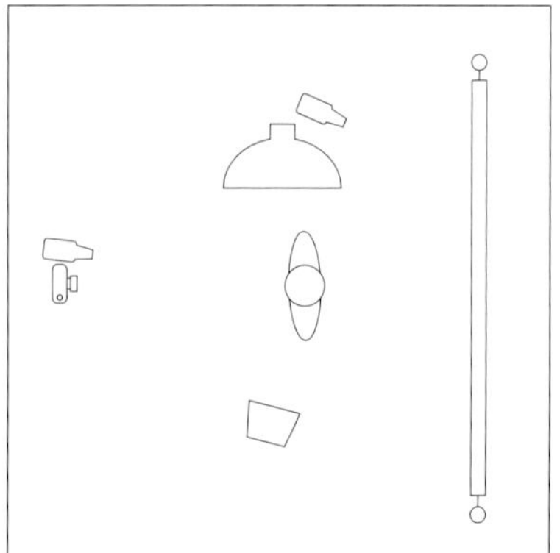

Plan View

B R E N D O N

▼

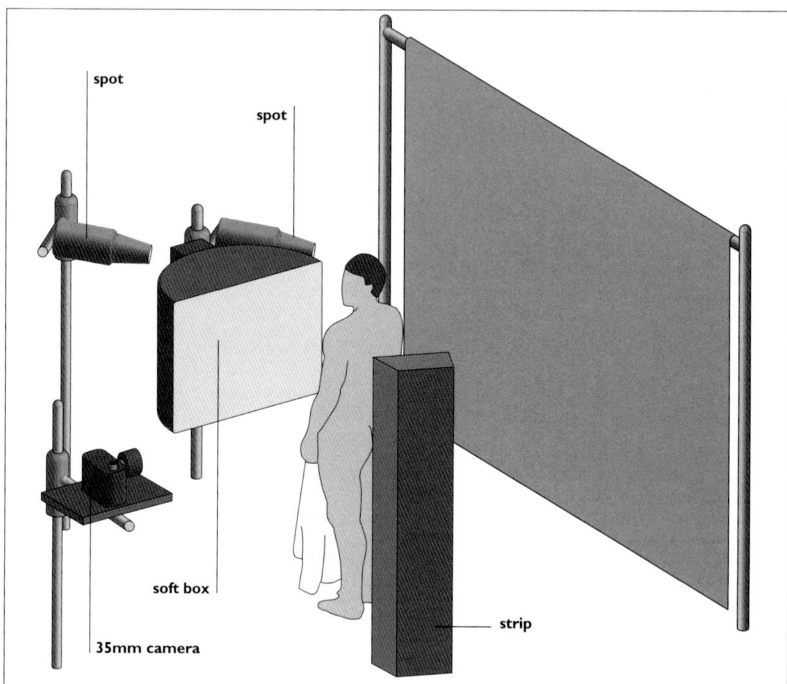

A MODERN MALE MODEL MAY BE CALLED UPON TO PORTRAY ALL KINDS OF ROLES, FROM VULNERABLE TO TOUGH, FROM FASHION ICON TO FASHION VICTIM. THIS IS A REMARKABLY VERSATILE PICTURE WHICH SUGGESTS SEVERAL ASPECTS OF THE MODEL'S CHARACTER AT ONCE.

The lighting is surprisingly complex. A strip light to camera right delineates the model's back and buttocks, while a soft box to camera left provides the modelling on his front; notice the change of emphasis in the shadows between the upper part of his body, so that both the strength of his legs and the breadth of his shoulders are emphasized. Then, a spot lights his face only, for personality and eye contact. Finally, a small snooted spot on the background creates the highlight to camera left, in front of the model. Cover that up, and suddenly the picture is clinical, or perhaps voyeuristic, instead of a nude portrait.

► *Body shape and facial expression often require very different types of lighting*

► *Mimicking naturalness with complex lighting is often more effective than genuinely natural lighting, which can be unidirectional*

Photographer's comment:

I normally use 6x7cm but in 35mm I love my Contax, especially with the 85mm f/1.4 lens.

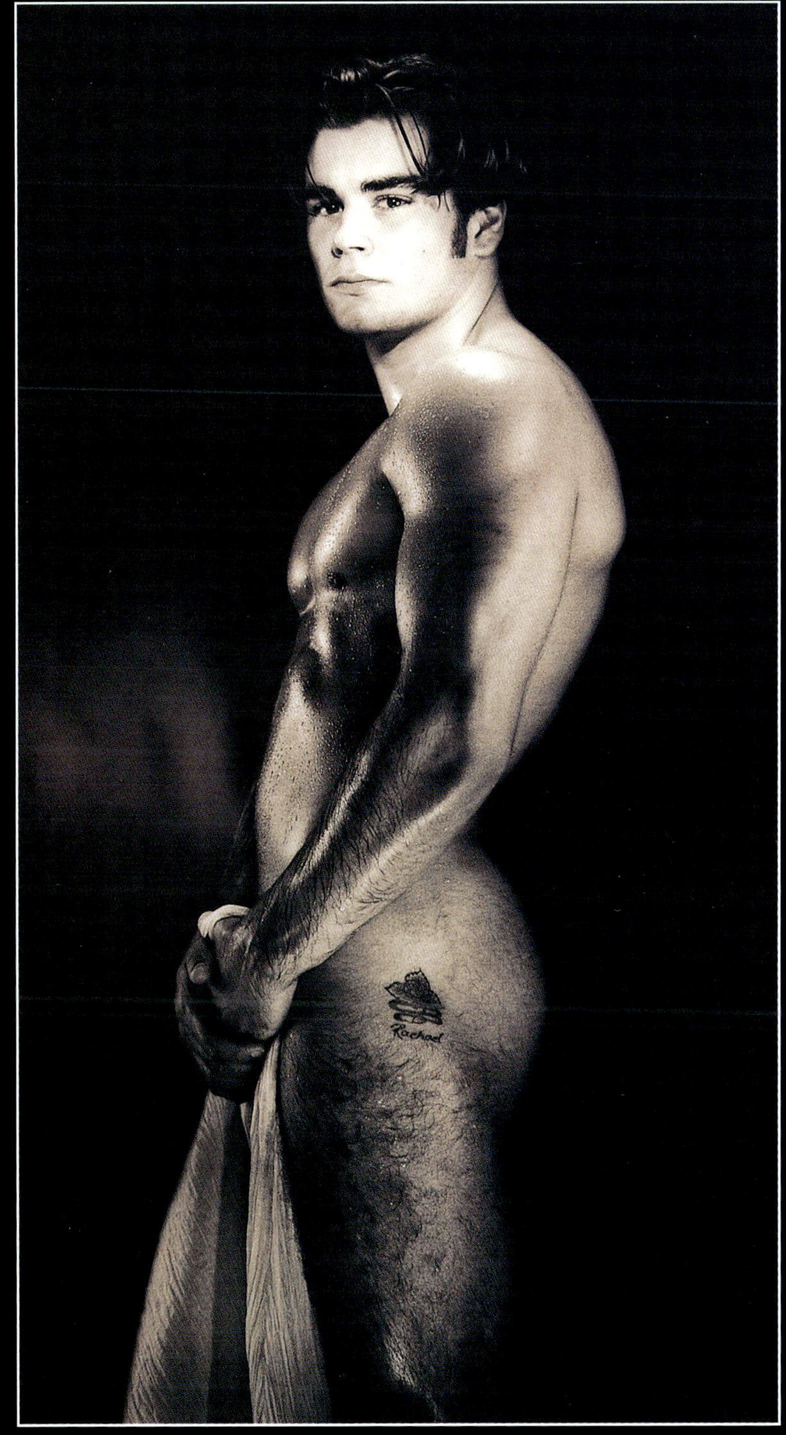

Photographer: **Stu Williamson**

Client: **Simon**

Use: **Model portfolio**

Camera: **6x7cm**

Lens: **140mm**

Film: **Ilford HP5 Plus**

Exposure: **f/11**

Lighting: **Electronic flash: 3 heads**

Props and set: **Lastolite black background, pickaxe handle**

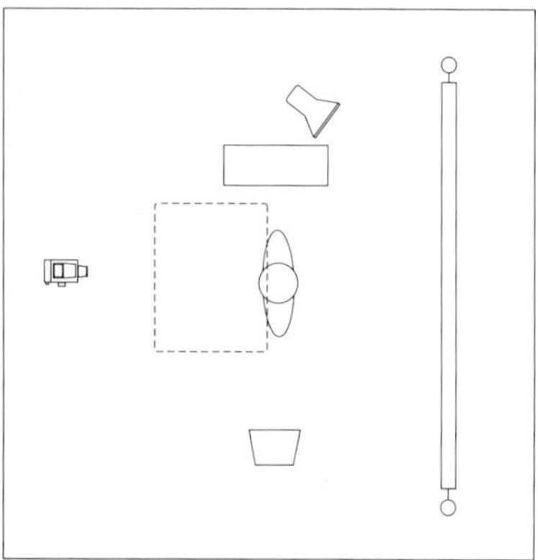

Plan View

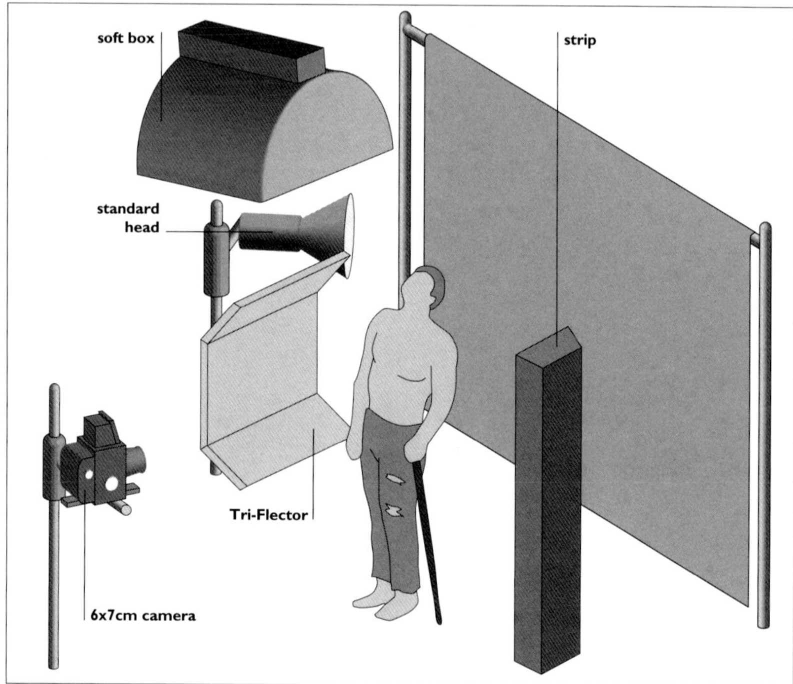

THERE ARE ECHOES HERE OF SOCIALIST REALISM — THE OLD STALINIST PICTURES OF HEROIC STAKHANOVITES TOILING FOR THE MOTHERLAND. THE POSE, THE PROPS AND THE LIGHTING ALL CONTRIBUTE TO THIS.

The jutting jaw is emphasized by the key light, which is a soft box almost directly over the model's head. The brightly lit face has quasi-religious overtones: seeing the light, a brighter tomorrow. The glancing light also emphasizes the texture of the torn jeans and the contours of the muscles and the veins. A strip light to camera right delineates Simon's left arm and provides a (very) modest amount of fill, while a "Tri-Flector" (see page 24) to camera left evens out the lighting somewhat on the model's right side. The background is separately lit with a standard head. Using HP5 Plus, a fast "old-technology" film (as distinct from the "new-technology" Delta series), gives a surprisingly long tonal range.

► *Direct overhead lighting is not normally recommended for photographing people but it can be made to work*

► *Strip lights can be useful for delineation*

► *Not everyone can look convincing in ripped jeans, partially undone; Simon can*

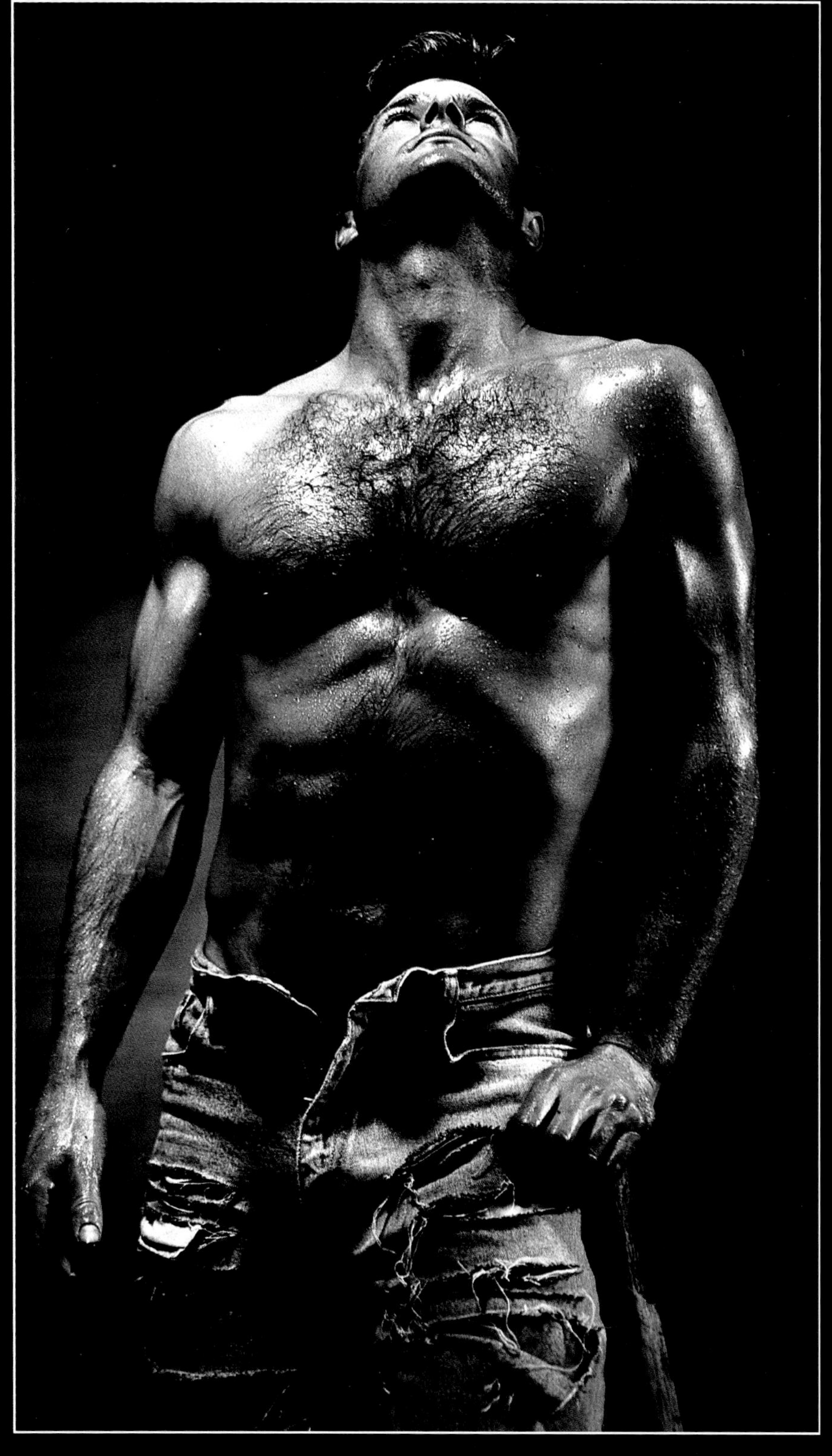

Photographer: **Stu Williamson**

Clients: **Simon & Correna**

Use: **Modelling portfolio**

Camera: **6x7cm**

Lens: **105mm**

Film: **Kodak Plus-X Pan**

Exposure: **f/11**

Lighting: **Electronic flash: 2 heads**

Props and set: **Rope; muslin; Lastolite
hand-painted background**

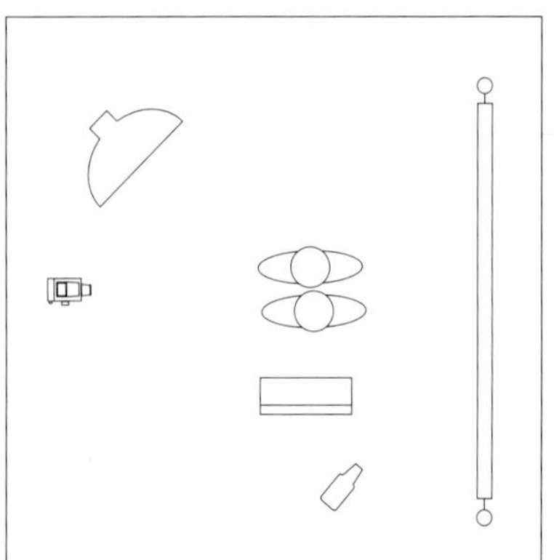

Plan View

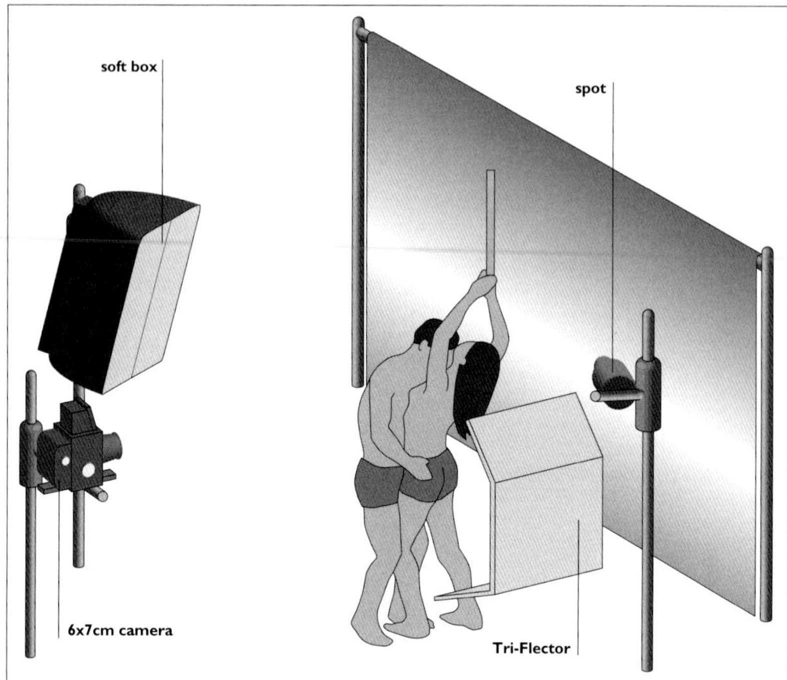

As with many of Stu Williamson's pictures, the resonances here are outside photography: the shape of Simon's back is reminiscent of Nijinsky in *L'Après-midi d'une faune*, while the overall pose brings to mind Caliban and *The Tempest*.

The lighting is remarkably simple. A large soft box to camera left is the key, and indeed the only light on the subject. It is however supplemented by a "Tri-Flector" (see page 24) to camera right, low behind Correna; look at the light on the cloth around her hips. A second light, a standard head, illuminates the Lastolite painted background. The film – Kodak Plus-X Pan – was carefully chosen and developed to give the appropriate tonality. After that a good deal of the impact depended on the printing: Stu prints all his own pictures, as this is an integral part of his vision.

► *With a transparency the image is effectively finished when it is printed; with a print, as Ansel Adams said, "the negative is the score and the print is the performance"*

► *Exercises with two lights – one on the subject, one on the background – should be an essential part of every photographer's education*

Photographer's comment:

The loin-cloths are just muslin; I have various ways of dyeing and ageing cloth – in effect, of getting it "dirty" under controlled conditions.

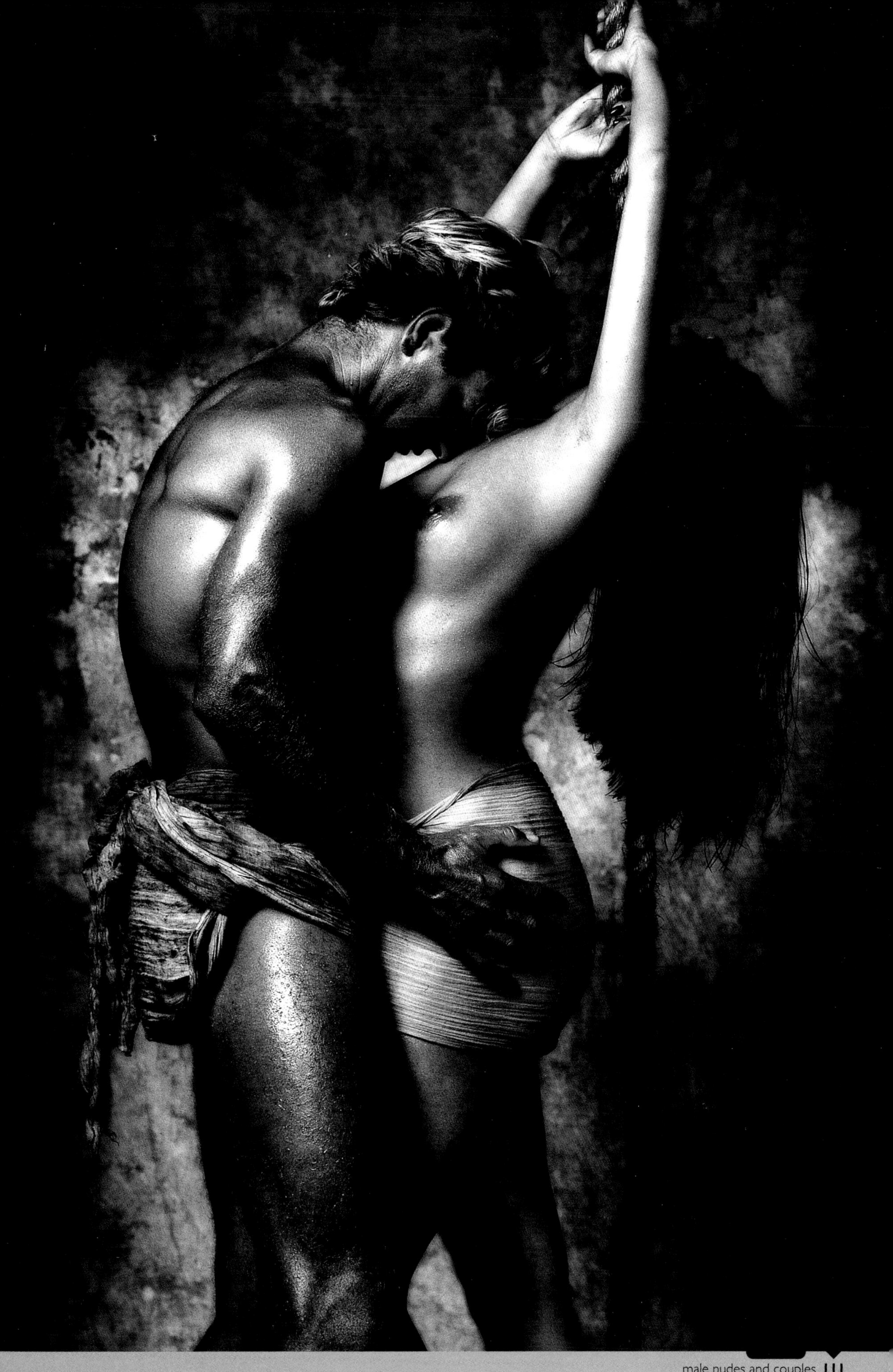

Photographer: **Julia Martinez**

Client: **Christiaan**

Use: **Model portfolio**

Camera: **35mm**

Lens: **50mm**

Film: **Kodak T-Max ISO 100**

Exposure: **f/11**

Lighting: **Available light plus on-camera flash**

Props and set: **Location: very small shower**

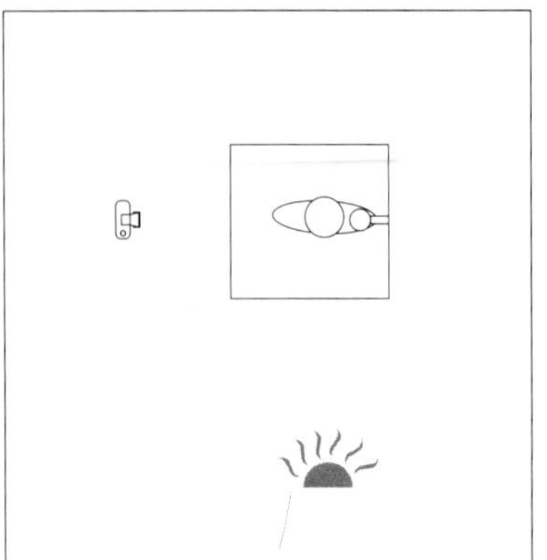

Plan View

CHRISTIAAN IN THE SHOWER

▼

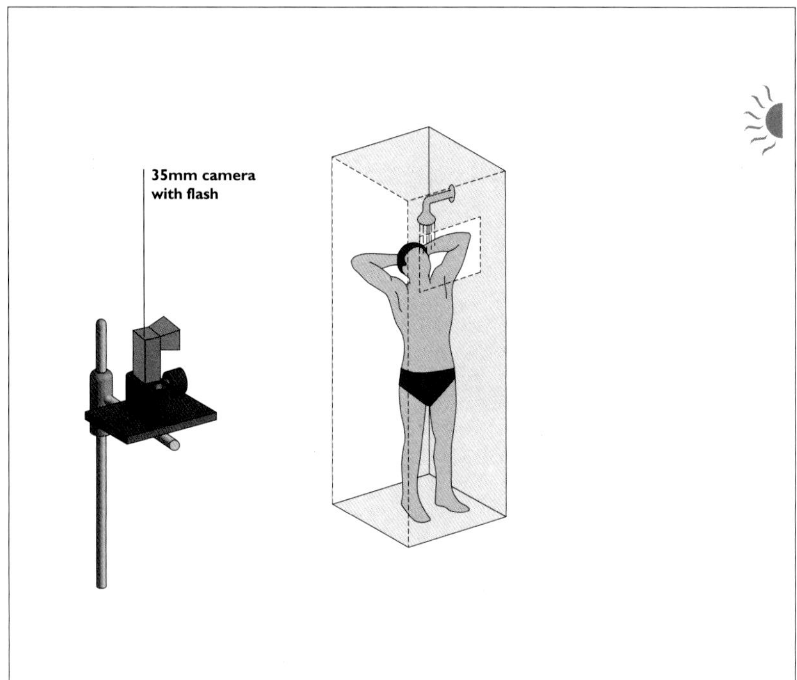

IT IS A COMMON JOKE AMONG PHOTOGRAPHERS THAT THE ONLY TIME THAT AN ON-CAMERA FLASH DELIVERS ITS FULL RATED GUIDE NUMBER IS IN A VERY SMALL WHITE-PAINTED BATHROOM — WHICH IS WHERE JULIA SHOT THIS PICTURE. IN HER WORDS:

"I say it's an available light shot, but really the flash is doing all the work. It's one of those tiny Spanish showers, with white-painted concrete walls. It was difficult to keep the camera dry, because I was getting splashed, but it was good to work with the bare minimum of equipment." You can see the highlights on Christiaan's chest, and the shadows on the wall behind him. There was a small window, rather above the model to camera right, which explains why the shadow above his head is paler than the shadow beside him. The white walls of the shower evened out the light considerably. The print was made on Kentmere Art Classic and selenium-toned.

► *On-camera flash can be a medium worth experimenting with*

► *Plenty of reflectors can even out the hardest light*

► *Electronic flash and water can be a dangerous combination*

Photographer's comment:

Christiaan is my best friend and wanted some pictures for his modelling portfolio.

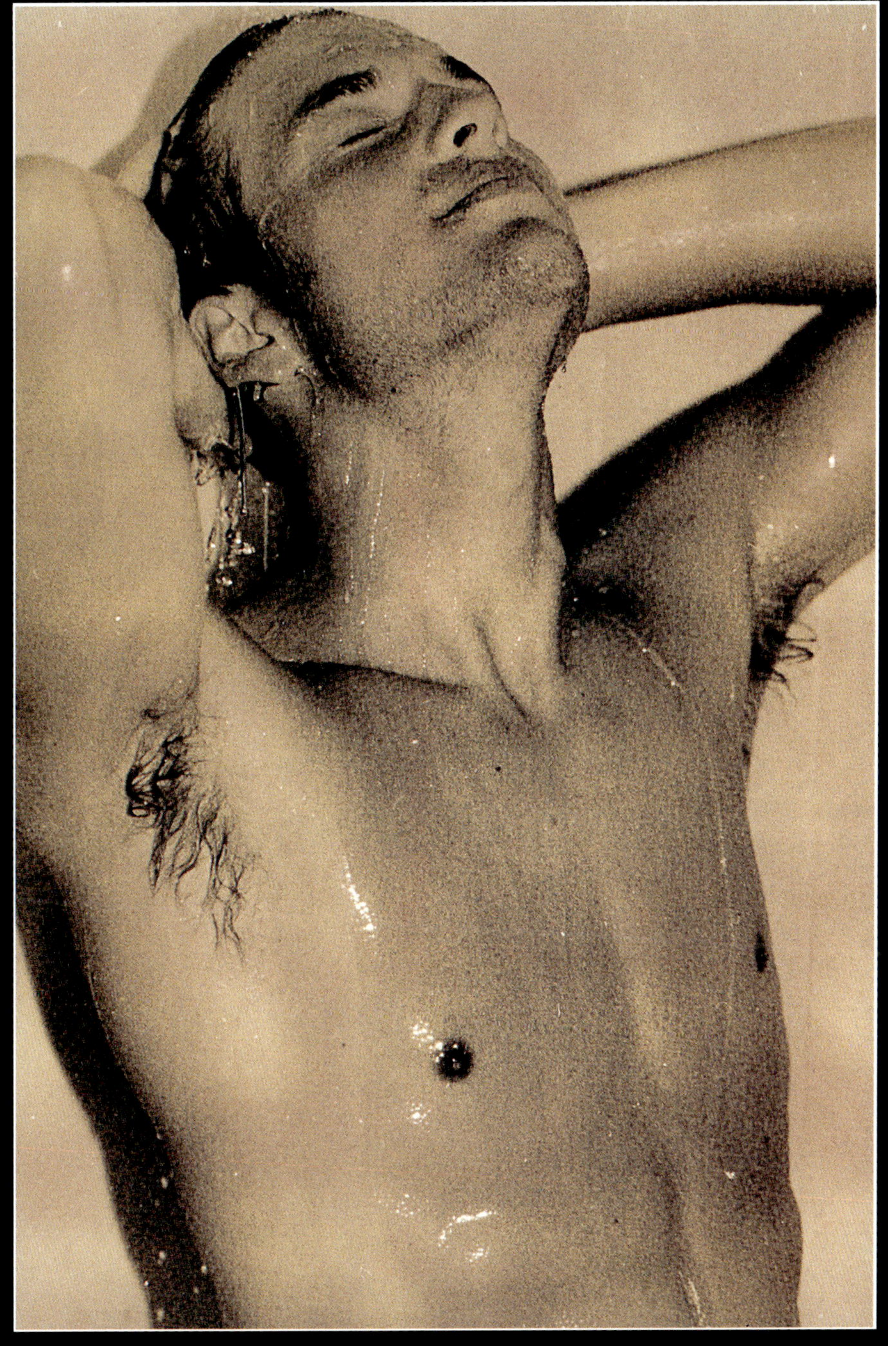

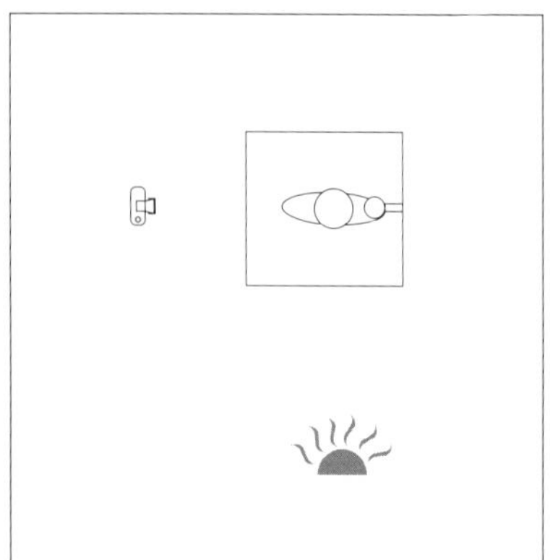

Plan View

C H R I S T I A A N

▼

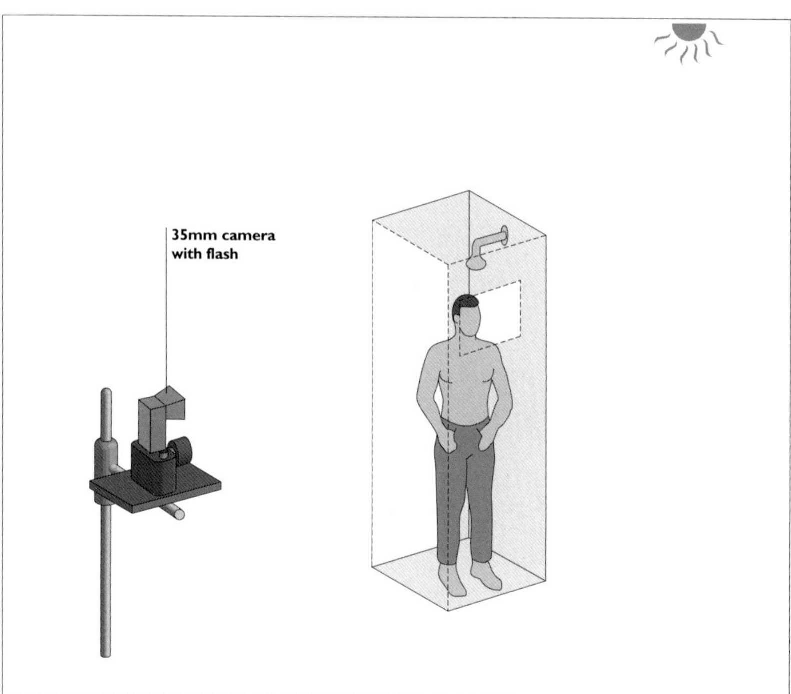

As soon as you compare this with the picture "Christiaan in the shower" (page 113) you can see that while the lighting is all but identical, the effect is very different.

The key light is an on-camera flash, as evidenced by the hard shadow on the model's right side (camera left) but the streak of sunlight on the background makes a considerable difference: the picture was shot around noon, when the sun was very high in the sky. As with the other picture, the small size of the shower cubicle and the highly reflective walls have made for a very different effect from what you would expect with on-camera flash, much more even but still with superb delineation of texture. Moreover, the water-slicked skin in the other picture is considerably more reflective than the dry skin in this shot.

► *Baby oil is the classic medium for
  making skin glisten, but water
  will do the same*

► *Separating the photographic potential
  of a shower cubicle from its everyday
  use is a step many might fail to take*

Photographer's comment:

We tried a number of shots in the shower.

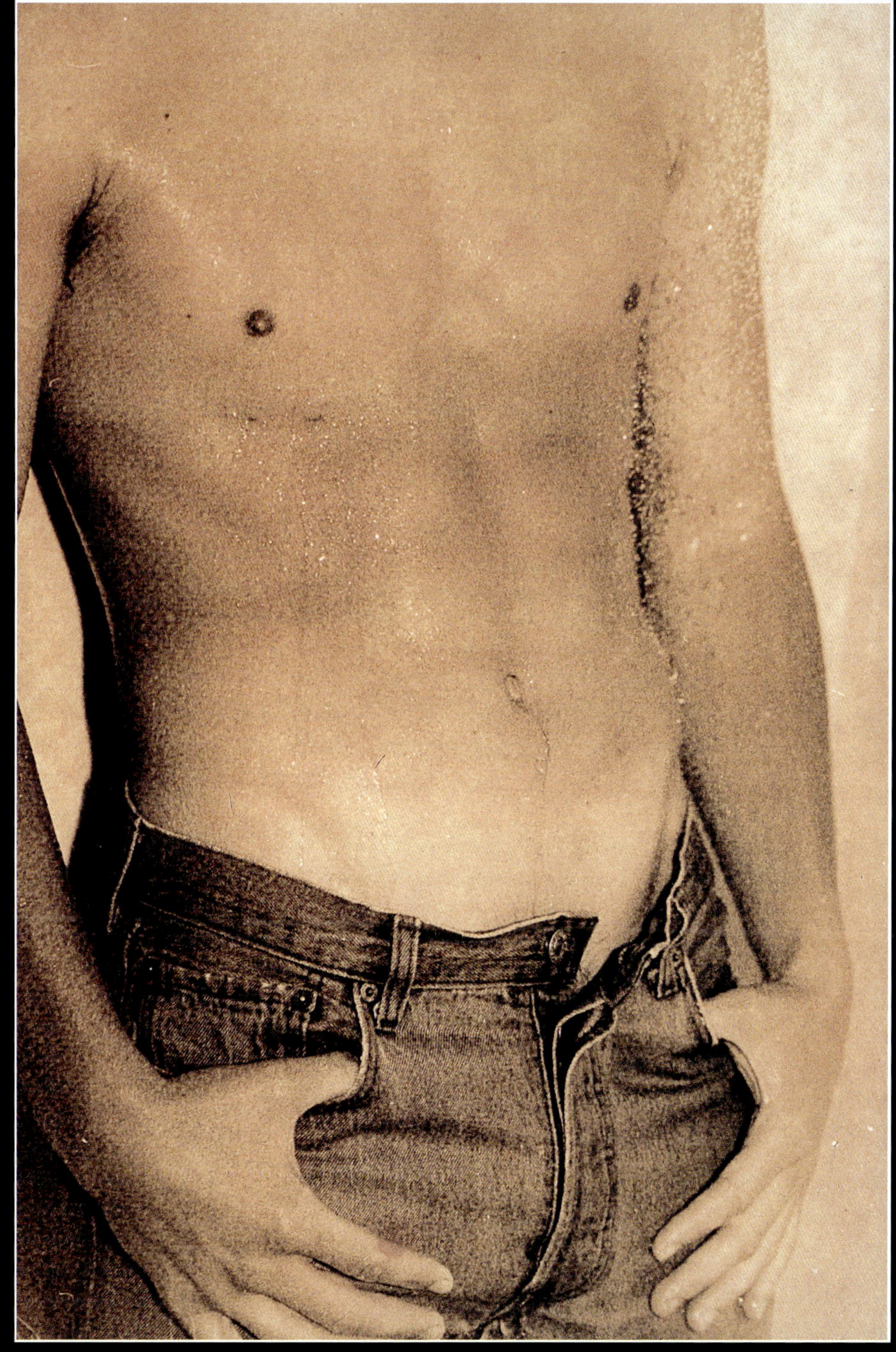

Photographer: **Struan**

Client: **Karl Lagerfeld**

Use: **Advertising ("Photo" cologne for men)**

Model: **Rob Simpson**

Camera: **35mm**

Lens: **105mm**

Film: **Kodak Tri-X Pan**

Exposure: **f/11**

Lighting: **Electronic flash: 1 head**

Props and set: **Black wall sprayed with moisture**

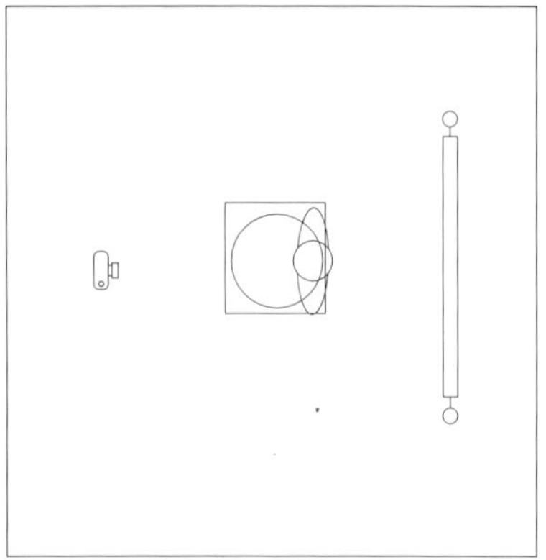

Plan View

P H O T O

▼

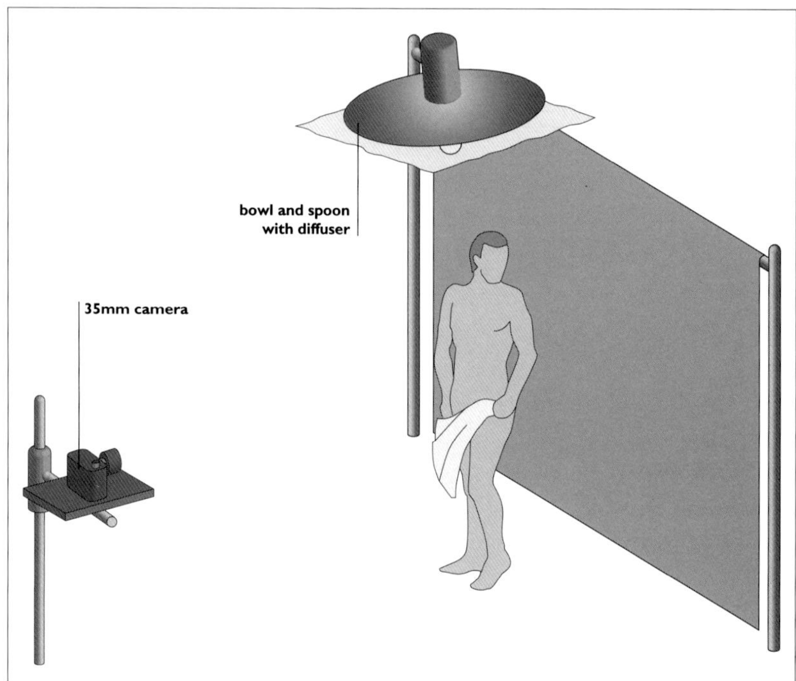

A NEW MEN'S COLOGNE CALLED "PHOTO" … BLACK AND WHITE PHOTOGRAPHY … A DYNAMIC ACTOR/MALE MODEL LOOK — THE LOGIC IS CLEAR ENOUGH. BUT IT TAKES A GOOD PHOTOGRAPHER TO CONVERT THE LOGIC INTO A PICTURE.

The lighting is surprisingly simple: a 500mm (20in) reflector on a standard head, mounted on a boom arm directly above the model and diffused with a sheet of tracing paper.

Overhead lighting may be of limited use out of doors, but it can be very effective in the studio. It can be particularly useful when the background is an integral part of the picture, as it is here: without the moisture on the wall (which was painted with black latex paint), the background is too bleak. The white towel completes the slightly diagonal composition of the picture; without it, the tones would simply peter out towards the bottom.

► *Use things like towels, books, flowers and so forth as areas of tone to complete a composition*

► *Light items like the towel must not be too near the light source or they may burn out*

► *White fabric is between five and ten times as reflective as skin*

Photographer's comment:

For the launch of Lagerfeld's new cologne/after-shave I arranged for six female photographers and two male (including myself) to provide our own interpretations of the product.

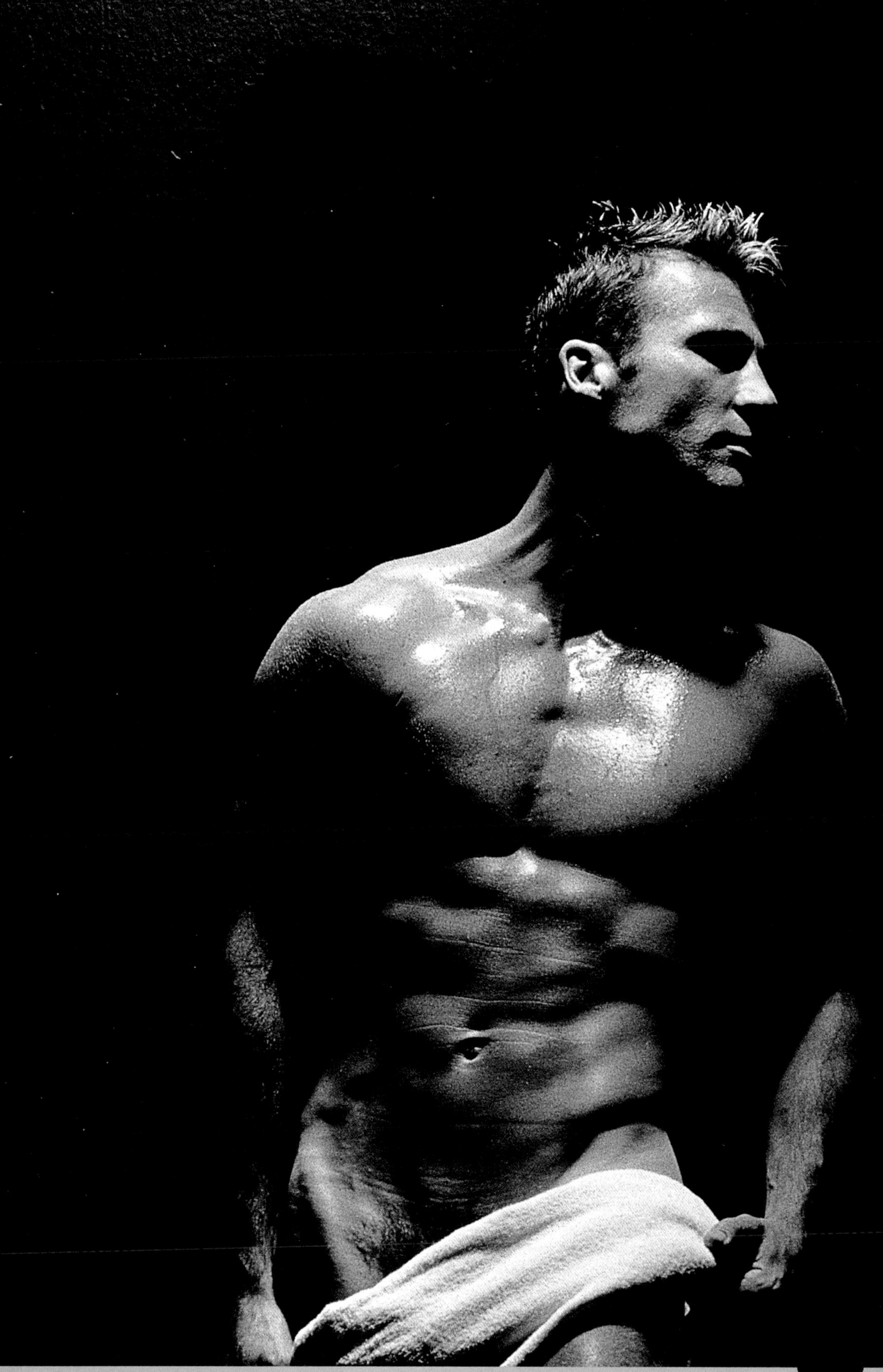

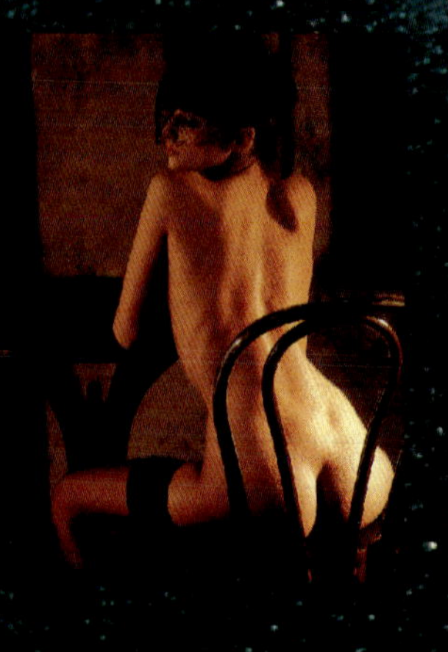

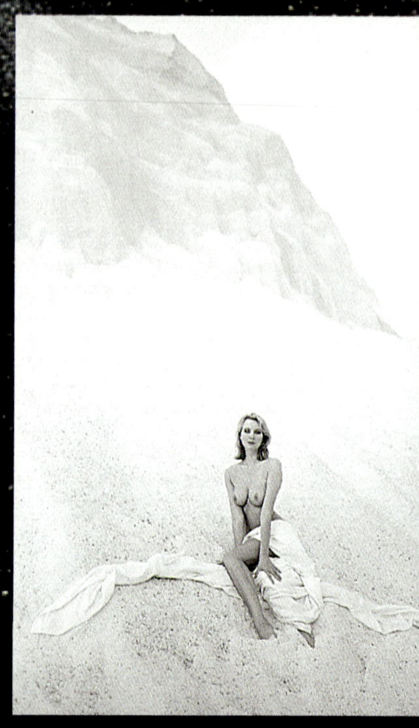

6

the

outdoor

nude

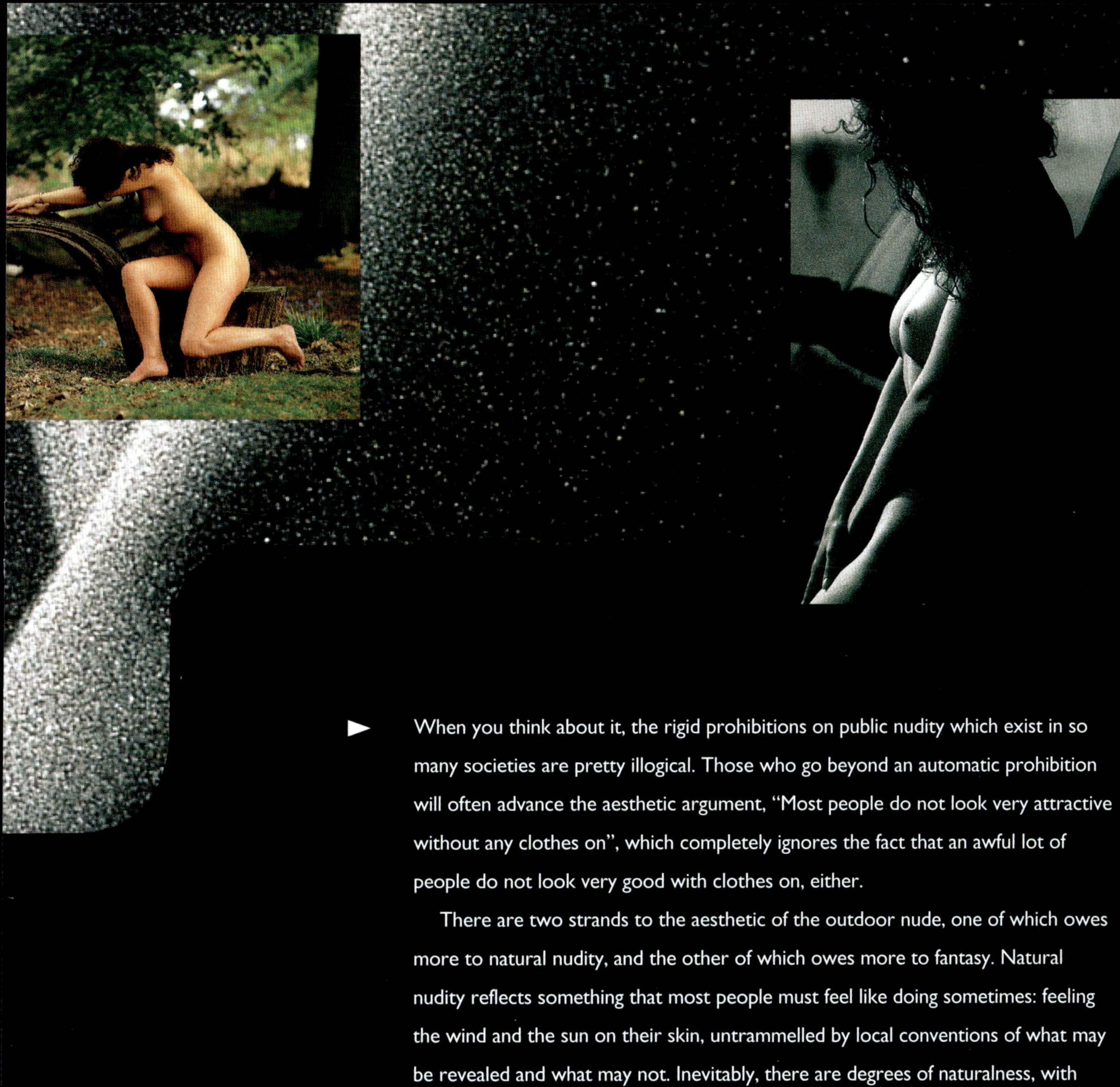

When you think about it, the rigid prohibitions on public nudity which exist in so many societies are pretty illogical. Those who go beyond an automatic prohibition will often advance the aesthetic argument, "Most people do not look very attractive without any clothes on", which completely ignores the fact that an awful lot of people do not look very good with clothes on, either.

There are two strands to the aesthetic of the outdoor nude, one of which owes more to natural nudity, and the other of which owes more to fantasy. Natural nudity reflects something that most people must feel like doing sometimes: feeling the wind and the sun on their skin, untrammelled by local conventions of what may be revealed and what may not. Inevitably, there are degrees of naturalness, with something like Struan's Blue Pool or Frank Wartenberg's Nude with Car looking as if the photographer just happened to take a picture of a girl who just happened to have taken her clothes off, while Harry Lomax's Outdoor Nude or Bob Shell's Heidi in the Palmetto are more self-consciously posed.

The fantasy nude is perhaps typified by Mike Dmochowski's Nude on Chair with Table, where a beautiful girl waits at a café table. Many men might wish that they were away from their desks on a rainy day, and sipping a cappuccino or a kir on a shady sidewalk by a sunny street. The girl simply expands the fantasy. Struan's Window and Shutters is another enduring fantasy: the beautiful nude glimpsed at a window.

Photographer: **Mike Dmochowski**

Use: **Glamour video**

Model: **Nella**

Camera: **6x6cm**

Lens: **150mm + warming filter**

Film: **Kodak Ektachrome EPP 120**

Exposure: **1/125sec at f/11**

Lighting: **Electronic flash: 3 heads**

Props and set: **Built set**

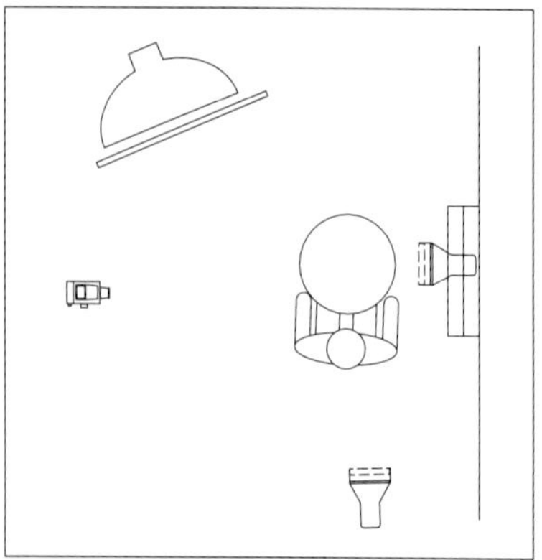

Plan View

MODEL ON CHAIR WITH TABLE

▼

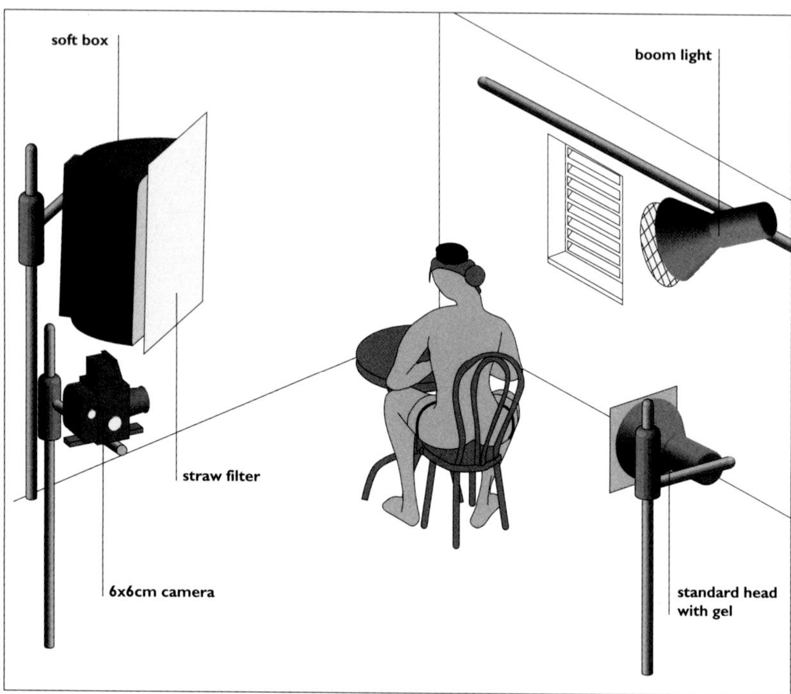

BUILT SETS ARE ONE OF THE SECRETS OF MANY SUCCESSFUL GLAMOUR PHOTOGRAPHERS — THEY ALLOW FULL CONTROL OF THE AMBIENCE AND LIGHTING, WITHOUT FEAR OF ONLOOKERS — BUT LIGHTING IS ANOTHER. THIS FORMS PART OF A LARGE NUMBER OF PICTURES SHOT FOR A VIDEO *CAPTURED SECRETS*, WHICH MIKE PRODUCED.

► *The illusion of sunlight is often harder to create than might be expected. Plenty of power will make it easier*

► *A good set will create its own expectations as far as lighting goes, and the eye will "read" whatever seems most appropriate*

► *Incident-light metering with a flat receptor (not a dome) makes it easier to determine lighting ratios*

A direct side light with a wide honeycomb, set to camera right and slightly back lighting the model, creates the impression of sunlight coming in under an awning or onto a balcony. This light is some 120cm (4ft) from the model and 150cm (5ft) above the floor. The exposure reading from this alone, pointing the meter at the light from the subject position, was f/11.

A small, square soft light with a straw filter provides the highlights on the left: this creates the impression of sunlight bouncing off ancient stucco. Again this is about 120cm (4ft) from the model, and about 150cm (5ft) from the floor.

Finally, a boom light some 240cm (8ft) above the ground provides a back light. Like the fill, the reading from this alone was f/8.

Photographer's comment:

This video is still available; my address is at the back of the book, in the Directory section.

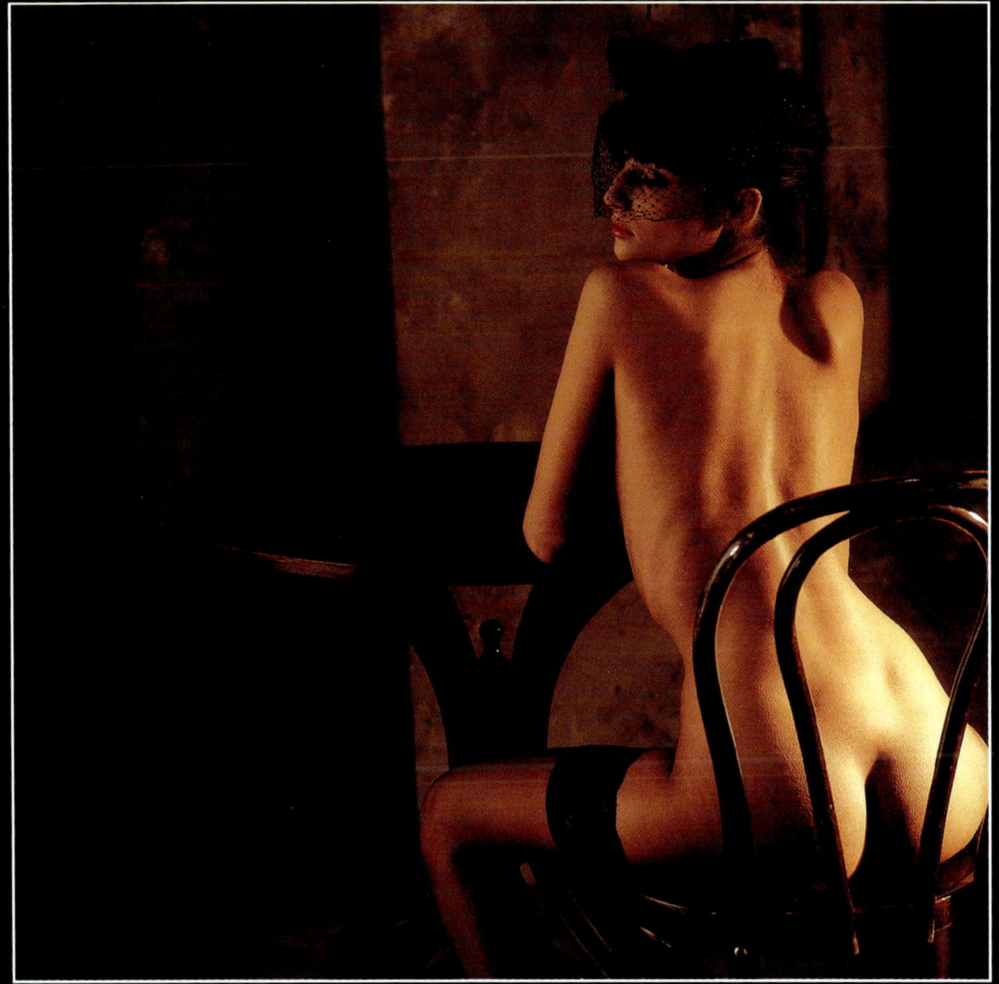

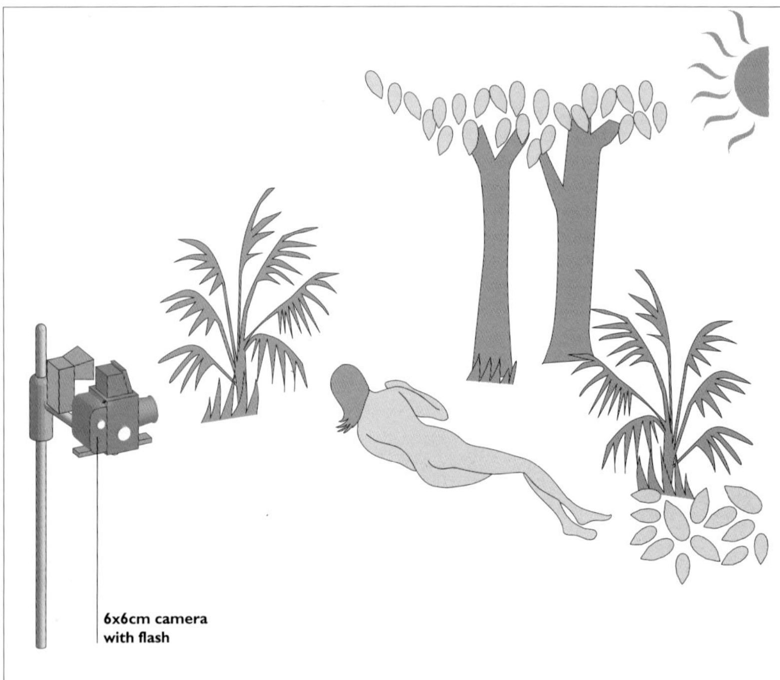

DAPPLED SUNLIGHT IS LESS OF A PROBLEM IN MONOCHROME THAN IN COLOUR BECAUSE OF THE INHERENTLY GREATER TONAL RANGE WHICH MONOCHROME CAN RECORD; BUT WITHOUT SOME DEGREE OF FILL THE CONTRAST CAN QUICKLY DEGENERATE INTO "SOOT AND WHITEWASH".

The direction of the sun – clearly the key light – can be seen here: it is effectively over the photographer's right shoulder. Fill for the dappled shadows came from an on-camera Vivitar 283 bounced into a Lumiquest, and from the white wall of the house immediately behind the photographer, reflecting indirect sky light. While painted walls can make excellent bounces, they can also introduce colour casts if they are any colour other than white – a point which is easy to forget, as the eye adapts easily to colour casts.

Rangefinder medium-format cameras can be remarkably effective for nude and glamour photography as they allow the photographer to establish an easier rapport with the subject, although long lenses (over about 180mm) are not very convenient.

Photographer: **Bob Shell**

Client: **Hove Books**

Use: **Editorial (Mamiya Guide)**

Model: **Heidi Guenther (acted as own stylist)**

Assistant: **Roger Bansemer**

Camera: **6x6cm**

Lens: **75mm**

Film: **Kodak T-Max 100**

Exposure: **1/30sec at f/11 ('I think!')**

Lighting: **Daylight + flash**

Props and set: **My friend Roger Bansemer's back yard**

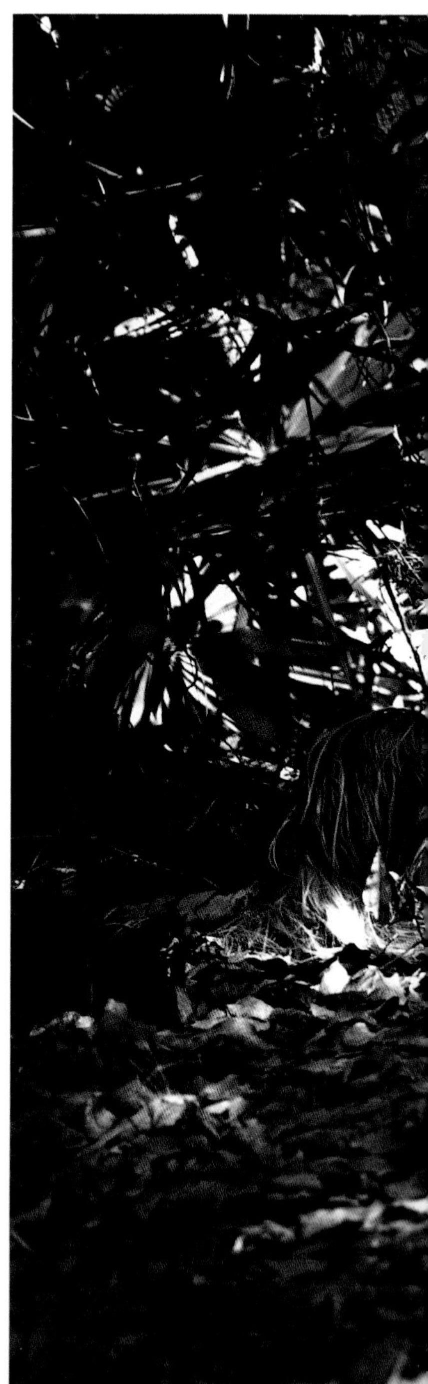

► *Lumiquests and similar small bounce diffusers can be extremely valuable for lowering contrast in this sort of situation as well as for adding catchlights in the eyes of portraits*

► *It does not matter in monochrome, but in colour, foliage can introduce an unattractive greenish cast*

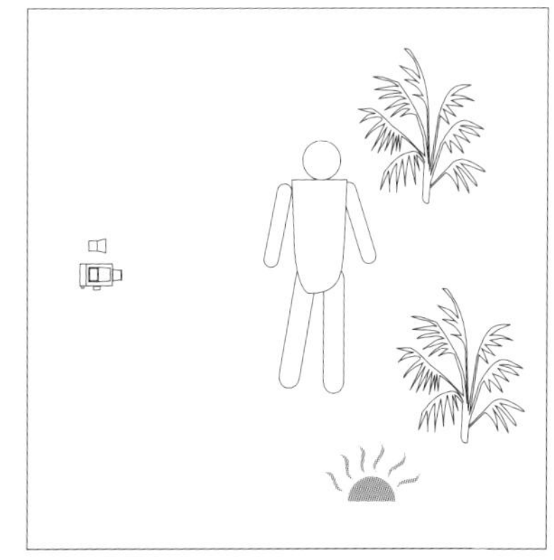

Plan View

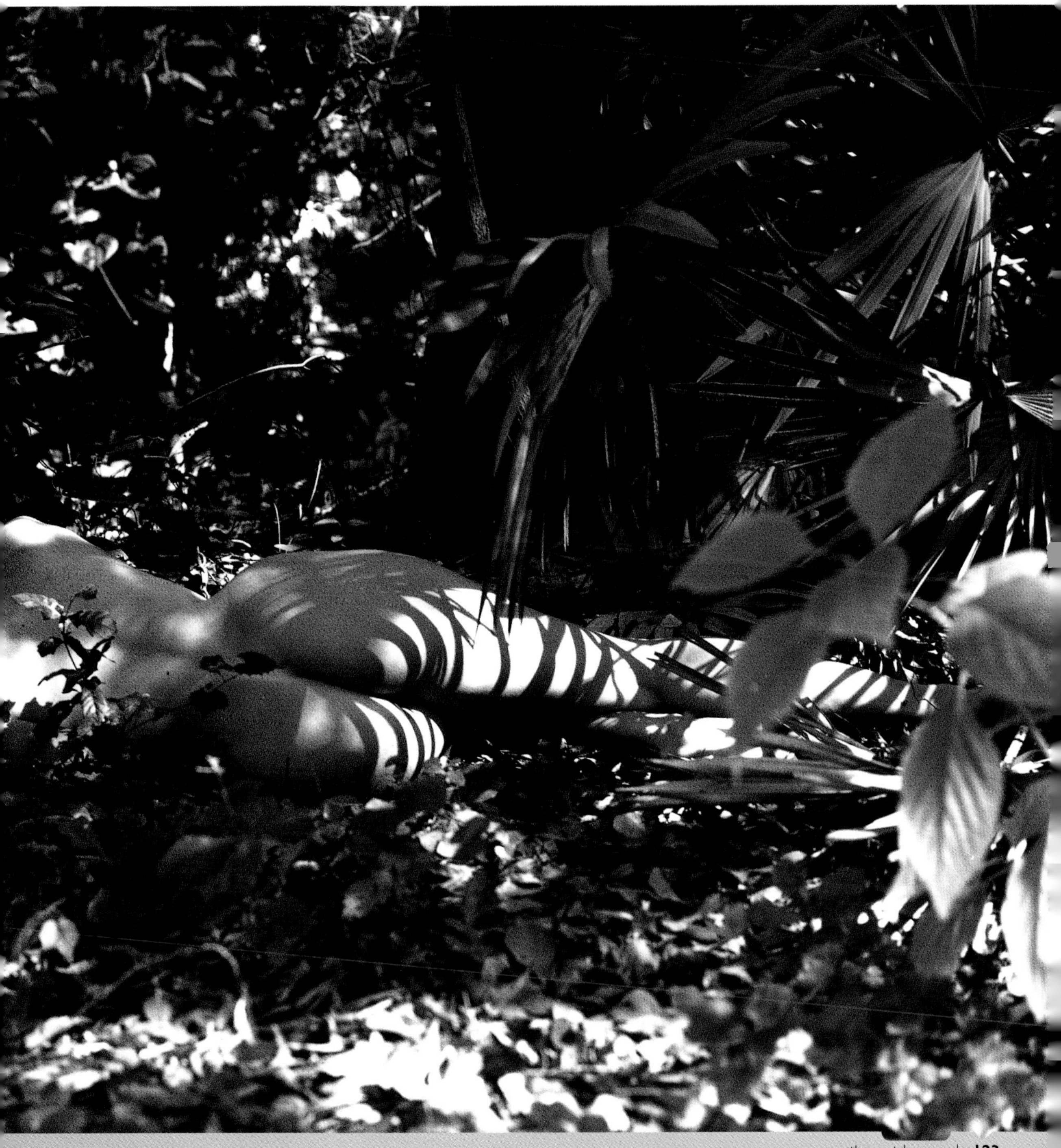

Photographer: **Harry Lomax**

Use: **Library**

Model: **Claire**

Camera: **6x6cm**

Lens: **150mm**

Film: **Fuji RDP ISO 100**

Exposure: **1/30sec at f/11**

Lighting: **Daylight plus flash**

Props and set: **Location**

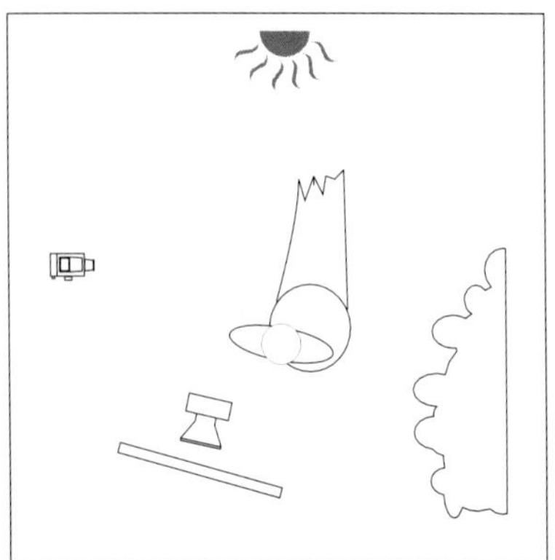

Plan View

▼

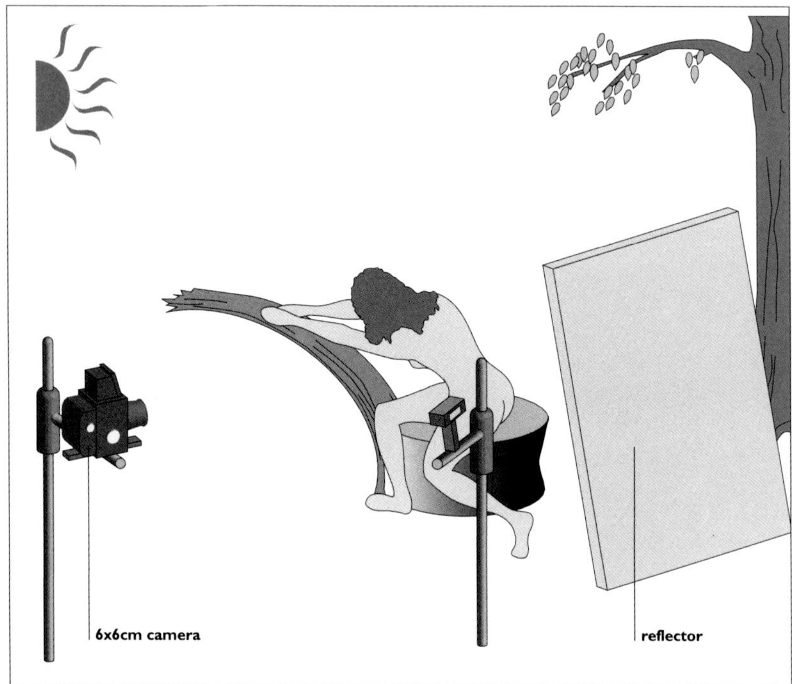

THE SURPRISE IN THIS ATTRACTIVE AND NATURAL-LOOKING PICTURE IS HOW MUCH DIFFERENCE CAN BE MADE BY A RELATIVELY WEAK FLASH AND A REFLECTOR AT QUITE A CONSIDERABLE DISTANCE – 4.5M (15FT) – FROM THE SUBJECT.

The key light is arguably sunlight from camera left, but it is supplemented by a Metz 45 CT flash bounced off a reflector (size not recorded) mounted about 2m (6½ft) off the ground to camera right. The reason for the flash was almost the opposite of a fill: the aim was to throw the inner curves of the model's body more fully into the shadow. The two sources are almost exactly equal in value.

A great deal of control is however afforded by the way in which flash is affected only by aperture, but ambient light is affected by both aperture and exposure time. Thus, if this same picture had been shot at 1/60sec instead of 1/30, the flash would have been dominant, but if it had been shot at 1/15 the daylight would have been dominant.

► *Aperture alone controls flash exposure, but aperture and exposure duration control ambient-light exposure*

► *Using flash reduces the problem of dappled sunlight and also reduces the greenish cast which is sometimes introduced by foliage*

► *A very weak magenta filter (CC05M) can counter a greenish cast without looking too obvious*

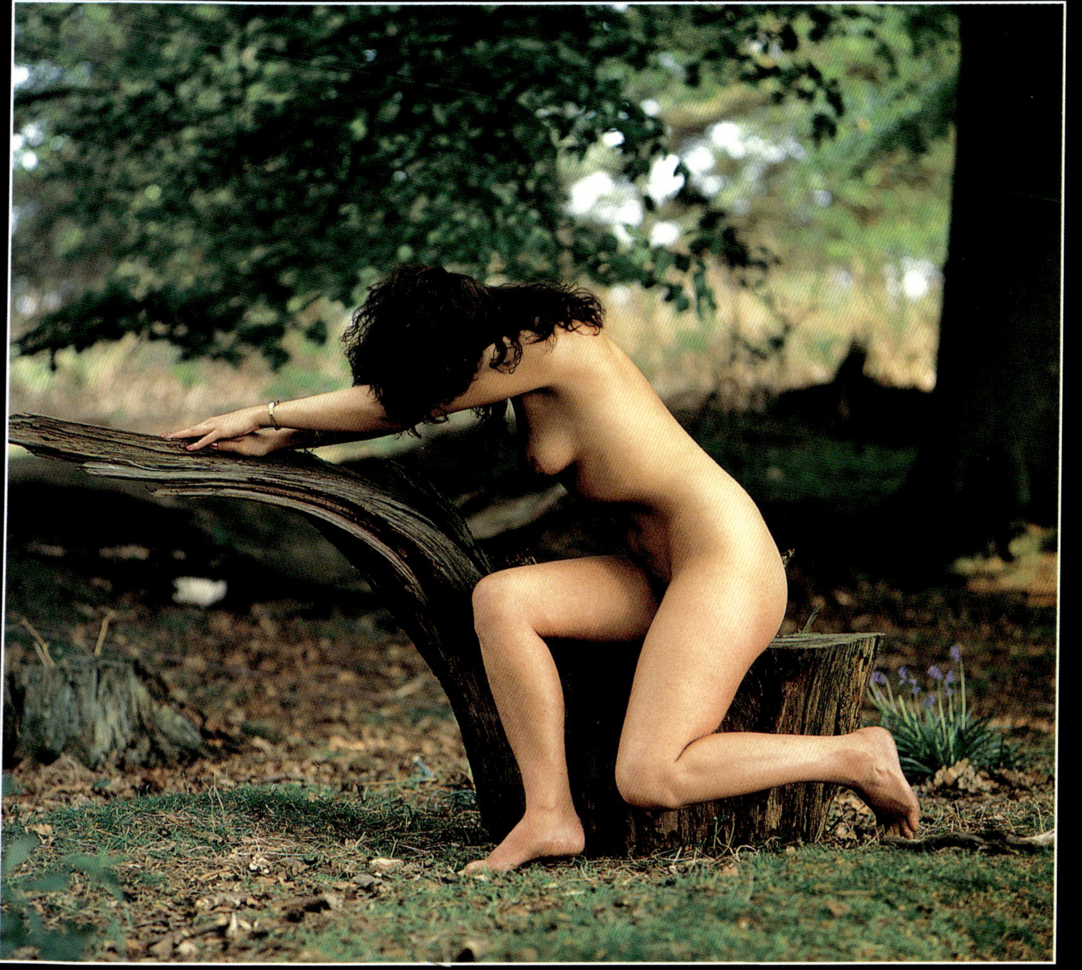

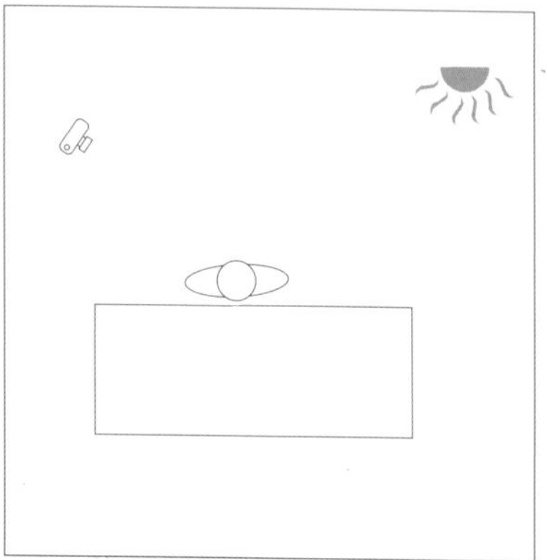

Plan View

N U D E   W I T H   C A R

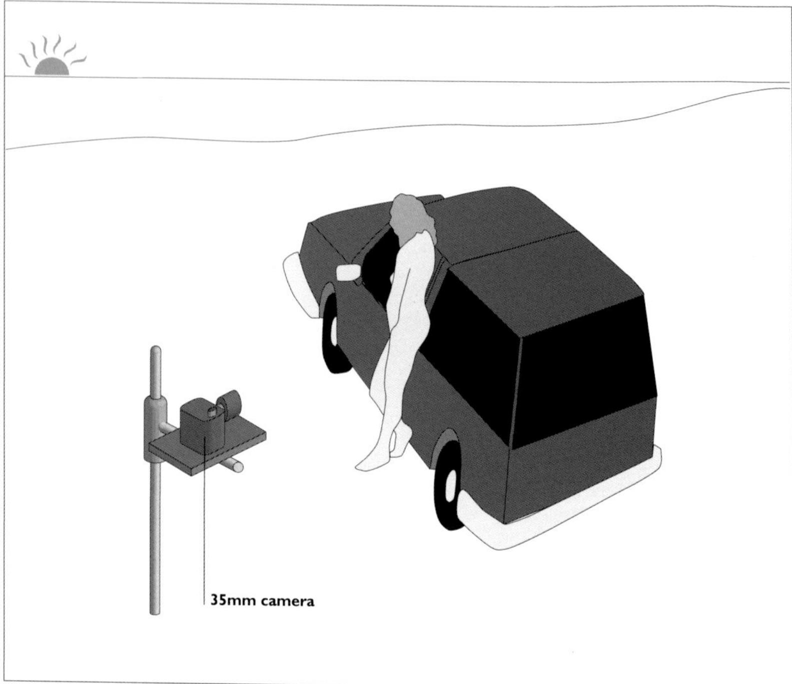

THE MODEL IS LEANING ON A CAR, WITH THE EARLY MORNING SUN BEHIND HER; SHE IS BACK LIT, WITH NO REFLECTOR TO ACT AS A BOUNCE. AS IS CLEAR FROM THE DIRECTION OF THE SHADOWS, THE SUN HAS JUST RISEN.

Very early morning sun has a wonderful quality, but the effect is short-lived – there are no more than a few minutes of that almost liquid red light – and the lighting changes very rapidly, doubling and doubling again as the sun rises; this makes metering difficult, and practically demands extensive bracketing. Also the initial light levels are surprisingly low, and long exposures may be called for. It is often as well to have several bodies loaded (or several backs, in the case of roll film) to obviate the need for reloading.

▶ *It may be as well to load several bodies with different films, to compare the different effects*

▶ *Alternatively, exhaustive exploration of a particular film stock may prove more rewarding*

▶ *You may need to use extensive bracketing, or have an assistant taking continuous readings, or (if you trust it) you can use automatic exposure*

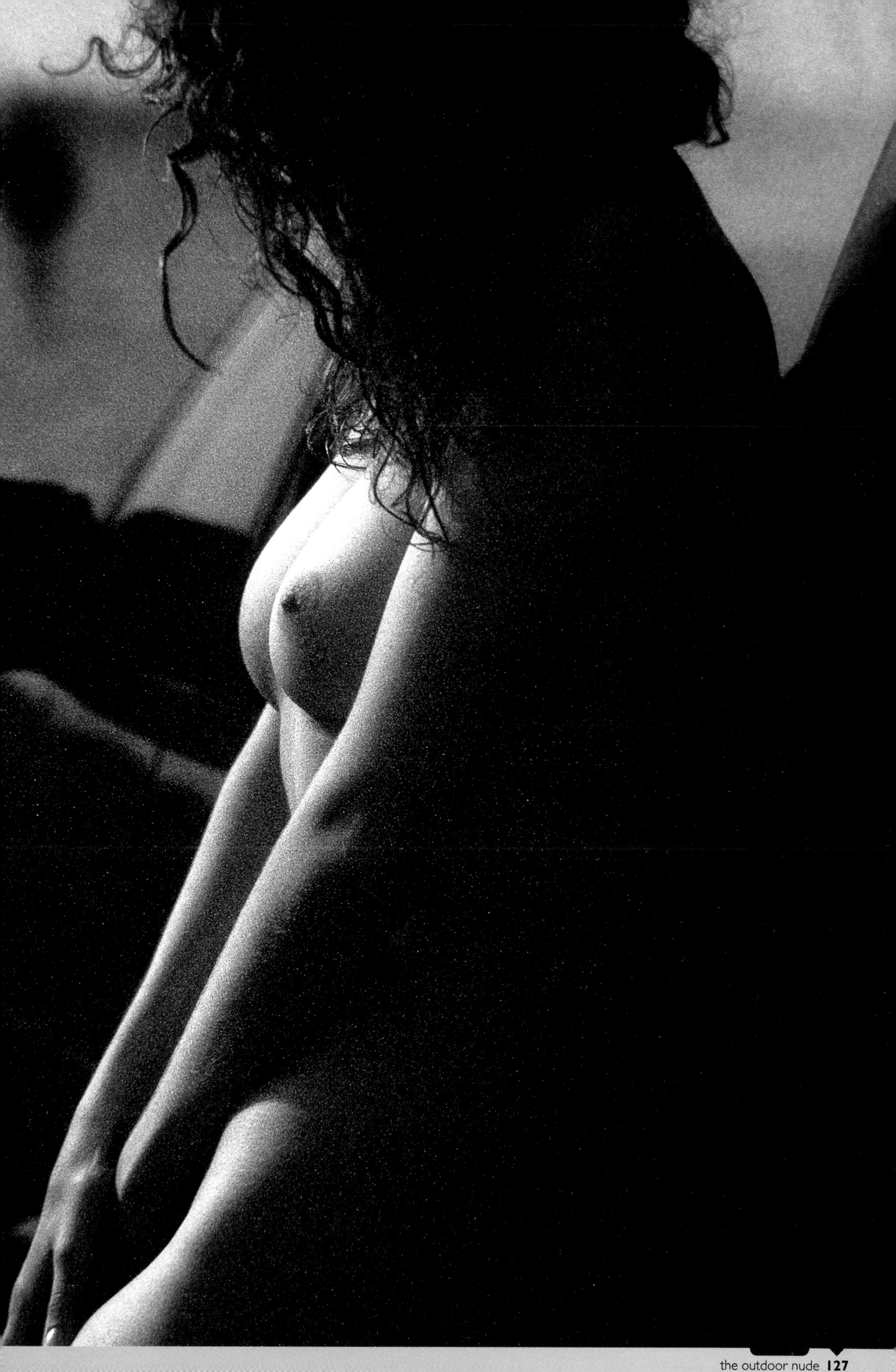

Photographer: **Struan**

Use: **Personal work**

Model: **Coralie**

Camera: **35mm**

Lens: **35mm**

Film: **Kodak Tri-X Pan rated at EI 200**

Exposure: **1/60sec at f/5.6**

Lighting: **Available light**

Props and set: **Salt, sheet**

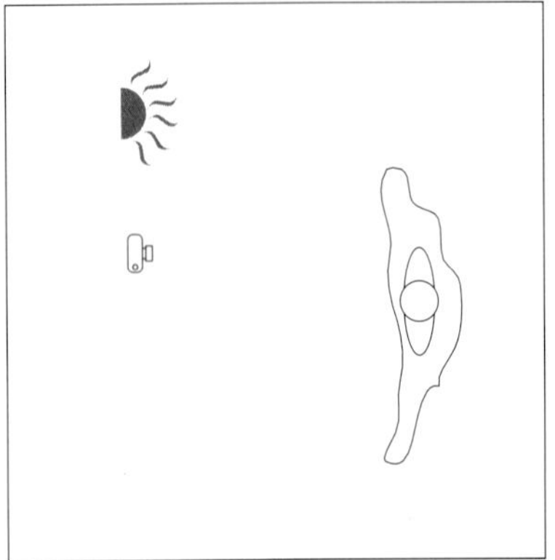

Plan View

SALT DUNES

▼

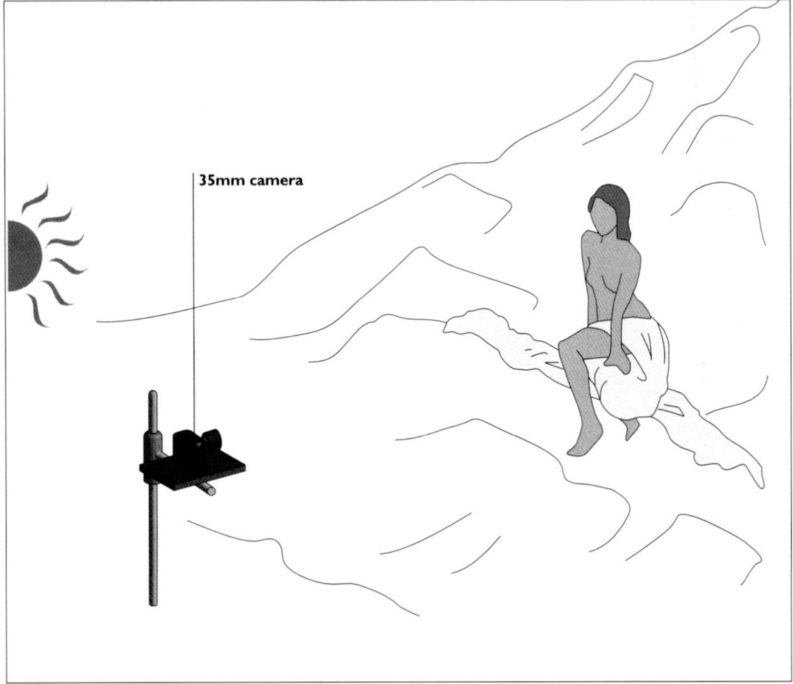

CONTRARY TO APPEARANCES THESE HUGE DUNES ARE NOT OF SAND BUT OF SALT. STRUAN HAD BEEN SHOOTING A BLACK DRESS FOR A CLIENT EARLIER THAT DAY; THIS WAS PERSONAL WORK, SHOT BY THE DYING LIGHT.

As he puts it, "When the paid shoot was finished, and everyone else was going home, I asked the model if she minded staying behind for some more portfolio shots. The sun was very low, and the evening was beginning to get hazy: a few minutes later, it was too dark to shoot. It was really nice light, though. Earlier, it had been rather harsh and contrasty, but this was really good".

The salt acts as a giant reflector, bouncing light everywhere and creating a very even light in these conditions, and one of Struan's trusty all-purpose sheets (see pages 69) was pressed into service as well.

► *Late-afternoon light is often hazy*

► *In the last quarter hour or so before the sun sets, the light changes very rapidly indeed*

► *The very red quality of the setting sun often seems to create an unusual effect in monochrome*

Photographer's comment:

If you just pack up and go home when the commercial shoot is finished, you can miss some really good personal shots.

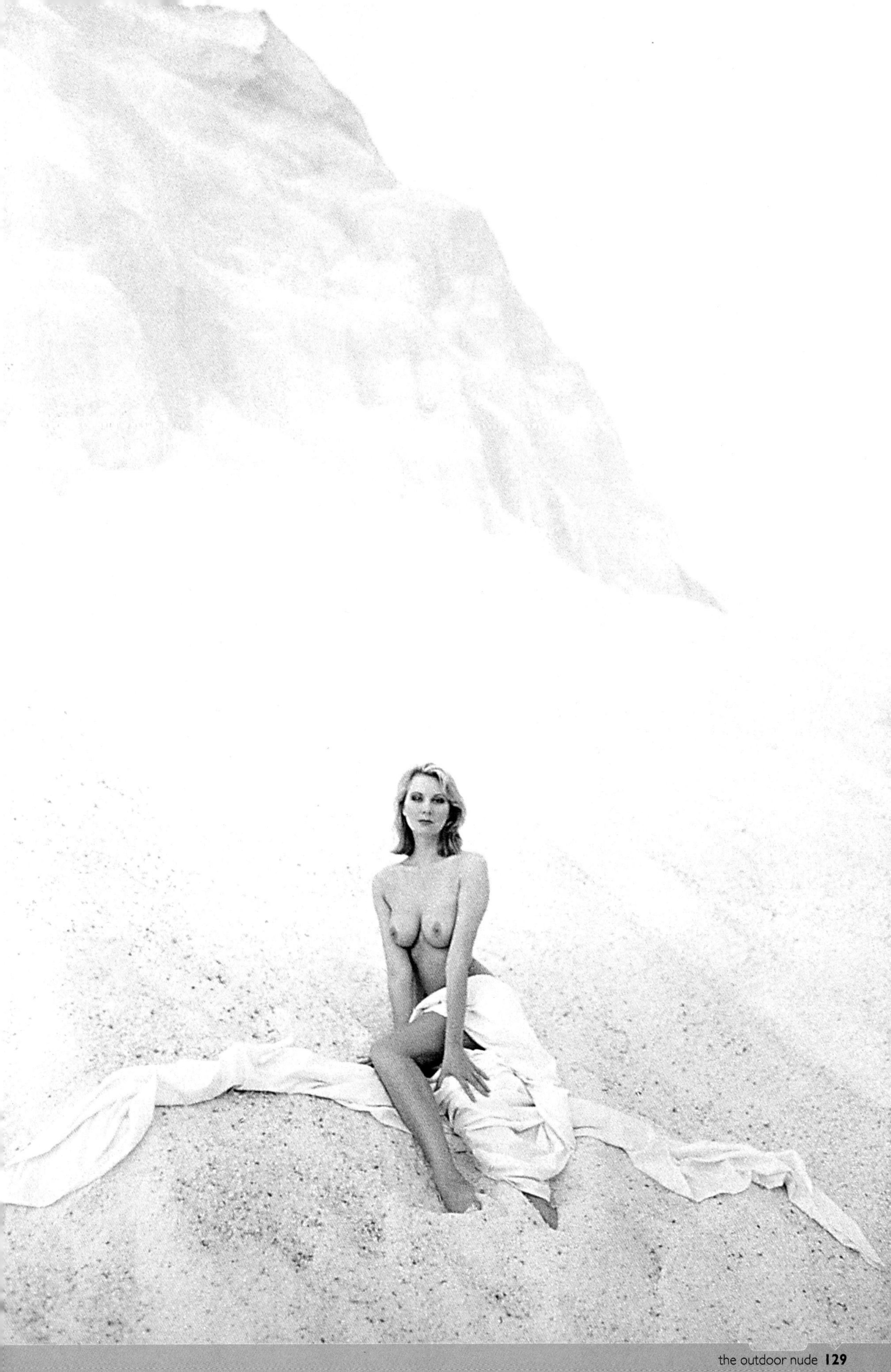

Photographer: **Struan**

Use: **Personal work**

Model: **Alex**

Camera: **35mm**

Lens: **35mm**

Film: **Kodak Ektachrome EPN ISO 100**

Exposure: **1/60sec at f/4**

Lighting: **Available light**

Props and set: **Li-Lo type bed; sheets**

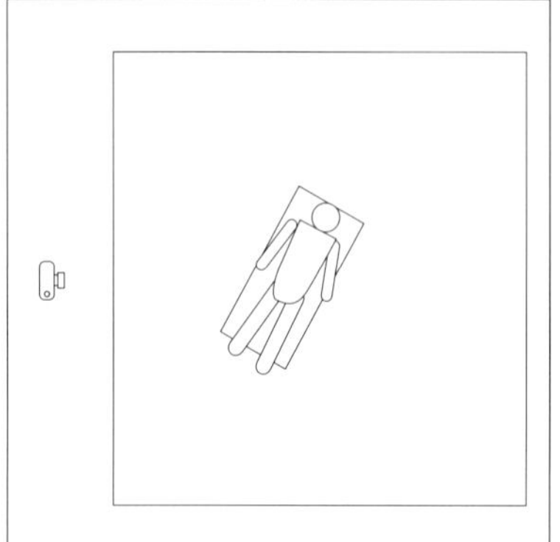

Plan View

BLUE POOL

▼

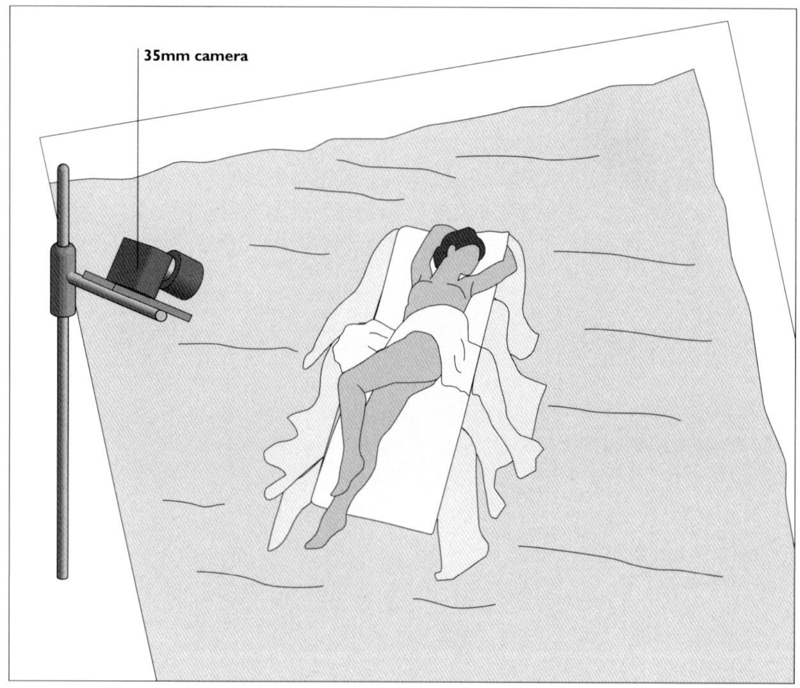

THE MODEL WAS AN ACTRESS VISITING FROM LOS ANGELES. STRUAN BORROWED A FRIEND'S POOL AS A GOOD SETTING. ONE SHEET WAS DRAPED OVER THE FLOATING BED, AND A SECOND SHEET WAS USED AS A PARTIAL DRAPE FOR THE MODEL.

The lighting was overcast daylight at about 3 to 4 pm. It was sufficiently diffuse that, in Struan's own words, "I had a reflector with me, but it wasn't doing anything".

It was therefore a matter principally of pose and of composition. This picture well illustrates that partial veiling is often more attractive than complete nudity, and the diagonal composition in a vertical frame has a very different mood from what could have been achieved with a horizontal composition. The generous amount of blue water above the model's head includes reflections as a part of the composition. The 35mm lens makes the subject's legs look even longer, but note how the toes are pointed to avoid making her feet seem too big.

► *Whether filtration is needed on an overcast day, and how much is needed, can depend very much on the film in use*

► *When the contrast of colours is strong, as here, there may be little need for filtration*

► *Sometimes a wide angle is necessary just to get enough in: it is not always used merely to make legs look longer*

Photographer's comment:

I find my sheets extremely useful for all kinds of things, though my laundry bills are sometimes pretty high.

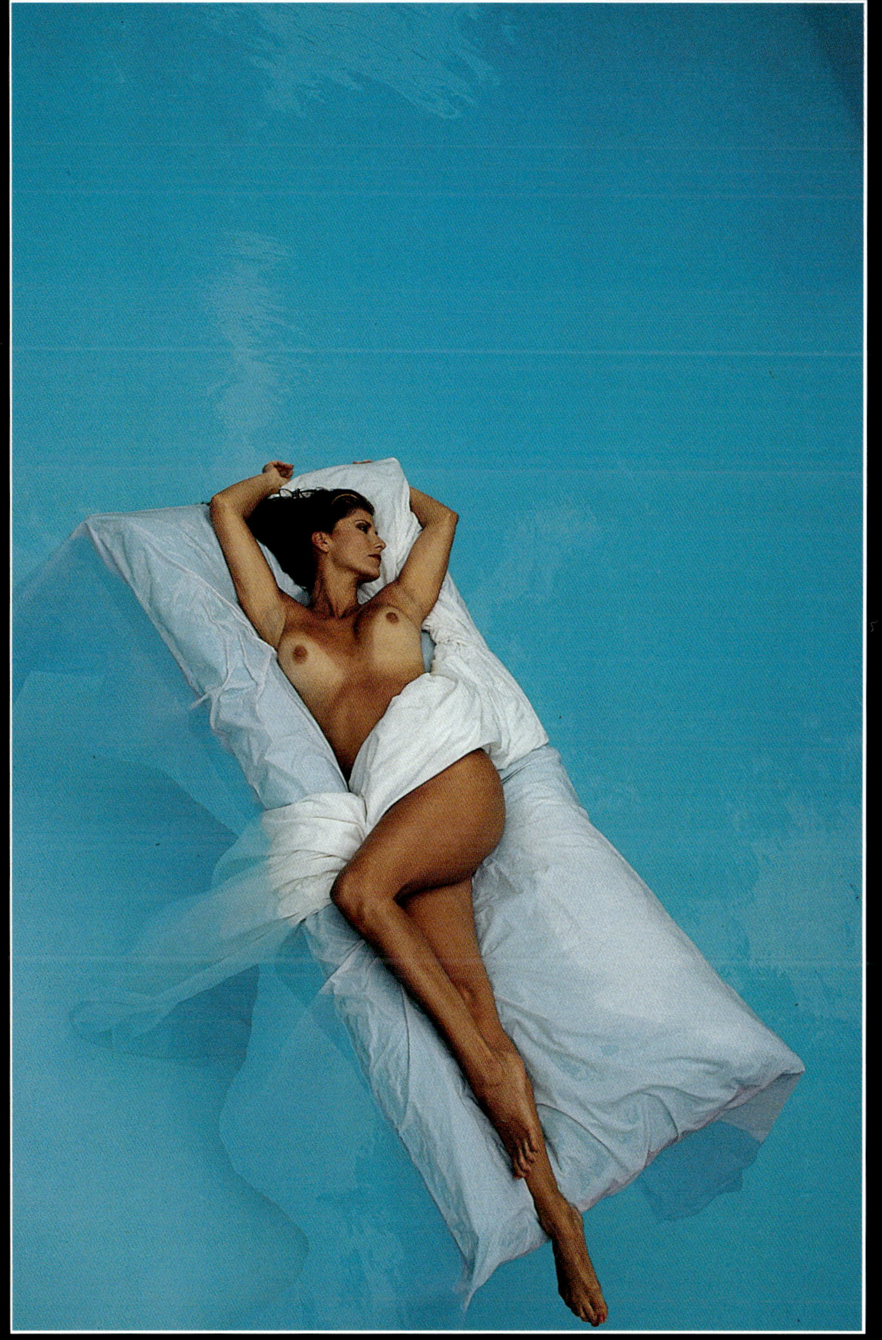

W I N D O W S   A N D   S H U T T E R S

Photographer: **Struan**

Use: **Poster out-take from magazine editorial shoot**

Assistant: **Michael Lee**

Camera: **35mm**

Lens: **85mm plus warming filter**

Film: **Kodachrome 64**

Exposure: **1/60sec at f/5.6**

Lighting: **Daylight, about 3–4 pm**

Props and set: **Location (Dubrovnik)**

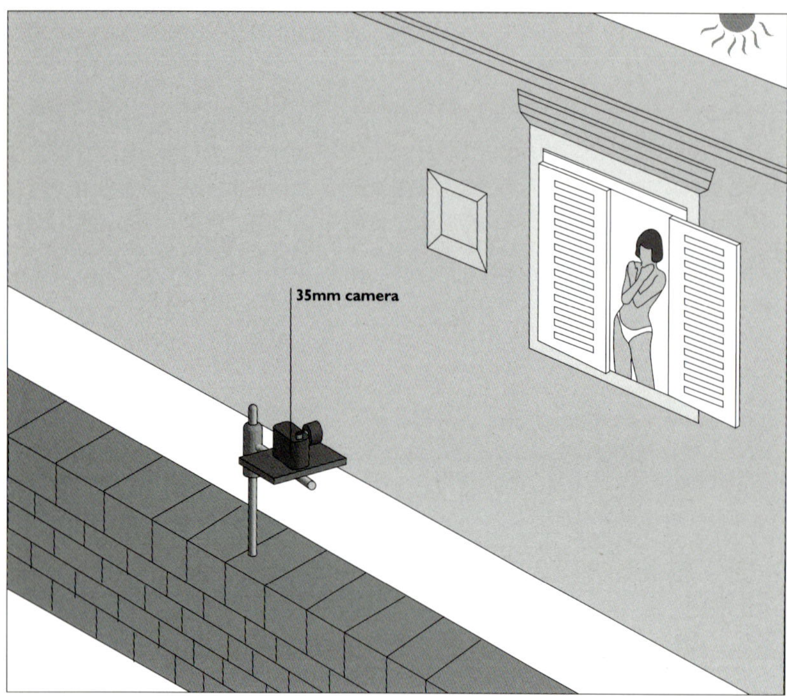

THIS WAS SHOT AT THE END OF A 10-DAY SHOOT IN DUBROVNIK, IN WHAT WAS THEN YUGOSLAVIA. STRUAN WAS INTRIGUED BY THE OCHRE WALLS OF THE HOUSE, AND IN ORDER TO GET THE SHOT HE GOT UP ON THE CITY WALLS.

He had to walk several hundred yards to get to the nearest steps; then climb them; then walk back to be opposite the window. The model was the one who had been modelling clothes during the shoot. Behind her there is a curtain; behind that are the art director, etc., drinking wine and celebrating a successful end to the shoot. Above the girl, out of shot, there were three young men on a balcony. One of them was leaning out in an attempt to see her. He almost fell: his friends had to haul him in by his jacket.

Apart from the warming filter, there was little Struan could do to modify the light, though opening and closing the shutters made quite a difference to the shot

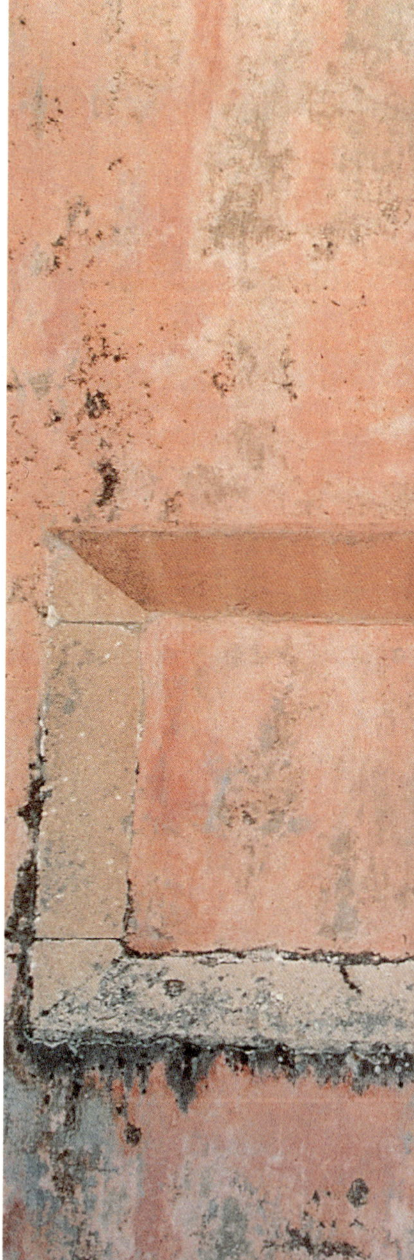

► *If the light is "wrong", there are always warming filters*

► *One advantage of standardizing on a limited range of films is that you know how they will behave under different lights*

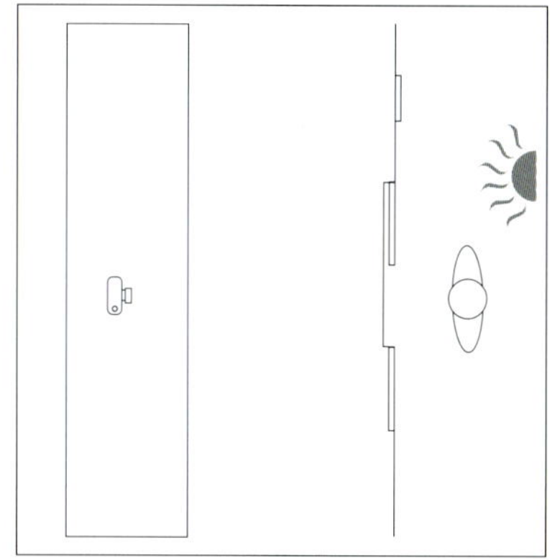

Plan View

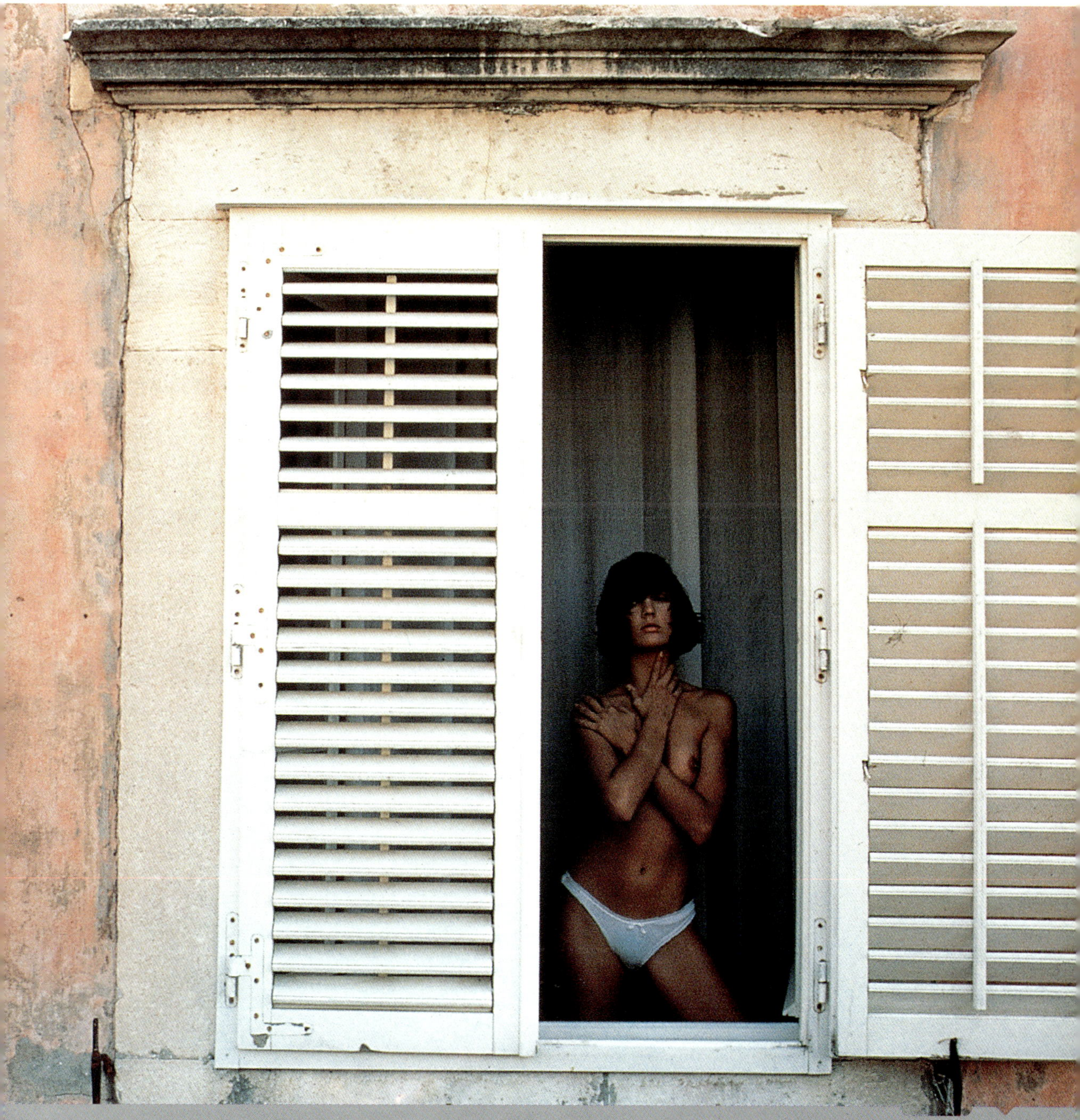

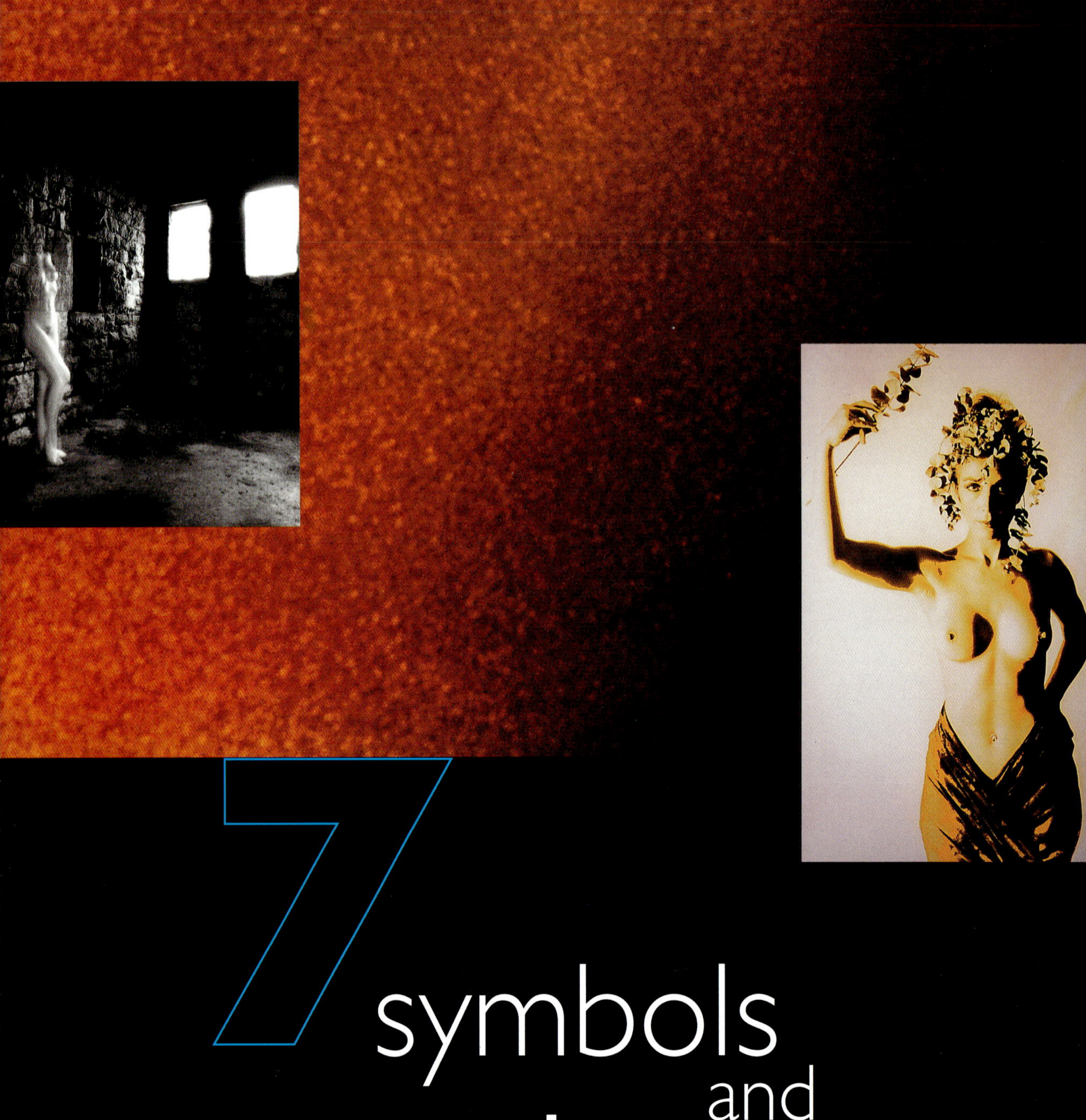

7
symbols and experiments

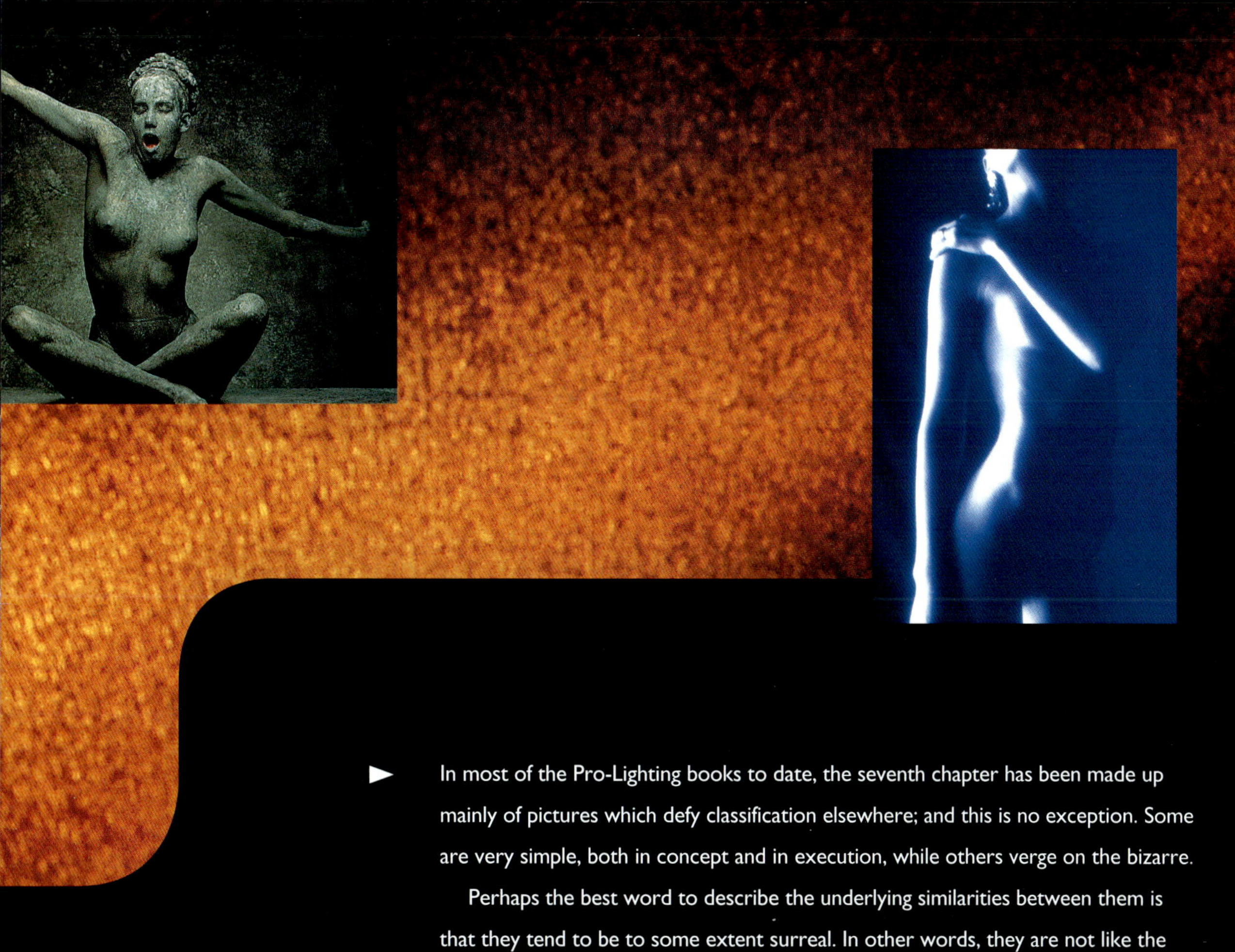

In most of the Pro-Lighting books to date, the seventh chapter has been made up mainly of pictures which defy classification elsewhere; and this is no exception. Some are very simple, both in concept and in execution, while others verge on the bizarre.

Perhaps the best word to describe the underlying similarities between them is that they tend to be to some extent surreal. In other words, they are not like the fantasies of Chapter 4; the twist which they impart to reality is often subtler, whether it be the architectural curve of a model above a shoe in Struan's advertisement for Charles Jordan, the uncertain presence of a ghostly model in Peter Goodrum's Infra-Red Nude, the abstraction of form and contour in Mike Dmochowski's Gold Close Up, or the impression of looking into another time in Ben Lagunas and Alex Juri's Maniki.

In this chapter 35mm predominates: the actual figures are four 35mm, three roll film, and (rather surprisingly) two on 4x5in. Extensive manipulation of the images – by toning, by hand colouring, or even by computer – renders it somewhat irrelevant which films were used; and the same could be said of the equipment. In fact, the message once again is that, always and above all, it is the photographer's eye that makes the picture. We hope that as you embark on this, the last chapter, you have been fired with new ideas and that you will find this book as much a source of inspiration as of information.

Photographer: **Ben Lagunas & Alex Kuri**

Client: **Private Art**

Use: **Gallery**

Assistant: **Isak de Ita**

Art director: **Ben Lagunas**

Stylist: **Alex Kuri**

Camera: **35mm**

Lens: **180mm**

Film: **Kodak LPP**

Exposure: **f/22**

Lighting: **Electronic flash: 4 heads**

Props and set: **White backdrop; flowers**

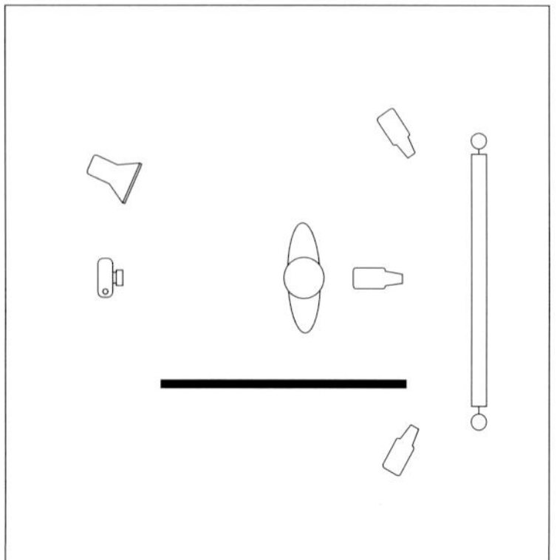

Plan View

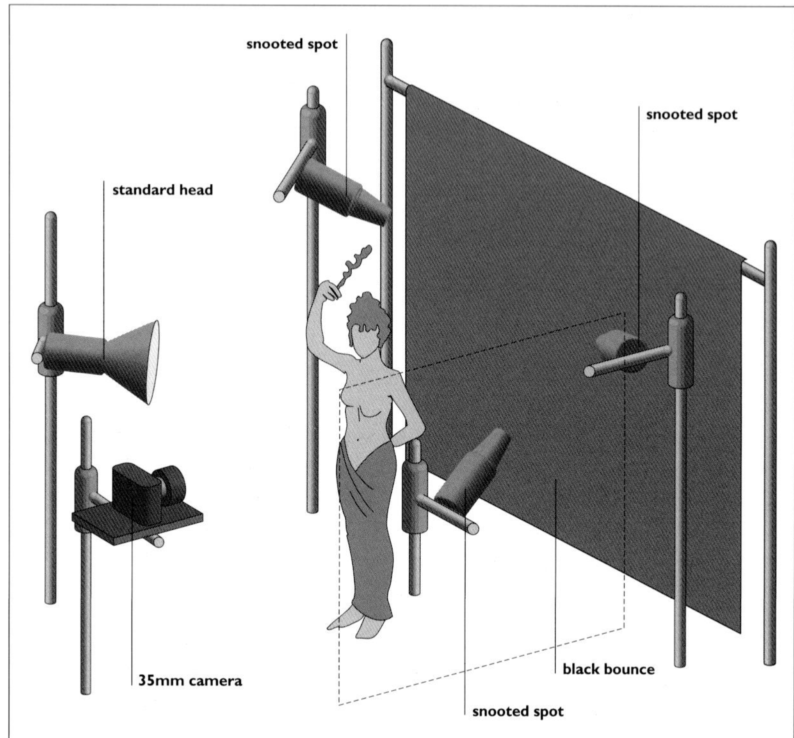

TONING AND DYEING CAN CONSIDERABLY INFLUENCE THE IMPACT OF A PICTURE — AND OFTEN, A TONED OR DYED IMAGE (BOTH TECHNIQUES WERE USED HERE) WILL CALL FOR CONSIDERABLY MORE DRAMATIC LIGHTING THAN WOULD BE USUAL IN A MORE CONVENTIONAL PHOTOGRAPH.

The lighting is actually quite simple. Three snooted spots illuminate the background brilliantly – lens flare from the brightness of the background reduces the model's raised arm to a sculptural mass – while the key light is a standard head to camera left. The extremely directional nature of the key light is emphasized still further by the use of a large black bounce to camera right, so there is no fill to speak of: this bounce absorbs light both from the key and from the background.

► *There are often several number of routes to a given effect. Instead of trying to duplicate an effect exactly, why not try another approach?*

► *Remember the possibilities for selective (limited-area) bleaching, toning, etc.*

► *Consider using lith films, printing mono negatives on colour paper, solarizing and more*

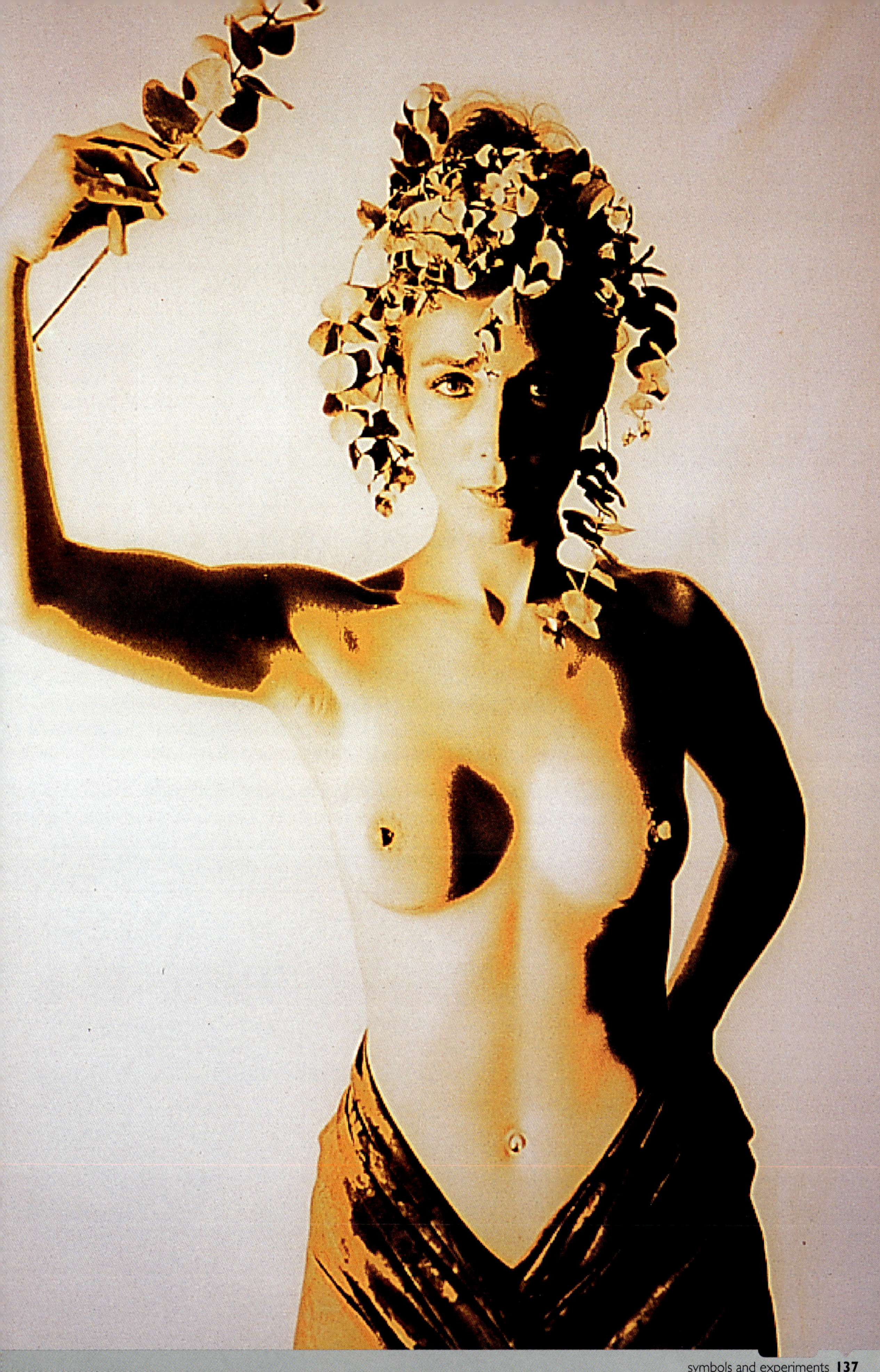

Photographer: **Ben Lagunas & Alex Kuri**

Client: **Private Art**

Use: **Gallery**

Model: **Kate**

Assistant: **Isak de Ita**

Stylist: **Manolo**

Camera: **35mm**

Lens: **180mm**

Film: **Kodak Ektachrome EPT**

Exposure: **1/60sec at f/8**

Lighting: **Tungsten: 4 heads**

Props and set: **Black background; colour
introduced with gels**

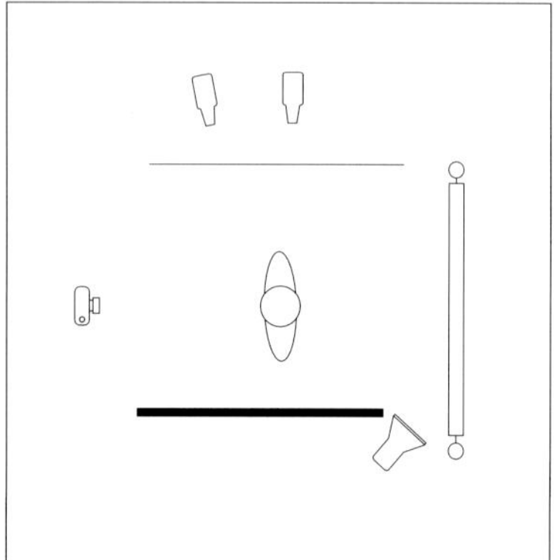

Plan View

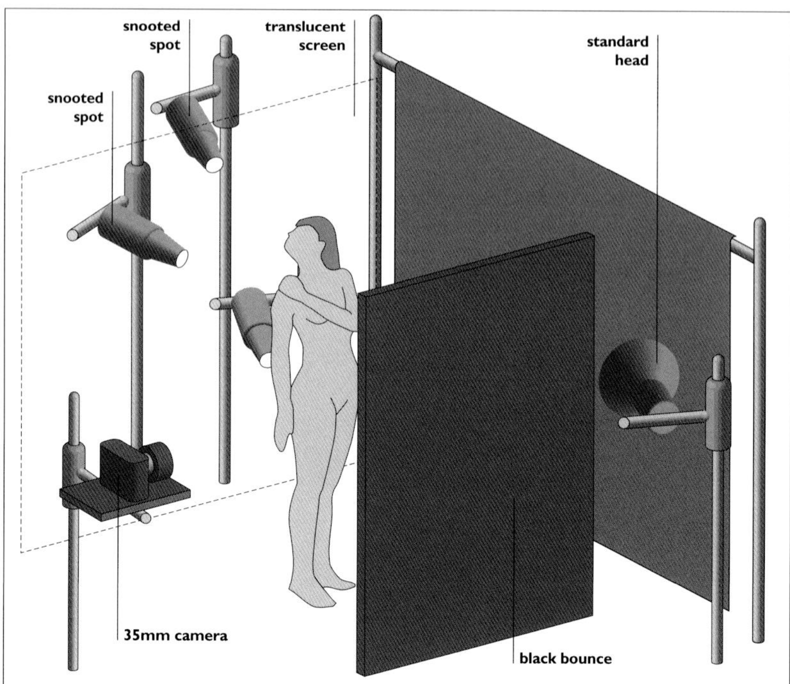

Again and again, photographers debate the question of literalness versus interpretation. There is no doubt that interpretation is riskier, because a literal image can be judged by objective criteria; but an interpreted image often has something which is missing from a mere likeness.

The key light is a big, soft source created by shining three snooted spots through a translucent screen to camera left. Snooted spots may seem an odd choice until you realize that they allow the accurate placement of diffused light: the effects obtainable are quite different from what one would get with a large, uniform diffused light source. A black bounce to camera right darkens the side of the model which is away from the light, while a fourth light introduces just enough light to the background to differentiate the model's figure from it. Despite the differences in technique, this resembles some of Brandt's pictures taken with an ultra-wide lens on large format.

▶ *Different focal lengths render an out-of-focus image in different ways*

▶ *Dramatic side lighting is often most effective with deliberately out-of-focus images*

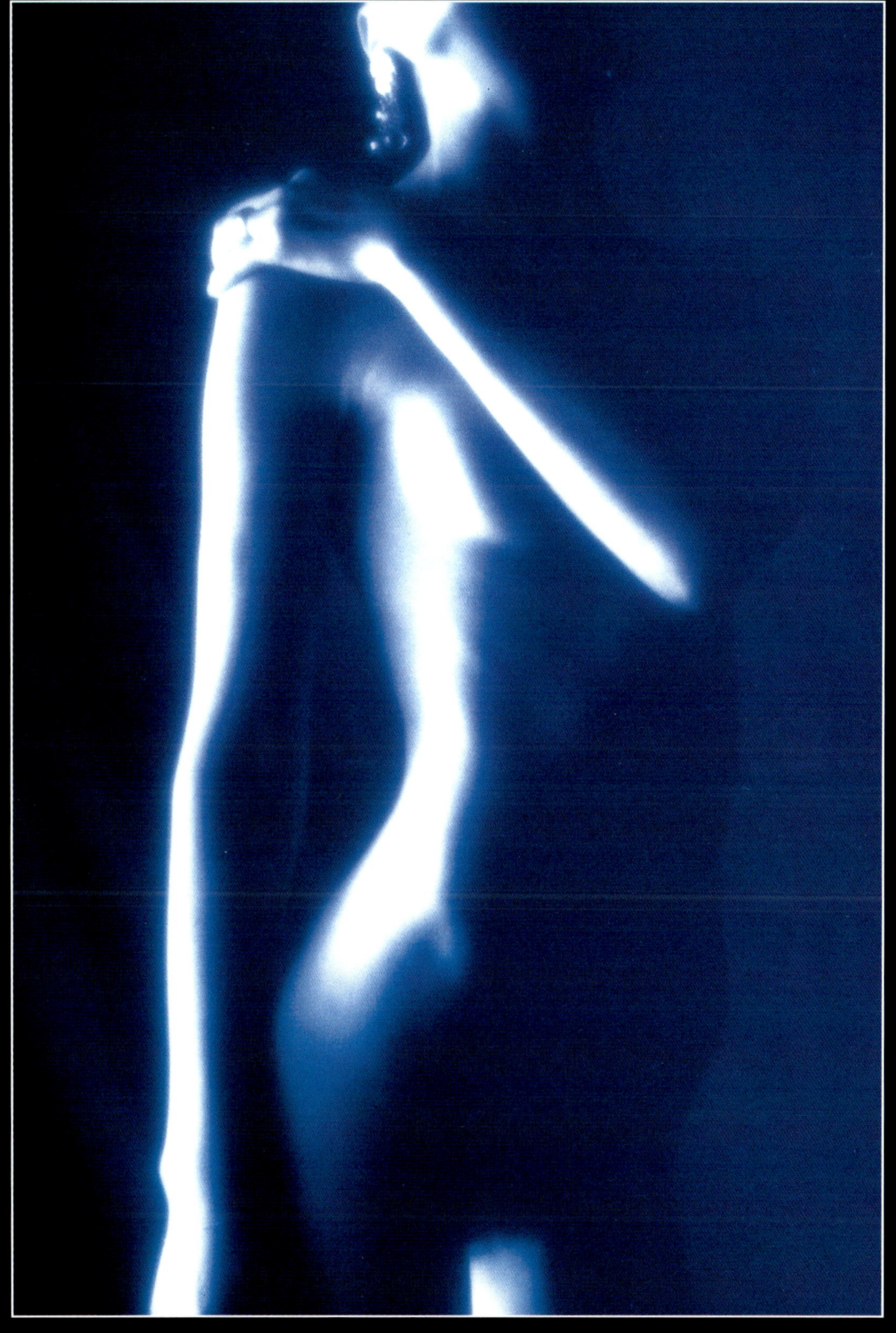

Photographer: **Ben Lagunas & Alex Kuri**

Client: **Private art**

Use: **Gallery**

Model: **Andrea**

Assistant: **Isak de Ita**

Stylist: **Michel**

Camera: **4x5in**

Lens: **210mm**

Film: **Kodak monochrome; image subsequently coloured**

Exposure: **f/16**

Lighting: **Electronic flash: 4 heads**

Props and set: **Dress, mannikin**

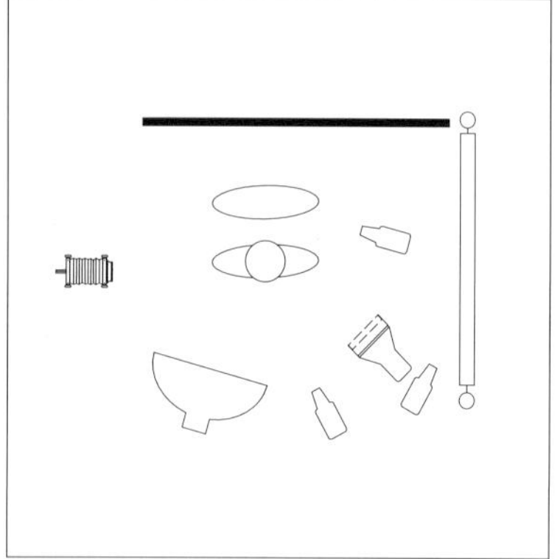

Plan View

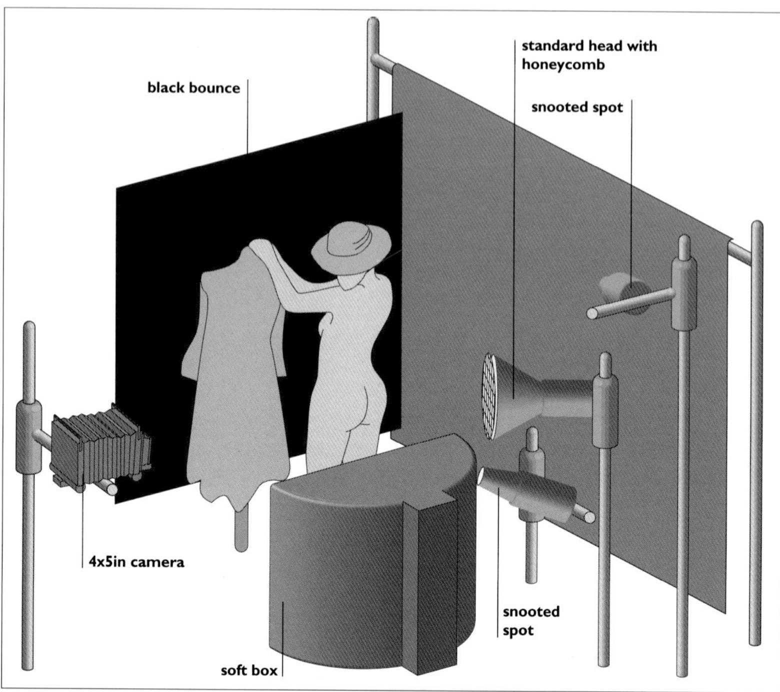

PARADOXICALLY, PHOTOGRAPHY CAN OFTEN SAY MORE ABOUT A SUBJECT (AND SAY IT MORE REALISTICALLY) BY MEANS OF CONTRIVANCE AND ARTIFICE THAN CAN BE SAID WITH A LITERAL LIKENESS USING ULTRA-REALISTIC COLOUR FILMS.

This is a monochrome image which has been toned, dyed and hand-coloured, but it manages to create a dream-like atmosphere which would be very hard to convey with a more conventional image.

The lighting from camera right is highly directional: a standard head with a honeycomb back lights the model very slightly (look at the shadows) while a soft box softens the directionality of the light slightly. A third light, this time a snooted spot, grazes the background to create the light patch above the model's head while a fourth (a snooted spot again) differentiates the side of the dress from the very dark background. A black bounce to camera left emphasizes the directionality of the lighting, ensuring that there is no fill to speak of.

► *Some photographers never use black bounces; others use them all the time. What could they do for your pictures?*

► *Use extra effects lights to differentiate small areas such as the side of the dress*

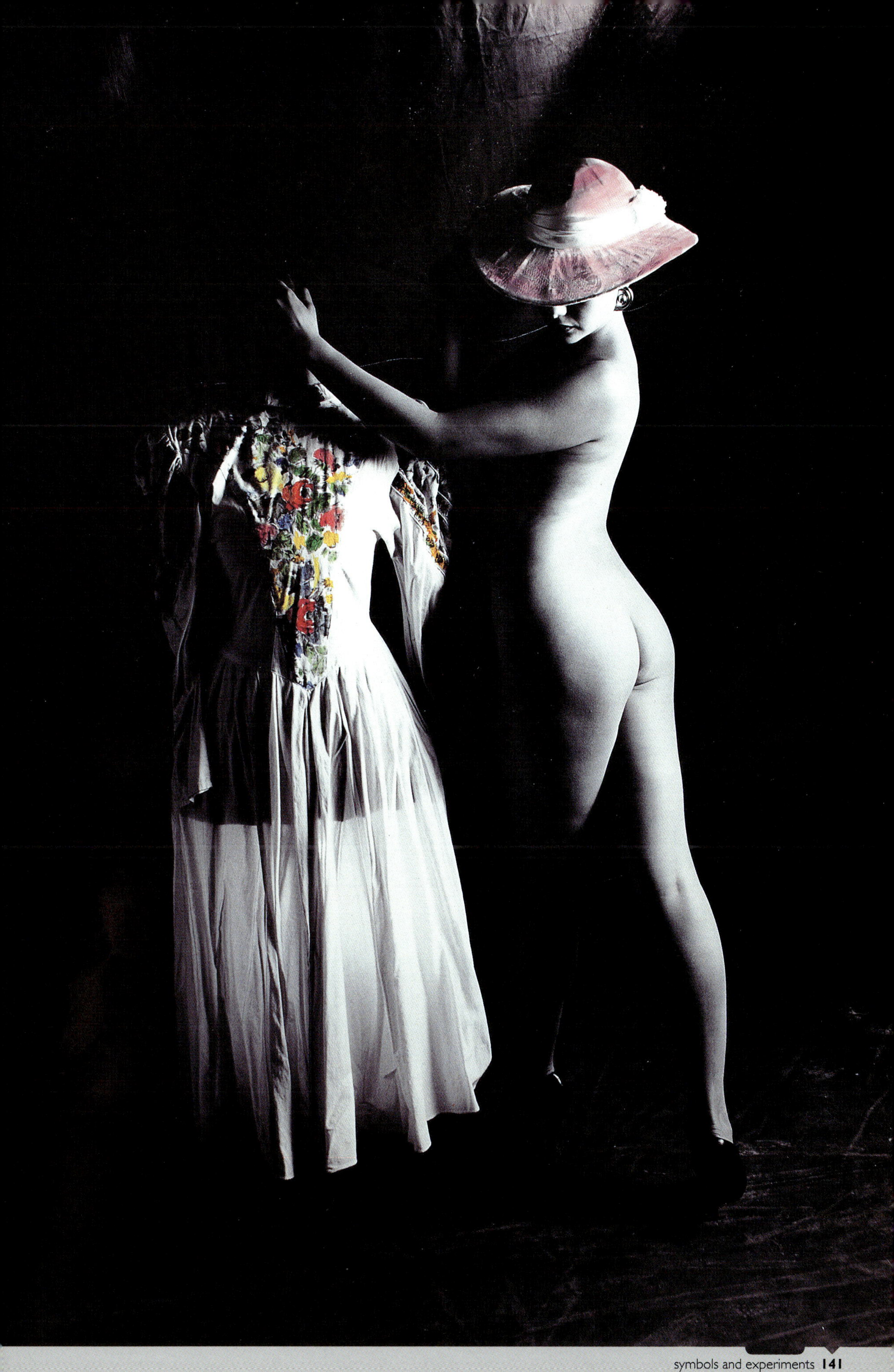

Photographer: **Mike Dmochowski**

Use: **Self promotional**

Model: **Dawn (who also acted as stylist)**

Camera: **35mm**

Lens: **200mm with warming filter**

Film: **Kodak Ektachrome EPP**

Exposure: **f/11**

Lighting: **Electronic flash: 1 head, filtered**

Props and set: **Gold body paint, black velvet, black paper**

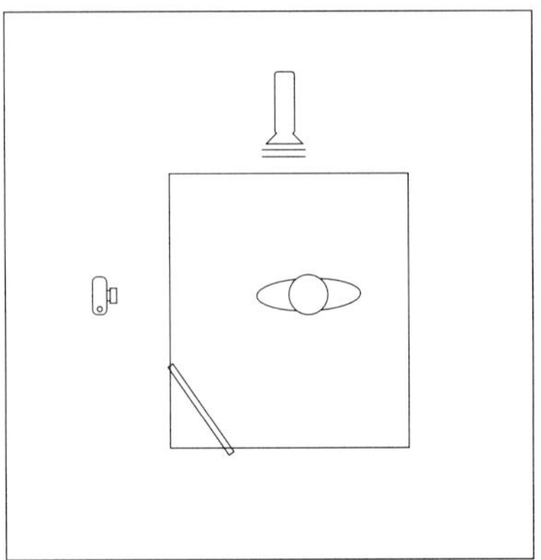

Plan View

GOLD CLOSE UP

▼

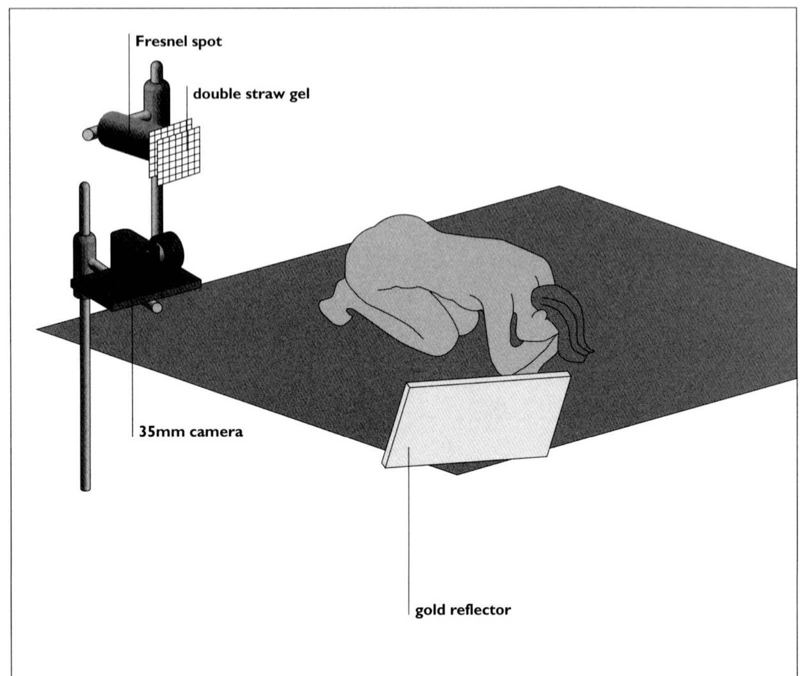

THERE ARE NO FIXED BOUNDARIES IN PHOTOGRAPHY. IS THIS A CLASSICAL NUDE? AN EXPERIMENT? AN ABSTRACT? FOR THAT MATTER, SOME WOULD NO DOUBT RAIL AGAINST IT BECAUSE IT DEPICTS THE NUDE HUMAN FORM. BUT THE DEFINITIONS DO NOT MATTER. IT IS A GOOD PHOTOGRAPH.

The model is painted gold with body-paint. A Fresnel flash to camera left is the key, and indeed the only, light. It is filtered with a double straw gel, and sits about 30cm (12in) above the floor, some 120cm (4ft) from the model. The fill comes from camera right, a gold reflector (size not recorded) about 30cm (12in) from the model. A warming filter over the lens adds still more to the intensity and warmth of the gold – and it is interesting to speculate what effects might have been obtained with other film stocks.

► *Black velvet photographs about a stop darker than black seamless background paper*

► *Gold can be intensified by colouring the lights; by filtration over the camera lens; by film choice; by exposure; and by push processing*

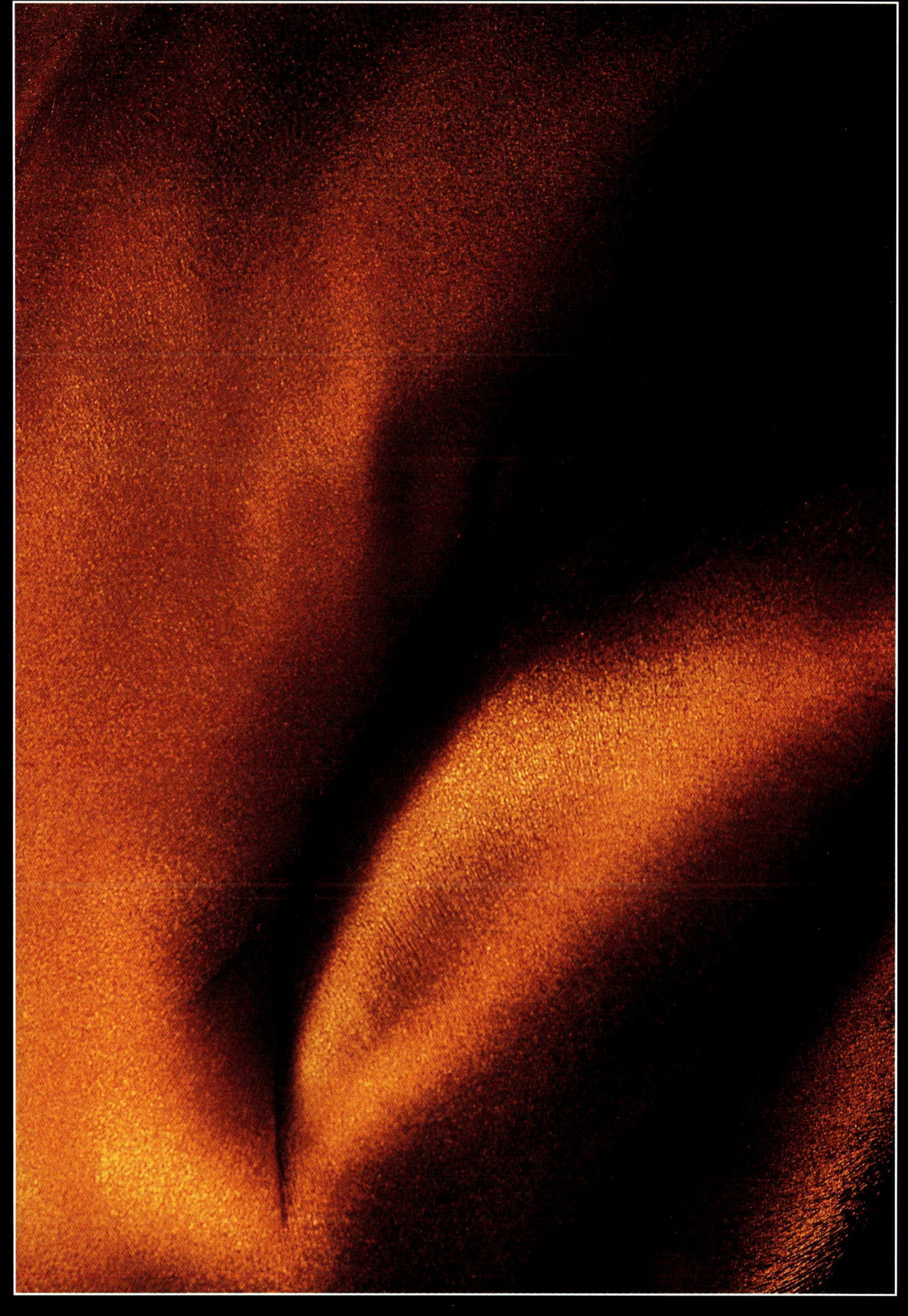

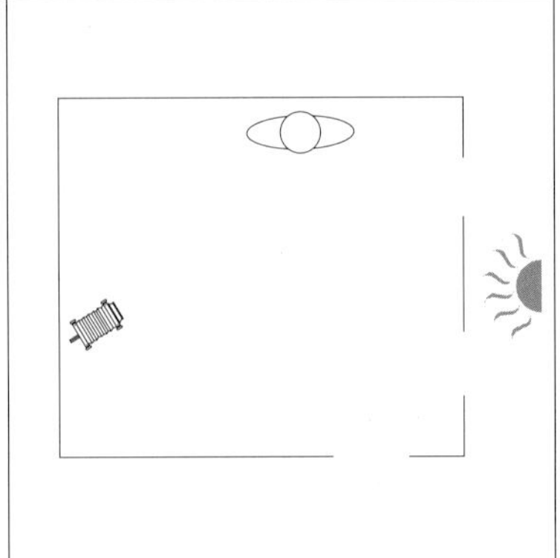

Photographer: **Peter Goodrum**

Use: **Portfolio**

Model: **Jo Rowden**

Camera: **4x5in**

Lens: **90mm**

Film: **Kodak Infrared**

Exposure: **32sec at f/6.8**

Lighting: **Available light**

Props and set: **Location: Brean Down fort**

Plan View

► *Infrared can give impressive flare and halation*

► *Pictures involving movement may need a good deal of rehearsal*

► *Polaroid tests are invaluable for checking the effects of movement*

INFRARED NUDE

▼

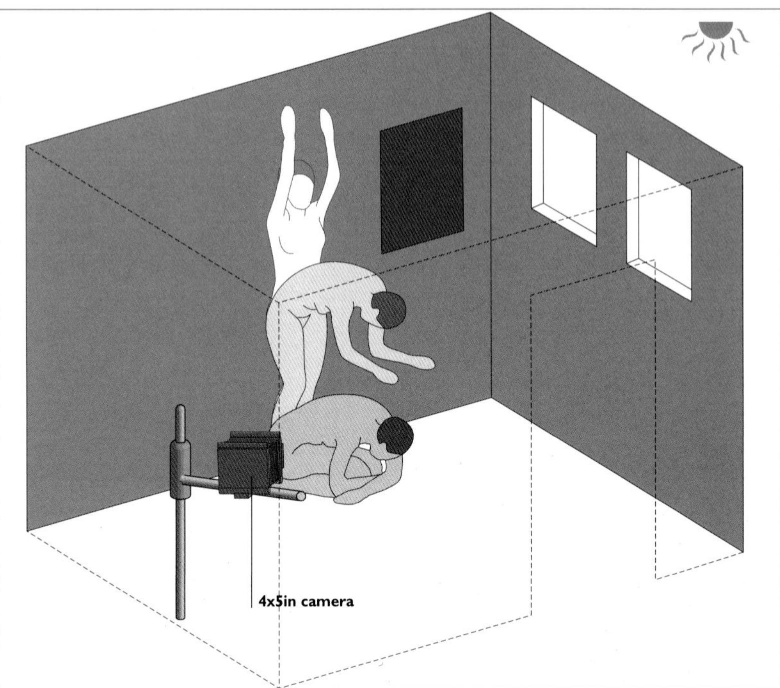

OLD SCHNEIDER ANGULONS ARE NOT SUPPOSED TO BE USED WIDE OPEN: THEY ARE NOT SHARP UNTIL ABOUT F/16. INFRARED IS NOT NORMALLY THE FILM OF CHOICE FOR NUDES. NOT MANY SHOOT NUDES ON 4X5IN.

Peter Goodrum let none of this stand in his way. This picture was shot purely by available light, from the two window apertures and a door behind the camera. At the beginning of the long exposure, the model was curled up in a ball on the floor. Next, she stood up so that her legs were more or less in the position recorded, but her body was at right angles to the wall: she was bowed at the waist. Finally, she straightened up, but moved her arms and head quite vigorously so that they would not record at all.

The flare around the windows is characteristic of infrared materials, which give a sort of liquidity to the light, and the effect is accentuated by the softness of the lens when used wide open.

Photographer's comment:

I made the print on Cotman watercolour paper coated with Silverprint Cold Tone emulsion, over-exposed a couple of stops and then bleached back before toning in Rayco Varitone Sepia.

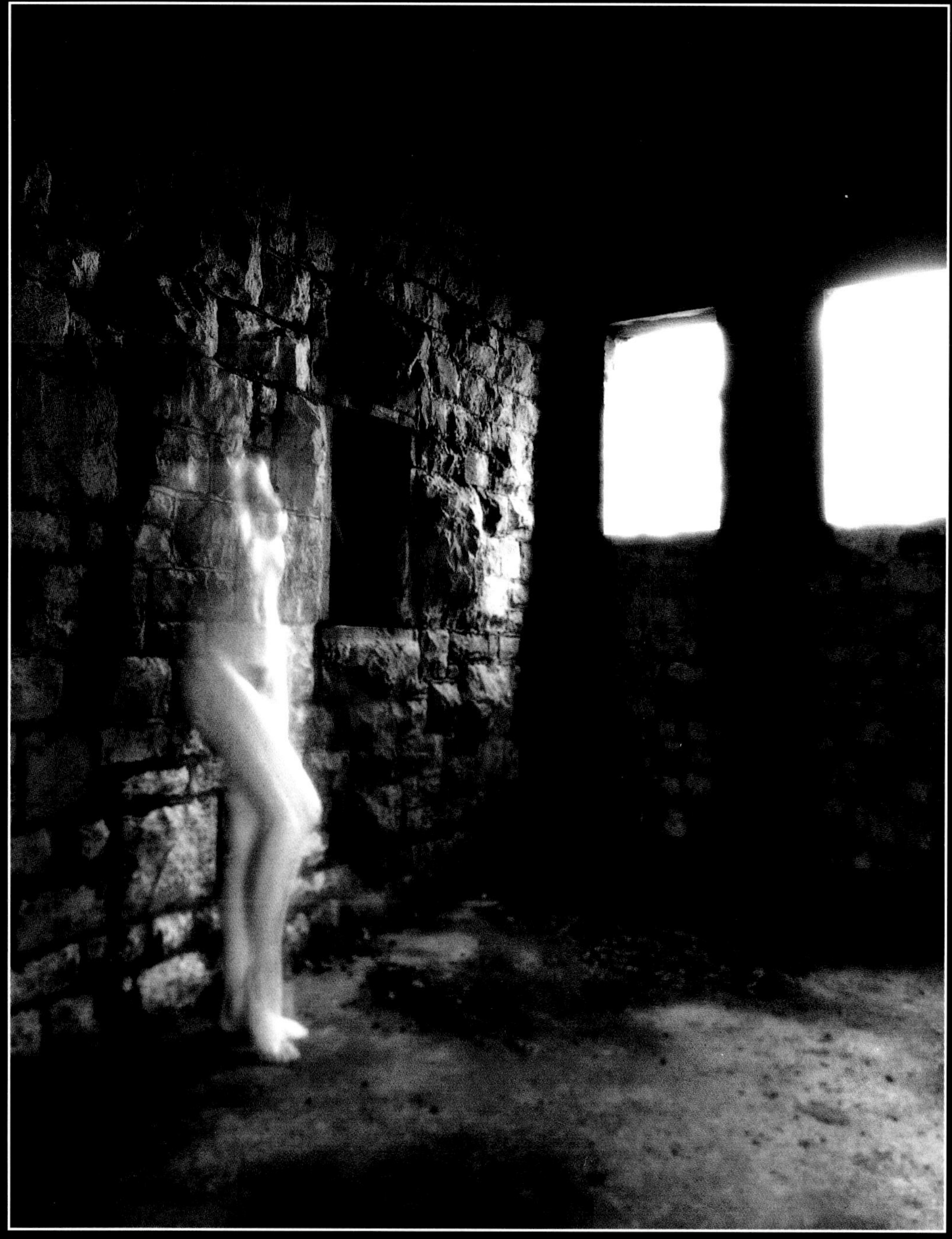

Photographer: **Rod Ashford**
Use: **Personal work, later sold as a book cover**
Model: **Geraldine Barrett**
Camera: **35mm**
Lens: **70-210mm**
Film: **Ilford FP4**
Exposure: **f/11**
Lighting: **Electronic flash: 1 head**
Props and set: **Sunflower**

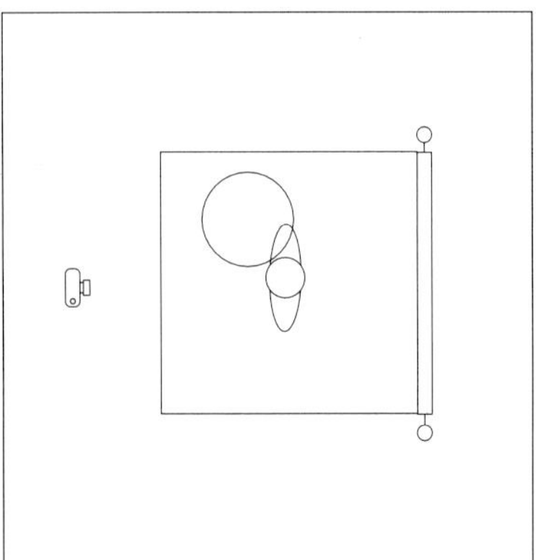

Plan View

GERALDINE AND THE FLOWER

▼

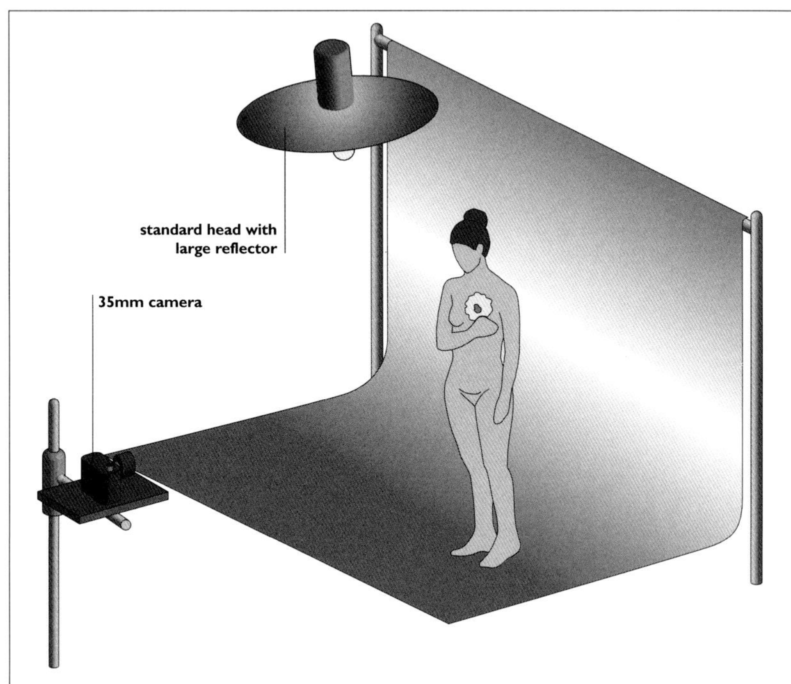

ROD ASHFORD IS FOND OF HAND COLOURING, ALTHOUGH, AS HIS WORK DEMONSTRATES, HAND COLOURING IS MOST EFFECTIVE IF YOU HAVE A GOOD PICTURE TO BEGIN WITH. IT ALSO HAS AN AFFINITY WITH SEPIA.

There is only one light in this picture, a single large-reflector head set high and to the model's right (camera left): from the shadows, you can see quite clearly where it was. The quality of this light, sold as a 65-degree reflector, is subtly different from that of a soft box: it is about 45cm (18in) in diameter, and it is not highly polished on the inside.

There is no bounce at all to camera right because Rod wanted dramatic chiaroscuro, although he says, "I may have overdone this – I think I had to bring her left side up a little in printing".

► *Many good photographers are critical of their own pictures, even if those pictures receive unqualified praise elsewhere*

► *Naturalistic colouring of green foliage is not as easy as one might hope*

► *Half-close your eyes and note the distribution of tones in this picture; it is superb*

Photographer's comment:

This was sold as a poster under the name "Passion Flower" but I like my working title better.

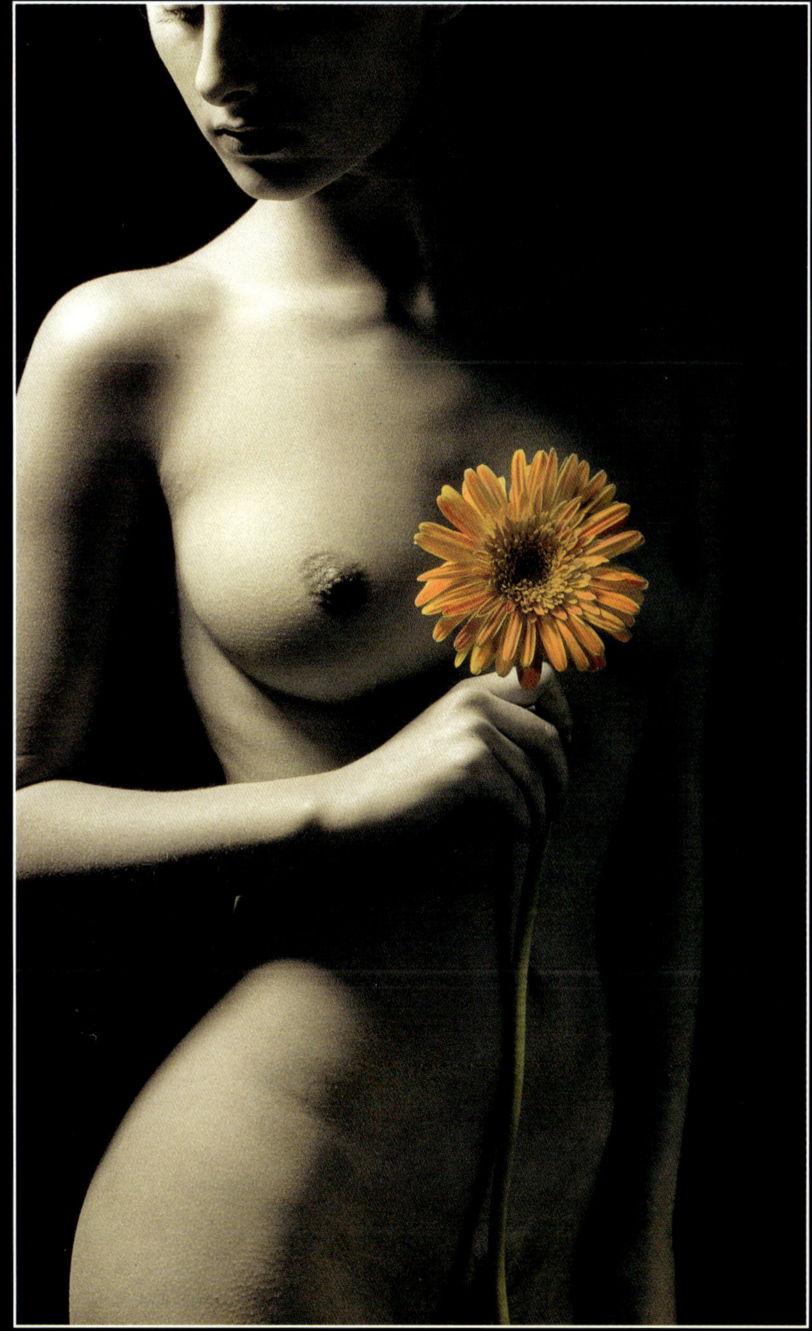

P A I N T E D   L A D Y

Photographer: **Struan**

Client: **Creative Source (out-take)**

Use: **Poster advertising**

Camera: **6x6cm**

Lens: **150mm**

Film: **Kodak Ektachrome EPN ISO 100**

Exposure: **f/11**

Lighting: **Electronic flash: 2 heads**

Props and set: **Green canvas (and see text)**

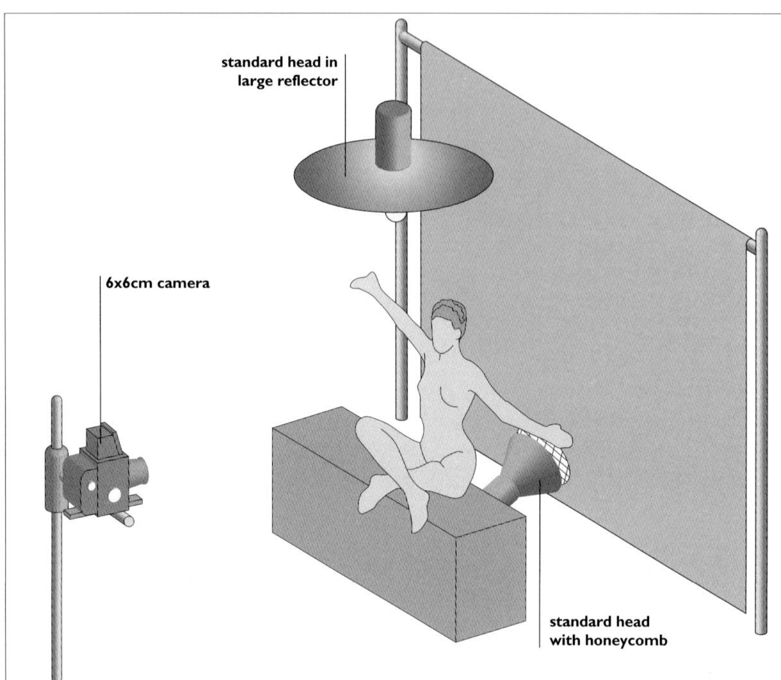

THIS IS ONE OF THOSE SHOTS WHICH TOOK SIX HOURS TO PAINT AND MAKE UP, AND ABOUT HALF AN HOUR TO SHOOT. THE MODEL WAS PHOTOGRAPHED IN VARIOUS POSES, AND THIS IS ONE OF THE ONES WHICH WAS NOT USED.

The lighting is straightforward. The key light is a standard head in a 90cm (3ft) round reflector, pretty much directly over the model: look at the shadows. The only other light is a standard head with a 40° honeycomb for the background.

Otherwise, what you see is what was there. The model was made up to match the background, and her head-dress was made up from plasticine and plaster of Paris – the same stuff that is used for arm casts. Only skilled and experienced make-up technicians should apply this stuff: if it sets into the model's hair, it can mean trouble.

▶ *Professional make-up is sometimes the only realistic way to get a picture*

▶ *Make-up and paints can reflect different amounts of UV, making for a mismatch on film*

▶ *Some pictures are the result of an evolutionary process; others must be fully visualized before they are taken*

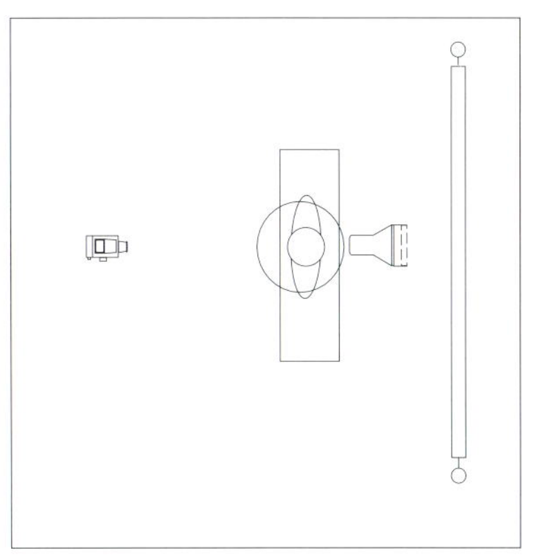

Plan View

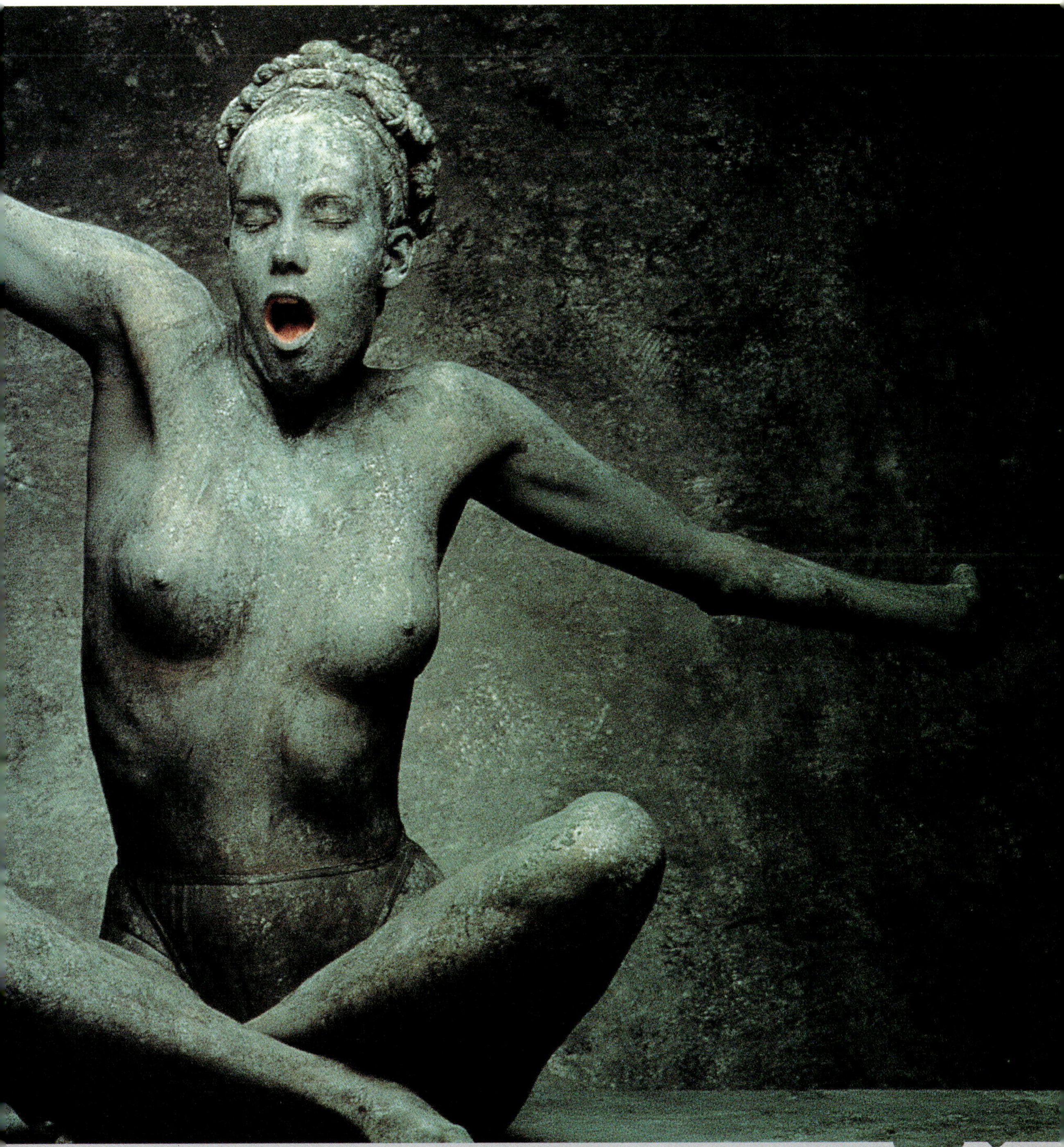

Photographer: **Guido Paternò Castello**

Use: **Self-promotion**

Model: **Telma Merces dos Santos**

Assistant: **Fernando Ribiero**

Camera: **6x6cm**

Lens: **50mm**

Film: **Kodak Verichrome Pan**

Exposure: **f/11**

Lighting: **Electronic flash: 3 heads**

Props and set: **White background paper**

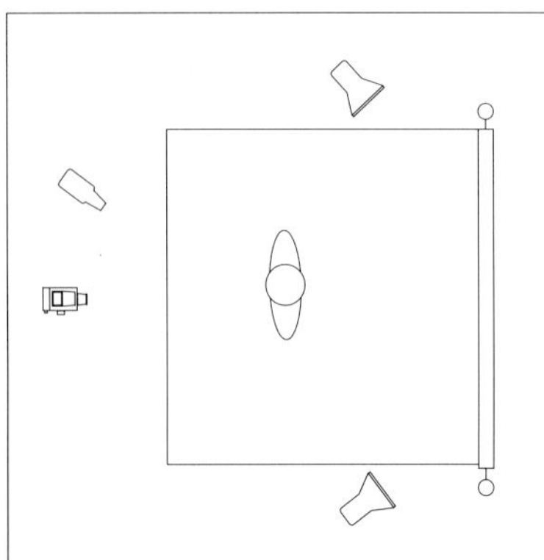

Plan View

► *Extreme wide-angle lenses can create fascinating distortions*

► *Be relentlessly self-critical with distorted nudes; compare your work with the very best*

► *Note how many successful nude distortions make use of out-of-focus areas in the image*

▼

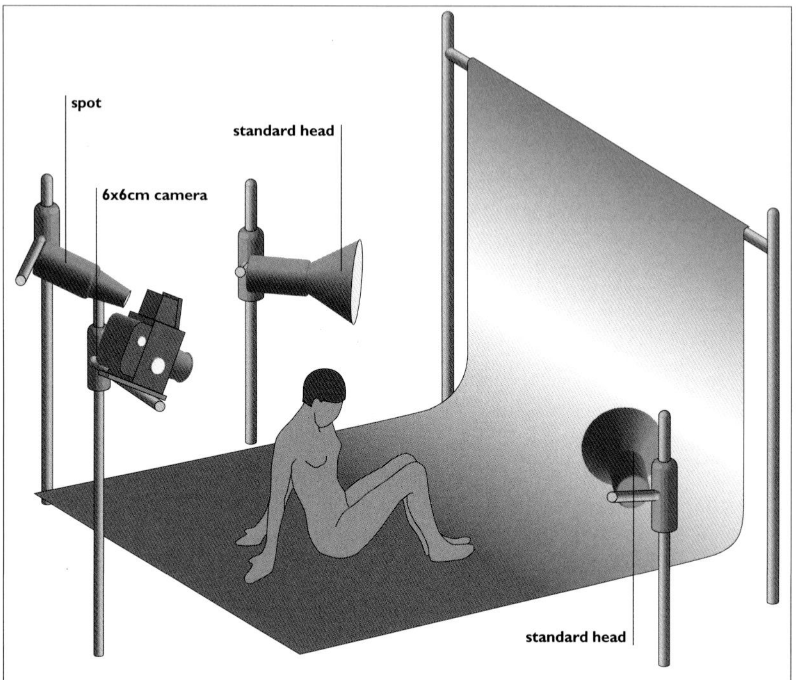

WIDE-ANGLE DISTORTIONS IN NUDE PHOTOGRAPHY HAVE BEEN EXPLORED BY MANY GREAT PHOTOGRAPHERS — BILL BRANDT SPRINGS TO MIND — BUT THEY ARE VERY HARD TO DO SUCCESSFULLY WITHOUT LOOKING AWKWARD OR (WORSE STILL) GROTESQUE.

A large part of the secret, as in most kinds of nude photography, lies in suppressing unwanted detail. Guido Paternò Castello achieved this by shooting on Verichrome black and white film; inputting the resultant image to a Power Mac; and then shooting the image off the screen using colour film.

The dramatic lighting emphasizes the graphic shape of the model's pose and makes her shadow an integral part of the composition. It is simple but effective: two standard heads on the background for a classic high-key effect, and one spot on the model herself from high on the camera left. The unusual camera angle makes it unclear at first whether the picture should be "portrait" (as printed here) or "landscape", with the model's head to the right and hands to the left.

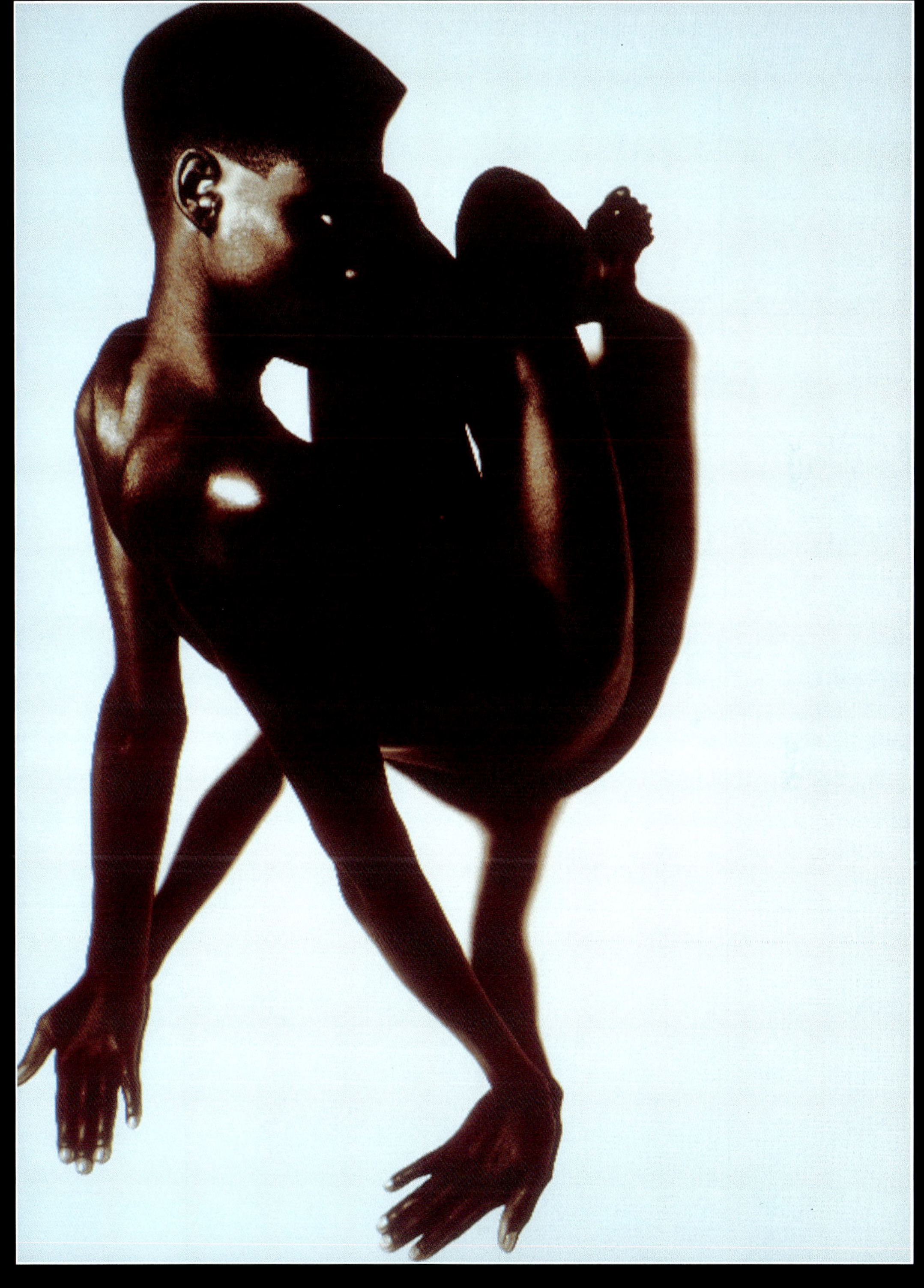

CHARLES JORDAN

▼

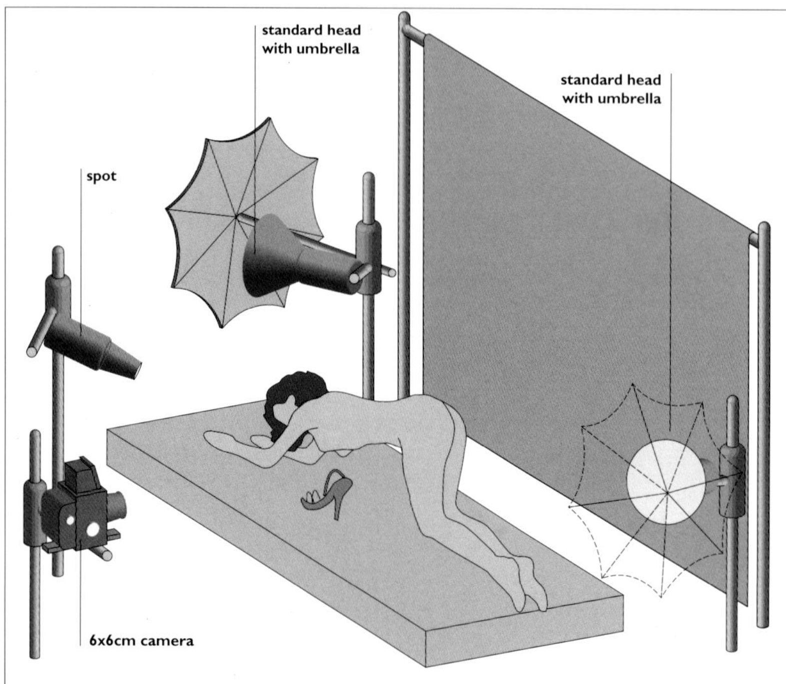

Photographer: **Struan**

Client: **Charles Jordan**

Use: **Billboard**

Camera: **6x6cm**

Lens: **150mm**

Film: **Kodak Ektachrome EPN**

Exposure: **f/11**

Lighting: **Electronic flash: 3 heads**

Props and set: **White paper and black Mylar**

THIS IS AN EXCELLENT ILLUSTRATION OF HOW A CONCEPT EVOLVES, OFTEN VIA LOTS OF POLAROID TESTS. ORIGINALLY, THE MODEL'S LEG WAS TO HAVE PARALLELED THE HEEL, AND THE SHOE WAS TO HAVE STOOD ON SILVER OR WHITE MYLAR; BUT NEITHER IDEA WORKED.

The model's pose had to be changed or it would have been next to impossible to keep a reasonable balance between her and the shoe: it was a question of scale. Also, the shoe just did not reflect properly, so black Mylar was substituted – and that is what you see here. Because Mylar is highly reflective, even black Mylar reflects the brightly-lit white background perfectly, while the reflection is much more saturated.

As for the actual lighting, there were two umbrellas on the white background to light it 2 stops up from the shoe, and a very tight spot (a narrow angle grid, maybe 10°) to illuminate just the shoe, not the model.

Photographer's comment:

When I first showed this to the client he didn't realize there was a nude in it. The image is now in the National Archives of Canada.

- *Always be prepared to modify a concept if it does not work*

- *With highly reflective plastics, black can often give better saturated colour in a reflection than you would get from silver or white*

- *Very tight honeycomb grids can be even more versatile than focusing spots for some shots*

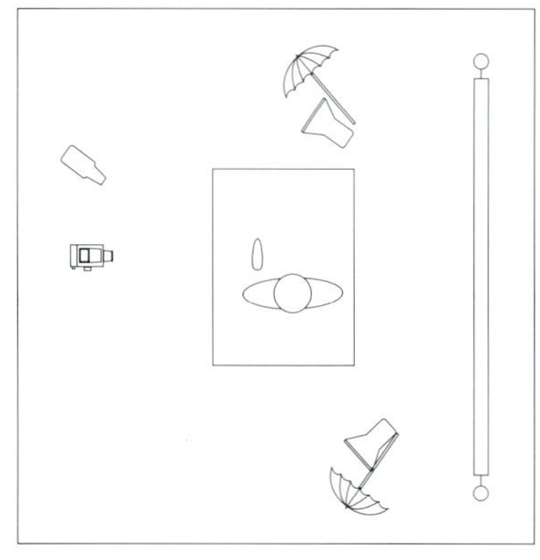

Plan View

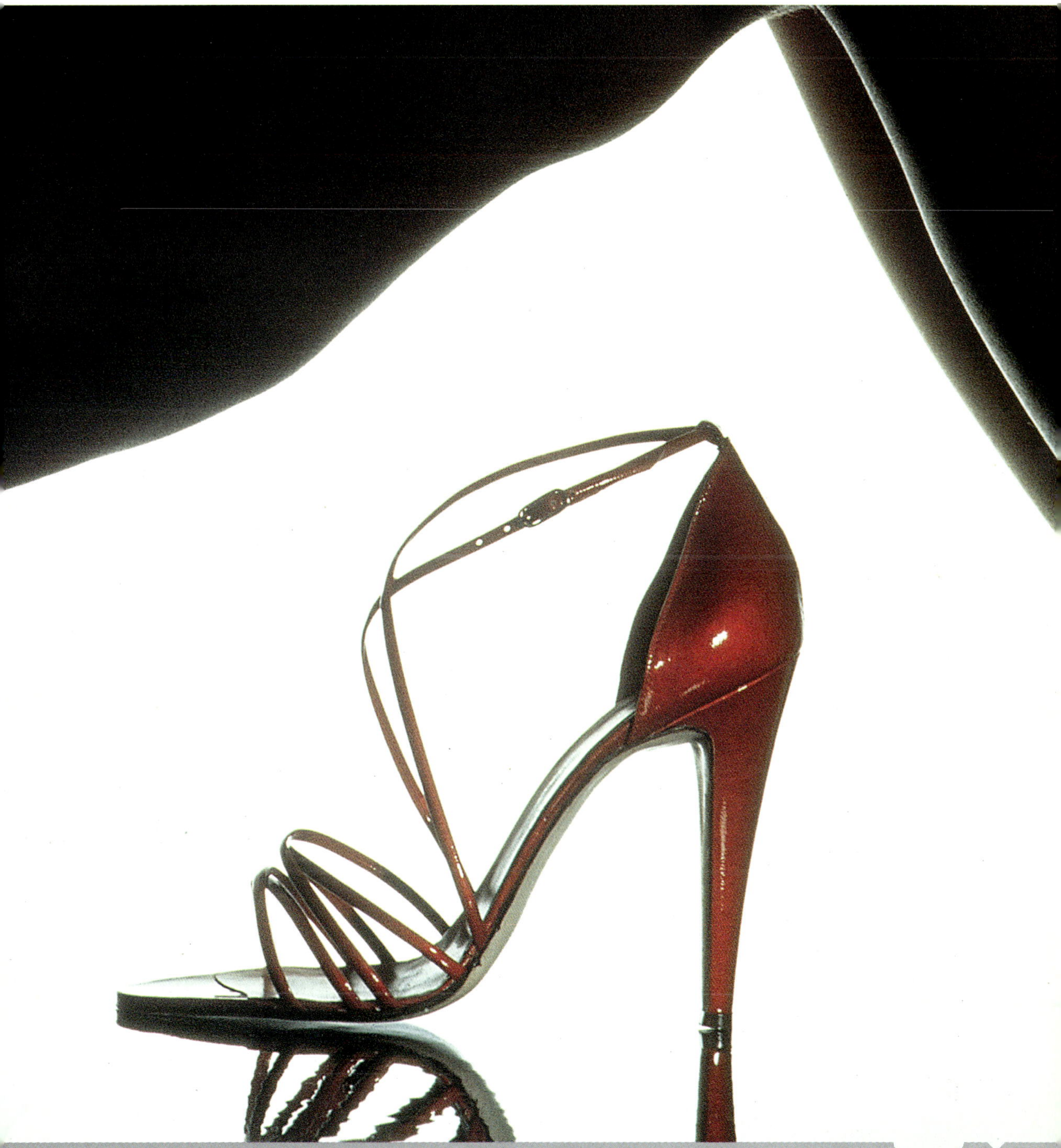

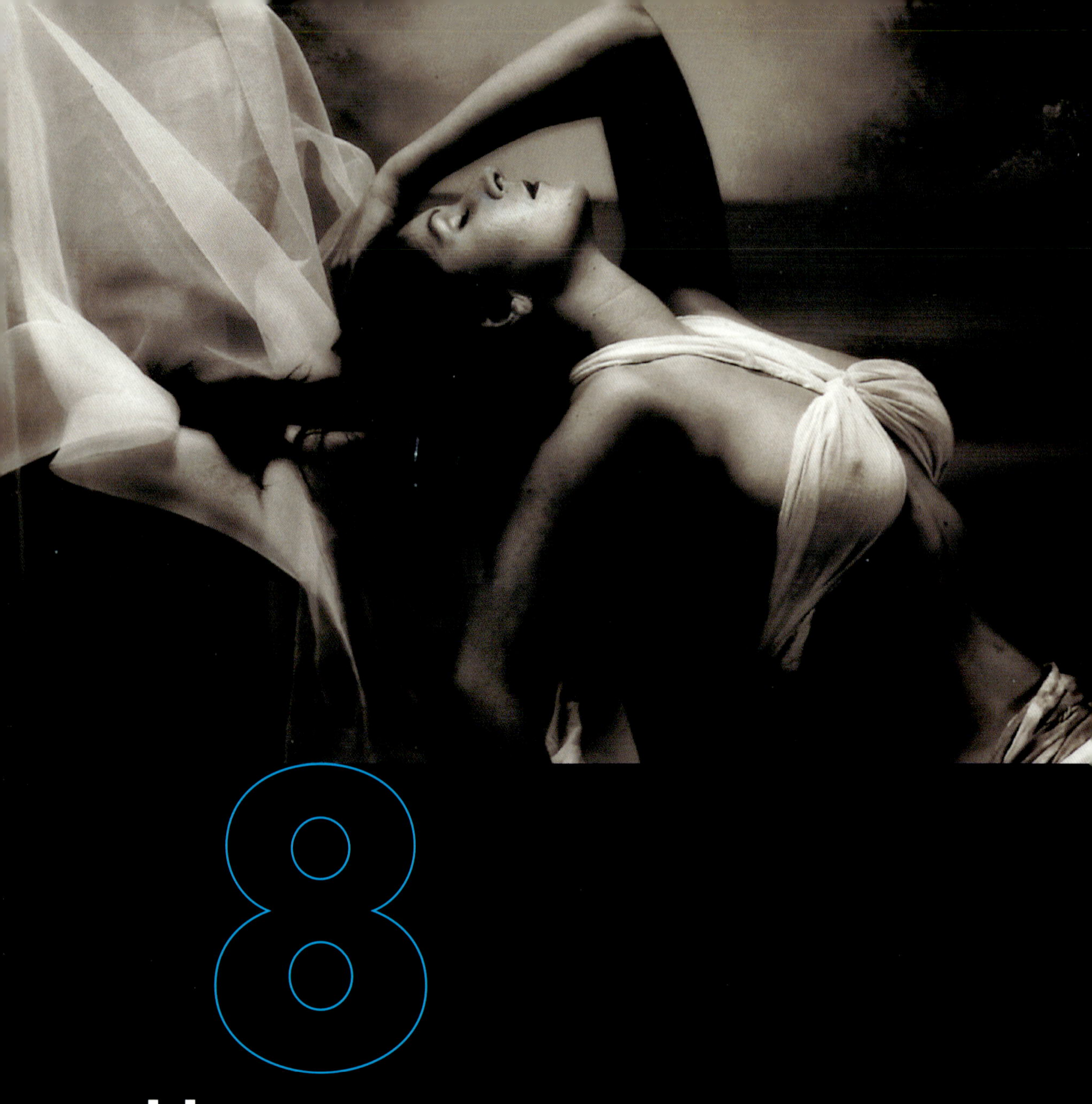

8

directory of photographers

Photographer: **ROD ASHFORD**
Address: UNIT 10
ARUNDEL MEWS
ARUNDEL PLACE
KEMPTOWN
BRIGHTON BN2 1GD
ENGLAND
Telephone: + 44 (0) 1273 670 076
Mobile Phone: + 44 (378) 036 287
Biography: *Rod runs a commercial photographic studio and a busy stock library. His personal work consists mainly of black and white and hand-coloured images which have been widely published as fine art posters and postcards. His work is in great demand for both hardback and paperback book covers in the UK, Europe and the United States. Commercial clients have included American Express, Elizabeth Arden, Revlon, Lloyds, South Eastern Electricity Board and Iceland Frozen Foods.*
Nudes: pp 58, 147

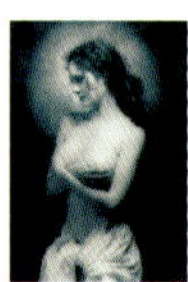 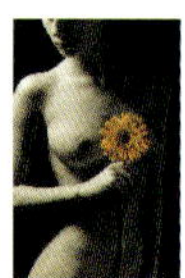

Photographer: **PETER BARRY**
Address: 57 FARRINGDON ROAD
LONDON EC4M 3JB
ENGLAND
Telephone: + 44 (0) 171 430 0966
Fax: + 44 (0) 171 430 0903
Biography: *Peter Barry's work is extremely varied — fashion, advertising, girls, still life and food — so every day is different, exciting and stimulating. Constantly learning and experimenting with new techniques, his two main passions are people and food. He has travelled all over the world and met many fascinating people and as a result he feels that photography is not so much work as a way of life.*
Nudes: pp 73, 93

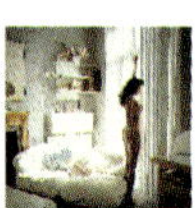 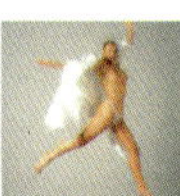

Photographer: **GUIDO PATERNÒ CASTELLO**
Address: AV. HENRIQUE DODSWORTH 83/1005
RIO DE JANEIRO 22061-030
BRAZIL
Telephone: + 55 (0) 21 5218064
Fax: + 55 (0) 21 2870789
Biography: *Born in New York City March 19, 1958. Associate Arts degree at the American College in Paris: June 1979. Bachelor of Arts degree in Industrial and Scientific Photographic Technology at Brooks Institute of Photographic Arts and Science: June 1984. Presently working in Brazil as a commercial photographer. His clients are all major agencies based*

in Rio de Janeiro. He has won various awards including silver medal in 1992 and gold medal in 1993 at the Prêmio Produçao from ABRACOMP (Brazilian Association of Marketing and Advertising).
Nude: p 151

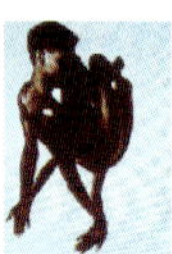

Photographer: **BENNY DE GROVE**
Studio: FOTOSTUDIO DE GROVE
Address: ZWIJNAARDSE STEENWEG 28A
9820 MERELBEKE
BELGIUM
Telephone: + 32 (0) 9 231 96 16
Fax: + 32 (0) 9 231 95 94
Biography: *Born 1957, he has been a photographer since 1984. Most of the time he works in publicity and illustration magazines. For some time now he has been fascinated by triptychs. He likes to make his pictures somehow symbolic: they must be a starting point for discussion, for thinking about.*
Nudes: pp 82-83, 85

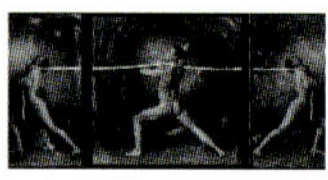 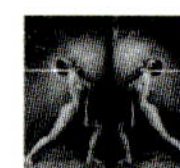

Photographer: **MIKE DMOCHOWSKI**
Studio: STILLS-IN-THE-STICKS
Address: PHOENIX FLAUNDON LANE
FELDON
HERTS HP3 0PA
ENGLAND
Telephone: + 44 (0) 831 321 202,
(0) 1923 211 077
Fax: + 44 (0) 1923 228 702
Biography: *Mike specializes in people and still lifes, often with complex built sets, working for major international clients. He used to do a good deal of "trick" and special effects photography, but increasingly supplies what he calls "jigsaw pieces" to be assembled electronically. He is well known for his glamour photography and has produced a video on lighting for glamour called CAPTURED SECRETS, which is available from the above address.*
Nudes: pp 41, 103, 121, 143

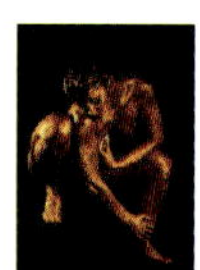 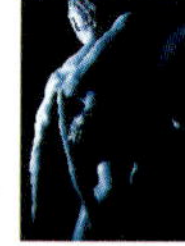
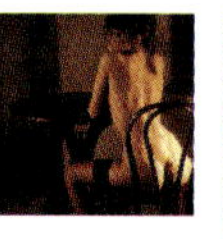 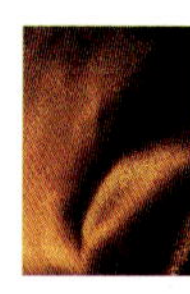

Photographer: **MICHÈLE FRANCKEN**
Studio: N.V. FRANCKEN
Address: VLAANDERENSTRAAT 51
9000 GENT
BELGIUM
Telephone: + 32 (0) 9 225 4308
Fax: + 32 (0) 9 224 2132
Biography: *Créer une ambiance avec la lumière et la composition. Travaillant beaucoup en location pour trouver plus d'intimité. Me sentant à l'aise aussi bien en mode qu'en publicité. Cherchant le moyen technique d'émouvoir le spectateur!*
Nude: p19

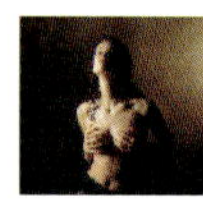

Photographer: **PETER GOODRUM**
Address: 2 HILLEND COTTAGES
KEWSTOKE ROAD
WORLE
WESTON-SUPER-MARE
AVON
ENGLAND
Telephone: + 44 (01) 1934 516 178
Biography: *Peter Goodrum has turned his hobby of the early 1980s into a career for the 1990s and beyond. As a book illustrator, he was hit hard by the recession: clients, art directors and advertising agencies vanished overnight, so in 1993 he decided to do a degree in photography at Cheltenham. He now looks upon this as the best thing ever to happen to him, both for exploring new ideas and techniques and for his personal development. He now specializes in photographing people — he particularly likes to photograph artists — and works for editorial, advertising and corporate clients as well as establishing a growing reputation as a photographic printer.*
Nude: p 145

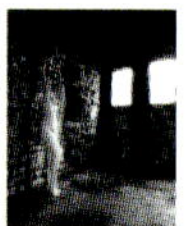

Photographer: **KAY HURST**
Studio: K STUDIOS
Address: 9 HAMPTON ROAD
GREAT LEVER
BOLTON
LANCASHIRE BL3 3DX
ENGLAND
Telephone: + 44 (0) 1204 366 072
Biography: *K's work is concerned with the positive representations of women: women seen as assertive without being viewed as aggressive, women seen as natural without being viewed as uncultural, women seen as feminine without being viewed as passive. Her images have been exhibited in a number of leading galleries and have received major*

Nudes: pp 49, 87

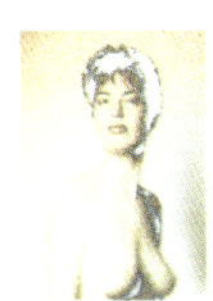
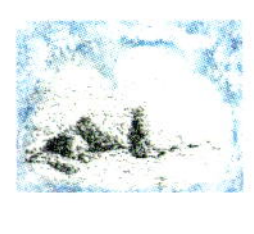

Photographer: **BEN LAGUNAS AND ALEX KURI**
Studio: BLAK PRODUCTIONS PHOTOGRAPHERS
Address: MONTES HIMALAYA 801
VALLE DONE CAMILO
TOLUCA
MEXICO CP 50140
Phone/Fax: + 52 (0) 72 17 06 57
Biography: *Ben and Alex studied in the USA,
and are now based in Mexico. Their
photographic company, BLAK
Productions, also provides full production
services such as casting, scouting, etc.
They are master photography instructors
for Kodak; their editorial work has
appeared in international and national
magazines, and they also work in fine
art, with exhibitions and work in
galleries. Their work can also be seen in
The Golden Guide, the Art Directors'
Index, and other publications. They work
all around the world for a client base
which includes advertising agencies,
record companies, direct clients and
magazines.*

Nudes: pp 137, 139, 141

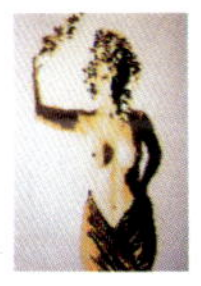
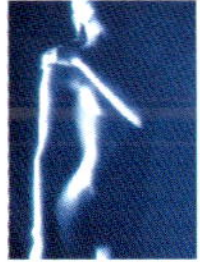
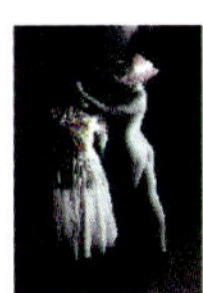

Photographer: **HARRY LOMAX**
Address: THE ANNEXE
NORMAN HOUSE
HENLEY-IN-ARDEN B95 5AA
ENGLAND
Telephone: + 44 (0) 1564 794 001
Fax: + 44 (0) 1564 794 752
Mobile Phone: + 44 (0802) 282 765
Biography: *Well known as an architectural
photographer and best recognized for
his interior work; buildings don't move or
answer back, or at least they shouldn't!
Harry, like most professionals, looks at
photography as a way of life rather than
as a business and so relaxes with a*

camera (plus a gin and tonic).
*He has – and who in this business has
not – shot glamour work for calendars
and magazines but likes to concentrate
on figure work, especially using complex
multi-images such as the girl and the
dragon. He much prefers to work on his
5x5 monorail, which is his favourite tool
because of ease of composition and the
discipline needed in any situation, but he
has sometimes been known to use
smaller formats for speed and
portability.*

Nudes: pp 81, 125

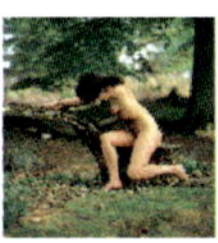
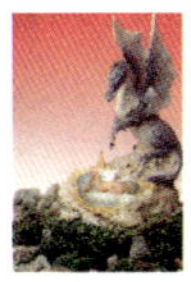

Photographer: **JULIA MARTINEZ**
Address: FLAT 2
37 LANSDOWN CRESCENT
CHELTENHAM
GLOUCESTERSHIRE GL50 2NG
ENGLAND
Telephone: + 44 (0) 1242 255 094,
(0) 1341 421 029
Mobile Phone: + 44 (589) 722 973
Biography: *After completing a degree in
photography in 1995, Julia finds that her
passion for the subject continues to
grow. Her forte is beauty photography,
in particular her ability to bend the light
in such a way that the bad points
disappear and a beautiful person
emerges. She agrees this may be
deceiving, but who says the camera
never lies? Her reputation and client list
is rapidly growing, by word of mouth
recommendation alone, and she spends
several months a year shooting abroad.
If she does not respond promptly to
messages on her answering machine,
please call the 1341 421 029 number
above.*

Nudes: pp 30-31, 33, 113, 115

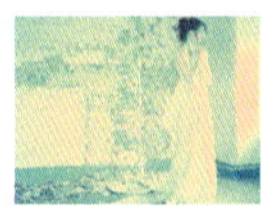
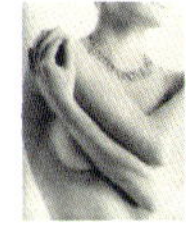
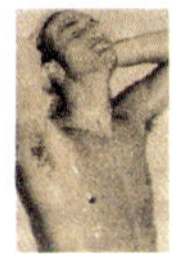
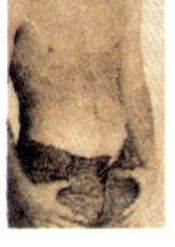

Photographer: **RON MCMILLAN**
Address: THE OLD BARN
BLACK ROBINS FARM
GRANTS LANE
EDENBRIDGE
KENT TN8 6QP
ENGLAND
Telephone: + 44 (0) 1732 866111

Fax: + 44 (0) 1732 867223
Biography: *Ron McMillan has been an advertising
photographer for over twenty years. He
recently custom built a new studio,
converting a 200 year old barn on a
farm site, on the Surrey/Kent borders.
This rare opportunity to design his new
drive-in studio from scratch has allowed
Ron to put all his experience to use in
its layout and provision of facilities
including a luxury fitted kitchen. Ron's
work covers food, still life, people, and
travel, and has taken him to numerous
locations in Europe, the Middle East
and the USA.*

Nude: p 23

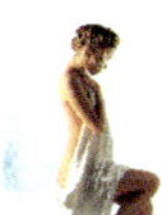

Photographer: **JORDI MORGADAS**
Address: DIPUTACIÓN 317
LO 08009 BARCELONA
SPAIN
and LOS NELEES S/N
22145 RADIQUERO
HUESCA
SPAIN
Telephone: + 34 (0) 3 488 25 68
Fax: + 34 (0) 3 488 34 65
Biography: *Born in April 1946. At 19, he decided
to concentrate totally on photography.
Self-taught, like many of his generation,
he found work in many fields from
portraiture to industrial photography
to magazine photography as a
correspondence for the EFE agency.
Later, his nude photography appeared
in such magazines as Playboy,
Penthouse and Interviù, including
a number of cover pictures. Now,
he works exclusively in advertising,
specializing in beach wear, lingerie
and nudes.*

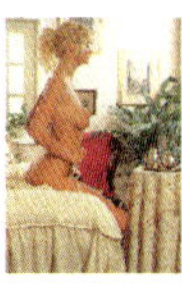

Photographer: **TERRY RYAN**
Studio: TERRY RYAN PHOTOGRAPHY
Address: 193 CHARLES STREET
LEICESTER LE1 1LA
ENGLAND
Telephone: + 44 (0) 116 254 46 61
Fax: + 44 (0) 116 247 0933
Biography: *Terry Ryan is one of those
photographers whose work is constantly
seen by a discerning public without
receiving the credit it deserves. Terry's
clients include The Boots Company Ltd.,
British Midlands Airways, Britvic,
Grattans, Pedigree Petfoods, the Regent
Belt Company, Volkswagen and*

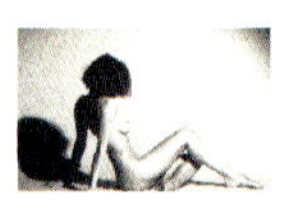 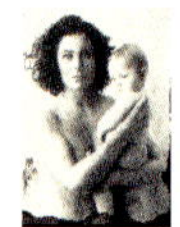

Photographer: **BOB SHELL**
Studio: BOB SHELL PHOTOGRAPHY
Address: 1601 GROVE AVENUE
RADFORD
VA 24141
USA
Telephone: +1 (0) 540 639 4393
Fax: +1 (0) 540 633 1710
Biography: *Bob is editor of Shutterbug, the world's
third largest monthly photo magazine,
and is on the technical staff of Color
Foto, Germany's major photo
magazine. He has also been editor
and publisher of a major UK photo
magazine. His photographs and his
writings about photography have been
published in books and magazines all
over the world, and he is the author of
fourteen books on photographic topics.
He holds several workshops a year
for professional and amateur
photographers, both in the studio and
in a variety of outdoor locations.*
Nudes: pp 21, 123

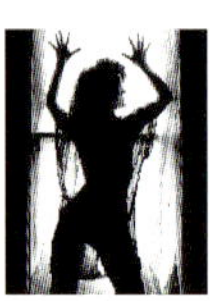 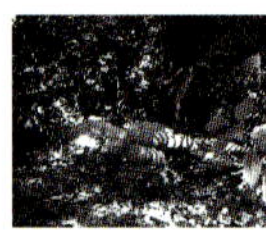

Photographer: **STRUAN**
Address: 60 HERBERT AVENUE
TORONTO
ONTARIO M4L 3P9
CANADA
Telephone: +1 (0) 416 698 6768
Fax: +1 (0) 416 698 3338
Biography: *"Intuition, simplicity and passion – these
are the ingredients I use to create the
images that keep me on the edge."
The early part of Struan's life was spent
mostly in Europe: London, Paris and
Geneva. After a year at Toronto's
Ryerson University in 1969, he opened
his own studio in Toronto in 1970, but
in 1989 he gave up his large studio and
full time staff, the better to operate on*

an international level.
*He has constantly been in the forefront
of beauty and fashion photography,
both advertising and editorial, and since
1982 he has also been directing
television commercials. He has won
numerous awards: Clios for advertising
in the US, Studio Magazine awards,
National Hasselblad awards, awards in
the National Capic Awards Show. His
work appeared in magazines in Japan,
the United States, Germany and Britain
as well as Canada.*
**Nudes: pp 37, 70–71, 77, 95, 97,
99, 117, 129, 131, 133, 149, 153**

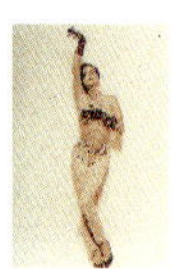 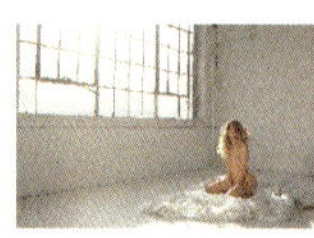
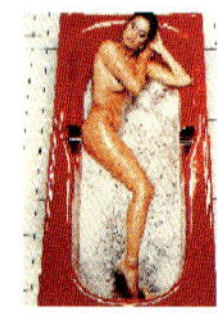 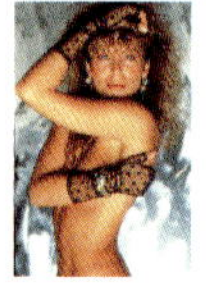
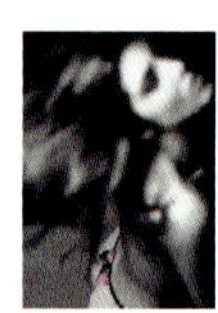 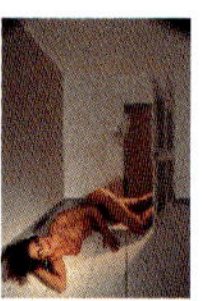
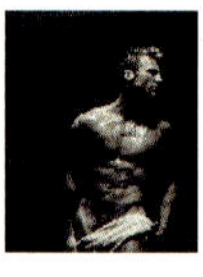 
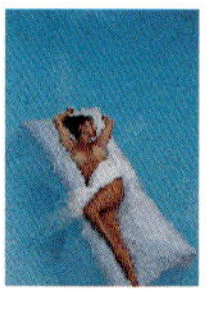 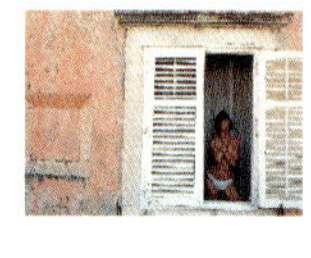
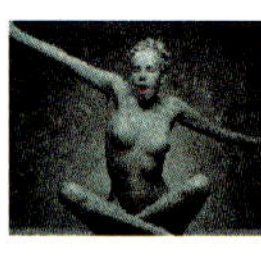 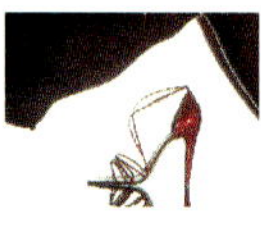

Photographer: **GÜNTHER UTTENDORFER**
Address: GÈLIEU STRAßE 9
12203 BERLIN
GERMANY
Telephone: + 49 (0) 30 834 1214
Biography: *Self-employed since 1987. Shooting
mainly fashion (especially lingerie and
bathing suits) but with many other clients.
Studio is 250 square metres in an old
factory. He used to shoot still life, but got
awfully bored with it – he has to work
with people, which is much more fun.*
Nude: p 89

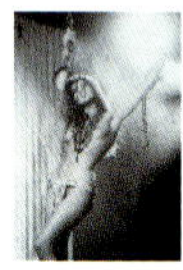

Photographer: **FRANK P. WARTENBERG**
Address: LEVERKUSENSTRASSE 25
HAMBURG
GERMANY
Telephone: + 49 (0) 40 850 83 31
Fax: + 49 (0) 40 850 39 91
Biography: *He began his career in photography
alongside his law degree, when he was
employed as a freelance photographer
to do concert photos. He was one of
the first photographers to take pictures
of Police, The Cure and Pink Floyd in
Hamburg.
After finishing the first exam of his
degree, he moved into the area of
fashion, working for two years as an
assistant photographer. Since 1990 he
has run his own studio and is active in
international advertising and fashion
markets. He specializes in lighting
effects in my photography and also
produces black and white portraits
and erotic prints.*
Nudes: pp 35, 51, 53, 55, 61, 66–67, 127

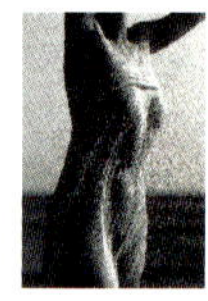 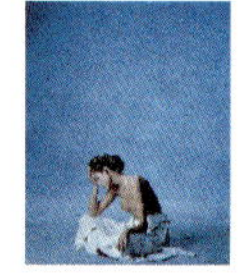
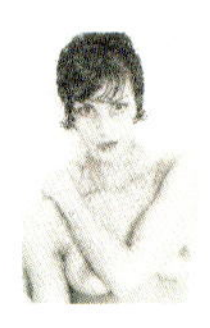 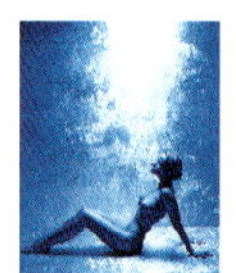
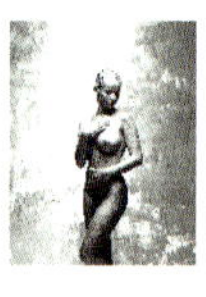 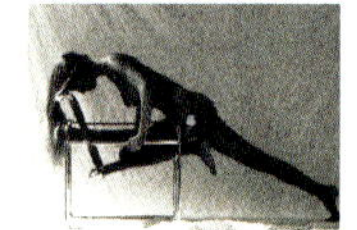
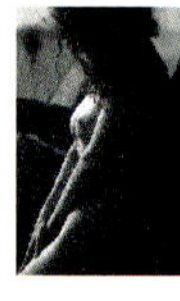

Photographer: **STU WILLIAMSON**
Address: CHAPEL COTTAGE
COVENTRY ROAD
FLUSHING
CORNWALL TR11 5TX
ENGLAND
Phone/Fax: + 44 (0) 1326 373 885
Mobile Phone: + 44 (0) 860 210 052
Biography: *A former session drummer, Stu turned
professional photographer in 1981
and has since won most of the major
photographic awards in the UK as well
as lecturing worldwide for Ilford, Kodak,
KJP (Bowens), Pentax, Contax, Lastolite,
BIPP and the MPA. In the late 1980s
he became very well known for his
"Hollywood" makeover style using the
Lastolite Triflector which he invented,
working in both monochrome and colour.*

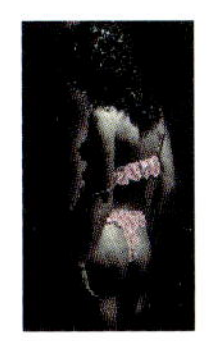
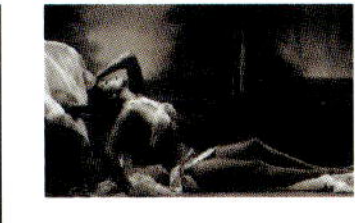
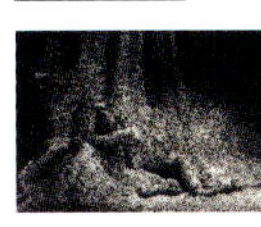
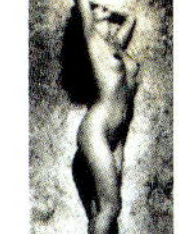
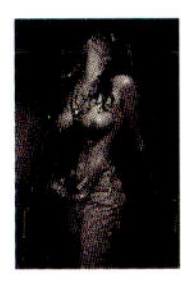
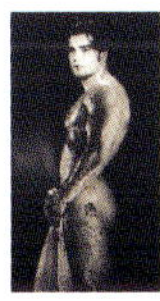

He now works almost exclusively in monochrome, both commercially and in fine art photography – his clients value his unique way of seeing – and sells to European calendar companies via his London agents.

Nudes: pp 25, 26-27, 46-47, 57, 91, 107, 109, 111

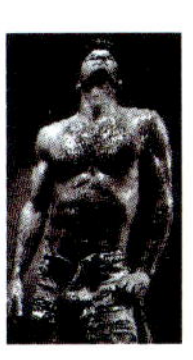
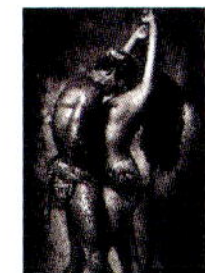

Photographer: **NICK WRIGHT**

Studio: STUDIO SIX

Address: 9 PARK HILL
LONDON SW4 9NS
ENGLAND

Telephone: + 44 (0) 171 622 5223

Fax: + 44 (0) 171 720 1533

Biography: *After twenty years in photography, he can turn his hand to most subjects though he is probably best known for his pictures of people and for still lifes. He has photographed many celebrities, and clients have included* Which? *magazine, W.H. Smith, Nestlé and E.M.I. Like any self-employed photographer, he is always looking for new and challenging commissions, especially in landscape: he has illustrated several books, wholly or in part, most notably Daphne du Maurier's* Enchanted Comwa

Nude: p 105

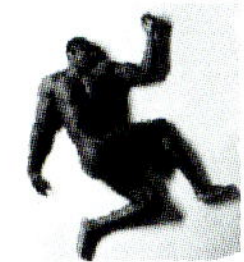

A C K N O W L E D G M E N T S

For this, the third series of PRO-LIGHTING books, we must as ever give our greatest and
most heartfelt thanks to all the photographers who gave so generously of pictures, information
and time. We hope we have stayed faithful to your intentions, and we hope you like the book,
despite the inevitable errors which will have crept in. It would be invidious to single out
individuals, but it is an intriguing footnote that the best photographers were often the most
relaxed, helpful and indeed enthusiastic about the series – though this is not the same thing
as saying they were the ones with the most time to spare.

We also owe a considerable debt to Brian Morris, whose idea the series was, and
we should like to thank the manufacturers who supplied the lighting equipment illustrated
at the beginning of the book – Photon Beard, Strobex and Linhof and Professional Sales
(importers of Hensel flash) – as well as the other manufacturers who support and sponsor
many of the photographers in this and other books; we have mentioned them in the text
or in the biographies wherever possible. Finally, Colin and Jenny Glanfield of The Plough
Studios in London (a major hire studio, call + 44 171 622 1939) were as ever a
constant source of help, ideas and introductions.